A 457   £8.50

GW00728946

Tigers

Tigers

The Story of No. 74 Squadron RAF

BOB COSSEY

ARMS AND
ARMOUR

Arms & Armour Press
A Cassell Imprint
Villiers House, 41–47 Strand,
London WC2N 5JE

Distributed in the USA by
Sterling Publishing Co. Inc.,
387 Park Avenue South, New York,
NY 10016–8810

Distributed in Australia by
Capricorn Link (Australia) Pty Ltd,
P.O. Box 665, Lane Cove, New South Wales 2066

© Bob Cossey, 1992
All rights reserved. No part of this book may be
reproduced or transmitted in any form or by any
means electronic or mechanical including
photocopying recording or any information
storage and retrieval system without permission
in writing from the Publisher.

British Library Cataloguing in Publication data:
Cossey, Bob
Tigers: story of 74 Squadron, RAF.
I. Title
358.41310941

ISBN 1-85409-143-3

Edited and designed by Roger Chesneau

Typeset by Wyvern Typesetting Ltd, Bristol
Camerawork by M&E Reproductions, North Fambridge, Essex
Printed and bound in Great Britain
Hartnolls Ltd, Bodmin, Cornwall

To the memory of
Wilfred Bertie Giles, old Tiger,
and of
Euan Murdoch and Jerry Ogg, Tigers both

CONTENTS

MAPS

FOREWORD

Group Captain Clifford Spink OBE RAF

When Bob Cossey asked me to write the Foreword to this book I was delighted—but somewhat daunted by the task: delighted because of my own experiences as OC 74 Squadron, but unsure of where to start to write about a fighter squadron which needs little introduction and must rank as one of the most famous in aviation history. From those early days of the First World War, when Mannock and his brave comrades set the mould of the Squadron, the Tigers have enjoyed a reputation second to none. That reputation was enhanced over the years, particularly in the Second World War when pilots such as 'Sailor' Malan wrote another glorious chapter in the story. Truly the Squadron motto, 'I Fear No Man', was never more appropriate.

In the years that followed, 74 remained at the forefront of RAF fighter operations and the lead it took in the introduction of the Lightning into RAF service was another chapter of excellence. Indeed, the story of 74 Squadron is one of dedication and service to this country where professionalism and high standards have been the hallmarks of its performance. I was privileged to command 74 when the Phantom F-4J was our capable steed, but as ever it was the wonderful spirit of the people that made my command so fulfilling.

Recently, in the Gulf War, I was able to see at first hand that spirit that so typifies the personnel of the Royal Air Force, and while 74 was not directly involved in that conflict it was fought by squadrons which in every way reflect the same laudable traditions.

Bob Cossey has spent countless hundreds of hours researching this comprehensive record of a unit that reflects the very best of the fighting service that is the Royal Air Force. I commend the book to you.

I am sure the Tigers can look forward to a future that is every bit as glorious as their past.

Clifford Spink
Coningsby, August 1991

PREFACE

Quite where one begins to say thank you after completing a project such as this is difficult to determine. Over the four years since 74 Squadron's 70th Birthday celebrations, when the idea of a new Squadron history was conceived, so many people have been willing to give their time that they could not possibly all be listed here. To all those whom I do not mention below I apologize; but they know who they are, and I would like to pay tribute to their enthusiasm and support.

It must be something of a record in itself that this should be the third book dedicated to a single RAF squadron, and it is indicative of the tremendous interest in its exploits during its 75 years and in the people who served in it. There is no doubt at all that 'Once a Tiger, always a Tiger', and, to the public at large, names such as Mick Mannock, Ira 'Taffy' Jones, 'Sailor' Malan, H. M. Stephen and Mungo Park are familiar ones. In the postwar years the Tigers will always be remembered as the squadron that brought the Lightning into operational service at Coltishall, and many still recall those times at the beginning of the 1960s when it seemed that you could not pick up a newspaper or magazine without seeing 74 and its aircraft somewhere in its pages. More recently, the acquisition of F-4Js from the US Navy and their appearance in British skies, proudly wearing their unique blue colour scheme and famous black fins, excited considerable interest amongst the aviation fraternity and the public at large.

My first thanks must go to 'Taffy' Jones, whose *Tiger Squadron* gives such a personalized account of 74's exploits during the First World War: I had the privilege of meeting his wife Olive shortly before her death and she recalled the many hours she spent typing the manuscript for Jimmy's book ('Jimmy' being her name for him). Thanks must go also to Doug Tidy, one of the minds behind the magnificent Malan Sword and whose *I Fear No Man* followed on from where *Tiger Squadron* left off. Doug's support for this new history has been unequivocal.

Cliff Spink was the Commanding Officer of 74 Squadron when research started and he has followed progress closely. To Cliff, and to Dick North-cote and Graham Clarke who have also commanded the Tigers since their re-formation in 1984, I must say 'thank you' for making me so welcome on my many visits to Wattisham and for allowing me access to people and documents: indeed, a special word of thanks must go to everyone on the Squadron for the interest they have shown and the support they have given. If any individuals must be singled out, they are Kevin Wooff,

Gordon James, Dave Allan, 'A. J.' Robinson, Tony Dixon and Iain Walsh—and John Sims, Bill Medland, Mike Castle, 'Spike' Whitmore and Steve Whitehead on the day of my unforgettable Phantom flight. Former Commanding Officers have also made themselves available and have accommodated many dozens of questions over the past four years—Sir John Lapsley, John Howe, Bill Maish, Ken Goodwin and Dennis Caldwell amongst them.

No book such as this can succeed without the facilities of the Air Historical Branch being made available, and in this respect I acknowledge the assistance of Air Commodore Probert and his team: 74 Squadron has had a succession of very good diarists over the years, and I have been able to draw considerably on their often inspired (albeit informal) record of Squadron life. Going back to the very beginning, Twist Giles recalled his days in 1917–18, demonstrating a brilliantly retentive memory in the process. Sadly, Twist is with us no more: I am sure he would have been tickled pink to have seen the results of our many conversations in print. From the 1930s and 1940s there is a potentially huge list of 'thank yous' to be recorded. Instead, I must restrict myself to acknowledging the help of Sammy Hoare, Bill Felstead, H. M. Stephen, Bob Spurdle (and his British correspondent Chris John), Tony Blythin, Joe Tombling, Allan Griffin, Don 'Llew' Llewellyn and Hugh Murland. From the Meteor and Hunter days, Dennis Brennan, Bernie McParlin, Boz Robinson and Arthur Bennett were particularly voluble about their time as Tigers, and, concerning the Lightning days, to Henry Ploszek, Ian McBride, Tony Craig, Simon Bostok, Jim Jewell, David Pugh, Norman Want, Henry Lether, Mike Cooke and David Jones go particular thanks. Photographically, Malcolm Gee has been of invaluable help and for this I most heartily thank him; and to my friends of the Norwich Airport Aviation Group, the Norfolk and Suffolk Aviation Museum and the Norfolk Aviation Society, many of whom remember the Tigers' presence at Horsham St Faith and Coltishall, I am indebted too. I must also acknowledge the support of NATO's other Tiger Squadrons, who have sent copious letters, literature and photographs and who have readily made themselves available when I have had the opportunity of talking to them. Perhaps the stories they have submitted may be the basis of another book one day. . .

There is no doubting that the compilation of this book has been a labour of love, but none of the work could have been accomplished without the support of my wife Angie, who has travelled many thousands of miles with me and written many thousands of words in her unofficial capacity as Private Secretary to the author! One of the biggest problems has been the need to précis over 350,000 researched words into the book you see here—a reduction of over 50 per cent. Inevitably there have been casualties in the process in the sense that there have been many stories and anecdotes, facts and figures that I have been unable to include. To some, the omissions may seem important ones and for that I apologize. There have been several instances where I have been given different versions of the same story and in these cases it has been a matter of bowing to the consensus of informed opinion as to which is the right one. I must stress that any errors that appear in the text are mine and mine alone—although they do not appear for want of verification and cross checking! I must also mention that there are in fact *two* RAF Tiger squadrons, the other being 230 Squadron currently based at Gutersloh and paradoxically flying Puma helicopters. I apologize to them for yet another book on their more celebrated colleagues . . .

Finally, I have a request for further information. Over the years, and through two disbandments, many Squadron artefacts have gone missing, including such diverse items as the inscribed silver Hunter that Chuck Sewell presented when he returned to the United States, the Battle of Britain Class locomotive nameplate '74 Squadron' that proudly announced the Tigers' offices in Tengah and the 1922 Rolls-Royce presented to the Squadron by Air Commodore Tester in memory of his son Nick in 1959. Does anybody know where they all may be?

Bob Cossey
Norwich, August 1991

CHAPTER 1

Formation and Training

WILFRED GILES—'Twist' to everybody at the time and since—saw the First World War through with 74 Squadron having joined the unit at Northolt on 1 July 1917 when, with the title 74 Training Depot Squadron (TDS), it was officially activated under the command of Major O'Hara Wood. Moving ten days later to London Colney with an initial complement of aircraft consisting mainly of Avro 504s, 74 TDS conducted training covering all aspects of air experience—formation flying, turns, glides, taxying and innumerable touch-and-goes—and an initial ten hours a week rose to over thirty during the first two months. No flying was allowed over 5,000ft until the New Year, when Twist and his colleagues celebrated by climbing to 6,000ft and proudly completing their first loop and spin. On 10 January 1918 Twist set off on his first cross-country flight. The route was from London Colney to Northolt and thence to Hounslow, where after three touch-and-goes he was forced to land with a broken ignition wire. A quick repair enabled him to return to London Colney the same day. In the ensuing weeks, the whole Squadron was employed on cross-country work around the Home Counties. By this time various other aircraft types were available for use, including Sopwith Pups and Scouts. Flying one of the latter, Twist actually managed to get lost over South Mimms and had to make a forced landing when he ran out of fuel! Aerobatics appeared next on the syllabus: on 12 February they were practised in 'very bumpy conditions'—conditions which, it would seem, extended to the grass strip, as Twist bent an axle on landing!

After six months the Squadron lost its training status and began to prepare for an impending move to the war zone. This was heralded by the arrival of the first S.E.5a:

> It was a magnificent machine to fly—we loved our S.E.5s and felt comfortable in them. A bit lonely, of course, being a single-seater, but usually we had plenty to occupy our minds so we weren't too bothered! We never hankered after anything new. I had a few of them in my time but then I crashed a few too!

Twist took his first S.E.5 aloft on 13 February: on the same day he was airborne in one of the Scouts but came down pretty quickly when the kingpost broke and the rigging started to unravel! Back on the S.E.5a his luck seemed to desert him, for on his first firing of the Vickers gun he contrived to shoot off two blades of the propeller!

I was sent up by our new CO, Twistelton-Wickham-Fiennes, to test the guns after the gunnery officer had been working on them. We had laid a tablecloth as a target in a field at London Colney and on my first pass in a shallow dive I fired, shot off two of the four propeller blades because of badly synchronized guns and went out of control. In front of me was a wood. Many a pilot had met their deaths by trying to do a turn with no engine and with this in mind I decided to clip through the tops of the trees ahead of me, which would effectively slow me down. This they did and I crashed into the field beyond, turning the aircraft on to its back in the process, I got out—shaken but okay otherwise, apart from a tear in my trousers.

Confidence was quickly restored in yet another S.E.5a the same afternoon, but Twist could only complete one circuit before he was forced to land in a hurry when more rigging problems asserted themselves. His misfortunes continued on the afternoon of 21 February when he lost all oil pressure, the engine seized and he crash-landed again, this time at Northolt. Once again he turned the machine on to its back, wrecking the undercarriage and propeller into the bargain. The comment 'Good landing' is underlined in his log book for the 25th, but the situation was reversed again on the 26th when he damaged the undercarriage and propeller of a newly delivered S.E.5a after landing in the rough!

At the beginning of March 1918, 74 (Fighter) Squadron (as it was now designated), under the command of Major Dore, migrated north to Ayr and No 1 School of Aerial Fighting, where the art was constantly practised during a week's intensive training. The return to London Colney was marred by yet another written-off aircraft for Giles when the axle broke on landing! However, Twist was not the only Squadron pilot to suffer such misfortunes: most had stories to tell of the 'bangs and prangs' incurred during training, and whilst these were expensive in terms of equipment, fortunately no lives were lost. It was all put down to experience and a realization that the aircraft were far from dependable and that their structural integrity was not always of the first order. Synchronization continued to be a common problem, and although there was no recurrence of Twist's experience of actually shooting off blades, many aircraft came back with them damaged.

Whilst 74 Squadron was at Ayr, another new Commanding Officer arrived, appointed specifically to complete the training programme and get men and aircraft to the Front. New Zealander Captain Keith 'Grid' Caldwell came to 74 from 60 Squadron, with whom he had been a Flight Commander, and it immediately became apparent that here was a man who would set such an example to all in the Squadron—to air crew and ground crew alike—that the unit's success would be assured. A daring and aggressive fighter (who was, paradoxically, neither a particularly good pilot nor a good shot), Caldwell was an inspired leader. He was with 74 through most of their time in France and he became, it was said, 'the fairest, squarest and most beloved of any squadron CO in France'. There were no half-measures about him: he would always lead patrols himself when possible, and he invariably took his aircraft far over the enemy lines regardless of the opposition. He had the ability to pick out promising fighting men from amongst those who were posted to the Squadron and he did not hesitate to get rid of those who would not make the grade. It is a certain fact that by patience, practice and leadership he welded together a unit that feared no man: the Squadron's reputation for determination and ruthlessness in the face of the enemy stemmed from Keith Caldwell. Morale was as high as it could be, and everyone possessed an unfailing sense of duty. In a few short months under his leadership in France, the Squadron shot down over two hundred enemy aircraft and, in the light of this tremendously aggressive spirit, was dubbed by others 'Tiger Squadron'.

A recollection of one remarkable incident serves to illustrate the courage of the man. Caldwell and his patrol were involved in a dogfight when he saw a lone enemy aeroplane below him. He immediately dived towards it, not seeing that another Squadron machine, piloted by Captain Carlin, had done the same. The two S.E.5s collided and hurtled earthwards out of control. Carlin was able to right his aircraft but, struggle as he may, Caldwell could not bring his out of the uncontrollable spin which was seemingly taking him to his death. In desperation, and with the ground rushing up towards him, he stood up and leant out over the wing, half in and half out of the cockpit, one foot holding down the rudder bar to its limit upon the side nearest to him, hoping that his weight, together with the pull of the rudder, would be sufficient to counteract the spin. Below, in the trenches, thousands of pairs of upturned eyes from both sides watched the damaged aircraft and men held their breaths for the inevitable crash. But slowly the spin became less violent until it finally ceased; the damaged wing held and Caldwell eased the stick back until his machine flattened out a mere fifteen feet above the ground and roared over the heads of the incredulous onlookers! His troubles were not yet over, however. As he throttled back, the plane became unsteady again and nose-dived. In the fraction of a second between realization of what was about to happen and the actual impact, he jumped. Hitting the ground, he rolled over and over, coming to a stop, unhurt, a few yards in front of a British dug-out. Before the eyes of the speechless infantry, he jumped to his feet and, with a grin on his face, calmly walked over to them and asked for a cup of tea!

Mick Mannock had arrived on the Squadron a month earlier than Grid Caldwell to take command of A Flight. A thirty-year-old Irishman, he had won his spurs with 40 Squadron and also brought with him to 74 a reputation for fearless aggression. As did Caldwell, he inspired pilots by personal example and an infinite patience in instruction. Mannock was considered to be one of the top five aviators on the British side. He was arguably the finest patrol leader in the RAF, and history tends to present a picture of an indestructible hero who flew swashbuckling missions, destroying the enemy at every opportunity. But those who knew him saw a different Mannock, one who did indeed enjoy the exhilaration of a good fight but who knew fear as did everyone else, who suffered recur-

SOUTH-EAST ENGLAND, 1917–1992

ring nightmares about being burnt in his aircraft and who was aware that he trod that very thin line between sanity and madness. The lectures which he gave to the trainee pilots introduced a radically new style of teaching—no longer dull theory but teaching spiced with personal reminiscence and *aides-mémoires*.

Twist Giles remembers Mannock as a man who would stand no nonsense but who was very good with the younger pilots. After one week at Ayr, the Squadron gave a display of formation flying, after which Skeddon cut away and performed some aerobatics on his own. 'Very pretty,' commented Mannock afterwards, 'but all those evolutions will be no damned use to you when you get a Hun on your tail!' Mannock's close study of the activities and strategy of the enemy led to some very practical advice to those around him:

If the Hun fires long bursts at you, you can be sure he is a beginner and windy. Fight him like hell, he should be easy meat. Remember that good flying alone will never beat the enemy. You must learn to shoot straight—that is one of the failings of some of our best pilots . . . and by the way I advise you to sight your own guns. It's no use leaving it to your armourer, he hasn't got to do the fighting. A pilot is not a machine. He is a man and must have certain weaknesses. The idea is to keep the plane under control and not let yourself down. A dead pilot is no good to anybody. Practising stunting is a waste of time. It is the quick turns that are needed more than anything in a fight.

Grid Caldwell wrote of Mannock:

His successes were largely due to his tactical approach to a fight and his extraordinarily fine deflection shooting once he was engaged. In an air fight most people try to get behind the other man to get an easier shot and where you cannot be shot at but Mannock was able to hit them at an angle. With two-seaters he usually came down in front where the pilot's vision was obscured by the top wing and if he missed in his approach he half rolled to come up under the tail and attack where the gunner had trouble getting at him. When he landed back after a successful show he was always in tremendous form!

By May 1918 Mannock was shooting down at least one enemy aircraft a day. Sometimes he broke his own records: for example, in one twenty-four-hour period he destroyed four Germans. On this occasion he had with him a young seventeen-year-old (who had lied about his age to get into the RAF), and during the course of one engagement he lined up a Hun for the youngster—an established practice of his which counted for at least twenty-five enemy aircraft. When Mannock died his score stood officially at seventy-three, but if these 'tutorial' combats were to be taken into account then his actual score would stand at ninety-eight.

CHAPTER 2

Opening the Account

B
Y MARCH 1918 all nineteen of the Squadron's S.E.5s were *in situ* at London Colney and all had been air-tested and declared fit for active duty. The aircraft moved to Goldhanger in Essex on 25 March and then to Rochford five days later. It was from Rochford that they took off to cross to France in bumpy conditions, flying at 8,000ft. The wind got the better of Twist when he landed on French soil for the first time, catching his machine and blowing it over on to its back whilst he was taxying in. Taffy Jones was in the same C Flight as Twist and he had taken the Squadron mascot with him—a little black puppy called Contact. The S.E.5 had a compartment built into the fuselage in which pilots used to put their shaving and mess kit when moving. Taffy put the puppy in here too, and a claustrophobic ride ended rather spectacularly when his S.E.5 hit some rough ground on landing and somersaulted as well. Fortunately man and dog were all right, although Contact was extremely sick.

The Squadron's South African 2nd Lieutenant 'Swassie' Howe wrote a contemporary account of the cross Channel flight:

We had a full requirement of machines in England but we had less upon arrival in France! The Squadron took to the air for France on March 30th after the transport had been well started and left the air at St-Omer. Taffy gave an exhibition of looping on the ground both for the benefit of the spectators and for the good of Contact the pup whom he had as a passenger. Poor little pup. He could not understand a gawd damn thing that was going on. Several other pilots demonstrated the poor quality of our undercarriages by crashing same. Just to show there was no hurry the weather came up dud and all hands were detained. When the weather finally became navigable the Squadron, headed by Grid, took to the air for Tetenghem and there joined the transport who had already arrived.

The 'transport who had already arrived' were the ground crew with motor vehicles, whose experiences during their move to France by road and sea were far from straightforward and represented a sorry episode of inefficiency and lack of communication which led to the section under Captain 'Youngski' Young taking eleven days to complete its journey. Having travelled from London Colney to Southampton then to Le Havre, where nobody knew what to do with them other than send them back to Southampton, the ground crew returned to London and were next sent on to Dover, where it took two attempts to get across to Calais before they could finally meet up with the airborne element of the Squadron across the Channel! Meanwhile the remainder of the motor transport, which was carrying the bulk of the stores and equipment under the command of Lieutenant 'Splitpins' Mansfield, was commandeered to assist in the stemming of the German March offensive as soon as it arrived in France, the stores being unceremoniously dumped on the roadside. The Squadron was finally reunited on 1 April 1918, the day the Royal Naval Air Service and the Royal Flying Corps amalgamated to form the Royal Air Force. The baggage and stores that Mansfield had abandoned had not been replaced, and all personnel were forced to make do and mend, eating with the aid of pocket knives and fingers. Some items were discovered back at St-Omer, and Mansfield was despatched to collect these although he nearly got into a running fight with members of 98 Squadron in the process who were adamant that the stores were theirs and not 74's!

Meanwhile gunnery practice commenced, mainly involving shooting at a target in the sea. Guns were sighted by each pilot with the assistance of the Gunnery Officer, Lieutenant 'Gibspring' Coverdale. Harry Coverdale was a much respected member of the Squadron, as much for his expertise with the guns as for the fact that he was a famous English Rugby international of the day.

The Squadron started the interminable round of patrols on 7 April. During the early days it snowed a lot—a most uncomfortable and unpleasant experience in an open cockpit, and a disorientating one too while patrolling the skies over Dunkirk, Ypres and Nieuport. To Taffy Jones fell the dubious honour of flying the machine that became the Squadron's first casualty when he was hit by flak (which was known universally as 'Archie'). Taffy Jones was another of those memorable characters that the Squadron produced in its formative years. He finished the war with twenty-six enemy aircraft confirmed as destroyed. A great admirer of Mick Mannock, he was determined to emulate his success and, being possessed of keen eyesight and the ability to shoot well, he soon found that he was scoring regularly. Held in high esteem by all his colleagues, he was considered to be the best flyer on the Squadron after Mannock—and, indeed, once Mannock had gone, the best.

On 10 April the Squadron moved to La Lovie, replacing 29 Squadron there, but its residency was short-lived for two days later it moved on to Clairmarais. This was a very small field, hardly big enough for aircraft to take off and land: 54 shared the aerodrome with 74 at the time, and it certainly could not have accommodated more than the two squadrons that used it. 'Swassie' Howe described it as being 'situated on the side of a hill with three impossible ways to land and, incidentally, crash!' Popularly known as 'The Tennis Court' because of its size, it measured just three hundred yards by one hundred and fifty and was bounded by a tall hedge and trees. There were three small prefabricated hangars per squadron, one for each Flight of six, the spare aircraft being squeezed in wherever there was space. NCOs lived in prefabricated buildings too, and the officers were quartered three to a hut.

April 12 was a red-letter day—the day the first contact with the enemy was made. At 0600 hrs Captain Cairns led his C Flight on patrol over the lines near Merville and was attacked by a mixed flight of German triplanes and Pfalzes. Taffy had a prolonged tussle with a triplane but was on the defensive most of the time and ended up by making a run for the safety of the British lines which the Huns decided not to cross. When C Flight landed, A Flight took off to take its place and the rest of the Squadron knew that it had been successful when it returned firing Very lights of all colours and diving and zooming at the sheds in excitement. Mick Mannock and 'Bolo' Dolan had both accounted for an Albatros Scout over Merville, Mick laying claim to the first enemy aircraft shot down by 74 Squadron. He got a second that day, whilst Grid Caldwell and Captain Young shared another Albatros. Taffy Jones partly offset the success when his crankshaft broke at 17,000ft during an evening patrol. He somersaulted as he tried to land in a ploughed field near Clairmarais.

Orders of the Day for the 12th dictated the fitting of bomb racks to all aircraft and the carriage of four 20lb bombs on patrols henceforth. These were used over enemy lines, instructions being to drop them 'anywhere'. The carriage of the bombs affected the performance of the S.E.5, the climb rate being quite seriously impaired, so they were always dropped at the earliest opportunity. Release was by means of a handle on the cockpit floor, and once were away the S.E.5 became the sprightly machine that the pilots preferred. The fitting of the bomb racks was one of the consequences of General Haig's famous 'backs to the wall' message which was a prelude to a mighty burst of sustained aerial activity all over the Front.

Following the successes of the 12th, bad weather set in and the Squadron was switched to ground-strafing. The enemy were flying similar sorties, and Clairmarais came under attack on more than one occasion during the April nights:

> . . . we all enjoyed the fireworks and the demonstrations of our dud Archie and gave vent to the same by laughing and parading in pyjamas. It was great sport dodging the dud Archie shells and as souvenirs the Hun dropped a few bombs on our 'drome.

So wrote the redoubtable Swassie Howe. The enemy employed the lumbering Gotha bomber on some of these raids, the aircraft coming in so low that the observers could be plainly seen hanging over the side, trying to shoot out the searchlights that surrounded the airfield. It would seem, from Howe's remarks, that the defensive fire of the flak batteries left much to be desired.

Giles' log book records his first dogfights with the enemy on 21 April. The weather had become fine again, and all the Flights were aloft several times during the course of the day. On the last patrol, C Flight encountered a gaggle of Germans over Armentières and very soon the sky was full of wheeling aircraft as both sides fought to win supremacy—'a grand fight although very frightening.' 74 Squadron lost its first man as from amongst the twirling mass of aeroplanes there came a blaze in the sky. Afterwards, Taffy Jones recalled:

I looked, and I saw it was Begbie's S.E.5. A sudden feeling of sickness overcame me. Poor old Begbie, I thought. How terrible. But the *kak-kak-kak* of a machine gun a few yards behind me warned me of my own danger. Poor Begbie had to leave us without a farewell wave. A Hun was still at him pouring more bullets into his machine. But while he pursued his victim Giles dived on his tail. The Hun dived away and he wasn't seen again . . . One by one the Germans left the fight and Twist and I flew towards Begbie's machine which was floating enveloped in flames. I hope he followed Mannock's advice and blew his brains out when he realised he was on fire. Perhaps the Huns saved him the trouble. Why have we no parachutes like balloon observers . . . ?

This was the day that the Germans lost the Baron von Richthofen and Mick Mannock was heard to say in the Mess that he hoped that he, too, died in flames. But he did not find many of his colleagues subscribing to such sentiments, for they felt deeply that no man should meet his death in such a way. All were for killing the enemy, but death by burning was not something to savour, whichever side you were on. Cheery 'Hup Dearie' Begbie's death hit the Squadron very hard, but Grid Caldwell was adamant that they must keep their spirits up, if not by drinking then by playing silly games in the Mess. The death of any Squadron member could never be allowed to affect morale, and it became a tradition that, when anyone was killed, a lively guest night be held in his memory. This was a tough proposition initially, but as time went on the sense of such a decree became apparent.

On 23 April Mannock added another German to his record, taking his pick from a formation of up to forty Pfalz Scouts west of Merville. Then the weather closed in again, lifting briefly in the evenings to allow one patrol a day. C Flight chased off seven Albatros Scouts towards Roulers on the 25th. On the 27th Taffy and Twist went up in the afternoon and the former endured the nerve-racking experience of becoming disorientated in cloud. Terrified of colliding with Twist, he finally emerged inverted over an enemy Archie position and only just pulled up in time to avoid disaster. Twist meanwhile had returned to Clairmarais. 'Sound old devil Giles', recorded Taffy. 'No flies on him. The South African Kiddie and he are very much alike. They are the type one knows will never let one down. Human Rocks of Gibraltar.'

On the 29th 'Zulu' Savage crashed on the aerodrome after being hit and wounded by German flak. The following day Dolan scored against a German who had strayed across the lines. A lorry with a trailer was sent out from Clairmarais to collect the German pilot and the aircraft, but heavy shelling prevented it from reaching either. 54 Squadron flew out on 1 May to take a well-earned rest at Calais, their place being taken by No 4 (Australian) Squadron—a fine bunch with whom 74 quickly got on good terms. Mannock and Dolan shot down one each of a flight of ten enemy scouts south-east of Ypres whilst 'Glynski' Glynn downed a triplane, and Roxburgh Smith, affectionately known as 'Dad' to his colleagues, destroyed a two-seat LVG and ordered champagne all round afterwards! Twist Giles:

> Actually it couldn't be said that successes were always celebrated by big parties on the ground. 74 were a pretty abstemious lot—not teetotal by any means, but they rarely drank in excess! The fact that I could speak a little French meant that I was given the job of buying all the wines for our meals. We all got on very well with the locals. At Clairmarais there was a farm on the edge of the airfield and we became very friendly with the owners who used to make butter and so forth for us. We had comfortable huts and good relations with the locals so our lot overall wasn't a bad one.

By the end of April, 74 Squadron had fifteen Germans to its credit—as Mannock would have said, 'good arithmetic'. But the Tigers had only just begun.

FIGHTING TIGERS

As the first days of May passed, 74's tally increased steadily. Mannock claimed another LVG on the 3rd and the following day he and his A Flight shot down three more, but on 8 May 74 Squadron was mourning the loss of three of its number. B Flight under Captain Young had taken off at 0715 to bomb Menin and C Flight, with Taffy Jones leading on this occasion, had done likewise fifteen minutes later. Climbing to 15,000ft, C Flight could see Young and his colleagues some way above them. But above them in turn was a flight of ten Germans, of which Young appeared to be totally unaware. Despairing in the knowledge that they could not warn them by any other means, Jones, Giles, Birch and Skeddon fired red flares in the hope of attracting Young's attention, but to no avail. They could only watch B Flight reach its objective, drop its bombs and turn to make for Ypres. As the British turned, the Germans did too and picked their moment to dive in to the attack. Still too far away and too low to help, C Flight made for a position under the mêlée above them, hopeful of being able to pick off any stray aeroplanes. Circling below his colleagues, watching them fighting for their lives in an unequal battle, Giles first saw Stuart Smith hit and burst into flames, followed by Bright who also burnt fiercely. Then it was 'Boy' Piggott's turn, chased down by a German triplane. Giles and Skeddon broke away to dive after him, firing for all they were worth: the German escaped but Piggott crashed. Fortunately his S.E.5 had not burnt and he survived, rescued from the wreckage by Australian soldiers. Young and Kiddie both escaped, Young's aircraft being so severely damaged that he crash-landed short of Clairmarais. Then a further tragedy struck. Skeddon threw his aircraft into a loop over the aerodrome when he returned, perhaps in celebration of his survival, but as he did so the wings folded and he spun into the ground and was killed instantly.

The Squadron felt very keenly that the Huns had had a day of success that must not be repeated, and from that moment on their determination redoubled. Jones brought down his first German in the evening of the

8th, and four days later Mannock's A Flight and Cairns' C Flight were both aloft for evening patrols when they spotted a formation of eight enemy aircraft comprising Albatroses and Pfalzes. Mannock shot down three, with Young, Roxburgh and Giles bagging one each. Giles' log book records the event:

I dived on an enemy aircraft from 10,000ft and fired both guns. The enemy turned over on to his back but recovered close to the ground and flew very low east as if to land. The aircraft was then seen to crash near Wulverghem by Lieutenant Jones who was with the patrol.

In a personal note he went on to echo Jones' thoughts:

There is no doubt the spirit of revenge should be cultivated during a war. It helps the fighter to put a little more ginger into his fighting.

The success of this particular scrap was tempered by the loss of 'Bolo' Dolan. The Squadron was suddenly short of pilots, but replacements soon arrived. 74 never had more than eighteen on strength and replacement was always one-for-one. There was always a high percentage of South Africans, Canadians and Americans, so much so that the Englishmen were usually outnumbered. It is sad to recall that, on this occasion, the trio of replacements quickly succumbed. Nixon was shot down on his very first patrol, and the same afternoon Barton took a direct hit from German Archie at 7,000ft. In the evening Russell crashed on the aero- drome as he was landing and was seriously injured. To help redress the balance for the day, Mannock and Jones shot down an Albatros and a Hannover respectively.

Mannock shot down his fortieth aircraft of the war on 17 May. Jones added to his score too, and the following day earned a commendation along with Kiddie for destroying an observation balloon—a rather more hazardous business than might be expected. The plan was that C Flight would escort Jones at 15,000ft to Armentières, where they hoped they would be 'archied'. When a burst came near, Jones was to pretend to be hit and go tumbling down out of control towards the balloon that had been selected. When half a mile away he was to pull out of his dive and have a go at the surprised occupants. The scheme worked. Two men jumped out of the balloon and deployed their parachutes, but, as Jones later said,

I immediately attacked them, seeing no point in setting the cumbersome look- ing sausage on fire if the observers were to get away with it with their informa- tion and their lives. I think I hit them. I hope I did. The balloon was going down in flames and a huge volume of smoke arose to signify the importance of the occasion.

That evening the Germans sent their bombers over the British lines once again and 74 attempted to hide their aeroplanes by distributing them around the airfield close to the hedge, noses well buried in the foliage. One bomb dropped in the centre of the landing strip but no damage was done. Two days later Mannock destroyed four enemy Pfalzes out of a flight of six (Grid Caldwell and Young getting the other two), and then with Howe and Jones appeared on the score sheet again the following day when each man claimed one aircraft destroyed. Mannock celebrated the news of a DSO by shooting down one of a flight of forty Germans on 26 May, Roxburgh claiming another in the same dogfight. On the 27th Taffy and Twist were out together to intercept two-seaters which were known to be working between Voormezelle and Ypres. Attacking a flight of four scouts north-east of Armentières, Twist got on to the tail of one of them but saw him apparently land safely in a field near Courtrai. They moved on to Merville and found another pair of two-seaters with a dozen scouts above them and went into the attack with the advantage of height on their side. Twist recalled:

> When you were actually in combat you found that fighting the enemy was the sole point of concentration. But at least concentration of effort pushed the fear to one side temporarily. When fighting, your eyes were on a single part of the enemy machine or on the pilot. They were all open cockpits so you could always see your adversary very well. You were looking at that head through your sights and that was all you were thinking about! You should have been thinking about what was behind you but there were times when you were so close in that you forgot to do so!

A few days later Twist nearly paid with his life for forgetting to watch his tail, allowing an enemy machine to pounce on him whilst concentrating on the destruction of a silver-grey two-seater. It was only by virtue of the fact that Caldwell was close enough to come to the rescue that Giles survived. Mick Mannock did the same thing for 'Clem' Clements, and then the following day added to his ever mounting tally with an Albatros over Armentières.

> There was also a very real risk of collision in a dogfight. The mêlée of your own and enemy aircraft was such that it couldn't be avoided and there were several instances when aircraft on both sides were lost in this way. [It happened to Grid Caldwell, as has already been recounted.] He was hit by the one-legged Carlin during a scrape which evolved from six of us going down to help the French one day. When we disengaged we went home and all landed except the CO whom we hadn't seen, but Carlin was in a real state because of course he knew he had hit Caldwell's aircraft. In fact, such was his distress that we had difficulty in stopping him from shooting himself.
>
> There was nothing as exhilarating as a dogfight between two large formations with aircraft whistling past each other at a furious pace. It was only afterwards that you realized that you had never been so frightened in your life! But we had a job to do and we did it. We had no time to think about the human consequences, about the fact that it was another man probably with a wife and family back home in Germany that you were pursuing. The moment you held back on compassionate grounds it was odds-on that you were the one that would be spinning to your death. There was really no room for the chivalry of the air concept that is talked so much about, except on occasions when we were on our side of the lines and there was no chance of the enemy escaping. Kill or be killed is a stark and clinical statement of truth when applied to the Western Front in 1918. Looking back at the whole episode, it is easy to level charges of callousness, of revelling in the horror of war when you consider the

pranks we used to get up to, the way we collected 'trophies' and so on. But if you didn't look after your own skin and if you didn't treat the whole affair in a decidedly eccentric way then you were heading for trouble. Many couldn't cope with the situation. You could understand the reasons why, but somehow we were still scornful of their mental state. There was no place for the pilot who couldn't do what he had to, because you would never be able to trust him. But it is also true to say that on 74 we rarely had anyone who failed through loss of nerve. We were all very afraid: we all abhorred the thought of burning; we all had nightmares. But we all coped with it in one way or another. And in some way this was an area of common ground which welded us together into the team that in reality we were.

It is interesting to compare the styles and success of the courageous Caldwell and the invincible Mannock. Grid never concerned himself unduly about tactics or orders and in terms of individual courage there was no equal, so much so that he would regularly frighten members of his patrol more than the enemy did by leading them into situations a wise man would avoid. And when he found an enemy aircraft, it was alleged that there was no man in France who would get nearer to it and yet still be unable to shoot it down! Giles recalls seeing Grid sitting resolutely on the tail of the enemy, pumping bullets into the machine—with nothing happening except that the German flew on and ultimately evaded Grid's attack; Mannock, on the other hand, with the skill of the true ace, could attack from the most unlikely quarter and with a masterful display of deflection shooting send his adversary into the ground almost effortlessly. Mannock's philosophy, too, was somewhat different from that of his Boss: if the odds looked unfavourable, he was not afraid to leave the fight. 'There are plenty more Huns', he used to say. 'We can have them tomorrow.'

Jones claimed his sixth and seventh Germans on 30 May and on the 31st Mannock was awarded a bar to his DSO. Twist shot down another two-seater and was then forced to drop out of a subsequent patrol with engine trouble. Once the problem had been cured, he and Taffy decided to go up by themselves in the evening:

At 7.10 p.m. I observed twelve Enemy Aircraft (EA) Scouts flying west from Menin at 10,000ft. Giles and I climbed to the north and east, eventually getting between them and Menin. We attacked them over Ploegstreet Wood. I fired a good burst at the rear machine, which half rolled and dived away. I then engaged the leader at 75 yards' range from above and behind. This EA got on its back and went down vertically from about 5,000ft when his wings collapsed and he crashed. The remainder dived east. On returning from this engagement, I observed another formation of ten EAs coming from Armentières at about 8,000ft. We again climbed north and got east of them, attacking at 7.35 p.m. After a short engagement, these EAs dived east without any decisive result being obtained. At 7.45 p.m. I observed three Pfalz Scouts just below, apparently trying to climb up to me. I half rolled and fired a good burst from both guns at the nearest EA, which got into a spin with full engine on. This EA was still spinning at about 2,000–3,000ft. I was unable to observe whether he crashed owing to my being engaged with the other two who eventually spun away and dived east.

Jones failed to score during the second engagement as a consequence of Twist becoming caught with a black-and-white chequered Pfalz on his tail, a situation caused by his engine choking and dying during a dive. Jones chased the German off and Giles' engine re-started. When Taffy and Twist landed, Grid Caldwell was there to meet them and tell Jones of the latter's award of the Military Cross, which had just been confirmed by General van Ryneveld at Brigade HQ.

It is not recorded precisely when 74 earned the sobriquet 'Tiger Squadron', but the grit, determination and fighting spirit displayed by the unit as the days of combat passed and as the score gradually mounted are the basis for its award and the adoption of the Squadron motto 'I Fear No Man'. There is no doubt that, despite the losses of the first few months in France, its successes and Grid Caldwell's courageous leadership welded 74 into a unit with a tremendous *ésprit de corps*.

Aircraft markings at this time consisted of a simple, white rectangular band about three feet long by six inches wide, carried on the rear fuselage in front of the toned-down roundel. Each squadron member had his individual code letter, carried alongside the white band, and pilots flew their own aircraft as much as possible in the same way that mechanics and riggers were allotted specific aircraft to maintain. It was the usual practice for the patrol leader to attach a narrow coloured signal flag to his rudder. Twist Giles recalls the system and how well it worked:

> If we got into a scrap and ours and the enemy's machines got all mixed up in the mêlée, we would look around for our leader so that we could re-form on him afterwards. This flag trailing from his fin would readily identify him. He also used to carry a Very pistol with a red cartridge, and if he fired that it was a signal to re-form on him. These were our only means of communication. Incidentally, the flag had a little pocket on the end with a lead weight in it. Its real purpose was to carry messages down to our troops below. If we sighted something of significance we would scribble a message on a piece of paper, put it in the pocket with the weight and toss it over the side!

June started badly when Captain Cairns was lost. Giles again:

> He was a nice fellow. Captain 'Glynski' Glynn took his Flight although I increasingly found myself leading it because of Glynn's poor health. I also gradually became the one on the Flight to show the new boys the ropes by taking them to see the enemy lines for the first time.

Giles was hospital-bound when returning from one such sortie his engine died. He saw what he thought was a hay meadow which had just been cut—the next best thing to an aerodrome's grass strip. But what he could not tell from the air was that beneath the hay were deep furrows caused by previous ploughing, and as soon as his wheels touched he was thrown into a terrifying somersault. The S.E.5 crumpled and Twist was trapped in the cockpit, hard against the control column and the machine guns, which went off and continued to fire as British soldiers ran across to help.

Once the ammunition was expended they were able to get close enough to haul Twist from the cockpit. He was hospitalized for a month with 'contusions of the back'.

The day Cairns died had been a day of very heavy fighting. Three Germans had been destroyed by the dawn patrols, and then later in the day A and C Flights chanced upon seven Pfalzes. After furious dogfighting, one of the enemy went down to Mannock. Cairns had his right wing shot off and he spun down to his death. A few days later, on 10 June, Mick Mannock was celebrating his fiftieth German destroyed. The new Squadron dog, Shell Shock, celebrated too by giving birth to five fine and healthy pups. Around the same time Coverdale received news from England of the birth of a baby daughter. Captain Young had just been awarded the DFC, and to mark the occasion a 'raid' on No 1 Squadron was organized, bombs being replaced by dozens of ripe oranges! Not to be outdone, No 1 retaliated with a well-aimed shower of bananas! All things taken together, there was indeed just cause for the champagne to be brought up from the cellar, for Roxburgh to set-to on the piano and for the rafters to reverberate to the uneasy metre of the Squadron Song:

> In France there is a damn good old squadron,
> Though the 'drome's on the side of a hill,
> It's a squadron of great reputation—
> It is 74 Escadrille.
>
> There was Mannock of fame in the Air Force,
> Hunarinos he shot down with ease,
> As happy as hell round the aerodrome
> As he shouted 'All tickets please!'*
>
> And Roxburgh, Youngski and Taffy,
> Men who are who in the air,
> And all of the rest in the squadron
> The best you could find anywhere.
>
> Now one toast I will offer in closing
> Just one it could easily be more
> A toast to the CO who led us—
> To Caldwell of 74.

At the end of June a deadly 'flu epidemic took its toll, and of the whole of 74's complement thirty men died, all ground crew, despite being splendidly cared for in the Duchess of Westminster Hospital at Wamereux. It was inevitably a very tough time for all concerned: the Squadron was not pulled back from the lines, and those who remained fit enough had to work all the harder to keep things going. Meanwhile the Tigers' tally mounted steadily. Jones, Roxburgh and Mannock all added to their personal scores before the last went on leave on 19 June. As he went, news arrived of his promotion to Major, the award of another bar

---

*'All tickets please' was one of Mannock's catch-phrases.

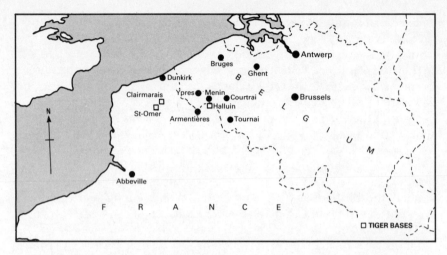

BELGIUM AND NORTH-EASTERN FRANCE, 1918 (SEE ALSO MAP ON PAGE 141)

to his DSO and the command of 85 Squadron. Taffy Jones was simultaneously promoted to Captain and took over command of A Flight, flying his first patrol as leader on the 21st. He took the Flight up to 18,000ft, searching for the enemy, but initially without success. Eventually, as he was thinking of turning for home, he saw a solitary LVG far below over Ploegstreet Wood and gave the signal to dive to the attack. Enemy Archie opened up but Jones continued his dive, his companions not far behind him but at this stage not knowing precisely where the enemy was. The LVG wisely chose to lose height, but with the S.E.5s bearing down on it the nervous observer opened fire at 500yds and almost immediately his guns jammed. Jones took his chance and closed in, destroying the German with a long burst of fire.

Jones' determination to make a kill on this occasion was a product not only of his wishing to make his mark in his first patrol as Flight Leader but because it was 74 Squadron's 100th victory since its arrival in France just seventy days previously. 56 Squadron lost its record of 100 victories in 74 days in the process, and so began that competition and rivalry that has endured through peace and war between the two squadrons, their fortunes having been intertwined ever since.

On 30 June Jones and Clements claimed four aircraft between them—a Hannover, a DFW, a Fokker biplane and a Rumpler. Clements' Rumpler came down on the British side, and once the pilot had returned to Clairmarais he drove out to the site to see whether there was anything worth salvaging. He found the remains—a charred skeleton amongst the desolate landscape of the reserve trenches. Of the German bodies there was no sign: the crew had fallen out as the aircraft fell to its destruction or else they had jumped rather than suffer the hideous pain of being burned to death. The aircraft's instruments had already been ripped out as souvenirs by soldiers. All that remained worth salvaging was a small black cross on the fin. This Clements hastily cut out and returned to Clairmarais, where he fixed it to the Mess wall alongside all the other trophies of war that had been collected.

July 1918 saw a further escalation in contacts with the enemy. On the 7th Giles claimed an LVG two-seater. His combat report was short and to the point:

At 11.30 a.m. when over Bailleul I observed an enemy aircraft diving out of the clouds. It flattened out and continued west at 8,000ft. I attacked from long range and on the EA sighting me it went into a left-hand spin and crashed into the ground.

A week later he engaged a flight of six Germans:

I attacked the formation with my patrol and a fight ensued during which I observed several members of the Squadron firing at enemy aircraft at close range. One enemy aircraft dived away vertically and I observed it break into pieces at about 7,000ft. Several enemy aircraft spun away apparently out of control, and one is confirmed by 70 Sqn to have still been in a spin when near the ground but it was not seen to crash,

Grid Caldwell returned from leave in the middle of the month and immediately went on to the offensive, leading his first patrol over the enemy lines in typical fashion—that is, with no regard for accepted tactics! Taffy Jones recalls the incident:

Crossing the lines at Ypres at 12,000ft, he made straight for Roulers aerodrome. Here he circled around until a large formation of Huns arrived from above to accept the challenge. Then an unholy dogfight started. About forty machines dived and fired like madmen at one another: zoomed, turned, twisted, dived and fired again and again . . . I saw an S.E.5 go spinning down with a cloud of Fokkers on his tail. It was poor old Grey . . . A mad merry-go-round had developed with death the price of faltering . . . Grid closed to within a few yards of a Hun's tail, pouring lead into him. Even a Fokker could not stand that . . . Soon everyone was flying all out to miss the floating pieces and one another. If the others felt like me, they gasped and felt sick as the bare fuselage, now turned coffin, dived vertically to destruction . . .

And so Freddie Grey's death was avenged. Swassie Howe was wounded in the fight too and crashed trying to get back to Clairmarais when he blacked out through loss of blood. After a few days in hospital he was shipped back to England, his association with 74 at an end.

B and C Flights were ordered to escort Bristol fighters on a bombing raid to Courtrai on the 19th, Roxburgh leading the patrol. Its bombs successfully dropped, the whole formation turned for home and almost immediately fell foul of a marauding formation of Fokker biplanes. Roberts, one of four Americans now on the Squadron, and Richardson were both shot down in the ensuing flight. The following day Carlin bagged a balloon.

Taffy Jones and Mick Mannock, the latter back from leave and now leading 85 Squadron, were honouring an earlier promise to keep in touch with each other on a regular basis—comparing personal scores and reliving combat—either by field telephone or, as on the 25th, by Taffy driving across to join Mannock for lunch, tea and dinner. At this stage of the war, flying at the pace he did day after day was beginning to wear at Mannock's nerves. Things which once formed the source of only minor irritation now became the basis of real anxiety and deep depression. His mind kept returning to the lack of parachutes (the use of which, it was said, would make cowards of airmen or at the very least offer them the opportunity of escape at the slightest pretext). His conversation became full of reference to burning aircraft and helpless pilots trying to beat out the flames with their bare hands in the last remaining seconds. And he became very fussy about carrying a loaded revolver on operations, with which he vowed to kill himself rather than suffer the agony of burning to death. When he arrived on the 25th Taffy found Mick to be in such a mood, constantly referring to his fear of fire and then finally taking him to one side, saying, 'Don't forget, Taffy, when that aircraft of yours goes sizzling earthwards it will kindle a flame which will act as a torch to others.' As Jones left, Mannock was at the bar, trying to calculate how many times a man who fell to earth without a parachute would bounce when he hit the ground. The next day Mick Mannock was dead, hit by ground fire and dying the death he dreaded in a fireball of an aircraft.

TURNING THE TIDE

The death of Mick Mannock hit the men of 74 very hard, none more so than Taffy Jones, whose self-styled motto 'Kill or Be Killed' seemed even more pertinent now in his quest for revenge. Taffy began to believe that he led a charmed life, for there were numerous occasions over the following weeks when an almost reckless disregard for his own safety led to his finding himself in situations out of which he had to be bailed by fellow members of his Flight. July 30 was such a day—an eventful one in several respects: one of the new arrivals, McHaig, killed himself on his first practice flight, Carlin downed a Fokker and one of the Squadron's Americans, Shoemaker, aided by George Gauld, destroyed his first German.

It was in the course of this engagement that Taffy almost died. He was chasing a suspected German reconnaissance machine, a highly camouflaged aircraft which did not show any national markings, but he began to have doubts about attacking it in case it was an unmarked Allied machine. Deciding that he needed to be absolutely sure of its credentials, he nosed up to it and was rewarded by a sudden burst of gunfire which spattered his aircraft. Diving quickly to get out of the line of fire, the German entered a steep dive himself but Taffy was loath to follow as his rear outer wing bay strut was badly shattered and he had visions of his wing folding. Fortunately, his companions were on hand to chase off the Rumpler (it had now been identified) and shoot it down. Despite his damaged strut, Taffy decided to complete his patrol time and was rewarded with a clear shot at an LVG over Estaires. It was easy pickings. The LVG came down close to where Mannock had met his death and

Taffy had his twentieth victory. When he landed back at Clairmarais his S.E.5 collapsed, so badly had it been shot about.

Later the same day, Taffy found himself embroiled in a dogfight with eight black Fokkers:

> Every Hun was having a go as the opportunity offered. They were so eager that at times I thought they were shooting at each other. I only got one good shot . . . then I noticed a formation of ten diving towards us. Thank God, here come the boys, I thought. They were the boys all right—unfortunately they all wore black crosses. That was when I decided to bolt for home. Like a scared rabbit among the bracken, I made the shooting as difficult as possible by zigzagging and diving flat out.

At the beginning of August, 74 flew several 'wireless interruption duties' which involved the interception of German aircraft using wireless to co-operate with their artillery. George Gauld and Freddie Gordon brought down such an aircraft on the Allied side of the lines on 3 August. After they had landed, they set off to claim the wreckage and bring it back to the Squadron, but when they arrived at the crash site they found that the Belgian Army had already packed up the LVG ready to transport it away. Something of a private war ensued with no little resort to physical persuasion, the net result of which was the transfer of the aircraft to 74's lorry!

On 3 August Captain Young was promoted to Major and given command of 1 Squadron at Clairmarais South. Roxburgh took over B Flight, and at the same time Taffy Jones was awarded a bar to his DFC. Grid Caldwell had still been awarded nothing, much to the embarrassment of his fellow officers who failed to understand why this should be so. Grid himself laughed it off: 'It's the honour of the Squadron that matters'. On 6 August Jones was

> . . . flying at 10,000ft when I observed a formation of nine enemy scouts coming up from an aerodrome east of Armentières. I got into position above and behind the rear machine and dived on it. At the critical moment my guns failed—in the excitement I had failed to cock them! Pulling up to do this, I found I was between the enemy and the sun and not noticed. I decided to follow the enemy closer to Allied lines before attacking again and flew thus for a full five minutes until, close to Merville, I saw an R.E.8 coming east from Mers. Two of the rear enemy aircraft left the formation and went towards the R.E.8. I dived after these and after firing at the nearest he got on his back and side-slipped towards the other who made a right-hand turn and collided with the former, both machines being interlocked. I then fired a long burst at them and both machines went down in flames. The other seven EAs attacked me but after a minute's engagement they all dived off.

Jones was awarded the DSO as a result of his success in this engagement, which took his tally to twenty-eight Germans destroyed.

There followed a period of massed Wing attacks on German aerodromes. Four layers of squadrons were used, three of S.E.5s and one of Bristol Fighters, the latter flying on top as an early version of a combat air patrol albeit with a big bomb slung underneath. Rendezvousing at a prearranged spot, the whole formation crossed the enemy lines and on the first raid attacked Linselles. Each S.E.5 dived in turn on the aerodrome, released its 20lb Cooper bomb and then climbed away but only after the Bristols had released their much more potent 112-pounders. There followed a concerted strafing attack on all ground personnel, administration buildings and messes. Much damage was done, and in the ensuing weeks such raids were repeated several times. This was the first time that these tactics had been used and the experience gained opened up new spheres of aerial operations.

At the end of August 74 moved to La Lovie but within a week the Squadron was back at Clairmarais. By now the enemy were slowly retreating and there was an air of gradual optimism that the war was approaching its end. Over the ensuing weeks, 74 moved to a succession of airfields following the line of the Allies' advance. During October the American Ferrand joined the Tigers. Like most of the American pilots, he was well liked and was immediately anxious to get into the fray, realizing that 'when I joined the Squadron I knew I would be expected to uphold the famous Tiger tradition by fighting like a tiger!' Uphold it he did, making history by shooting down three Fokkers on his first offensive patrol and returning with his S.E.5 riddled with bullets.

Twist Giles welcomed the chance to get back to England for a couple of weeks' leave and on his return to France he began to keep a diary:

October 28th 1918: A quiet but good leave in England. I arrived in Calais and stayed the night at the Officers Mess. I left Calais by motor on 29th and found the squadron near Courtrai on an old German aerodrome. The officers were billeted in a fine chateau nearby with plenty of furniture and also two grand pianos with which to entertain ourselves.

Giles was soon back to flying:

I did one patrol on the 30th at midday over the River Scheldt east of Roubaix and Tournai. At night the Huns dropped bombs on the aerodrome and put a dozen machines out of action and also all of our motor vehicles. Rather disastrous!

The raiders obviously knew the aerodrome well—at one time it had probably been their own—and their accuracy was uncanny. Two bombs fell on the hangars, completely destroying the aircraft in them. The motor transport met a similar fate, and a fourth bomb fell on some huts which were temporarily sheltering some members of the Middlesex Regiment who were passing through. Fifteen soldiers were killed and the aerodrome itself was pock-marked with craters. It was fortunate indeed, that, of all the remaining bombs that fell, not one hit the château where all the pilots were quartered. Because of the proximity of Courtrai to the German lines and the consequent continual bombardment of the aerodrome, 74 were moved to Cuerne. Twist complained:

The billets compared with the chateau were pretty rotten, and I was put into a farmhouse.

There were various and increasing numbers of rumours of imminent peace. The French and Americans had crossed the Scheldt in three places and the Germans were fighting a desperate rearguard action. 74 devoted itself to ground-strafing the retreating army. On 4 November the weather was fine and at least two offensive patrols were mounted between Tournai and Ghent. Twist wrote:

We saw Holland quite well from Ghent . . . a country of patchwork design.

On Guy Fawkes' Day the Squadron turned tourist:

We went into Bruges in the afternoon. It is a wonderful City and had not suffered damage by the Germans. Inhabitants told us that a damaged Hun submarine used to come up the canal every day for repairs. A very interesting visit.

The weather stayed 'dud' for several days thereafter. On the 8th the Tigers went to 41 Squadron at Halluin and saw a complete Fokker biplane that had been brought down by that squadron. In the afternoon they completed a line patrol in rainy weather but on the 9th the weather was much better and they completed two more offensive patrols from Tournai (which had only recently been retaken) to Ghent. Twist recorded:

The Germans are retreating hastily on this front and we flew quite twenty miles over their lines without any trouble. There was very little Archie and no Huns. We repeated the exercise on the 10th, once again meeting no opposition in the way of enemy aircraft. At one time we were almost in sight of Brussels. East of Ghent though we were severely strafed by Archie and incendiary shells. The air was absolutely swarming with British machines and at one time I counted sixty. No wonder there were no Huns about! There were rumours of the Kaiser's abdication and then after we had landed there was official news of the armistice having been signed at 8 p.m. Everybody went into a wild frenzy. A wonderful firework display immediately took place and bells rang in neighbouring towns, factories hooted and the army trains whistled various tunes! On the aerodrome we started bonfires with petrol and paraffin and used up all our rockets. We got through 600 gallons of fuel! A wonderful night never to be forgotten. It was hard to believe that all the fighting was over! At 7.30 on the morning of the 11th I led a patrol to the lines with orders not to cross them on any pretext whatsoever. I went east of Seselghem, Ath and Grammont but there was, not unexpectedly, no sign of the Germans. As we passed low over villages the inhabitants were all out in the streets waving Belgian flags at us and everywhere there was a scene of excitement and joy. When I landed at Courtrai I found an official wire from GHQ stating that hostilities had ended as from 11.00 a.m. that day. To celebrate we went into Bruges again and had tea and dinner there.

It was later learned that the German Air Force had spent that historic morning either busily destroying its machines or risking flying homewards trying to avoid the Allied patrols which continued to be flown for a while. Taffy Jones recalled those last moments as well:

As the hands neared 11 o'clock we flew closer to the retreating armies. As the hour passed we flew right over them. They took no notice. For the last time 74 Squadron turned back towards its own lines. As each aircraft reached the

aerodrome its pilot stunted wildly, diving, looping, zooming, rolling and spinning before landing from his last wartime patrol.

DISBANDMENT

For the next few days the Squadron still flew line patrols as a security
measure, but without incident: it seemed that the Germans had accepted
the Armistice without exception, and there was no sign of any violation.
By the 15th, Squadron members once again took the opportunity to relax
in the welcome new air of peace, already pushing the harsh routines of
war behind them and looking forward to a return to England and their
families. After the Armistice, 74, along with the other squadrons remaining in France, found itself on the move again, first to Froidmont near
Tournai on the Belgian border. This aerodrome had been occupied by
Gothas and was well camouflaged. Giles and his fellow officers were
billeted

> . . . in a nice clean *estaminet* in the village and the people made us exceedingly
> welcome and comfortable. Before retreating from this village the Huns had
> blown up the railway station and mined the permanent way. Shell holes were
> scattered all over the aerodrome, making landings difficult. But our Mess was
> fine!

Snow fell and temperatures dropped. Mail from home, the event of the
day most looked forward to, was delayed. But within a week the skies
cleared and on Friday 19 November several of the Squadron flew to
Clairmarais and had lunch with the mayor and his daughters.

> These people were awfully good to us. They invited us to fly over on Sunday
> next and have lunch again. We had great trouble starting our engines owing to
> the cold. Joy riding continued on succeeding days—Taffy and I flew to Ris-
> seghem to lunch with No 4 Squadron of the RAAF and my old squadron, 43,
> were there too and I met many of the old mechanics.

On 27 November Giles flew to Halluin as the advance party to take over
the sheds and billets from 70 Squadron:

> Our quarters are old German huts built alongside a church and are not so bad.
> On the 1st December we flew to No 1 Squadron at Izel-le-Hameau and saw
> Major Young, the CO, one of our old Flight Commanders. But the following
> day joy rides by air were forbidden except with the Wing Commander's
> express permission and in their place machine gun lectures and other forms of
> 'hot air' were instituted.

After the Armistice, Grid Caldwell, having led the Tigers throughout
their victorious stay in France, was promoted and posted to command 65
Wing and was later awarded a long overdue DFC and the Belgian Croix
de Guerre. On 9 December 1918 Ira Jones was given command of his
beloved 74 Squadron. But there was little to do. Life became rather dull
and routine, with restricted flying consequent upon the new orders. This
state of affairs lasted until the end of the year. Christmas proved to be a

welcome interlude, although Giles spent Christmas Day in bed with toothache and neuralgia:

The other officers had a wonderful dinner at night which I couldn't share. Never have I been so unlucky. On Boxing Day I paid a visit to the dentist and had an extraction. I feel ever so much better now. I was intrigued to find out that there are three or four men with sprained ankles after last night's celebrations!

Almost unbelievably, there were security problems:

December 27th. My hangar was broken into and the watch taken out of my machine. Those Belgians! During the past few nights one complete motor cycle, four motor lorry lamps, two flying suits, petrol and fire extinguishers have been pinched from the squadron. Motor cars are disappearing from all units by the tens. Although hostilities have ceased, some more ammunition will have to be used one of these fine nights!

Further problems arose on the 29th. Taffy Jones and twenty-four men were admitted to hospital at Courtrai, victims of the latest 'flu epidemic. This meant that they missed the New Year celebrations, but Twist took the opportunity to look back:

The year has had its pleasures and disappointments. Perhaps it has been my most enjoyable one in the service for I have been associated with a fine set of fellows and exciting events have been plentiful. My squadron, of which I am lucky to be one of the few survivors, has earned its laurels during the time that it has been in France, and although I have not been so fortunate as others in downing Huns I have done my very best and I feel quite satisfied that I have done my share to have made the success of 74. Many of my friends have lost their lives in aerial battles. Wonderful fellows the whole lot of them, always out to win and fearing nothing. All honour to you. You are real men. The past year saw the cessation of hostilities and I shall always be proud of the fact that I was out here to see the end. May the New Year see peace and prosperity for all gentlemen whom I have met during the war!

The Squadron ended the war with a total of 224 victories, made up of $140\frac{1}{2}$ enemy aircraft destroyed, 15 balloons destroyed and $68\frac{1}{2}$ probables—a total achieved in just seven short months in the front line. It is easy to forget that the Squadron consisted of far more than the few top-class fighters. Mannock, Caldwell and Jones are the names that immediately come to mind when considering the successes of 1918 in the same way that the likes of Malan, Stephen and Mungo Park dominate the days of the Battle of Britain, but it must never be forgotten that the success of any squadron is due to its work as a unit. The other major factor determining the success of 74 was the leadership of Grid Caldwell. He went on to pursue a distinguished career and died at the age of 85 in his native New Zealand in 1980, having attained the rank of Air Commodore.

Shortly after the New Year, news filtered through that the Squadron was to be demobilized:

January 23rd. We bid farewell to our machines tomorrow which we will be flying to Cerny. From there they will be flown to England by pilots of 32

Squadron. On the day I felt awfully sorry to part with my old bus which served me so well in the later stages of the war. Farewell old warhorse.

January 26th. Snowed during the night and all day. Very fed up with life and nothing doing· all day.

January 29th. Poor old 74. You must feel very sorry, old girl, to see all your children leaving you like this. Especially as we have all been so happy with you too. You will soon be able to put RIP after your title—but never mind, you are dying a glorious death.

Then it was Giles' turn to leave too:

January 31st. I bid farewell to 74 and reported to 91st Wing HQ from whence I was sent to 32 Squadron at Cerny. Snow and mist is preventing any flying and we are waiting for it to clear before we can start ferrying machines to England.

Taffy Jones flew down to hand over his aircraft to the Pool. He was pretty depressed at the time, for next day he was due to take the remains of the Squadron to Boulogne for trans-shipment back across the Channel. On 10 February the men arrived at Lopcombe Corner and then went their various ways. 74 Squadron remained in existence on paper only until 3 July 1919 when it was officially disbanded. The Tigers were left to slumber undisturbed for sixteen years.

CHAPTER 3

Reawakening

A T 1430 HOURS on 3 September 1935 the troopship *Neuralia* set sail from Southampton, bound for Malta. Amongst those on board were officers and airmen who had been drawn from a number of existing RAF squadrons, and from this complement a new squadron was formed under the command of Squadron Leader H. G. 'Jim' Crowe whilst in transit to the Mediterranean. No number was allocated, the unit simply being known as the 'Demon Flights', after the aircraft they would fly. None of those on board was aware that Malta was to be the destination until after the *Neuralia* had sailed. The reason for this secrecy was an attempt to hide the fact that the RAF were sending a squadron of fighter aircraft to Malta in response to Mussolini's threat to occupy Abyssinia. The brief was quite simple: defend Malta against Italian air attacks. Other than the men's own equipment, no other stores were carried aboard the ship: the aircraft, the motor transport and most of the maintenance stores were on board the SS *Maihar*.

Ten officers, eighteen senior NCOs and seventy-nine airmen formed the three Demon Flights, whilst the aircraft aboard the *Maihar* were, like the men, drawn from a cross-section of the squadrons flying Demons in Britain and still retained their old squadron markings—much to the confusion of any watching Italians! The original plan had called for the unloading of aircraft and equipment in Marga Scirrocco Bay, but the swell proved to be too much for the lighters to go alongside and so the freighter was brought around to Valetta and a 200-ton floating crane was used to offload the motor transport and aircraft. The ship's own derricks lowered the crates containing the wings, tailplanes and fuselages of the dismantled Demons into lighters, which then took them to the RAF Wharf where the slow process of unloading them with just one hand-operated crane began. Much credit went to the packing depot at Sealand for the aircraft's safe arrival in Malta and to the Warrant Officer and three airmen riggers who travelled with the dismantled Demons, inspected their charges twice daily and then supervised their transfer from ship to shore. By 16 September all twelve aircraft had been landed, and it took the rest of the day, and that following, to tow the fuselages and transport the crates to Halfar.

By cease-work on the 19th, eight of the aircraft had been re-assembled and were ready for use. Pilots began flying them the following day. Those who had not flown Demons before converted without any instruction and encountered no problems. The armament, by contrast, did prove troublesome, by virtue of the fact that it was old. Nevertheless, the ground crew pronounced the overall condition of the aircraft to be good. Spares were to be a problem for a while, and many signals were exchanged between Malta and Britain before the situation improved. The result was initially a very low flying rate per pilot—just half an hour in a twenty-four-hour period, most of which was by day. It was not until an experiment with two Navy searchlights mounted on a Morris six-wheeler to aid night landings had proved successful that the night total increased. Halfar was equipped with paraffin flares which were laid out to mark the landing path, the only problem being that they were visible well out to sea and would have been an easy target for marauding Italian fighters had they been in the vicinity.

The Demon Flights had quickly been made very welcome at Halfar when the Station Commander threw a Demon Cocktail Party. This was not restricted to military personnel: there was a virtual open invitation to the whole island, and the merrymaking lasted through the night and well into the next day. Amongst all the stations from which 74 has operated, Halfar was the only one which had a working pub next to the Squadron hangar on the airfield. Beppo's Bar had been known to a whole generation of Fleet Air Arm pilots and was allowed to remain because of some legal complexity in the Maltese land laws. Unfortunately the Germans succeeded in removing it in 1942 when it received a direct hit. It must be said that the privilege of having such a convenient bar was never abused, temptation being successfully mastered by each individual in the Squadron. It follows that the owner of the bar never got very rich from the proceeds!

Camouflaging of the aircraft began during the first few days of October, using locally available dopes and copying designs that had evolved during 1918. The job had been completed by mid-November. Flotation gear was fitted to all Demons, which meant that had any aircraft been forced to land in the sea it would have been held just below the surface to facilitate its salvage. Training now began in earnest and included affiliation with 202 (Flying Boat) Squadron.

MALTESE TIGERS

The Demon Flights received a signal from the Air Ministry on 14 November instructing them that they would be known henceforth as No 74 (Fighter) Squadron and in fact that this nomenclature would be back-dated to 3 September. So the Tigers were at last back in existence, now destined to serve for an unbroken 33 years. Just how conscious they were in Malta of the precedent established by their forebears in France in 1918 is difficult to judge. What is remembered is the 'work hard, play hard' policy adopted by the Squadron as a whole, and over the next few months many successful relationships were struck with sister squadrons and with the Royal Navy, with whom 74 trained closely. The first task following official recognition was a nine-ship flypast to welcome the new

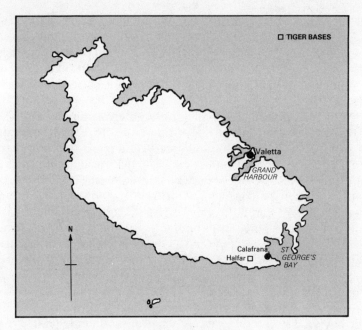

MALTA, 1935—1936

Governor, His Excellency Sir David Campbell, to the island on 17 November. Then came a combined 'attack' on HMAS *Australia* in concert with 22 Squadron's Vildebeests, followed by attacks two days later against 202's Scapa flying boats.

Against a background of non-aggression pacts signed by Italy and Germany and by Germany and Japan and the subsequent increased tension in the world, training in the Demon (the only two-seat aircraft that 74 Squadron were to fly until the arrival of the F-4J Phantoms in 1984) continued. The programme was varied—a low-flying attack against the 1st Destroyer Flotilla at the beginning of December, then height-finding exercises in conjunction with anti-aircraft batteries, followed by attacks on anti-aircraft posts and firing at towed sea targets. A war test was carried out on 18 December with the aircraft sheltered in stone pens built around the perimeter of the aerodrome. It took twenty minutes from the opening of the hangar doors to the completion of the taxying of the aircraft to the relative security of their revetments, for camouflage engine and cockpit covers to be fitted and for armed sentries to be posted. It then took five minutes for a Demon to become airborne from a pen when the alarm was sounded, the beginnings of the process which, over the years, has resulted in a steady whittling down of the time for such take-offs when the RAF's current air defence aircraft respond to the QRA scramble.

The increasing co-operation between the Tigers and the Navy resulted in an increase in the number of goodwill visits between Halfar and the Fleet, and this extended to opportunities for Navy personnel to fly in the back seat of a Demon—with the Tigers trying to give the sailors the ride of their lives! However, there was one occasion when the back-seat ride went very wrong. This involved not the Navy, but one of 202 Squadron's men whom 'Brookie' Brookes took up, initiating some manoeuvres which caused considerable *g* forces. Unbeknown to Brookes, his passenger had hooked his feet under the gun ring in the back cockpit and the *g* had broken one of his legs.

The New Year initially saw something of an escalation in training, with night flying playing an increasingly important role. By day a turnround exercise proved that the Tigers could rearm and refuel their total complement of aircraft in just 9½ minutes after landing from an hour's sortie. One of the three Flights carried out a low-level raid on Fort St Elmo. On 1 February Sergeant Papworth made a forced landing on an unfinished landing ground at Ta Kali, his engine having cut out at 4,000ft. Ta Kali was one of two emergency strips on the island, the other being across the polo ground at Marsa; Malta posed its own particular set of problems as far as operational flying was concerned, there being very few spaces in which to effect an emergency landing. Sergeant Papworth's effort was the only one away from base that 74 had to make during its tenure at Halfar—which is just as well, for the Maltese' liking for small fields bounded by solid stone walls gave very few options to the pilot in trouble. The diagnosis of the engine failure was a fractured camshaft housing. Eight other aircraft had their engines removed after inspection as a consequence, and at one stage 74 had just three serviceable Demons on which it could call. Fortunately this situation did not last long, and further affiliation with 22 and 202 Squadrons and the live bombing of an uninhabited island off the Maltese coast were a precursor to participation in flypasts in honour of the C-in-C Mediterranean Fleet and the Governor of Malta.

Brookes assumed temporary command of 74 when Jim Crowe returned to England for some leave on 13 May. By this time the Squadron members were beginning to feel that their presence in Malta was becoming somewhat superfluous. The great resolve shown by the British Government over the Abyssinian Crisis a year earlier had dissolved into an acceptance of a policy of appeasement. Mussolini took Abyssinia and formed the Rome–Berlin Axis with Hitler. Events were beginning to move with increasing rapidity, and it was becoming obvious that the issue was developing into a wider European argument. Politically, the damage had been done: 74 could serve no useful purpose where it was. It had spent a year training hard, but now it was time to return home, and orders to do so were received on 13 July 1936. The Demons immediately began to be dismantled and were repacked in their cases at Calafrana prior to despatch. By the 27th Halfar had been evacuated and men and equipment were ready to board the troopship *Somersetshire*, although some of the equipment found its way aboard the *Neuralia* and *Manela*. The orders were that, as soon as disembarkation in England had been completed, all personnel were to report to Hornchurch. This done, twenty-two days' overseas leave was granted to all, with reassembly due on 21

September. By this time Jim Crowe, who had been promoted to Wing Commander, had moved on and Brookes had been confirmed in his role as Commanding Officer.

HORNCHURCH

On its formation in 1936, Royal Air Force Fighter Command nominally numbered sixteen squadrons, although these figures were misleading because they included squadrons such as 74 who were in transit home and whose aircraft were all in packing cases. The most modern fighter in service was, for the moment, the Gauntlet, although the introduction of the Gladiator was imminent. The country's early warning system was primitive, consisting of a few concrete sound mirrors on the Kent coast and some mobile sound locators manned by the Army. It was comforting to those worried about the problem in 1936 to know that radar would soon be available.

As the men returned from leave in that warm September of 1936, Brookes reviewed his new command and found to his dismay that more than half his complement of pilots had been posted to active squadrons. 74 were temporary victims of Expansion, but the way to recover the situation was to get the aircraft reassembled and back into the air, and to this effect the CO took his men off to the Sealand packing depot to get on with the job. At Hornchurch the aircraft were organized into two Flights (instead of the three that had been the norm previously) and over the next few months the complement of pilots and ground crew slowly increased. A frequent visitor to the Tigers was Taffy Jones, who had made a point of keeping in touch with his old squadron. There was one particularly memorable evening in January 1937 when not only did Taffy arrive but he brought with him four old 1918 Tigers, Carlin, Hunt, Clements and Twist Giles, who recalled that

> . . . my lasting memory of that evening were the numbers of barrels of beer on tap—74 weren't so abstemious then as I recall them being during 1918! We were given accommodation, and when the orderly woke me up at 8 o'clock the following morning he asked me very politely whether I wanted a cup of tea or a glass of beer!

It was on this night that Taffy produced a drawing of the unofficial crest that the Squadron had used during 1918—a tiger's head and the inspired motto 'I Fear No Man'. Brookes, who had been considering the adoption of an official crest, took the drawing to the Chester Herald. The final design was complete within a matter of weeks and the King had approved it by the end of February 1937. A few days later a glass panel went up beside the Squadron notice board covering a newspaper article on ex-Tiger Mick Mannock and detailing the number of kills he had with 74 during the War there for all the new postings to see when they first arrived. This, allied with the inevitable strains of Harry Roy's 'Tiger Rag' (which the Squadron had adopted as its signature tune) emanating from somebody's gramophone left no doubt as to which squadron they had joined!

Hornchurch was a typical peacetime RAF station—grass runways, three hangars in a crescent and an approach path straight over the Ford factory at Dagenham. When 74 arrived they joined 54 and 65 Squadrons. All three units were technically self-supporting, although station workshops provided back-up for major repair work together with special facilities. To put this into perspective, it is worth remembering that the only engineering officer on the station was a Flying Officer. In other matters the station provided administrative and logistic support—equipment, accounts, education, medical and so forth. There was no Secretarial Branch as such, nor were there any WAAFs, so many station and squadron non-flying functions had to be carried out by squadron officers.

The working week was 5½ days, and each day, Monday to Friday, started with the Colour Hoisting parade at 0830 hrs. The parade was formed up by squadrons and consisted of a cursory inspection of airmen by squadron adjutants, raising the RAF Ensign, short prayers by the station padre and then a march-off to places of work. There was little doubt that this was a rather tedious way of starting each day: there is also little doubt that, after the parade, squadron routines were rather leisurely. Tiger pilots would assemble in their Flight Commander's office for a chat whilst the airmen moved the aircraft out of the hangar and prepared them for flying. Weather permitting, this would start at around 0945. Everything would stop for lunch between 1230 and 1330. In the Mess, some officers would indulge in a single glass of beer—never more—whilst others would read the day's newspaper or a periodical. As there was no bar, drinks would be ordered and served on a silver salver by a civilian Mess orderly. After lunch there would be more flying. Once or twice a week, 'living in' officers were required to dress in Mess Kit for dinner and occasionally a formal guest night was held which all officers attended. Otherwise evenings were free and informal. Once during the year the whole Squadron would close down for a month's annual leave. This still left officers with thirty days to take at other times.

Operationally, pilots would fly between 180 and 200 hours a year—one forty-minute flight per working day—and would do so in accordance with the Fighter Command Training Syllabus of formation flying, sector reconnaissance, aerobatics, practice attacks, radio direction finding (RDF), night flying and so forth. Special commitments such as the annual air firing camp, cross country flights and air displays provided a welcome change. Group Operations were planned for once a week, though these amounted to little more than practice scrambles and in fact were more often cancelled than put into effect. With only that one forty-minute flight, pilots were often hard-pressed to occupy the rest of their working day, particularly when the weather was bad. There were, however, many routine station and squadron tasks which had to be carried out, such as kit inspections, pay parades, audits, enquiries, Mess secretaryship and barrack block inspections and the duties of Orderly Officer. Dormitories (fifteen beds ranged either side of a single coke stove) were always kept spick and span by the occupying airmen, two room orderlies being responsible for ensuring that the quarters were ready for inspection by the Duty Officer at 11 o'clock every morning. Any station activity, however small, had an officer in charge.

Arriving at Hornchurch to join B Flight as a wireless mechanic in January 1937 was Jim Tufnail. In those days each Demon had a fitter and rigger assigned to it and there was an armourer to every three aircraft. There were no electrical or instrument trades: the wireless man covered those as well, and with just two to each Flight it was as busy a time for him looking after the six aircraft on the Flight as it was for the armourers. The cross-training element of servicing with the wireless mechanic meant additional work—for example, putting a patch on to the fabric-covered aircraft or clearing a gun. A Flight Sergeant, with a Corporal Electrician under him, took charge of each Flight, each of which was completely independent of the others. Servicing patterns demanded that there was always one aircraft from A and B Flights on deep servicing after a predetermined number of flying hours (120 in the case of the Demon) and these would be situated in the centre of the Squadron hangar with the other aircraft positioned around them overnight.

Jim and his counterparts used to fly regularly on air tests. In those days it was the vogue for a wireless operator to be a rear gunner too, and to wear the brass bullet above his 'sparks' badge, although some, such as Jim, resisted the opportunity and retained their interest solely in the wireless trade. That loyalty to the chosen trade did not preclude the obligatory Saturday morning duty of washing down the aircraft. The Demons were camouflaged and so did not require polishing—just a cleansing with petrol! Saturdays also offered the opportunity of cleaning hangars and billets, a job to which considerable attention was paid as Brookes made a point of a weekly inspection of at least one billet and the hangar. The ground crews saw their CO as a tough leader and a great disciplinarian who saw *his* squadron as the best in the RAF and was determined to keep it so. Inter-squadron rivalry at Hornchurch was inevitably very keen. 54 and 65, who occupied the other two hangars, were just as determined to prove that they were the best. In the air, rules regarding dogfights were not always complied with when aircraft from the three squadrons met in the Hornchurch sector, but most encounters were harmless and were actually good training even though unauthorized.

Rivalry was not restricted to operations and training and it spilled over to the sportsfield and even to the NAAFI and Messes, with arguments often approaching potential violence! The ground crews were as proud of their traditions and achievements as their counterparts in the air. Squadron loyalty was of paramount importance and has always been a notable feature of 74. Naturally, not everyone likes everyone else, and there have always been occasional squabbles. But within the bounds of the Squadron hangar and offices throughout the Tigers' existence, everyone has known that he is part of an élite team and everyone has always worked towards maintaining that. A good Commanding Officer, of course, makes all the difference. 'Brookie' Brookes, for example, was so successful because he was determined that 74 Squadron would be *the* squadron—the one that the rest of the Royal Air Force would look up to.

GAUNTLETS

Between 21 and 29 April 1937 the Squadron re-equipped with the single-seat Gloster Gauntlet. For a brief moment it was thought that 74 was going to receive the brand new Gladiator—one example had been issued to the Squadron during March—but there was a change of mind and the Gauntlet was delivered instead. Thrusting disappointment aside, air and ground crew alike soon warmed to their new silver aeroplanes even though 54, in the hangar next door, flaunted the Gladiator they had received in 74's place! A considerable step ahead of the Demon as far as electrical systems were concerned, the Gauntlet was nevertheless not as reliable. One big improvement which the pilots did appreciate, however, was the aircraft's new type of radio, the TR9, which transmitted relatively clear speech, air to ground and air to air, without the horrible background noise of the radios carried by the Demons—although, compared with modern VHF radio equipment, the TR9 was still primitive. In the absence of Air Traffic or Fighter Control, its use was also limited, despite the fact that, by careful tuning, pilots could sometimes find the popular music of the day from the BBC!

The Gauntlet's silver finish quickly invited the application of the new Squadron markings. The tiger's head was applied to the fin, and Brookes designed the famous black and yellow alternating triangles which were considered to be dangerously unconventional at the time and which the Air Ministry took some persuading to accept.* With the Squadron having overcome its initial disappointment and now keen to fly its new aircraft —and well aware of its potential—Squadron Leader Brookes took seven of the Gauntlets to Aldergrove towards the end of May 1937 for affiliation work with 502 (FB) Squadron. The opportunity was also taken to participate in the famous Empire Air Day displays, in Northern Ireland and at Hornchurch. The Aldergrove detachment returned to Hornchurch on 31 May, completing the 405-mile flight non-stop in three hours. The following month 74 found itself leading a line of five fighter squadrons during the 250-aircraft flypast which was the highlight of the last of the RAF Pageants at Hendon. The Squadron, with a few ground crew, had moved to Duxford for the event. Brookes treated the affair as a drill exercise and, given the job of organizing the Duxford Wing of fifty aircraft which was to fly on the port side of the formation, he ensured that the timing was exact. It was drummed into the Tigers that they should move in a smart

---

*Elsewhere in this book, these black and yellow triangles are referred to as 'asymmetric dicing', or simply 'dicing'. These terms, although not strictly accurate as descriptions of the markings, are to be found in many official papers.

and airmanlike manner on the ground as well as in the air (shades of the precision of modern display teams), a routine which other squadrons saw and emulated. It was Brookes' philosophy of command which dictated that 74 were to be the archetypal Royal Air Force Squadron—precise, neat, efficient, and with a very evident high level of morale, with everyone believing that without exception they were the best. This was an admirable attitude and one which stood the Squadron in good stead in the difficult days ahead.

On 12 July, 74 moved to Tangmere for coastal defence exercises, charged with the night defence of Portsmouth. During such exercises 74 worked frequently with the Heyfords of 10 Squadron. The wireless mechanics would put in a 12-volt battery for night flying to power the port, starboard and tail navigation lights and also to power the gun heaters and a small light which illuminated the compass; a wind-driven generator attached to the lower starboard wing would ensure that the battery remained charged. Interceptions at night were really a matter of chance, but the Heyfords were quite large aeroplanes with open exhausts which stuck out like sore thumbs.

More air defence exercises, during daylight hours this time, occupied the Tigers during August. One of the big occasions of the year was (as it still is) the annual armament training. In 1937 it was held at Woodsford in Dorset. Fairey 111Fs and Audaxes acted as towing aircraft, hauling drogues aloft over Chesil Bank, and, with two hundred rounds of ammunition loaded (and dipped in different coloured paints to identify the firers and to enable scores to be counted), pilots took off, only to be frustrated by their seeming lack of ability to hit the target. The reason for this was quickly identified—too much firing at long range—and it was not long before the faults were rectified and things improved radically. Of the twenty pilots who achieved a good score, there was one who did significantly better than the rest. This was Malan, a natural deflection shooter much as Mannock had been during the Great War.

The return flight from Woodsford proved to be quite exciting. Rain and low cloud delayed the early morning departure, and only at lunchtime did Brookes decide that the weather was fit for flying. Twelve aircraft took off in squadron formation and headed for Hornchurch, rapidly catching up with the weather front which had only recently cleared Dorset. As they approached London the rain got worse and the cloud base lower—and so did the twelve Gauntlets! Keeping formation was difficult because of turbulence, but once the Thames was reached everyone relaxed. South of Hornchurch and on the north bank of the Thames there runs a stream alongside the Ford Motor factory; this stream (its size hardly qualifies it to be called a river) flows north-east to the eastern boundary of the airfield and was affectionately known to all Hornchurch pilots as 'Shit Creek'. So the favourite bad-weather route back to base was always 'find the Thames, follow it until you see Ford's, turn on to 045 degrees, up Shit Creek, and you will see the airfield on your left'—which is exactly what the Squadron did on this occasion. It was quite common for pilots to fly singly over London at fairly low altitude, but it had probably never been done before by a squadron in formation. In the crew room later, one of the pilots remarked that it was the first time that he had had to look *up* to Big Ben for a time check!

New arrivals on the Squadron included the Canadian Don Thom, an expert gymnast and diver of near-international standard who passed many idle hours in the crew room standing on his head or practising backflips into a specially constructed sandpit; perhaps that was why he had some early problems with the Gauntlet, particularly with the use of brakes whilst taxying. On one occasion Paddy Treacy had cause to congratulate him for having taxied from the end of his landing run back to the hangar with his tailwheel two feet above the ground, an almost impossible feat were it to be tried intentionally! Sammy Hoare recalls his own arrival at Hornchurch:

We reported to the Squadron office and were greeted by Tom Rowland, the Squadron Adjutant at the time, whose pleasant but formal welcome left us in no doubt that we were joining a very good squadron and that he was a very senior pilot in it! It was a day of excitement tinted with some disappointment —excitement because it was my first fighter squadron after Flying Training School and disappointment that I would be continuing to fly biplanes instead of the Battles or Blenheims which were at that time entering service in bomber squadrons. There were no monoplanes then in Fighter Command, but I would have been well satisfied with the Hawker Fury which I had flown at FTS and which I liked enormously. But 74 had the Gauntlet, which, although a delightful aircraft to fly, itself was only slightly faster than the Fury and indeed looked rather less modern with its two-bay interwing struts, bracing wires and open cockpit. My disappointment was not lessened when I found that our neighbours at Hornchurch had the superior Gladiators!

In the New Year, events in Europe continued to provoke deteriorating relations between Germany and its neighbours. April saw a change in command for the Tigers, Brookes moving on and Squadron Leader G. E. Sampson arriving to take the reins. Sammy Sampson had as his adjutant Sammy Hoare and so the two were inevitably known as Sammy One and Sammy Two. In contrast to Brookes, Sampson was not a Commanding Officer who was able readily to identify with his men and he was only seen in the Mess on formal occasions. Soon after his appointment the European situation demanded a General Mobilization Exercise, for the purposes of which 74 was brought up to its intended war establishment with personnel from reserve units. During the exercise Bomber Command 'raided' London and the South East with Blenheims and Battles. 74 attacked the raiders with their Gauntlets but 'combat' was non-existent because even when they saw the attackers they could never catch them! For the purposes of the exercise, however, sighting alone was considered a success since at that time there was no effective radar or ground control.

Searchlight co-operation took up a week of August and then the time for the annual armament camp came round again. This was to be held at Sutton Bridge in Lincolnshire, but the Squadron had scarcely arrived and tested its guns and sights before it was hastily recalled. The aircraft were all camouflaged, the pristine silver finish disappearing under virtually any shade of green and brown dope that could be found, with the result that the Tigers possessed probably the most bizarre collection of Gauntlets anywhere in the Air Force. When regulation dope later arrived, the riggers took on the task of making a proper job of the camouflage and the Squadron looked respectable again, although there were those who said that the new finish was not nearly as effective! The crisis which had prompted the early return from Sutton Bridge resolved itself with the Munich Agreement, although Chamberlain's assertions about 'peace in our time' prompted the general feeling that the problem had been merely postponed. Sammy Hoare:

Until the summer of 1938 I cannot recall having taken any great interest in international politics nor having been concerned about the possibility of war. We all realized that our ultimate purpose was the defence of the UK and that our probable opponent was Germany, but the likelihood of war seemed remote. Nor did we feel unduly disturbed about the prospect of competing against the Luftwaffe in our rather antiquated Gauntlets. Unbelievable as it might seem now, we had little idea of the strength of the Luftwaffe and we were unaware that many of its squadrons were already equipped with modern monoplanes of considerably greater performance and firepower than any RAF aircraft.

Munich was a landmark for all the RAF's squadrons. Life from then on became far more active and training was carried out with real meaning. The Officers' Mess became notably fuller than previously as various classes of reservists were called up. Another immediate effect of Munich was the giving up of the daily working parades and dining nights in the Mess. An occasional Station Commander's parade would help to maintain standards of discipline and military deportment. On the Squadron, more time was devoted to formation flying, inter-flight interceptions, RDF practice and Fighter Command tactics, standard forms of attack which proved to be quite inappropriate when the war started. And the Tigers maintained a small number of pilots at readiness who were for a while required to sleep at night in the crew rooms.

The experienced hands of A Flight qualified for the finals of the Sir Philip Sassoon Challenge Trophy for Fighter Attack at North Weald, which they proudly went on to win. Victory was all the sweeter as they beat off the challenge of their colleagues in 54 and 65 Squadrons. The competition was the only one in the RAF which called for teamwork as opposed to individual performance, and this meant a tough time for the ground crews as the demand for six serviceable aircraft was constant. What made the victory even more significant was that other competing units had Hurricanes or Gladiators: only 74 were soldiering on with the outmoded Gauntlet. But the Squadron had been promised Spitfires, and at the year's end news came that re-equipment was imminent. This was confirmed when Malan and Treacy were sent on an induction course to Duxford, and in December 1938 Hornchurch took delivery of a brand new piece of equipment, a Link Trainer with an instrument panel as fitted to the Spitfire—the forerunner of all flight simulators.

SPITFIRES

The first Spitfire I arrived at Hornchurch on 13 February, delivered by Brookie Brookes, who was now the RAF overseer at Vickers. Flying from Eastleigh, he had been met by Malan and Treacy in their Gauntlets and escorted to the airfield, where the envious eyes of 54 and 65 followed the Spitfire's every movement. Conversion by the Squadron's pilots over the next few weeks presented no major problems, although it did take a few flights to get used to the two-speed propeller and the use of the flaps —and, most of all, the retractable undercarriage, which had to be pumped up and down by hand, leading to many an unusual-looking take off. As it took fifteen seconds to pump it up, pilots initially felt that they really needed three hands—one for the throttle, one for the stick and one on the hydraulic pump handle! Even the bravest pilot allowed a little more distance between aircraft on formation take-offs until he was used to the new technique.

The arrival of the new aircraft was followed by a series of visitors of rank to the Squadron, and several demonstration flights were flown. There were inevitably several incidents with this new generation of air-craft, the most common of which seemed to arise from the pilots' forget-ting to lower the undercarriage prior to landing! In fact the Flight Sergeant on 'A' Flight reached the stage of keeping a loaded Very pistol in the Flight hut and using it many a time to warn an incoming pilot to get his wheels down! Sammy Hoare quotes the story of Paddy Treacy com-pleting a first-class demonstration for a party of visiting Army officers and, on coming in to land, failing to pump down his wheels fully into the locked position. After an impeccable landing, the aircraft slowly sank as the undercarriage retracted neatly into the wings. This impressed one of the watching Army types: 'What a beautifully controlled manoeuvre to finish off such a good display!'

Along with the Spitfires came a Fairey Battle, which was to be used for blind-flying instruction. Bill Felstead, who joined the Squadron as an LAC Fitter 2 in 1938 and left as a Sergeant in 1941, remembers the Battle well—and in particular the occasion he was a passenger in the aircraft on a test flight with Mainwaring as pilot. One of the things to be tested was the undercarriage—which, when it came to it, suffered a lock breakage and subsequently jammed. With little choice other than to attempt to land with just the one leg extended (after employing every trick in the book to get the second leg to extend), the Battle almost inevitably ground-looped. Against all the rules, Bill had not been in communication with Mainwaring; furthermore he could not get through the well to talk to him as it was full of experimental wireless equipment. So he was left to speculate as to exactly why the aircraft was being thrown violently around the sky. Bill was extremely sick as a result of all this unorthodox activity. When, after assuming straight and level flight again, Mainwaring turned and started pointing over the side, this was wrongly interpreted as an indication that he was finally going to land. In fact he was trying to tell Bill to bale out! It was only after Mainwaring had given up in his efforts to get Felstead out and flown at low-level across the aerodrome in view of a line of trucks and personnel on the tarmac that Bill realized that something was very wrong. Both pilot and passenger survived the ground loop and in fact it fell to Bill Felstead to organize the aircraft's rebuilding. When completed, honour dictated that Bill accompany the aircraft on its air test but, in communication this time, when a warning was given of an impending roll he decided that that was not for him, grabbed hold of his stick and hauled the opposite way to the pilot's input! The roll did not materialize, but, after landing, Bill endured the most colossal ticking-off for allowing the aircraft to be released with such stiff controls!

As war clouds continued to gather, the Squadron busied itself developing new tactics which would allow full advantage to be taken of the Spitfire's superior performance. Air exercises and detachments to Upper Heyford for affiliation with 18 and 57 Squadrons were all part of this build-up, as were continuing 'unofficial' dogfights with 54 and 65. Arriving on the Squadron at this time was Pilot Officer Derek Dowding, whose father, 'Stuffy' Dowding, was Commander-in-Chief Fighter Command. Young Dowding was a delightful chap but somewhat untidy as regards dress and deportment—certainly not what would have been expected of an officer just out of Cranwell and the son of an Air Marshal. Not surprisingly, he quickly acquired the nickname of 'Scruffy' Dowding! Also posted in was Sergeant Gower RAFVR, who was to be killed within a few weeks of his arrival. Having gained his wings just one month previously, he had taken off as part of a three-ship formation practice training flight. For some unexplained reason his aircraft was suddenly seen to part company from the other two—probably an evasive action to avoid a collision —but was soon apparently in some kind of trouble. An eyewitness saw him attempting to guide the Spitfire away from a housing estate and towards a school playing field at Grays, ready for a wheels-up landing. Just over the boundary fence the aircraft stalled, dipped a wing and dived into the edge of the field.

Soon afterwards the Tigers were stunned by the suicide of Pilot Officer Norman Pooler. Towards the end of an informal party, he appeared in the anteroom in an unusually subdued mood carrying his revolver. After chatting for a while with those present, he insisted on saying goodbye to everyone; and, being in such a depressed state, he was escorted to his room by fellow officers. The following day he was missing from duty and his body was found lying in the Mess gardens, his revolver at his head. The funeral was a private one and the Squadron was not represented, but shortly afterwards an urn containing Pooler's ashes was delivered to the Squadron offices with a request from his parents that they be scattered over the airfield. Norman Pooler had been one of the finest rugby players in the Air Force and had represented the Service in many competitions. A popular and capable pilot, he was also a daring one with a bit of a wild streak, and he was certainly one of the most colourful characters on the Squadron. In the months subsequent to his death there were reports of Pooler's ghost being regularly seen. It would walk through the hangar towards a Spitfire on dispersal and then return in the direction of the crew room, only to disappear. So real was Pooler's image that one of his old ground crew suffered a nervous breakdown.

Despite the urgency of training and the build-up to inevitable conflict, the Tigers still found time to detach to Le Bourget to help the French Air Force celebrate the Fall of the Bastille in July. Then, as a mark of Anglo-French solidarity, a formation of bombers from each country flew a cross-country route over each other's territory, thus providing an opportunity to test London's air defences. 74 were ordered off and shortly after reaching altitude they sighted the antiquated French aircraft over the Thames Estuary. But no sooner did the Tigers see them than they had passed them. A quick 360-degree turn brought them round to get some camera gun shots, but only by throttling right back and virtually hanging on their propellers could they do so. It was little wonder the French encountered the problems they did when they faced Me 109s a few months later.

In August Fighter Command squadrons were involved in the Home Defence Exercises. As in previous years, the forces were divided into 'Eastland' (hostile) and 'Westland' (friendly). This exercise was in fact the first *full scale* practice for the defence of the United Kingdom to take place, involving as it did fighter and bomber squadrons, anti-aircraft divisions, air-raid warning organizations and the Observer Corps. The systems evolved during the course of the exercise were still in force when war finally broke out a few weeks later. This was the first occasion on which 74 had experience of radar—so secret that squadrons had scarcely been told of its existence.

CHAPTER 4

Battle Stations

O N 3 SEPTEMBER 1939 Neville Chamberlain announced that Britain had declared war on Germany. At Hornchurch, squadron markings had already been deleted from the aircraft (leaving just roundels and the code, 'ZP') and the Spitfires had been dispersed around the aerodrome. All three squadrons were brought to readiness, each with personnel busily filling sandbags and building aircraft pens. Bell tents were delivered and pitched close to dispersals, the pilots and ground crews sleeping and working from them; short-lived attempts by enthusiastic fitters to sleep under the aircraft's wings were quickly scotched by the Flight Commanders. This was a return to scouting days—but without the need to cook since men were released in rotation to go for food and baths. Security was undertaken by members of the Local Defence Volunteers (the forerunners of the Home Guard), armed initially with nothing more than pieces of wood to serve as 'rifles'. Flying was on a much reduced scale for a while, although the Tigers were fortunate in that their pilots had been together for a long time and each man had already flown between 50 and 100 hours on the Spitfire. Meanwhile more changes on the station itself became evident. The Officers' Mess began to fill up even further as Controllers, Intelligence Officers and Admin Officers arrived. The anteroom would be packed, ready for the main evening news from the BBC. Squadron adjutants spent a lot of time in the office dealing with incoming signals concerning mobilization plans and other matters.

THE BATTLE OF BARKING CREEK

The first operational patrol of the war by 74 Squadron was on 4 September when it was ordered to intercept an enemy raid approaching the coast from Holland, a 'raid' later identified as the twenty-two survivors of the first Allied attack of the war on the Kiel Canal. On the bright sunny morning of 6 September both A and B Flights were ordered aloft once again to intercept a supposed enemy raid. This time they found a formation of Hurricanes from 56 Squadron operating out of North Weald and there followed one of the blackest incidents in the Tigers' history, the Battle of Barking Creek, when, in the excitement of the interception and in the wake of unreliable IFF procedures, the Hurricanes were wrongly identified as enemy escort fighters and Paddy Byrne and Johnny Freeborn shot down two of them. There were various reasons why such a tragedy could have happened. Allied to poor IFF procedures was the apparent breakdown of the 11 Group control system. Both procedures were in their infancy at that time and most Controllers were recently called up reservists and therefore inexperienced. The Observer Corps were in the same position at that stage in the war too. But it must be said that both pilots were fully trained—although not necessarily in aircraft recognition, lessons for which were not formally conducted at that time. Nevertheless, Hurricanes had been in service for two years and everyone knew what they looked like; the weekly aviation journals were full of photographs, silhouettes, pictures of Luftwaffe markings and performance details of German aircraft. The question must be asked: what prompted Byrne and Freeman to break away from A Flight and pursue two Hurricanes flying straight and level in the vicinity of their base at North Weald, thinking they were hostile fighters? The Controller might not have known what aircraft they were, nor whether they were friend or foe, but both pilots might reasonably have been expected to make some attempt at positive identification before opening fire. Sammy Hoare has his own thoughts:

There can be little doubt that the whole affair had originated at 0600 with a blip appearing on the screen at the RDF station at Canewdon indicating one or more aircraft approaching the coast and flying westwards. At about the same time an AA battery reported engaging some twin-engined aircraft approaching Clacton. It was later learned that they were Blenheims of 64 Squadron, one of which was shortly afterwards shot down north-east of Hornchurch. The Controller at 11 Group was apparently not aware that the blip he was seeing was friendly because of a technical problem which resulted in false plots on the table and a breakdown in communication.

Tom Rowland, who had by now been posted to 11 Group, recalls that North Weald had scrambled a flight of 56 Squadron Hurricanes without reference to the Controller:

In the gloom of early morning an airman had walked outside, looked up and saw what he immediately took to be a formation of enemy bombers flying high overhead and raised the alarm. The Station Commander, only recently posted in and not as yet fully conversant with procedures, bypassed the system and ordered his fighters up to investigate. Unfortunately it was realized too late that what had been seen was actually a formation of *geese*!

The aircraft from 56 Squadron suddenly appeared on the Controller's screen, together with the blips of the Blenheims which he had still not identified as friendly. Classifying them in the absence of other information as possibly hostile, he ordered off a section of six from Hornchurch—74 Squadron—to investigate. Sammy Hoare:

It is reasonable to assume that a degree of panic and confusion would by now have arisen at Canewdon and that a conclusion was erroneously drawn that something big was about to happen. More squadrons would have been brought to readiness, including those in adjacent Sectors; other RDF stations would have been alerted, as would the Observer Corps and AA batteries, all of which would have resulted in a flood of information being fed to the Controller. More Sections or Flights were ordered off to intercept and identify those already airborne, each in turn appearing as unidentified plots on the table as a result of the technical problem. The picture now was one of aircraft being directed and redirected all over the sky, chasing each other and probably sometimes even themselves. One has to sympathize with personnel at Canewdon, below ground and with inadequate and unreliable IFF and consequently less able to sort friend from foe than anyone above ground. The fact was that no one could have reported seeing and positively identifying an enemy aircraft as of course there were none anywhere in the vicinity. It was all a classic example of the 'snowball effect', and who eventually ordered a halt to the situation two hours later is not known.

Strangely perhaps, there appear to have been no repercussions or Group directives following the affair. The two Tigers were immediately grounded after the incident, but the resultant Court Martial acquitted them. There was little discussion on the Squadron—in fact there was an overall feeling of embarrassment for Freeborn and Byrne, and neither the CO nor Malan made any comment to any of the other pilots. Johnny Freeborn, the often blunt northerner, and Paddy Burne, the jovial Irishman, both appeared to get over the incident quickly. Freeborn had scored $12\frac{1}{2}$ confirmed victories by June 1941 when he left the Squadron; Paddy Byrne had been shot down over France and taken prisoner within eight months of Barking Creek.

THE PHONEY WAR

Over the next few days, B Flight was involved in happier undertakings with its participation in the filming of *The Lion Has Wings* with Ralph Richardson and Merle Oberon. Meanwhile Malan and Treacy were busy trying to bring the new boys on their Flights up to scratch: it was now that the expertise of the old hands was to play such a vital part in encouraging the raw youngsters. Squadron formation flying and formation landing on the grass airfields of 11 Group was practised. Conservation of fuel was imperative as the 87-gallon capacity of the Spitfire was enough for just $1\frac{1}{4}$ hours' flying, and landing singly after a long patrol could mean that the last few aircraft coming in were likely to run out of fuel, especially if they were forced to go round again. Landing twelve aircraft at once was certainly a hazardous operation and it required a great deal of concentration. For those more experienced pilots, night flying was included in the programme, and a night fighting modification was tested by Squadron Leader Sampson. The original Spitfire was a difficult aircraft to fly at night because of the 'kidney' type exhausts which, at high revs, belched sparks and incandescent gases rearwards either side of the canopy and just below the pilot's eye level. Thus, in total darkness, forward vision was almost impossible, take-off was tricky, and any manoeuvre at full power, such as overshooting after a missed approach, was decidedly hazardous. The modification, which made a big improvement, involved fitting large 'blinkers' over the exhaust stubs (although these were removed by day since the blinkers themselves also obscured forward vision).

Whilst the training continued, the Squadron undertook its share of operational patrols, none of which produced any contact with the enemy. Ground crews had to be taught the rights and wrongs of their duties —what they could and could not do. Bernard Stebbings had recently joined the Tigers as an armourer and he considered himself to be the keenest man on the Squadron:

... so keen in fact that for the first few days I used engine oil and petrol to polish the two B Flight aircraft I had been allocated to look after until they shone. This had not gone on too long before Paddy Treacy came over to me one morning and said, 'Come on, I'll take you for a jolly'. We took off in the Station's Tiger Moth and I thoroughly enjoyed myself for I had never flown before! We circled the aerodrome, gaining height, until Treacy shouted back at me, 'Look down there and tell me what you see.' 'What am I looking for?' I asked in all innocence. 'Can you see anything bright and shiny?' Standing out conspicuously were my two bright, gleaming Spitfires. 'Those are the aircraft you have been polishing non-stop. Don't do it any more!'

There had been a potentially serious accident towards the end of September. Very few aircraft were kept in the hangars, other than those for maintenance and repair. Two Spitfires had been flown in for painting and coding. Flight Rigger John Gill takes up the story:

Two airmen were looking round one of the Spits. One was an armourer who was showing his friend around the cockpit and explaining the function of the different controls, which led to the airman sitting in the cockpit holding the control column and being shown how the guns were fired. I had just walked past the aircraft when there was the biggest bang I have ever heard in my life. All eight guns had been fired! Luckily the other aircraft was not in the line of fire but the hangar wall was peppered with bullet holes and some had gone through the door of Flight Sergeant Etteridge's office. At the time he was enjoying a short nap, sitting back in his armchair with stockinged feet on his desk. Above his head on the window sill was a row of potted geraniums. The bullets had taken them all out, as well as the windows, and he was very rudely awakened by a shower of earth and glass! The sight of him coming out of his office on hands and knees was one to behold. The offending airmen were rooted to the spot in horror. Their defence was (predictably) that they didn't know that the aircraft was armed. But it was not too long before they found themselves in the guardroom awaiting charges! It was normal practice for armed aircraft to have notices to that effect hanging from one of the gun nozzles and for the safety cover on the firing tit to be in position. The fact that this cover had been slid across to reveal the red firing button was the cause of all the trouble!

On 22 October thirteen aircraft moved to the satellite aerodrome at Rochford for a week, the first of many such deployments. During October and November, 74 suffered a spate of accidents, fortunately without serious injury to any of the pilots, although Browne was particularly lucky to escape when he hit high tension wires between pylons in bad weather near Rayleigh. Treacy taxied his Spitfire into another when his vision was impaired by tears forming in his eyes after being in the other aircraft's slipstream. This problem, and oil on the windscreen, became relatively common causes of ground accidents, involving one aircraft colliding with another whilst taxying. Any single-seat, tail-dragging aircraft suffers from poor forward vision whilst on the ground, and the Spitfire, with its long, flat nose, was no exception. Continual zigzagging when taxying was therefore essential, although this was an acquired art.

The Tigers registered their first victory of the war on 20 November when Measures, Temple-Harris and Flinders intercepted and destroyed an He 111 off Southend. On the following day three Spitfires were on patrol near Cherbourg but eventually had to force-land in France, short of fuel, having been vectored on to a 54 Squadron aircraft and straying out of R/T range. Unfortunately Thom wrote his aircraft off. Treacy and Bushell refuelled and took off successfully the following day for the return to Hornchurch. Thom took a slower route home by rail and sea. Making a long and careful approach to Hornchurch, Paddy Treacy landed and taxied slowly across to dispersal. He beckoned his rigger over and told him to kneel by the flap cover of the aircraft's parachute flare tube and not to drop whatever came out. The flap opened and, instead of a flare, out slid three bottles of champagne which were dutifully taken to the Squadron's crew room and savoured!

Over the next few months, the 'Phoney War' represented a period of routine patrols and training for Fighter Command squadrons. At Hornchurch, crews relinquished their tents as the tension relaxed and moved back to the Messes and crew rooms. At Rochford they used the flying club buildings. Operational life became relatively mundane and air crews soon found themselves wishing either that the whole sorry situation could be resolved so that they could stand down and return to normality or that there could be some military movement so that they could play their part as fighter pilots. To help alleviate the boredom at Rochford, a low flying competition was organized by Mungo Park whilst the CO and Flight Commanders were absent. The idea was that participants would fly one circuit and make one low pass over the centre of the aerodrome. Mungo managed to get three others interested. Each participating pilot put half a crown into the kitty and he who was adjudged to have flown the lowest over the airfield won the money. 'Chiefy' Etteridge was not too happy about the situation, but he was in no position to do anything about it. Each 'competitor' took off in turn and completed his pass. But there was no doubt about the winner—Mungo Park was the only one to clip the grass with his propeller! Ground crews watched in anticipation of disaster as they saw the turves fly but Mungo was able to retrieve the situation and land with bent propeller tips. Etteridge could not restrain himself and a few choice words were uttered, Mungo trying in vain to fend off his deserved castigation with apologies! If there were winners on the day they were ironically the riggers, who had to straighten the blades using hide-faced hammers and wood blocks, and all the winnings were handed over to them (and spent in the local pub!). The whole incident was smoothed over and Mungo Park escaped official reprimand.

Ground crews remember Rochford for other reasons too—those

involved with refuelling the aircraft, for example, because the system there was not of the quickest. To replenish a 400-gallon bowser took a very long time because ordinary forecourt pumps were used. The method was ingenious: insert nozzle into top of tank; tie the lever in the up position with string; retire to the shade of the hangar; and emerge to dip the tank from time to time! At Hornchurch the process took about ten minutes at the fuel dump. It became general practice for the fuel bowser to visit each aircraft after the morning engine-run as usually another gallon or so could then be squeezed into the Spitfires—a gallon which might make the difference between a safe return or a sticky landing at another airfield. In fact, such was the importance of ensuring that every aircraft was filled to its limit that the morning 'top up' round soon found its way into Standing Orders.

It was around this time that the Squadron's aircraft were re-fitted with constant-speed propellers to replace the two-pitch, coarse-and-fine props. This initially entailed a lot of work and a considerable number of man-hours, but Bill Felstead saw a way of reducing this and designed a spanner which enabled the job to be done without draining the coolant system and removing the header tank. He recalls:

> Workshops made it up, and by next day almost it was in use throughout Fighter Command! Hornchurch's Engineering Officer got the credit but got me promoted to Sergeant.

Whilst Bill Felstead was helping solve the problem of changing propellers, armourers Bernard Stebbings and Johnny Johnson were trying to think of ways of preventing the guns' freezing at heights above 28,000ft:

> We tried everything. We lubricated them with an anti-freezing oil, paraffin, used graphite and even tried sending them up dry, but they still froze up. It occurred to us that the problem centred around the very cold air at the heights we were talking about and the direction of the airflow above and beneath the wing. Perhaps the ejection opening on the underside was too vulnerable. We decided to test our theory by obtaining permission to design and fit a metal baffle to one aircraft which would deflect the sub-zero air past the openings. It worked so well in conjunction with the application of a 50/50 mixture of paraffin and anti-freezing oil on the prototype that the baffles were quickly fitted to the remainder of the Squadron aircraft. Within weeks they started to appear on Spits throughout Fighter Command and we were never sure whether our idea had been conveniently borrowed or whether the scientists had coincidentally come up with the same solution at the same time as we did!

On 11 January, 74 finally made another interception—but only of Blenheims at 10,000ft off the East Coast. For a while the Tigers involved themselves in tests to prevent windscreens icing up, using the anti-freezing agent glycol. Mayne, Ritchie and Skinner carried out a series of cloud-flying sorties in an effort to induce the device to work before heavy snow grounded all Spitfires.

At the end of February Squadron Leader F. L. 'Droguer' White arrived to take command of the Tigers. The nickname 'Droguer' was earned when White was in Malta as a member of the Station Flight towing drogue targets for anti-aircraft practice. His arrival at Hornchurch prompted little change in Squadron practices, although rather more air-to-air and air-to-ground work seems to have been undertaken. An influx of new boys arrived to replace experienced pilots posted out, and almost predictably another series of accidents ensued. Duckenfield crash-landed after a session of aerobatics, Stevenson force-landed on mud flats off Canvey Island after engine failure (he was rescued, but the aircraft was irrecoverable) and another Spitfire was wrecked the following day when Sergeant Skinner crashed at Rochford. All were losses incurred during the course of training sorties, but, very soon now, operational flying with real chances of meeting the enemy would dominate all 74 Squadron activity.

DUNKIRK

The invasion of Norway in May 1940 marked the end of the Phoney War, and shortly afterwards Luxembourg, Holland and Belgium fell to the fast-advancing Panzer Divisions. 74 acted as escort to the destroyer bringing Queen Juliana of the Netherlands to Britain after her country was over-run. Even at this stage it seemed as though Britain were immune from air attack, but the reasons for the Luftwaffe not launching such an offensive were largely based on its conviction that the desired results could not be achieved from airfields in Germany: whilst the campaign against the Low Countries was underway, it would not waste its strength on activity against England. This self-imposed restriction lasted until the German Army entered the smoking ruins of Dunkirk.

After eight months of prolonged operational inactivity, all leave was stopped on 10 May. Standing patrols over the Thames Estuary were followed on the 16th by the first offensive patrols near Ostend. By this time the situation in Belgium was becoming desperate and that country's army, together with the British and the French, was being pushed unrelentingly back to the coast. It was during this retreat that Fighter Command made its first sustained contribution, flying 300 sorties daily, often at extreme range, in an effort to prevent the Luftwaffe's bombers and fighters from attacking the retreating men. The threat that Fighter Command had been deployed to resist on its formation had become reality: the Luftwaffe was now ranged in a gigantic arc from southern Norway to Brittany.

On 21 May the Tigers were heavily engaged. Shortly before noon, Malan's Flight was scrambled to patrol over Dover. The cloud base was a mere 800ft and visibility was down to $1\frac{1}{2}$ miles. There seemed to be little hope of intercepting any enemy formation in those broken clouds, and initially it looked like being just another patrol. However, 74 came out of cloud at 17,000ft and almost immediately saw black smoke puffs over Calais—which could only mean that Allied anti-aircraft fire from that beleaguered town was attempting to shoot down counter-attacking German aircraft. Malan increased speed and set course for France. A dramatic newspaper account of the ensuing action was later published which, although full of 'journalese', does portray something of the excitement of his first engagement:

There were more clouds between them and Calais and the Spits dodged in and out of towering fleecy tufts as they pressed on. Sailor Malan was flying across the top of a great hummock of a cloud when without warning he came on a He 111 so suddenly that he almost collided with it. It was moving so fast that only by pulling his stick hard back and swerving violently did he manage to avoid ramming him. He was so afraid the German might escape by dropping down into the cloud 100ft below that he began firing while he was still doing a steep banking turn on the German's tail. The bullets ripped into the Heinkel from tail to nose. Pieces flew off and the Hun belched heavy smoke; his undercart fell out and he dropped helplessly into the cloud. The Heinkel had bought it. As Sailor saw the enemy bomber breaking up he yelled to his section over the radio 'Reform! Reform!' Suddenly Sailor spotted a Ju 88. He got on to the German's tail and fired when he was about five hundred yards away. He saw his bullets hammering home against the Hun's starboard wing root. But the Junkers kept on flying. Sailor manoeuvred his Spit into a better position. Then when he was one hundred and fifty yards away he saw his bullets bursting all over the Hun. And then came the end. The German aircraft fell into a dive with flames trailing behind. Sailor Malan had tasted blood at last. He found the release from tension terrific, the thrill enormous. He had been wondering too long how he would react on his first show. Now he knew. Everything he had learnt had come right. Sailor found there was hardly time ever to feel scared. He had scored two kills in his first engagement.

Bill Skinner, twenty years of age at the time, later recounted to Taffy Jones his feelings on his first Dunkirk patrol:

I had a feeling of trepidation as I crossed the Channel and saw the smoke curling high into the sky from the town. I wondered how I would feel when I got into a scrap. As Malan was leading I had complete faith in him. We got into a fight all right. I picked out my man but failed to keep as cool as I should have done, so was off my target. However, when it was all over and I was on my way home, I came to the conclusion that it was not so frightening as I had expected.

Bertie Aubert was reported missing from this same patrol after downing a Ju 88 and damaging an He 111 and news later came through that he had force-landed near Calais. Freeborn also shot down a Ju 88. The following day Malan, Freeborn and Mould shared one of the same type.

Meanwhile the increased activity in the air was keeping ground crews very busy, but they responded with predictable enthusiasm. In common with most stations, there was a very good NAAFI at Hornchurch and the twice-daily visits by the NAAFI van to the dispersal area dispensing Chelsea buns and doughnuts were always looked forward to. In the evenings, entertainment began to be laid on, with many well known stars of the day appearing. A regular favourite was The Gang Show. Time off was well organized too, so although the work was hard there were ample opportunities for recreation when the men were off duty. There always seemed to be plenty to do with a couple of pubs, a dance hall and picture house close to the camp, although the men often ventured further afield.

On 23 May Paddy Byrne was reported missing over Calais and Dunkirk, having been hit by anti-aircraft fire from Clairmarais Wood, the Tigers' old stamping ground from the First World War, and the CO was also reported missing in the same area after sharing an Hs 126 with Measures. His aircraft was traced to Calais, where he had been forced to land with an engine problem. White returned to the Squadron following a quite remarkable rescue by 54 Squadron in which a Miles Master trainer was flown across the Channel in the hands of Flight Lieutenant Leathart, who landed at Calais, located and picked up White and returned with him to Hornchurch. Whilst this was going on a pair of 54's Spitfires, flown by Al Deere and Johnny Allan, were engaging Me 109s overhead and success-fully preventing any harm coming to the Master and its passenger. On his return to Hornchurch, White reported his Spitfire as needing only minor repairs to make it airworthy again. A Blenheim was despatched with Corporal George Higginbottom and LAC Cressey on board and flown, with a Spitfire escort, to Calais to repair the aircraft. When the two ground crewmen arrived they found the problem to be far more exten-sive than their Boss had diagnosed. They were therefore brought back to Hornchurch, the necessary equipment and spares were collected and they were returned to France and left with the Spitfire, the idea being that they would be picked up the next morning when the Blenheim returned with a pilot on board to fly the Spitfire out. The whole Station seemed to turn out to see the Blenheim off, but those present will never forget the disbelief when it was announced that the Blenheim would not be going back for Higginbottom and Cressey after all as the situation over the Channel had deteriorated sufficiently to make the operation too dangerous. The Blenheim pilot was a very angry man. He wanted to go; and in retrospect the whole operation had been an utter waste, with the Blenheim and escorting Spitfires risked four times, *possibly* to save one aircraft when others were being abandoned and destroyed in France by the dozen.

On 24 May Malan shared in the destruction of a Do 17. Later in the day he accounted for an He 111, during the engagement with which he was hit in the starboard wing. One shell broke his ring reflector sight, another severed electrical leads and yet another tore a piece out of his flying boot. Climbing steeply into the sun to avoid his attacker, Malan decided there and then to fit the spare ring-and-bead sight which he carried. He quickly slipped it into place and rejoined battle, but by this time the dogfight had moved on. Malan returned to base. At 6.00 a.m. on the same day Sammy Hoare took off from Rochford with B Flight to patrol the Channel area around Calais. The pilots had been briefed not to cross the French coast unless in pursuit of enemy aircraft. After half an hour B Flight leader Paddy Treacy called that he had sighted a Henschel 126 reconnaissance aircraft low down and a mile or so east of Calais. Both sections went into line astern and dived, getting within attacking range of the Henschel when about fifteen miles inland from the French coast. Hoare did not get a chance to fire his guns: by the time he was in position the 126 was at tree-top height and on fire, thanks to the attentions of his colleagues. Shortly afterwards it hit the ground and exploded.

Treacy gave the order to return to base and the aircraft turned westwards. As the section was approaching the French coast again, Hoare's engine started boiling, glycol vapour streaming from it. A quick check of the instruments showed radiator temperatures off the clock, oil temperature high and pressure low. Sammy had a difficult decision to make. Flying at just 1,500ft, he could not be sure that the engine would get him home, or even across the Channel. Should he land in France and hope to get a quick repair done? At the time they were overflying Calais Marcke, from where Squadron Leader White had been rescued. Sammy also knew that the airmen Higginbottom and Cressey were still in the vicinity, and so the sensible decision would be to land straight away, therefore avoiding further damage to his engine. Judging by the state of the airfield which had been cratered by recent bombing, a forced landing seemed to present some difficulties but, following normal procedures, he prepared for a wheels-down landing using minimum engine revs. He had selected a line of approach which would take him between the many craters on touch-down: but, to his astonishment, at about 400ft on the final approach all the craters seemed to disappear. It was not until he actually landed that Hoare discovered why—the grass was about three feet high! Fortunately he kept straight during the final stages of his approach and the aircraft quickly came to rest without disappearing into a hole in the ground. Higginbottom and Cressey ran up as he climbed out of his cockpit and after a brief explanation they had the engine cowlings off in a matter of minutes. The trouble was soon located: a bullet hole in the pipe from the header tank to the engine had allowed most of the glycol to leak out. As there was no other visible damage to engine or airframe, Hoare called Treacy, who had remained overhead. Paddy Treacy promised to see that spares were flown out to enable the aircraft to be repaired. As to how the bullet hole had got there in the first place, the most likely explanation was that his Section had crossed the German line in its pursuit of the Hs 126.

Sammy Hoare's first thoughts were to have his Spitfire towed to a hangar so that it would not become a target should another bombing attack on the airfield be made. Higginbottom told him that it was almost deserted, there being only a handful of French Air Force personnel remaining in the domestic area and who were at that time having breakfast. Hoare called at the Mess to ask for assistance, but all he could get out of them was 'C'est fini: la guerre est fini'. And for them it probably was, for in fields adjacent to the airfield German tanks were already arriving. There was no option but to destroy the Spitfire. Sammy returned to the airfield and ran towards it with Higginbottom. They still had some way to go when the Germans started to attack, a few tanks appearing in full view on the far side. A hail of small-arms fire whistled through the long grass and, realizing that there was no hope of reaching the aircraft, the two men threw themselves flat, crawled away and spent the following twenty-four hours trying unsuccessfully to escape from the area. The sound of gunfire was coming from all directions and both Calais and Dunkirk were ablaze. Early in the evening they found themselves on the beach, together with refugees and British Army survivors from Calais, sandwiched between German tanks moving along the dunes from both east and west. Hopelessly trapped, they were all rounded up. It seemed so unbelievable. For Sammy the real war had only been fought for the past two weeks. As he stood on the beach he could see Spitfires and Hurricanes patrolling above him, the former perhaps flown by his colleagues from the Squadron. And just visible on the horizon were the white cliffs of Dover. They might just as well have been a thousand miles away. Sammy was to spend many months contemplating the activities of the Squadron he had served for nearly three years, wondering what had happened to Cressey and Higginbottom, with whom he lost contact, and also wondering whether or not a boiling Merlin engine would have got him across the Channel.

The stories of those Tigers who suffered the indignity of capture by the enemy during the Second World War could fill a book in themselves and it would be impossible to catalogue the experiences of them all here. However, tribute can be paid to their courage and resourcefulness in captivity. Throughout the days of their internment they considered themselves still to be Tigers—albeit caged Tigers—and their thoughts were often with their colleagues they had left behind. At one of the camps in which he was held, Oflag VIB, Sammy met up with Bill Skinner, who had often flown with him in B Flight, and then with Boulding, Parkes and Sandeman, all of whom had joined the Squadron after Hoare had been captured. The fact that they did not know each other mattered not. Once it had been established that they were all members of 74 Squadron, they were chatting like old friends. The Tiger spirit prevailed.

Pilot Officer Bertie Aubert returned to Hornchurch the same day that Hoare went down in France, 24 May, having left his damaged Spitfire at Calais where he too had force-landed three days previously. He took off within hours on a further patrol twenty miles south of Dunkirk from which he was reported missing once again. This time there was no happy ending, confirmation coming through that he had been shot down and killed. 74's successes on this eventful day were a Do 17 credited to Dowding and a Ju 88 to Skinner, whilst Mungo Park suffered a slight flesh wound to the left arm after an engagement with the enemy. Success continued on the 26th when, on the first patrol of the day, another Henschel 126 was shot down at low level, the kill being shared by Stephen, Mayne and Cobden. Stephen recalls that the army co-operation aircraft exploded in mid air:

This was my first engagement and that explosion was pretty horrifying. I wasn't expecting it and it came as a terrible surprise.

It was on this day that the British Admiralty signalled 'Operation Dynamo must begin'—the start of the evacuation of troops from the

Belgian and French coasts. On the 27th Ernie Mayne and Treacy claimed an Me 109 each. Two Do 17s were accounted for by Skinner and Stephen in a mid-afternoon sortie. Treacy was also involved in this but was later listed missing once again, this time over Lumbres. His escape back to England on this occasion was not to be the formality it had been a few days earlier. He found a route through Spain, whence he reached Eire. He did not return to 74, going instead to command 242 Squadron. Pilot Officer Stevenson, too, was reported missing in the Dunkirk/Calais sector but he had returned to the Squadron by the end of the month.

This short period of sustained activity had left men exhausted. They had destroyed twenty-six Germans (fifteen confirmed and eleven probable) and damaged four in seven days for the loss of three pilots—Aubert killed and Byrne and Hoare prisoners-of-war. Sailor Malan's personal quota of five led to the DFC which was announced a few days later. To give the tired pilots a chance to recuperate, 74 flew up to Leconfield on 27 May—sufficient ground crews to support the Spitfires were transported in a venerable old Bombay—and the ensuing week was spent in training. The day after Dunkirk fell, 74 returned to Hornchurch. In the night of 5/6 June, thirty Luftwaffe bombers crossed the East Coast to attack airfields and other objectives. Convoy and reconnaissance patrols were ordered, but there was no sign of the enemy in the sectors the Tigers flew until Ben Draper damaged an Me 109 and a Do 17 on 10 June. Sailor Malan flew down to Farnborough to participate in a flying trial against a captured Me 109 on the 13th.

Night raids continued to be flown by the Germans, and several of the Tigers' pilots volunteered to attempt interceptions. Taking off at 0020 during a raid on Southend and using the local searchlight units to pinpoint enemy aircraft, Malan found an He 111 whose crew failed to see him approaching from the rear quarter. Once within range, he opened up with his Brownings, saw his tracers bury themselves in the Heinkel's fuselage and then was temporarily blinded when oil from the stricken German spewed over his windscreen. Sailor almost immediately saw another raiding He 111 coned in searchlights and fired two five-second bursts. One of the crew baled out as the aircraft caught fire, later to crash near Chelmsford. This was the first occasion on which any pilot from any squadron had destroyed *two* enemy aircraft in one night. Incidentally, for night flying a flare path had to be laid out at Hornchurch—a trailer-mounted Chance light at one end of the landing field and gooseneck flares in a 'T' pattern away from it. The flares were paraffin-fuelled and had to be individually lit as and when required, this job usually being carried out by the Squadron armourers.

At the end of June, King George VI visited Hornchurch to confer Malan's DFC and also award 54 Squadron's Al Deere, Johnny Allan and 'Prof' Leathart their decorations for the part they played in the rescue of Squadron Leader White. New arrivals included the CO's namesake, Sergeant White, who was killed just nine days later when his Spitfire was struck by lightning and crashed in flames near Margate. As July progres-

sed, offensive patrols continued to be flown. The emphasis of the Luftwaffe's attack was still at night, although on the 6th Tinky Measures and
Derek Dowding sighted and attacked a pair of He 111s by day. Measures
damaged one, followed it to the French coast and saw it crash into the sea.
Dowding also badly damaged the other one but because of cloud was
unable to confirm its destruction. Two days later the same pair were again
in the fray when, together with Skinner, they were scrambled from
Manston. A solitary He 111 was sighted and all three attacked one after
the other. Skinner saw the German dive to the sea in flames. In the
afternoon of the same day Mould and Stevenson were on patrol over
Manston when they saw a quartet of Me 109s. Mould attacked one of
them and by dint of very accurate gunfire forced it to land at Elham. The
pilot was uninjured and taken prisoner. Stevenson meanwhile had
accounted for another of the Messerschmitts.

THE BATTLE OF BRITAIN

July 10, 1940, marked the beginning of the Battle of Britain—the date on
which the Luftwaffe commenced their concentrated daytime operations
against British ports and ships in the Channel and North Sea. 74
Squadron had already flown a number of shipping and convoy patrols in
an attempt to protect vessels from raiding bombers and were now
frequently operating from Manston, flying in from Hornchurch in the
early mornings and returning after the day's fighting in the evenings, an
arrangement which gave the Spitfires more time over the sea and thereby
allowed them to become a more effective fighting force.

The Squadron entered the fray bright and early that showery morning.
Patrolling in the Deal and Dover area, a formation of eight sighted twenty
Do 17s, forty Me 109s and forty Me 110s. The Tigers immediately
wheeled into the attack despite the odds being stacked so formidably
against them, and within minutes a whirling dogfight filled the skies, with
aircraft twisting, turning and diving around each other in a mêlée
reminiscent of the aerial battles of just twenty-two years earlier.
Measures badly damaged an Me 110 and a Do 17 and saw two enemy
aircraft collide. St John damaged an Me 109, whilst Stevenson crippled
two Me 110s. Draper in turn damaged a Do 17. The credit for the first
confirmed enemy aircraft to be destroyed by the Squadron in this opening
phase of the Battle of Britain went to Mungo Park, who attacked a Do 17
and watched as it turned lazily on to its back after its starboard engine had
burst into flames and dived into the sea. Cobden also went after a Do 17
but was himself riddled with bullet holes as he was delivering a second
attack on the damaged bomber. Engaging emergency boost, he broke
away in a steep climbing turn and, having evaded his pursuers, made an
emergency landing at Manston.

Red and Yellow Sections took off and were in action again mid-morning when they found a single Do 17—probably on a photographic reconnaissance mission—escorted by thirty Me 109s. Once again the Tigers

went straight into the attack, Freeborn immediately downing an Me 109 at fifty yards. Stevenson crippled one and destroyed another. St John, Draper and Cobden damaged one Messerschmitt each. Both Johnny Freeborn and Tony Mould successfully force-landed, their aircraft damaged by return fire from the German fighters. Two days later 74 were flying interception and convoy patrols when Red Section was vectored to a position fifteen miles north-east of Margate, where it quickly sighted AA fire from a ship which was being bombed by an He 111. Malan gave the order to attack in line astern, opened up at 300yds and silenced heavy fire from the Heinkel's rear guns. Mould and Stevenson attacked in turn and sent the German crashing into the sea.

A week of indifferent weather restricted the activities of the raiders and gave the defending squadrons a breathing space. Piers Kelly, an experienced Fleet Air Arm pilot, was posted on to the Squadron during this period and was quickly recognized as a very good bad-weather flyer. Most of the Squadron pilots subsequently flew with him on formation practice, as H. M. Stephen recalls:

> I don't think I have ever had such a terrible flight in my life—through thunderclouds, torrential rain, turbulent air. All I knew was that I hadn't a clue where we were and if I lost Kelly then I would be in trouble. So I didn't take my eyes off him the whole time we were in the air. I seem to remember we landed at Leuchars to refuel before returning to Hornchurch. We did as much training of this nature as we could and it is thanks to that that 74 were so proficient at close formation work.

On 19 July twelve aircraft were scrambled from Manston to intercept enemy aircraft over Dover, but they arrived only after the raiders had bombed the harbour. Sailor and Peter Stevenson saw two Me 109s and a Hurricane in a tight circle and attacked. Both the 109s were badly damaged and recorded as probables. The next contact with the enemy was on the 24th. In the early evening, A Flight took off to patrol the Channel and once again its pilots were detailed to intercept a raid near Dover. They found three Do 215s flying at sea level but as soon as these saw the Spitfires they immediately turned tail, one of them opening fire at 2,000yds, presumably in an attempt to scare the fighters off! 74 gave chase but were forced to break away over the French coast. The following day Malan's patrolling Red Section found a flight of Me 109s heading towards Calais and attacked but, short of fuel, was forced to return to Manston, running the gauntlet of Royal Navy gunners who misidentified the Spitfires as the enemy.

On 28 July the Squadron scrambled twelve aircraft in good visibility. Vectored on to fighters escorting another raid on Dover (leaving the bombers to a Hurricane squadron), they found thirty-six Me 109s: 'Tally Ho! The Tigers!' Another hectic dogfight ensued, with 74 emerging as the victors: Malan—one destroyed and one damaged; Kelly—one destroyed; Freeborn—one destroyed, and landing with damage to his own aircraft; Stevenson—one destroyed and two damaged, he too landing with damage to his aircraft; Stephen—one damaged; Gunn—one destroyed; St

John—one damaged. But a price was paid: Pilot Officer Young was shot down over the Goodwin Sands and was killed, and Tony Mould successfully baled out of his stricken aircraft despite being wounded.

The Tigers went on to bring July to a less successful close when sent to help counter a further build-up of enemy raids. Only B Flight made contact with the enemy. Kelly was leading and saw fifteen Me 109s 2,000ft above him and approaching on the port beam. The Spitfires formed line astern and turned towards them, forcing the Germans to split into two groups of six and nine, also in line-astern formation. The first group of six took the initiative by opening the attack. Sergeant 'Tiger Tim' Eley was hit during the first pass and went down in flames, hitting the sea just outside Folkestone harbour. Gunn was also quickly shot down. Piers Kelly turned to get on the tail of one of the enemy but a second Messerschmitt got on to *his* tail and opened fire at short range, damaging the cowling and armour plating, piercing the upper petrol tank and damaging the port wing. The aircraft was difficult to control and went into a short spin, but Kelly managed to recover, only to find 109s on either side of him and above. He fired at one to keep it off and then turned towards the other, but his damaged Spitfire again entered a spin. Once again he pulled out, and once again two Germans moved in above and below. The aircraft below executed a slow roll and dived away as though to act as a decoy whilst the second 109 stayed up into the sun, ready to attack. Kelly climbed towards the second but the damage to his aircraft prevented him from getting within range. Breaking off, he managed to limp back to Manston at low level.

Meanwhile, as Green Section climbed with Mungo Park leading, the other nine Me 109s turned in towards it. A pair of the enemy aircraft dived past once again, apparently acting as a decoy, but they were ignored and the climb continued, although by this time Mungo had lost sight of the remaining Germans and failed to regain contact. Bill Skinner, who had become detached from his section during the first climbing turn, saw a wide 'vic' of three Messerschmitts 5,000ft below him and made a diving attack from astern on to the centre aircraft, sending it seawards belching smoke and flame. But the odds on this occasion had been in the Germans' favour. For the loss of Sergeant Eley and Pilot Officer Gunn, one Me 109 had possibly been destroyed. However, the totals for the Squadron overall since hostilities began were thirty aircraft confirmed destroyed and nineteen unconfirmed, with seven of its own pilots missing. And news had come through of a DFC for Johnny Freeborn and a bar to the DFC that Sailor Malan had already won.

At the beginning of August Hitler issued a directive for the preliminary stage of the invasion of Great Britain, Operation 'Sealion'—the subjugation of the RAF. To this end, the German offensive against coastal airfields and radar stations began. Air Vice Marshal Keith Park, CO of 11 Group, which was to bear the brunt of the German onslaught, was very popular with those he commanded. It was his skill and experience, and that of Air Chief Marshal Hugh Dowding, that in some measure offset the British inferiority in numbers. At squadron level the dedication of 'The Few', as they came to be known, was paramount in securing the ultimate victory in the Battle of Britain. Of all those who served with the Tigers during those dark days, the name of the South African A. G. Malan is the one most often remembered; indeed, it is perpetuated by the Malan Memorial Sword, which is still carried by the Squadron Commander today on ceremonial duties. Sailor—the nickname came from his early days in the Merchant Navy—was appointed Commanding Officer of 74 Squadron at the time the Germans launched the second phase of the battle and was, in the public's eye, the archetypal ace. A handsome man, he was a fine shot and a determined fighter who had crossed that thin line which often separates the expert from the genius. But he was always the first to acknowledge that it was the backing and support of the Squadron that enabled him to achieve what he did. He was well loved by all who served with him and under him. He was strict but very fair, expecting everyone to give 100 per cent. Ground crews adored him. Bill Felstead speaks for them all when he says,

> Those were the days. Churchill was so right. What bloody marvellous men they were. Malan, Stephen, Treacy, Mungo Park. I think Malan was the most wonderful man I ever met. Certainly, in all my long service in the RAF, I never met another like him.

Bob Spurdle, who flew alongside Malan on numerous occasions, considered him to be somewhat aloof but puts that down to a measure of shyness:

> But he was without doubt a great leader of men and he gave us all tremendous confidence and faith in our squadron as a fighting unit.

Malan came to 74 from 3 FTS at Grantham at the end of 1936, had been promoted to Pilot Officer in early 1937 and while holding that comparatively humble rank was appointed Acting Flight Commander of A Flight in August 1937. Further promotion to Flight Lieutenant during the early days of the war was now followed by command.

There are many stories which illustrate Malan the fighting man. The media of the time portrayed him as being indestructible, ruthless and determined:

> This job of killing the Hun in the air is a serious business [he is quoted as saying]. When you go up make your target four enemy planes every sortie. You won't do it of course but it is no use going for just one man and then coming home.

But Malan also attached great importance to the avoidance of unnecessary risk to life and aircraft, just as his counterpart twenty-two years earlier, Mick Mannock, had done. Cuthbert Orde, who painted many famous pilots during the war, gave Malan pride of place in his book of portraits of RAF fighter pilots:

> I have seldom been more impressed by anyone as I was the first time I saw him. A very quiet manner and an air of authority made it obvious that here was a

leader of great determination and ability. He would undoubtedly improve a squadron, however good, not by sword waving but by strength of mind and integrity.

Malan was a perfectionist who insisted on absolute efficiency in everything connected with flying. H. M. Stephen recalls that all the pilots new to the Squadron held Malan in some awe and could even admit to being a little afraid of him:

I certainly was for a while, but that soon turned into respect for a man who was undoubtedly a fine leader and a fine disciplinarian. Any of the youngsters who flew with him would be sweating hard within minutes and then when they got down he would tell them that they would have to work harder next time! He pushed us hard but he quickly made us very aware of what we were capable and what was expected of us and of the Squadron.

Malan's outstanding flying characteristic was his aggressiveness. He himself once said:

This is the first quality of a successful fighter pilot. He must think in terms of offence rather than defence. He must at all times be the attacker. Both his mind and body must be alert and both must react instinctively to any tactical situation. When you are flying you have no time to think.

It was over France, the Low Countries and Dunkirk that the inadequacy of RAF tactics became very apparent. The Luftwaffe, with its experience of the Spanish Civil War, had been able to modify its own tactics to take account of the new generation of aircraft it was flying. Dunkirk was the turning point regarding where the air war was to be fought. Up to that time the RAF flew its patrols at around 8,000ft. During Dunkirk that altitude was pushed progressively up to 25,000ft in the course of seven days. Stephen remembers:

Our patrolling heights were initially low, but we responded to the Germans and the heights at which they flew. For us that meant ensuring that we were always above the enemy. As we got higher, so the Army on the beaches below began to ask, 'Where are the bloody RAF?' The answer was at 25,000ft, making sure we were above the enemy otherwise we would be losing aeroplanes as well as soldiers. Defence of the ground meant flying at heights where we could combat the Germans.

The RAF tactics which evolved during the Battle of Britain were formulated 'in the field'. Keith Park would work with Squadron Commanders on a day-to-day basis, formulating the revised approach. Most squadrons persisted with the three-aircraft 'vic' formation (one of the biggest drawbacks of which was the need for concentration in keeping formation at the expense of keeping a look out for the Luftwaffe) with a 'weaver' behind to protect the formation from enemy attack (which, if taken out by an enemy fighter without the alarm being raised, meant that the rest of the formation was at risk). There were exceptions, and Sailor Malan and 74 provided one of them. They began to fly in two pairs, usually line astern (although sometimes side by side), which, as Tiger Roger Boulding says,

. . . meant that we were far more manoeuvrable than those units flying in vics. Aircraft flying as a pair could do almost anything—stand on their heads, stall their aeroplanes—and stay together in the same sort of airspace.

H. M. Stephen again:

In combat a pair would fight according to the situation. We would all have learnt a number of attacks that were going to produce results but we would all have our own preferences. Mine was to attack from an angle of 15 degrees or 20 degrees, a regime that demanded a fair degree of judgement and skill—a skill that I had learnt on pheasant shoots and the like before the war.

SAILOR'S DAYS

During the first ten days of August there were no engagements with the enemy although 74 flew a heavy schedule of patrols from Hornchurch and Manston with up to seventy offensive sorties a day. On 5 August the first two Poles to be posted to the Squadron arrived, Flight Lieutenant Brzezina and Flying Officer Szczesny—who were immediately christened 'Breezy' and 'Sneezy' as an alternative pronunciation of their names! The exploits of the Polish pilots in the Battle of Britain are legendary and those who survived were proud to have been numbered amongst The Few. Szczesny in particular was very popular with all the ground crews. He was very much 'one of the boys' and would always share his cigarette ration with them; they in turn would make a fuss of him, rejoicing in his undisguised and excited delight when he shot down a German aircraft.

Malan could hardly have wished for a more decisive start to his period as Commanding Officer of the Tigers when, on 11 August, his Squadron flew into battle on no fewer than four occasions between dawn and 1400 hrs against enemy aircraft which for the main part were bombing East Coast ports and shipping. At the end of the day the Squadron's claim was for twenty-three enemy aircraft destroyed, one probable and fourteen damaged—an achievement which the Tigers proudly claimed as a record and which led to a telegram from the Chief of Air Staff:

A magnificent day's fighting 74 . . . This is the way to keep the measure of the Boche. Mannock started it and you keep it up.

Winston Churchill had, characteristically, kept himself informed of the day's events, too, for he arrived at Hornchurch in the evening to add his personal congratulations to pilots and ground crews alike, stopping to spend a little time in the Mess and then to watch the armourers and riggers at work on the Spitfires.

The first operational order to intercept a hostile raid approaching Dover had been received at dawn. Twelve aircraft led by Malan climbed to 20,000ft and surprised eighteen Me 109s flying towards the Kentish port. In the subsequent engagement, eight of the 109s were destroyed and four damaged. One went to Malan, one to Nelson, one (and one damaged) to Mungo Park, two (and two damaged) to Stephen, one to Stevenson, one (and one damaged) to Hastings and one to Smith. Sailor Malan tells the story in his combat report, which cites the Squadron callsign as 'Dysoe':

. . . Some of the Me 109s adopted the usual German fighter evasive tactics, that is a quick half roll and dive. On this occasion the air seemed clear of German aircraft above us. I followed one down and overtook him after he had dived 2,000ft, opening fire during the dive at two hundred yards range with deflection. He levelled out at about 12,000 ft so I gave him a couple of two-second bursts at one hundred yards. He was in a quick half roll and dived towards the French coast. I closed again to one hundred yards range and gave him another two or three two-second bursts when he suddenly burst into flames and was obscured by heavy smoke. This was at 4,000ft one mile north-west of Cap Gris Nez . . .

Stevenson's aircraft was hit by enemy fire after he saw a solitary Me 109 above him:

I climbed up to him. He must have initially thought I was an Me 109 too but when he suddenly dived away I followed him and gave him a two-second deflection burst. The enemy lurched slightly and went into a vertical dive. I kept my height at 15,000ft and watched. I saw him dive straight into the sea fifteen miles south-east of Dover and disappear in a big splash of water. I then climbed to 23,000ft up-sun and saw a formation of twelve Me 109s 2,000ft below me. It was my intention to attach myself to the back of this formation from out of the sun. As I was diving for them a really large volume of cannon and machine-gun fire came from behind me. There were about twelve Me 109s diving from the sun. There was a popping noise and my control column became useless. I found myself doing a vertical dive, getting faster and faster. I pulled the hood back. I got my head out of the cockpit and the slipstream tore the rest of me clean out of the machine.

Stevenson's trouser leg and both shoes were torn off by the blast but he suffered no debilitating injury and was able to pull the ripcord. When he hit the water his harness would not detach itself and he was dragged along, half-unconscious, before his struggling finally freed it. Now unencumbered, he started swimming, although he found this difficult because there was a heavy sea running. After an hour and a half, with Stevenson getting weaker by the minute, a motor torpedo boat came looking for him in response to a request from the Squadron. He was seen, picked up and taken to Dover.

The second combat took place mid-morning when twelve aircraft again took off to intercept enemy fighters approaching Dover. Several small groups of Me 109s were sighted in mid-Channel. One was destroyed by Freeborn and four were damaged by Malan and Mayne. Radio difficulties prevented the rest of the Squadron from engaging for they could not hear Sailor's orders as his radio had been damaged by an enemy bullet. The third combat started at 1145. This time eleven aircraft, led by Johnny Freeborn, took off to patrol a convoy twelve miles east of Clacton and it was not long before about forty Me 110s were spotted, approaching in close formation. When they saw 74, the Messerschmitts formed a defensive circle, but Freeborn led the Squadron in a dive into its centre and set to work on the Germans. Ten of the enemy aircraft were destroyed and five damaged—but at a cost: Don Cobden and Dennis Smith were shot down and killed. Freeborn had destroyed two of the enemy, Stephen two, Mungo Park one, Nelson one, Kirk one, Mayne one and Skinner two. With the exception of Freeborn, all these pilots had claimed a damaged Me 110 too. This was the last combat to be flown by Ernie Mayne, who had been with the Squadron since its re-formation. He had blacked out and fallen 20,000ft before coming to, but the drop had caused his eardrums to burst and he was grounded.

A very tired Squadron took off for the fourth time in the early afternoon, with Malan once again leading. Unserviceabilities had left just eight aircraft available, and they were detailed to patrol Hawkinge and Margate. Ten Ju 87s and twenty Me 109s were quickly seen, and 74 went into the attack. The 109s immediately dived for cloud but did not escape: once again the Tigers came out on top, with four destroyed and one damaged and with no loss to themselves. The top scorer for the Squadron on this remarkable day—quickly dubbed 'Sailor's August 11th'—had been H. M. Stephen, who claimed five Germans shot down and three damaged.

The Squadron was not called into action on 12 August, allowing the hard-worked ground crews to patch up the Spitfires after the previous day's fighting. August 13 was labelled 'Adler Tag' (Eagle Day) by the German High Command and was the day on which the RAF was to be defeated in the air once and for all, but the Luftwaffe lost forty-five aircraft against Fighter Command's thirteen. The Tigers patrolled Manston and found an incoming raid. Four Do 17s and two Do 215s were destroyed, with four Do 17s and two Do 215s claimed as probables. One Do 17 was damaged. Once again, there was no loss to 74.

At the height of this phase of the Battle of Britain, the Squadron withdrew from the front line and flew up to Wittering to rest and recover from the intensive patrol work and fighting of the previous few days. After a couple of non-flying days, local training started, utilizing Wittering's relief landing ground K3. The whole affair was hastily arranged, with everyone packed up and gone within a matter of hours, and personnel at Wittering were somewhat nonplussed by 74's arrival, no sleeping or feeding arrangements having been made. In the end they were accommodated in some old farm buildings. The Squadron had been on a real 'high' after the successes of the previous few days. To be suddenly thrust into this situation away from the fighting precipitated something of a drop in morale amongst all ranks, particularly when they learnt that they had missed some of the fiercest fighting thus far and also some of the heaviest raids, including those on 15 and 16 August—which were the most extensive in the whole of the Battle of Britain.

It is significant that eight or nine of the pilots on the Squadron when we were withdrawn on this occasion were the same as those who had gone to Leconfield when the Squadron had been withdrawn for a rest at the end of May. Experience was certainly beginning to count.

So says H. M. Stephen. Then aircraft and personnel were on the move again, this time the short distance to Kirton-in-Lindsey, where training continued, although not without incident. Two aircraft collided in mid-air during formation practice and Bill Skinner was compelled to bale out when the tail of his aircraft was sheared off. Neither he nor Wally Churches, who had pulled into him, was injured. Skinner's aircraft was burnt out; Churches force-landed with a bent propeller.

It was whilst at Kirton-in-Lindsey that ground crews found evidence of possible sabotage to the Spitfires. Several pilots had been reporting problems with lowering the undercarriage, and whilst no wheels-up landings were ever initiated the problem became sufficiently regular for a specific check to be made on all the Squadron's aircraft. Bill Felstead recalls finding that in the selector gear of some of the aircraft the nut securing the operating piston on the spindle had not been split-pinned and was not even tight:

> It would obviously have eventually vibrated off, the spindle would have pulled through the piston and the gear would have been left in the permanent 'up' position. I showed all this to Squadron Leader Malan who agreed that it was probably deliberate and he reported it to the proper authorities. All Spitfires were subsequently checked and as far as we were concerned there were no further problems.

On 3 September Malan and Freeborn attended Buckingham Palace to receive the decorations they had been awarded in July. On 8 September Piers Kelly was posted out and John Mungo Park was promoted to Flight Lieutenant to take command of B Flight. On the 9th the Tigers moved to Coltishall in preparation for their re-entry into the fight, ready to put into practice all that Malan had been teaching them over the previous three weeks. It was whilst at Coltishall that they exchanged their Spitfire Is for Mk IIs, which were basically Mk Is powered by 1175hp Merlin XII engines.

The Squadron's initial reintroduction to the fighting was to involve a flight down to Duxford to operate as part of the Duxford Wing, eight aircraft led by Sailor Malan taking off from the Cambridgeshire airfield as the rear component, with 19 Squadron in the lead and 611 in the middle, to intercept raids over the City of London. All the pilots returned safely to Coltishall after a hectic engagement, during the course of which they claimed one enemy aircraft destroyed and ten probables. The indifferent weather of the next two days prevented the Germans from launching any more major raids either by day or by night. On the 14th, however, both sides were involved again, 74 this time operating from Coltishall itself against targets around the East Anglian coast. Mungo Park, Ricalton and Boulding attacked a pair of Me 110s and damaged them both, although intensive fire from one of the Messerschmitts' rear gunners damaged Mungo's aircraft in turn. Later on the same date Ben Draper's Yellow Section was ordered to intercept hostile aircraft (which had just bombed Great Yarmouth) and found and probably destroyed a Ju 88. Red Section had meanwhile damaged an He 111 near Lowestoft which, after a hide-

and-seek engagement in and out of cloud, disappeared out to sea with its starboard engine smoking. In the afternoon it was the turn of Green Section, led by Wally Churches, to intercept a raid to the north-east of Ipswich. Roger Boulding sighted a lone Ju 88 heading north and the attack commenced. The Junkers was quickly damaged and, with smoke pouring from its fuselage, was seen to jettison two bombs. Roger Boulding also saw what were apparently hand grenades being thrown from the aircraft as he closed with it, presumably as a precaution against their exploding on board. They had obviously been primed before being thrown out, however, as they exploded after a few seconds!

Local skirmishing was all very well, but the Tigers were very much aware of the tremendous battles that were being fought around London as they languished in rural Norfolk under the auspices of 12 Group. On 15 September the failure of a last-ditch effort by Göring to deal a death blow to Fighter Command resulted in the cancellation by Hitler of the invasion of England. The Tigers did, however, continue to make spasmodic contact with the Luftwaffe, and David Ayers was lost whilst chasing enemy aircraft 1½ miles off Southwold. His body was recovered two weeks later when it was washed ashore. The following day, Franklin's Green Section sighted a Do 17 off the coast at Sheringham but, despite repeated attacks, it escaped—although the German's luck finally gave out when he crashed near Antwerp having managed to cross the North Sea safely. These contacts with the enemy and the requirement to fly regular patrols apart, Malan kept up a stiff training schedule for pilots and ground crews alike, knowing that before too long the Squadron would be returned to the thick of things as the German offensive entered its final phase. And now news came of more decorations for the Squadron: H. M. Stephen and Peter Stevenson were both awarded the DFC.

Despite the postponement of 'Sealion' and the turning of Hitler's mind to the Eastern Front, the Germans continued to maintain pressure on Britain by sending over fighters and fighter-bombers—modified Me 109s—in place of their far too vulnerable long-range bombers to attack industrial towns and ports over the country. Night attacks intensified, too, and these were a threat which the RAF could counter only gradually as techniques with radar and Ground Controlled Interception (GCI) improved. But there were times in the Royal Air Force when the numbers of air crew lost in training accidents seemed almost to equal those in combat. Training had to be as realistic as possible for any benefit to be gained, and inherent in this was the danger of collision. 74 lost Hastings and Buckland in such an accident whilst engaged in practice attacks on 8 October. Both aircraft crashed near Beccles, one of them hitting an area of hard ground, disintegrating and throwing wreckage over a wide area. The other descended in a flat spin close to a spot where a farmer was ploughing. He was the first person on the scene and found the aircraft still largely in one piece and upside down, having hardly penetrated the ground. Pilot Officer Buckland was still in the cockpit, hanging in his harness, but he had been killed on impact.

BIGGIN HILL

On 15 October, 74 flew their seventeen aircraft down to Biggin Hill to rejoin 11 Group and 92 and 66 Squadrons. Biggin had been the most heavily bombed station in Fighter Command and the damage was plain for all to see. Much of the airmen's accommodation had been laid flat and ground crews lived initially in a collection of wooden huts nicknamed 'The Warren', although during the first few days after the move from Coltishall a few slept wherever they could find space around the dispersal area. Others were fortunate to be billeted in old married quarters. Air crew, on the other hand, were accommodated in the lovely local country house that belonged to Waldren Smithers MP. For food and entertainment, many Tigers went to Knockholt, where the Elliot family, who ran 'The Crown', unofficially adopted them and treated them to many an excellent breakfast. Closer to Biggin itself was 'The White Hart', and here, too, good food was available to the pilots in the form of steaks, discreetly tucked away behind curtains.

Biggin Hill itself was constantly undergoing repair, the bomb craters caused by the latest raids being quickly filled in by airfield maintenance gangs, very often assisted by the Station's airmen. This forced a halt to the old practice of mass squadron take-offs (where up to twelve Spitfires ranged across the grass would take to the air simultaneously) as the risk of damage on the uneven ground was too great. The amount of equipment used to fill the craters and level the ground that was left on the airfield did lead on at least one occasion to a potentially fatal accident. Three aircraft returning from patrol attempted a formation landing. One of the outer aircraft, piloted by Brzezina, came in a little too low and hit the arm of a mechanical digger standing close to the landing path. The collision sheared off the oleo leg and wheel on the port side but the Pole was able to make a perfect landing, holding the Spitfire on just the one leg as it slowed until the speed was insufficient to keep it in that attitude, whereupon the wing dropped and the aircraft slewed and stopped.

Most routine servicing of aircraft was carried out in the often flooded dispersal bays as the hangars were considered to be unsafe. No major maintenance was carried out other than engine, propeller or oleo leg changes which would, when possible, be done in the single temporary blister hangar. All major repairs went to the Maintenance Units. It is often said that various ploys were thought up to keep aircraft in the air during the Battle of Britain, but as far as ground crews were concerned an aircraft was either serviceable or it was not: no technician would allow a pilot to take off in an aircraft known to be unserviceable. There was no pooling of maintenance resources as such. Each squadron was autonomous but, although there was no cross-training between armourers and fitters, everyone learnt very quickly to rearm and refuel aircraft, and ground crews were soon boasting of their ability to do this in less than ten minutes. At the height of the battle, officers, pilots and even the Station Commander would be on the pan assisting. Speed was of the essence as very often Sector Ops would want the aircraft back in the air again immediately. Ground crews would descend on an aircraft returning from patrol before the propeller had stopped turning and would ply their specialist trades whilst MT drivers brought up the 900-gallon fuel bowsers. Refuelling, rearming, engine checking, topping up oil and glycol, replacing oxygen cylinders, testing the radio—all would be done simultaneously.

As a panacea to the hectic and often dangerous work carried out by ground crews, the rostered off-duty moments at Biggin whilst the Tigers were resident were filled with the usual activities of servicemen—pubs, pictures or the dance halls. Crews were able to leave camp most evenings, after working on the Spitfires to ready them for the next morning's operations. Transport into Bromley by bus was easy. If the really bright lights beckoned, there were local trains to Waterloo. The same applied to the pilots, who all pursued their pleasures actively. H. M. Stephen recalls:

> We fought hard and we played hard. The great thing was that whatever time you flopped into bed someone was bound to get you up within a very few hours and expect you to be up and at it. And we were. We could cope with the hectic social life and then switch off completely and concentrate on the job in hand, never the worse for wear and always at the top of our form. We were young—that was the simple secret.

Within two days of its arrival at Biggin Hill, 74 was in action when eleven of its Spitfires intercepted enemy aircraft approaching London from the south. Guided by bursts of anti-aircraft fire over the Thames Estuary, the Tigers found the Luftwaffe over the Maidstone and Gravesend area. Sailor Malan attacked an Me 109, damaging its elevator controls and sending it into a vertical dive streaming black smoke. Ben Draper also attacked and damaged a single Me 109 before turning his attention to seven others which were flying slightly below him. He sent one down in flames. The Canadian Willie Nelson attacked another which immediately half rolled and dived vertically into the clouds, emitting white smoke. Peter St John went for a third and watched as it rolled on to its back with flames streaming from the engine. During the same action Alan Ricalton was killed when he was shot down near Hollingbourne.

Daily interception patrols did not always result in tangles with the enemy though, and it was three days before further contact was made. 74 was patrolling with 66 Squadron and found thirty Me 109s over Maidstone which broke formation as soon as they saw the British coming. Single aircraft were picked out of the general scramble and attacked. Mungo Park destroyed one. H. M. Stephen attacked a formation of four which promptly dived away in the direction of Dungeness and it was not until they were down to 900ft that he was able to pick one out. The tailplane broke up and the top of the cockpit flew off, but 'H. M.' was forced to break away when the other three Germans tried to get above him. In the mêlée that followed, he fired into one, the pilot baling out and the aircraft crashing into a wood. Draper fired a six-second burst into a

109 but was then himself hit, his oil radiator being shot away. His engine seized but he was able to glide down and belly land in a field. On his way down he saw his target crash near Woolwich. Sergeant Kirk was also shot down but was seriously wounded and lay for several days in Maidstone Hospital before dying of his injuries. Another Sergeant Pilot, Hilken, came to grief too, but he survived and was soon back on the Squadron.

Two days later 74 lost Peter St John whilst patrolling with 92 Squadron. Six 109s were intercepted over Ashford, 92 calling the 'Tally Ho!'. Malan sent one crashing into the sea and Mungo Park did the same with another. Bill Skinner was involved in a tussle with a pair of 109s but they got the better of him and he was forced to spin away to escape. Bob Spurdle baled out after being attacked: he was uninjured but had a lucky escape when his assailant returned to fire at him as he floated to earth. Newspapers got a whiff of a story and descended on the Squadron to talk to Bob:

As the New Zealander swept down on the yellow nosed fighter he felt his aircraft shudder. In a second he saw the right wing of his Spitfire crumple and rip away like tissue paper. A split second later the cockpit hood was shattered by a blast. Spurdle, as he expressed it afterwards, found himself 'shot out' of the Spitfire. The speed at which he was travelling caused his helmet and sheepskin-lined boots to be plucked from his spinning body. At that height it was icy cold and, divorced so abruptly from his oxygen supply, he became semi-conscious. But instinct prompted him to pull the ripcord of his parachute and he began a leisurely four-mile drift to earth. Dazed, and with his yellow Mae West lifebelt scrappled [*sic*] around his head, he could see nothing of the fighting he had left so unceremoniously as he swung backward and forward under his silken umbrella. A Nazi spotted him however and sent a stream of bullets in his direction. The odds were against him landing alive.

But the Nazis' hope of killing a 'sitter' was quashed abruptly by Churches and H. M. They circled around the suspended pilot until eventually Bob landed safely in a ploughed field. His chief emotion at that moment was one of silliness at finding himself in his stockinged feet!

On the 27th twelve aircraft took off from Biggin to patrol with 66 Squadron at 33,000ft over Maidstone. Flying so high was physically exhausting, and very little was known at that time about sustained flying at such altitudes. The increasing German use of faster, more manoeuvrable fighter-bombers called for greater vigilance on the part of the British and the need for almost continuous standing patrols, with the result that squadrons probably flew harder and the pilots became more tired than during the previous month's operations against the massed German raids. On this occasion they encountered thirty Messerschmitts and attacked out of the sun. Malan fired at two of them but was himself attacked by three Germans and his aircraft was hit. He was able to return to Biggin safely. Stephen set an Me 109 alight. Nelson, now OC A Flight, opened fire on Me 109s that came across his bows, getting so close that he was struck by debris. The Messerschmitt he had hit smoked badly and half rolled down and then pulled steeply into the sun so that Nelson could only follow him by the smoke trail; after two minutes he closed once more and gave a ten-second burst at point-blank range. The 109 again shed pieces of its fuselage, which again hit Nelson's aircraft, this time damaging the spinner and propeller, before finally crashing south of Rochester with the pilot apparently dead in the cockpit. Mungo Park had to break off his particular engagement when his guns froze. Bill Skinner took over where Mungo had left off and watched the 109 going down with black smoke pouring from it. Peter Chesters' chosen Messerschmitt attempted to turn on to the Tiger's tail but Chesters managed to pull his Spitfire round and put a burst into its engine. The German force-landed at Penshurst with his wheels up, Chesters landing beside him and personally taking him prisoner—an incident which provided the British pilot with a talking point for a long time afterwards! Nobody had seen Sergeant Scott disappear from the battle: he had crashed at Elmstead and was killed as the Spitfire exploded.

The Tigers took to the air again during the late afternoon of 29 October alongside 92 Squadron. They found more 109s, and Mungo Park, who was leading, scored two. Nelson attacked a singleton out of a group of six, and

> . . . the other five immediately disappeared and I was surprised and delighted to find my Me 109 climb to port and put up a fight whilst smoke was issuing from his engine. I circled it one and a half times before closing to point-blank range to fire two two-second bursts. The enemy aircraft did a half-roll and a third two-second burst sent it crashing to the ground in the East Grinstead area.

Churches saw and attacked an He 111 at 10,000ft over Tunbridge Wells whilst his Tiger colleagues were dealing with the Me 109s. It was last seen trailing smoke and gently diving towards Dungeness with Churches unable to catch it.

BIGGIN'S SIX HUNDREDTH

Historians have determined that the Battle of Britain was over by 31 October. The Luftwaffe had certainly failed to destroy the Royal Air Force: instead, they stepped up their night bombing campaign against British industry and the British people. November began for the Tigers with Sergeant Soars being wounded whilst on an interception patrol but managing to land safely. Willie Nelson was posted missing from the same patrol. Due for leave during August, he had turned it down, fretting over the number of untrained pilots that were being thrust into the fray. On 2 November the Tigers and 92 Squadron were patrolling Biggin Hill at 15,000ft and sighted sixty 109s over the Isle of Sheppey. Mungo Park was thwarted in his attack by a freezing windscreen which he was unable to clear. Churches shot one into the sea as did Morrison. Bill Skinner destroyed one, whilst Bob Spurdle dived down on to a formation of four and closed to point-blank range, firing as he went. The German he targeted took no evasive action, burst into flames, disintegrated and crashed near Ashford. Celebrations in the Mess on 5 November were ordered when it was learnt that Mungo Park had been awarded the DFC and Stephen a bar to the DFC he had received in September. Both were rising stars in the Fighter Command firmament and had been responsible for plenty of fireworks over the preceding few weeks.

It was 14 November before the Germans next launched a mass raid against London—fifty Ju 87s escorted by Me 109s—and the Tigers pounced on them. In Sailor's absence on leave, the honour of leading fell to Mungo Park. The Stukas were formed in tight 'vics' of five, in line astern, with the escort of Messerschmitts circling above them. The Tigers went for the port flank and 66 Squadron the starboard. Mungo attacked one 'vic' of Ju 87s and destroyed two aircraft: Stephen also engaged a section of three and after firing into one watched it roll into the aircraft next to it. Both went down out of control. He then attacked another Stuka, which burst into flames and dived to the sea. Ben Draper's first chosen Ju 87 crashed on the shore just behind Dover Harbour; his second hit the sea. The escorts, which had initially seemed stunned by the ferocity of the onslaught, now attempted to protect the remaining aircraft in their charge, but the first to come into Draper's sights was damaged with a short burst of fire and scurried into cloud for protection. Churches fired a four-second burst into another, the German attempting some half-hearted evasive tactics before a further burst finished him off. Thick black smoke poured from the engine, pieces flew off his wings and he rolled over and went down vertically as flames licked his canopy.

Meanwhile Franklin had shot another Stuka into the Channel whilst Glendinning picked out the leader of a 'vic' of three, closed in a head-on attack and set it on fire. Yet another Stuka was hit with a perfect deflection shot and it started to disintegrate as it fell away. Spurdle sent a Ju 87 into a vertical dive, claimed it as a probable and went on to attack two others in the formation and damaged them, blowing the entire cockpit cover from a third and killing the rear gunner. Skinner sent one seawards and destroyed a second which he caught at sea level scurrying back towards France. Freese attacked a Stuka from astern and it went down in an almost vertical dive with Freese following. He attacked a second Ju 87 which also hit the sea in flames. Armstrong was the one Tiger casualty of the fight, but not before he had scored a probable, closing in on a Ju 87 which jettisoned its bombs as soon as it was fired at. The German gunner returned Armstrong's fire but his aim was wayward. Further bursts from the Spitfire sent the Stuka flicking over and diving towards the Channel. Armstrong immediately turned his attention to a second Junkers which also dived towards the sea but which he could not follow as it would have meant flying into a heavy AA barrage from the coast. It was whilst attempting to re-form with the Squadron that he was hit by a stray cannon shell: his engine exploded and caught fire and Armstrong had no option but to bale out. He came down near Worth uninjured and quickly made his way back to Biggin Hill.

In the course of just fifty minutes the Tigers had destroyed fourteen Ju

87s and one Me 109 and claimed two 87s and two 109s as probables. They had also damaged a pair of each type. It is interesting to note that, just prior to the interception, both they and 66 Squadron had been fired upon continuously by AA batteries from the Isle of Sheppey. Such had been the accuracy of the fire that the formation had been obliged to break up to avoid a catastrophe. The leader of 66 complained over the R/T, but to no effect, and the matter was taken up vociferously by both squadrons after their return. During the course of the war there were many instances of friendly aircraft being fired upon, initially through a mixture of poor recognition techniques and keenness on the part of the battery crews. At this stage of the war there was really no excuse.

Two days later 74 was sharing a patrol with 92 mid-afternoon but this time the Tigers were caught off-guard and surprised by around twenty Me 109s. The enemy attacked in pairs. In the resultant dogfight Draper picked out a Messerschmitt below him, got on to its tail and fired. The enemy aircraft rolled slowly and lazily on to its back and crashed into the sea. Freese chased two and hit one: the front half of the fuselage burst into flames. The second 109 was also hit, the cockpit bursting into flames, but Freese did not see the outcome as he had to break off when he was himself attacked by three of the German fighters. Glendinning saw four Me 109s diving on to a Spitfire and attempted to follow, but he could not get close so he broke away and climbed to 18,000ft, where he saw another 109 on his port side and delivered a beam attack. The German rolled on to its back and for a few seconds seemed to hang in the air as though waiting for the second attack which would inevitably follow. Pieces flew off the aircraft, which went down in a series of rolls. Still chasing it, Glendinning fired a third burst and the tail broke away. The enemy crashed east of Bognor Regis.

On the 17th ten Spitfires left Biggin Hill once more to pursue eighteen Me 109s but only Johnny Freeborn, who was leading, and Stephen got in shots, both at the same aircraft, which crashed off Brighton. It was almost a week before the Tigers took to the air again—a prolonged period of abominable weather precluding any flying and, indeed, any raids by the Luftwaffe—and when they did Malan chased a Messerschmitt to the French coast before closing to fifty yards, firing and seeing it burst into flames and the hood coming away. Chesters baled out over north-east Kent on the 27th, having stayed with his aircraft to steer it away from a village before doing so. He had been bounced by three Me 109s and was hit and wounded in the foot. This was during the course of a fight over the Isle of Sheppey in which Malan once again closed to within fifty yards of a Me 109 before delivering the *coup de grâce* which saw the German's engine blow up and the aircraft disintegrate. Sailor left a second Messerschmitt to Squadron Leader Wilson, a test pilot from the Royal Aircraft Establishment at Farnborough who had been attached to the Tigers for operational training, to finish off. Wilson duly obliged.

The morning of the 30th dawned a damp and foggy one—typical of November. Not many people were about except for Mungo Park and

Stephen, who were very much on the alert and awaiting a call from the Duty Controller. H. M. remembers the day very well:

The evening previously Mungo had come up to me in the Mess, taken me to one side and told me quietly that the next German aircraft to be shot down by one of the Biggin Hill Wing would be its 600th of the war. Malan had also been told, and he had sanctioned an attempt by Mungo with another—me—to claim that valuable prize, valuable not only in terms of Squadron pride and achievement but also money, for a sweepstake had been organized amongst air and ground crew. Everyone knew that the 600th was not very far away, and the chance of a lottery was too good to miss. Armed with that information, we set off for the airfield to sleep. At around 6.00 a.m. a call came through from the Controller asking whether we could get off, given the conditions we had awoken to. Mungo took the call and I remember him saying that we were Tigers, a bit of fog couldn't deter us, of course we could get off, and where was the enemy? I didn't feel too put out about Mungo's supreme confidence, given the fact that we were pretty experienced in working as a team. We donned our flying gear and, with a man on each wing, were guided out to the runway's end. We took off as a pair, wing tips literally overlapping, and climbed. Operating in such a way was second nature to us. Malan had the whole Squadron capable of such tight formation flying and it really gave us all a great kick to be able to do it. Not only did it increase our confidence and faith in our colleagues, but it gave us a boost to know that they had complete confidence in you as well.

After climbing for a couple of minutes, we broke out of the fog into a day of brilliant sunshine and seemingly endless visibility. We were vectored initially down towards the coast, where Ju 87s had been attacking a coastal convoy. But they disappeared and, searching the skies around us, we could see other Germans high above and to the east, approaching the Kent coast. We started to climb, keeping down-sun all the time so that we would not be seen. Finally we arrived at 34,000ft in a position above and behind the German formation. It seemed to us that we had the choice of two aircraft to attack, one of which was acting as top guard for the rest, and this was the one Mungo and I agreed on. We dived and in the excitement of the moment we found that we were much too fast and overshot. We did manage to do a spot of damage on the way through and then pulled round and got back into position again for a second shot before the surprised German knew what was happening. This time we were slower by about 80 knots or so. This was a much more telling attack and I got in a decisive shot which spelt the end for the 109. Mungo fired as well and caused more damage. We broke off and returned to Biggin, where the weather had cleared and enabled us to get down safely, to be greeted by an enthusiastic and congratulatory Tiger Squadron and perhaps a less than enthusiastic group of pilots from 66 and 92. And I claimed a welcome £35 as my share of the prize money!

Such achievements as those that the Tigers had notched up over the previous month could not go unrewarded. H. M. Stephen was awarded the DSO—he was the first Pilot Officer to be so decorated—on the personal recommendation of Sholto Douglas, who had recently replaced Dowding as C-in-C Fighter Command. Malan was also awarded the DSO, whilst Ben Draper got the DFC. Bill Skinner was awarded a much deserved DFM.

The Tigers started December by patrolling Canterbury and taking on nine Me 109s. Eight of the enemy fled back to the French coast; the one which bravely (or foolishly) stayed to fight was destroyed by Malan and Szczesny. 74 found more 109s the following day: Malan consigned one to the Channel fifteen miles from Dungeness and Szczesny fired on another which also dived seawards with black smoke pouring from its fuselage. Glendinning accounted for a third which went straight into a spin, spewing black oil and glycol, and Morrison shot down another which was later confirmed as having crashed into the sea by shore watchers. Stephen badly damaged a fifth before re-forming as many of the by now scattered Squadron as possible and climbed to 20,000ft towards another formation of 109s on its way to the coast. Whilst 74 circled for position, more Messerschmitts came down from above and, severely outnumbered, the Tigers decided that discretion was on this occasion the better part of valour and a return to base was ordered.

The Squadron was next in action on the 5th. Stephen was, as usual, in the thick of things, destroying one Me 109 and damaging another, becoming the first pilot on the Squadron to reach twenty victories in the process. Murray sent one into the cold Channel waters and Freeborn another into the sea off Dungeness before climbing and attacking a second German and damaging its cooling system. He went in pursuit of a third aircraft and set it on fire: it went down ten miles off Boulogne. To complete a personally successful day, Freeborn picked out a fourth aircraft, one of several fleeing back to France, damaging it before being forced to break off when he ran out of ammunition. Szczesny increased his tally with another 109 into the Channel whilst Boulding pursued his target towards the French coast, firing and damaging it. The 109 was trailing smoke and did not quite make its haven, suddenly diving vertically into the sea. Bob Spurdle meanwhile flew between two Me 109s which were about sixty yards apart, not realizing until they flashed past that they were the enemy because oil on his screen was obscuring his vision. He straightaway turned and got on to the tail of one of them, opening fire from 250 yards. Strangely, the German took no evasive action whatsoever but flew on straight and level. Spurdle could see strikes all over its fuselage, and finally it half-rolled and dived out of control, streaming coolant, to crash into the sea five miles off Dymchurch.

The action on 5 December was the last for the Tigers in 1940, for, despite flying patrols for the rest of the month, they made no further contact with the enemy. Since war had been declared, the Tigers' tally stood at 124 aircraft confirmed destroyed and 47 damaged; by far the biggest proportion of the aircraft destroyed had been Me 109s. 74 had lost eleven pilots to enemy action. In cold statistical terms this equates to over twenty-four German casualties for every Tiger killed. In human terms it underlined the determination and skill with which the Squadron approached the job in hand.

Tigers in name and tigers by nature: Mannock would have been proud of them.

With the adoption of a new strategy by Fighter Command, many changes in Squadron personnel and a move away from 11 Group, the year 1941 was destined to be a very different one for the Tigers. The invasion threat had been defeated and now squadrons were to take the offensive with forays over French coastal regions, encouraging the Luftwaffe to fight. A corollary of this was a significant increase in losses, and 74 certainly had its share during the first half of 1941.

The first of the old guard were posted out when H. M. Stephen went to Turnhouse and 59 OTU. He had left 74 with a personal score of twenty Germans destroyed and three probables, second only to Malan. These are the figures quoted in the Squadron records at the time but, as with all recorded victories, they have been subjected to much discussion ever since. The point to be made is that, at the time, very few people in the Squadron—or indeed in Fighter Command—made much of their personal scores. To this day H. M. does not know exactly how many he has been credited with:

I don't know. I never have known. I don't really care how many I shot down. Much has been written about the competition between individuals in their quest to be top scorer. Such competition in my experience did not exist. We all did our job, which was to destroy as many of the enemy as we could. If the opportunity presented itself then we took it as an individual, a section or a squadron. That opportunity either arrived or we went out and searched for it. There were also occasions when discretion became the better part of valour and we pulled away from the chance of engaging the enemy because it was patently obvious that we would come off the worse. We were not in there for personal glory but as part of a team, and in 74's case a very well disciplined team.

Sergeant Freese was killed while force-landing at Detling after running out of fuel on a sweep over the French coast. At the beginning of February the Tigers flew as top cover to bombers pounding the invasion barges at Boulogne. Their escort task complete, they broke off on a roving air patrol along the French coast, Malan and Sergeant Payne claiming an Me 109 each in the process. Three days later 74 flew a defensive patrol over Dover and destroyed a Do 215. The third Pole to fly with 74, Sergeant Jan Rogowski, arrived on 9 February. In common with most of his countrymen, he was fearless, a little reckless—and one for the ladies.

Johnny Freeborn learnt that he had been awarded a bar to his DFC on the 17th. His tally at that time stood at twelve enemy aircraft destroyed. On the 19th the Squadron moved on detachment to the huge airfield at Manston. The first days' operations from there were singularly uneventful, but there was a flurry of excitement when Churches and Morrison shared an Me 110. Jock Morrison was reported missing whilst on patrol shortly afterwards.

Arriving at Biggin Hill on 10 February had been Sergeant Pilot R. H. 'Peter' May. Posted in to the Tigers from 57 OTU at Hawarden, Peter had a relatively brief career with 74. Fighter squadrons during the early part of 1940 had been manned largely by experienced regular RAF pilots and some experienced Volunteer Reserve pilots. The Battle of Britain altered the balance, the numbers of experienced air crew decreasing as the numbers of aircraft coming off the production lines increased, so that by the end of the year the pilot/aircraft ratio was firmly in favour of the aircraft. The need for operational air crew was pressing and the only source became the comparatively inexperienced reserve pilots whom the RAF had been endeavouring to train since the outbreak of war. Peter May was one of these.

It was a gamble to send men off in Spitfires at the OTU with only a minimum of experience, but it was a necessary one, with the squadrons calling constantly for replacements; it was an even bigger gamble to send them to front-line squadrons without adequate training:

> At OTU we had no opportunity to practise firing the aircraft's guns nor did we have any instruction in aerial combat. But our enthusiasm to join a front-line squadron in the 11 Group area overcame any doubts about our ability to come to terms with operational flying—that is, until we tried it. Those on my course who joined 74 and 92 at Biggin Hill were really thrown in at the deep end.

Peter May kept a diary:

> Feb 11th: Flew the Spitfire II for the first time. 1-hour trip.
> Feb 14th: A very busy day. 1½ hours' air drill this morning.
> Feb 15th: Two trips to the Isle of Sheppey for air firing. Hit target every time. [This was the only opportunity Peter May had of firing the Spitfire's guns between his leaving OTU and firing them in combat. There was no facility for drogue flying and no opportunity for practising aerial combat.] Low flying back up the Medway past Chatham and over the hills.
> Feb 22nd: Clear morning and many Jerries overlying very high. Jock Morrison shot down an Me 110 off Herne Bay. Twelve Me 109s bomb 'drome and kill a corporal in the decontamination centre. Sixteen bombs dropped.

Manston, only five minutes' flying time from occupied France, was subjected to regular hit-and-run attacks by the Luftwaffe during the Tigers' stay. Ted Mansfield, who joined 74 as a corporal armourer in January 1941, recalls one such attack:

> Five Me 109s came out of the sun, machine-gunning and dropping bombs. One of our Spitfires had landed a few minutes earlier and had a puncture in the port wheel. Twenty or so ground crew were sent out to bring it in by lying on the starboard wing and tail and the pilot taxying slowly and carefully. Then all hell was let loose around us and we threw ourselves to the ground but amazingly no one out on the airfield was hurt or Spitfires damaged.

A little-recognized fact is worth repeating here. More ground crew were killed during the Battle of Britain and its aftermath as a result of German raids on RAF airfields than were air crew in the air.

Peter May also recalls the Manston raids from the pilot's point of view:

> As soon as we heard or saw the Me 109s there was a wild rush from the crew room into a nearby shelter, coupled with much confusion and laughter.

Although rank took no preference, it was invariably the CO and the officers who got to the shelter first! I cannot recall anyone giving chase as the Jerries would be out of range before we could get airborne. We also had regular visits from high-flying aircraft heading towards London, no doubt to photograph the results of the previous night's bombing. Senior members of the Squadron were often sent off to try an interception on their return, invariably without success. The extreme height at which they flew meant that they had all the advantages.

Accommodation at Manston was quite comfortable. On base, facilities had not been hit so hard as at Biggin and barrack blocks still stood, as did the Messes. The billiards room, too, had escaped unscathed and was a popular place. Bill Felstead:

You could nearly set your watches by the consistency of the lunchtime raids, but on at least one occasion they tricked us by coming over a little early and caught us in the middle of a game of billiards. When the alarm sounded we all immediately took cover under the very solid table and felt quite safe there. Then suddenly, with bombs exploding close by outside, the swing doors burst open and a sergeant ran through and dived for cover. Unfortunately his outstretched arms went either side of a table leg which he hit with his head with a sickening thump and he knocked himself cold. It struck the rest of us as so funny that we burst into laughter and quite forgot to pull the poor sod in! Quite unkind of us in retrospect, but he recovered despite a case of slight concussion.

On 10 March a very significant change to the Squadron complement came about with the promotion of Sailor Malan to Wing Commander and his appointment as Officer Commanding Flying of the Biggin Hill Wing. The loss of Sailor as Commanding Officer was compensated for in part by the knowledge that the Tigers would still fly under him as part of that Wing and that the ever-popular John Mungo Park had been promoted to assume command of the Tigers. Mungo, as we have already seen, was a determined fighter and a fine leader of men and was never averse to indulging in a little harmless skulduggery when the occasion arose. Once leading the Squadron, he was of course forced outwardly to adopt a different attitude, but he was well aware of the sort of things that went on and when possible would turn a blind eye to them . . . as he did over the incident involving 87 octane. Operational pilots were allowed to use private cars and were given a meagre petrol allowance which was regularly supplemented with the help of the ground crews. 87 octane (used for all the station transport as well by private vehicles) was regularly syphoned from the bowser and stored in drums in the outhouses behind the air crew's billets. All was well until an airman was caught red-handed doing this and was brought before the newly promoted Mungo Park on a charge. With what must have been a twinkle in his eye, Mungo tore him off a strip and confined him to camp for seven days—which amounted to virtually no punishment as there were few places to go anyway! Mungo, together with his fellow officers, was of course one of the main recipients of 87 octane.

H. M. Stephen remembers Mungo Park with fondness:

He possessed a certain *joie de vivre* which was infectious. He came from the Fleet Air Arm into the RAF and when he first arrived on the Squadron he had immediately hit it off with Paddy Treacy. They were great chums. After Treacy went missing over France for the second time in May 1940, Mungo and I started to fly together and we found that we complemented each other very well in the air. Whenever we flew into a spot of trouble we would stick to each other and fight our way out together. We became known as The Deadly Twins: there were other pairings on the Squadron, but none perhaps as successful as ours.

The weather remained good, and a heavy schedule of patrols included Lysander escort duties to France. Flight Lieutenant Tony Bartley DFC (who was later to marry actress Deborah Kerr) joined the Squadron; in time he would take over command of A Flight. Meanwhile Peter May continued with his diary:

March 1st: Sweep to France. Spurdle two 109s and Glendinning one. Very good show. Sqn Ldr Wood was shot down just off Ramsgate. He crash-landed on the beach. Move to our new quarters at Manston and find them tip top with a nice fire going and every comfort.

March 2nd: Posted to Farnborough for an experimental course on the effects of high altitude flying. No doubt I have been chosen to be the guinea pig as I am the least experienced member of the squadron. [May was at Farnborough for ten days, enduring over a dozen sessions in 'The Chamber' and reaching altitudes of 41,000ft with no lasting ill effects. He was back at Manston with the Squadron by the 17th.]

March 17th: Poor old Glendinning shot down and killed over Folkestone while I was away. He was flying as Tail End Charlie at the time. I can well remember talking to him whilst he was placing a photograph of his wife and children on the mantelpiece. I said that after only twenty hours on Spitfires and one hundred and fifty hours in all I found it difficult to cope. 'Be patient' he said, 'Once you have mastered it it's as easy as flying a Tiger Moth!' We all had a soft spot for Glendinning for he was always endeavouring to bolster our spirits although perhaps he was becoming a little over confident himself.

March 18th: Mike Halahan crashes in the Magister and dies in hospital. I saw Mike spin in on the perimeter of Manston aerodrome

On the same day Wally Churches shot down another Me 109. Bob Spurdle was having a good month too: he shared a Ju 88 with Sergeant Dales on the 24th after chasing it from Ramsgate to Dunkirk and the same team struck again the following day when they damaged a Do 215. Squadron Leader Wood, who had recovered from injuries sustained in his previous engagement, shared a probable Me 109 with Pilot Officer Smith, although the latter was to be lost before the patrol finished. This brought the Squadron's tally for March to four destroyed, one probable and two damaged.

April 6, 1941:

We crossed the Belgian coast near Gravelines and flying just below cloud headed in the direction of St-Omer. Over the 'drome we saw no aircraft dispersed and no AA fire. There was little traffic on the roads and visibility was very limited owing to the low cloud base. There was a little tracer coming from what appeared to be an ammunition dump. We came on an Me 109 in a field. It appeared to have force-landed so we came low and machine-gunned it. I saw a big cloud of brown smoke go up after Bartley had shot at it. We climbed up under the clouds again and shortly after were attacked by an enemy aircraft which we didn't see to identify. I received two cannon-shell hits and four machine-gun bullets. I gained cover in the clouds, losing sight of Bartley. My machine was shaking and control at low speeds very poor. I tried to fly blind but my gyro instruments were upset so after about three minutes' circling in cloud I came down to get a horizon and let them settle down. I came out of the clouds and saw an Me 110 just in front and slightly to my left, flying in the same direction at approximately 400ft. I opened fire and the enemy turned left and crash-landed in a big field. The rear gunner got out and on turning back I gave him a quick squirt. He fell down but I don't think he was hit. My machine was shaking heavily . . . I landed at Manston. My port aileron controls were shot away and I had a cannon shell through my airscrew blade.

This was the combat report filed by Bob Spurdle after a 'rhubarb', the codename given to a sortie to attack targets of opportunity on the ground. The following day Rogowski shot down an Me 109 and during a period of heavy involvement in patrols and attacks Peter Chesters claimed another on 10 April. This engagement was fought in the blue skies above Manston and crews stood and watched the drama being enacted before them. So elated was Chesters with his success that he could not resist performing a victory roll on his return to the airfield. Sadly it all went wrong and he crashed on to the parade ground, coming down by the water tower, and killed himself. How many times did such exuberance cost unnecessary lives during the war?

As the month progressed and the Squadron continued to fly heavily, Wally Churches went missing from a convoy patrol. Peter May had begun to find his operational feet:

I cannot recall being nervous on my first patrols because I felt we had the advantage of being over our own base, and as the Germans were concentrating on bombing or shooting down barrage balloons the element of surprise was ours. But it is worth saying that I am sure the few remaining battle-hardened experienced pilots did not relish having to go on patrol with pilots straight from OTU.

His diary continues:

April 7th: Patrol Dover at 25,000ft and see balloons in flames as Jerry beats it home. Landing in formation with Churches I hit the hedge of the aerodrome and knock off starboard leg but manage to ease it down gently on one wing.

April 10th: Tons of Jerries over at terrific height. Have scrap at 31,000ft. My Spitfire a complete wreck after. Flying in squadron formation with the throttle wide open and hanging on our props, we were jumped by 109s coming at us from above. At this height the Spitfire is no match for the direct-injection 109. After being ordered to break and seeing a 109 on my tail, I turned so sharply I almost blacked out. When I recovered, my Spitfire was shuddering quite badly due to violent handling. I found myself alone over the French coast but with no sign of the 109s. Now being used to the Spitfire II I can make a few objective observations. It is a very good aeroplane but we wish we had direct-injection petrol feed. The two big disadvantages of gravity feed are that the engine cuts out with any rapid change of height and that the aircraft is sluggish at height.

April 21st: Take off to patrol base at 25,000ft. Hit wireless and sock mast on landing. Fractured knee. Taken to Margate General Hospital.

So ended Sergeant Pilot May's time with the Tigers.

GRAVESEND

The Tigers moved to Gravesend at the beginning of May. Lying just outside the town, the airfield was a small and deceptive one, with rising ground, which led to a succession of heavy landings and a cartoon being drawn on the hangar wall by ground crews showing two Spitfires in the circuit and one saying to the other 'Can't land yet Joe: someone's bagged the recovery crane!' Stored at the back of the hangar was the uniquely beautiful twin-engined de Havilland Comet now restored and owned by the Shuttleworth Collection. Other than the hangar, there were few buildings on the airfield. Accommodation at Gravesend was at Cobham Hall, a lovely old Elizabethan mansion, and the local pub, 'The Leather Bottle' in Cobham village, soon became a favourite.

May 6 turned out to be a bad day for the Tigers. Eleven Spitfires took off to act as escort to three Blenheims of 101 Squadron but returned three aircraft short with Howard missing, Arnott later confirmed as a POW and Sergeant Wilson having had to bale out just as he crossed the Kent coast when his engine caught fire. There was some retribution the next day when Poulton, Boulding and Sandeman respectively destroyed, probably destroyed and damaged Me 109s when they were scrambled to intercept a force of ten over Canterbury. Successes continued on the 9th, Armstrong shooting down one German and Roger Boulding bringing down a Heinkel 111 over Ashford at midnight. Roger recalls the engagement:

By now the Squadron was operating at night from West Malling from time to time. On this particular occasion we were sent to patrol over central London. I had been on patrol for forty minutes or so when I experienced some problem with the pitch control on the propeller so started back for Malling. As I set course I saw just ahead of me in the brilliant moonlight what was obviously an enemy bomber, so I lined up and pressed the firing button. As the bullets hit him an enormous cloud of sparks flashed in front of me and I flew through them. He dived sharply and I tried to follow but that left me clearly visible to his rear gunner against the moonlight sky whilst I could barely distinguish him against the dark background of the earth. His gunner fired with uncomfortable accuracy but we were soon down at low level and I chased him across the Kent countryside. Suddenly he disappeared. I circled the area and called for a radio bearing from West Malling which fixed the spot. Subsequently it turned out that either by good luck or by superb skill he had put his Heinkel down on its belly in a small field.

Johnny Freeborn, who had been a Tiger since 1938, now left for pastures new. Bill Skinner and Tony Mould were commissioned, and new aircraft began to arrive in the shape of Spitfire Vs, which were phased in over the course of the ensuing month. Amongst them were a number of presentation aircraft, funded by public subscription or by private sponsorship and carrying appropriate titles chosen by the donor. The scheme had been conceived by Lord Beaverbrook and 74 had already received a number of titled Mark IIs, 'Nuflier' (donated by the Norwich Union Insurance Societies), 'Goldcoast 2', 'Miners of Durham 2' and 'The Lewis and Harris Fighter' amongst them. A Mr Black had paid £12,677 11s. 10d. for two Mark IIs which the Squadron took on charge and which were named 'Black Varieties' and 'Black Velvet'. Amongst the presentation Mark Vs were 'Huddersfield 1', 'Henley on Thames', 'City of Salford', 'Newport Hundreds and Wolverhampton U.D.C.' and 'The Peruvian Oilfields'—not all names that tripped off the tongue by any means!

The Squadron continued its successes in the air over France, Baker destroying an Me 109 whilst on a 'rhubarb' with Sandeman on 26 May. June saw an escalation of contacts with the enemy as bomber escort duties and offensive sweeps increased: the Squadron's tally climbed accordingly, but a new round of Squadron losses began on 9 June when Bergen crashed into the sea whilst on convoy patrol off Folkestone. During the same patrol Sandeman claimed one probable Me 109. On the 11th Carlson destroyed a Messerschmitt whilst leading A Flight. On the 16th Mungo Park disposed of a pair of Me 109s whilst escorting Blenheims; Stuart shot two down on the same trip, with Sandeman and York each claiming a probable. On 17 June both Boulding and Parkes were posted missing although their colleagues were subsequently relieved to hear of their capture by the Germans rather than their deaths. Boulding recalls the moment:

It was a beautiful summer's evening and Sailor was leading. We were flying top cover when I saw some yellow-nosed characters sneaking up under us and informed Sailor who led us down on to them. I was chasing a 109 who was in a vertical spiral dive and couldn't line myself up for a good shot, so after a while, in accordance with the current practice, I broke away to re-form. At that period we were told not to follow right down to low level because too many of our boys were picked off trying to get home on their own. I followed Sailor, climbing towards the sun in a weaving pattern—again the normal practice —with one of ours following me until I heard Sailor warning somebody to 'look out behind'. Then, just as I saw what must have been Sailor rocking his wings and heard him telling someone 'to do something', I felt a thumping behind my seat and the aileron controls packed in. My aircraft threw itself all over the place and the only thing I could do was get out. That proved to be a bit difficult but as the elevator controls still worked I was able to more or less eject by pushing the stick forward. I floated down from 10,000ft into a field occupied by an assortment of Germans who chorused the sickening 'For you the war is over!'.

The Tigers met with better success on the 21st when, on another sweep led by Malan, Carlson destroyed a Messerschmitt and claimed a probable, Cole shot one down and Mould also claimed a probable. The following day 74 were part of a massive offensive which included squadrons from Biggin, Kenley, Tangmere, Northolt and North Weald. Malan again led the Biggin component and shot down two Me 109s whilst Tigers Sandeman and Mould got their names on to the score sheet too, with, respectively, two shot down and one damaged. The Squadron diaries still hold a message from Leigh Mallory sent to all those participating in the offensive:

My heartiest congratulations to you all on your magnificent performance yesterday. We are getting the Hun down; we must get him right down.

Poulton claimed a probable on the 24th and Wilson damaged one, but these successes were a precursor to a black day indeed when Hilken, Sandeman and Mungo Park were all posted missing after flying sweeps over France. Clive Hilken was hit first by unidentified German aircraft which came at them, unseen, out of the sun:

I can only surmise that they were hit during the same pass by the enemy formation. They were flying slightly behind and below me at the time but I was too preoccupied with getting out of my damaged aircraft to see what was going on.

Both Hilken and Sandeman became POWs, but Mungo Park was never heard of again and the mystery of his disappearance has long been one to exercise the minds of historians and colleagues at the time alike. He is the only serving Commanding Officer that the Tigers have lost in action.

Within three days Squadron Leader S. T. Meares (who had been a Tiger during the Squadron's Hornchurch days) returned as the new CO. Sweeps and patrols continued unabated. The tally mounted quickly during the first week of July. On the 2nd both Krol and Evans went missing from sweeps and both were made POWs. On the same offensive Malan and Lockhart shot down a 109. Carlson and Poulton claimed one each the following day but these victories were set against the loss of Cochrane, who was later also confirmed as a POW. Henderson was not so fortunate on the 4th—he was posted missing, presumed killed—whilst Lockhart (after shooting down two Messerschmitts), Carter and the long-serving Bill Skinner all disappeared on the 6th, only Carter and Skinner subsequently being confirmed as prisoners. Meanwhile Meares had claimed a probable 109 and had strafed an E-boat whilst on convoy patrol and Sergeant Trott claimed one destroyed and one probable.

These were to be the last successes and losses of 74 Squadron as a component of the Biggin Hill Wing, for on the following day personnel were all ordered to Acklington in Northumberland to become a component of 13 Group. Behind them they left a truly glorious chapter in the Squadron history—a chapter that encapsulates all the elements that go to make up the Tiger spirit. Many had given their lives in the defence of their country. Many had survived to tell the tale. But all had been supremely proud to be part of one of the greatest Fighter Command squadrons.

BACKWATERS

When the Squadron moved north it was with a modified nameplate, for from mid-June it had been officially retitled 'No 74 (Trinidad) Squadron'. The Fighter Fund Committee in the colony of Trinidad and Tobago had donated £100,000 to the Air Ministry for the purchase of fighter aircraft for the Royal Air Force. An article in the *West India Committee Circular* of the time records that a 'famous squadron of Spitfires had been named the "Trinidad" in recognition of the donation' and that from henceforth all the Squadron's Spitfires would have 'Trinidad Squadron' stencilled on to the engine cowlings. It became the tradition for a keg of Trinidadian rum to be sent to the Squadron each Christmas, from which a potent 'Tiger's Blood' cocktail was quickly concocted and consumed! The links with the West Indies were maintained for twenty years and it was only when Trinidad sought and gained independence from Great Britain that they were broken.

The Squadron's move heralded a period in its history which was in direct contrast to the sustained months of operations it had just completed. Squadron personnel changed constantly and it became a time for intensive training for the new and mainly non-commissioned pilots who arrived for a short stay with the Tigers; indeed, 74 found itself to be a post-OTU squadron, giving pilots newly emerging from these establishments some first-hand experience in flying patrols and very occasionally combat prior to their moving on to squadrons in the south which were continuing with the offensive. 74 embarked on a programme of air firing, AA co-operation, formation flying, aerobatics, GCI co-operation, camera-gun practice, practice attacks (often against Whitley bombers), practice scrambles, mock dogfights, circuits, altitude climbs, battle climbs, cross-countries, R/T exercises with convoys, dusk landings, night flying, searchlight co-operation and army co-operation. Operationally it conducted convoy patrols. 74 had exchanged aircraft with 72 Squadron, the latter moving south to take up 74's Spitfire Vs. Unfortunately for the Tigers, 72 had left them their old Spitfire IIs!

In the three months that 74 were in residence at Acklington they made contact with the enemy just once, on 6 August, when Pilot Officer Winterbeek, a Belgian, and Sergeant Edwards damaged a Ju 88 east of Whitburn. The Squadron's biggest problem was trying to maintain a closely knit team, such were the huge numbers of postings in and out. Also changing was 74's Commanding Officer. Charlie Meares was posted to 71 Squadron and arriving to replace him was Squadron Leader H. M. Richey who, in keeping with the continual turnover of air crew at the time, did not stay with the Squadron very long himself. The intensity of the training during this period contributed to the loss of two pilots. Pilot Officer Douglas Steven was killed on 2 August. Flying with six other Spitfires, he suddenly left the formation and went into a spin, hitting the ground near Sarington Hall at Ousten, possible causes of the accident being carbon dioxide poisoning or oxygen failure. The other fatality was that of

Sergeant Coxon, who while practising night landings undershot on the approach and hit a pillbox.

On 3 October 74 Squadron moved to Llanbedr in West Wales and continued its programme of training, allied with a routine of sector reconnaissance and convoy patrols. The Tigers soon fell foul of the religious fervour of the locals when they started flying on Sundays. Within three days of the first occasion they did this, the CO received a letter from the local minister complaining of the disregard for the Sabbath. A few weeks later, after one of the Spitfires had crash-landed on a Sunday, he received another, this time proclaiming the accident to be just retribution and an Act of God. Flying continued on seven days each week, however.

For the most part, the Spitfires were dispersed around the perimeter at Llanbedr and readiness was undertaken on alternate days by A and B Flights. The procedure was that a single aircraft would be at the runway's end, with engine warmed and parachute draped over the wing leading edge and with the pilot and ground crew in attendance. The scramble signal was given by a single Very pistol shot from the control tower. As one aircraft took off it was replaced immediately by another. Ted Newson recalls the day on which, as a member of B Flight, he was on readiness:

I was waiting with the pilot Steve Winterbeek and my ground crew colleague Roy Durrant. The Very pistol was fired from the tower and the first aircraft took off, to be replaced by the next in line. We accordingly moved up one position (second to go) and within a minute moved up to the runway's end as another flare was fired. Ground crew were loath to walk as the aircraft taxied on these occasions and instead it became the procedure to duck under the aerial wires extending from the fuselage sides to the extremities of the tail and sit on the tailplane!

Winterbeek accelerated along the peri track with Roy and I safely aboard and turned on to the runway. As he did so the Very pistol was fired for the third time and without hesitation our Belgian pilot opened up the throttles! I couldn't believe what was happening as we thundered down the runway, Roy and I hanging grimly on to the rudder, fighting against the slipstream and hot exhaust gases. Winterbeek was slowly realizing that something was wrong as he struggled to coax the Spitfire into the air. He did manage to get it six feet off the ground before looking in his rear-view mirror and suddenly realizing that he had totally forgotten about us! He immediately throttled back: we landed with a bump and came to rest a few feet from the runway's end.

Postings in and out continued apace and the Tigers counted Belgians, Canadians, Australians, a Trinidadian and a Rhodesian as well as a few Britons amongst their numbers at this time. New Zealander Cedric Hesketh recalls his welcome at Llanbedr:

I was immediately made to feel very much at home and quickly became one of what I now realize was definitely a close-knit circle of friends. The Mess was not over-large but on that account was all the cosier. The view was quite good as it was built on a hillside overlooking the airfield and beyond it to the sea. Furniture was somewhat the worse for wear but I soon gathered that this was because of boisterous activity on the part of air crew! Hanging on one wall was

Above: The result of several incidents that Twist Giles endured with S.E.5s (and other types) during training. Some were far more destructive than this! (W. B. Giles)

Below: 74 Squadron's 'mechanical transport' leaves for France, 18 March 1918. (W. B. Giles)

Above: Frederick 'Mike' Hunt with his S.E.5a 'somewhere in France' in the summer of 1918. (F. J. Hunt)

Left: Outside the Officers' Mess at Clairmarais. In the doorway is Roberts and, to his left, Taffy Jones; centre left is Mansfield; under the Officers' Mess sign is Gould, Twist Giles (with the cat on his shoulder) and, far right, Haines; and seated at the front are Carlin (with the pipe) and Kiddie. (W. B. Giles)

Above: 74 Squadron at Halluin soon after the Armistice: (back row, left to right) Sheppard, Carew, Goudie, Hale, Hobhouse, Lambert, Wallace, White, Ackland and Kilpatrick; (front row) Gould, Gordon, Hunt, Giles, Kiddie, Jones, Skinner, Coverdale, Mansfield, Chipper and Allen. (C. D. Skinner)

Left: Unloading the fuselage section of a Hawker Demon for 74 Squadron from the SS *Maihar* in Grand Harbour, Valetta, Malta, in September 1935. (74 Squadron)

Overleaf: Effectively camouflaged Demons over Malta. Note the differing positions of the roundels on the upper wing surfaces. (Jim Tufnail)

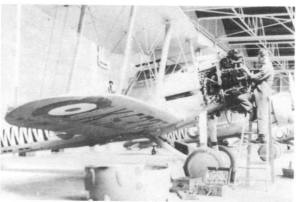

Above: The Tigers' first Gloster Gauntlet, K5337. The Gauntlets were the first of the Squadron's aircraft to receive the distinctive black and yellow dicing and a tiger's head (the latter just visible on the fin). (74 Squadron)

Left: One man and a tool kit: working on the Bristol radial of the Gauntlet. (Tom Rowland)

Below left: Hornchurch 1938: (left to right) Sammy Hoare, Charlie Meares and Tinky Measures. (Tom Rowland)

Right: B Flight Commander's 'office' (!) at Hornchurch at the outbreak of war, September 1939. (Gp. Capt. D. S. Hoare)

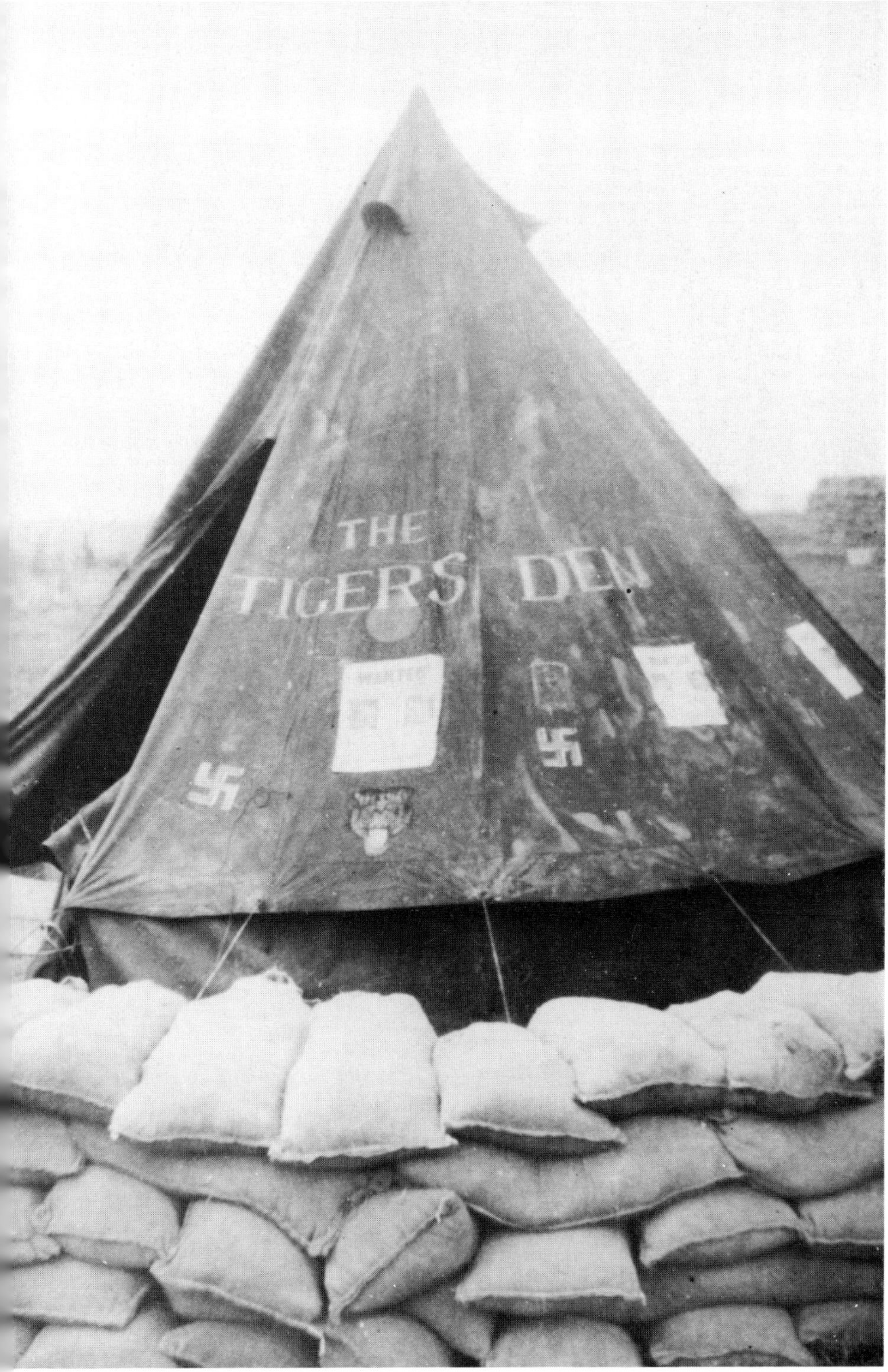
THE
TIGERS DEN

Left: Hornchurch, late 1939. In the cockpit of the Spitfire is Johnny Freeborn and from left to right are Ian Hawken, Tinky Measures, Sailor Malan, Polly Flinders, Temple-Harris and Tony Mould. (Bernard Stebbing/Ron Stone)

Left: John Colin Mungo Park (left) and H. M. Stephen, who, finding that they complemented each other very well in the air, regularly flew together and became known as The Deadly Twins. There were other such pairings on the Squadron but perhaps none was quite so successful as these two—as epitomized by the downing of Biggin Hill's 600th in November 1940. (74 Squadron)

Left: Sailor Malan admires a gift of a carved Javanese statue from the Dutch East India Company at Biggin Hill, December 1940. The Squadron received many letters and gifts from well-wishers that Christmas. Looking on, to Sailor's right, are Franklin, Bob Spurdle and, in the flying jacket, Armstrong. (Bob Spurdle)

Right: Biggin Hill crew room, February 1941: Ben Draper, H. M. Stephen and Sailor Malan with his dog, Peter. (Ernest Toms)

Right: Biggin Hill crew room, February 1941: Roger Boulding, the Pole Henry Szczesny and Johnny Freeborn are playing cards and H. M. Stephen is attending to the gramophone. Note the aircraft readiness board beside H. M. (Ernest Toms)

Below: Spitfire II 'ZP-Y' at Manston, April 1941. (Peter May)

Left: The remains of Spitfire II P7740 after Peter May's collision with the windsock by the perimeter fence at Manston, 21 April 1941. (Peter May)

Centre left: Long Kesh, February 1942: Spitfire V 'ZP-D' awaits attention after an undercarriage collapse. (Ted Mansfield)

Below left: The New Zealand-registered SS *Rangitata*—which took 74 Squadron personnel out to Durban, South Africa— *en route* to the Middle East, April 1942. (Ian Shand)

Right: Squadron pilots at Meherebad (Teheran), December 1942, Standing, left to right, are Macpherson, Jimmy Grey, Frank Twitchett, David Maxwell, Tony Reeves, Pete Lovell, Allan Griffin, Speed Norman, Besley, Bill Alston, Mitchell Wilson and Bunny de Pass; squatting are Titch Harris and Bobby Waugh. (Allan Griffin)

Below: Squadron ground crews begin their Middle Eastern meanderings: Jack Thornton, Harold Kirk, Frank Hubbel and Joe Tombling head for Palestine from Egypt, in July 1942. (Joe Tombling)

Above left: The Tigers' much-loved Medical Officer, Doc Ferris, who won the Military Cross on Simi for his valiant efforts in trying to save two soldiers buried under a bombed building. Ferris loved to fly and if ever the opportunity arose he was not slow to take it—hence the parachute and helmet. (Frank Twitchett)

Above right: Green Section's Hurricanes about to scramble, Meherebad, February 1943. (Allan Griffin/Frank Twitchett)

Below: In March 1943, A Flight and the requisite ground crews left Meherebad for Abadan in the Persian Gulf. On the road convoy's first stop, B Flight paid them a low flying visit! (Joe Tombling)

Above: Some of the difficult terrain which road convoys had to negotiate in Persia: *en route* to Abadan, April 1943. (Allan Griffin)

Left: 74 Squadron's Gremlin, which was regularly ousted in the Mess! It was during such a party, at Shaibah on 15 May 1943, that Spud Hayter received a signal ordering the Tigers to North Africa. (Frank Twitchett)

74 SQDN's GREMLIN.

Left: Wide open desert spaces: a solitary Hurricane undergoes its 0730 daily inspection at LG 106, El Daba, July 1943. (Joe Tombling)

Below left: Escape! Safely on board a Greek caique and approaching Bodrum in Turkey, having been taken from the beleaguered island of Cos, October 1943. (74 Squadron)

Above: The Tigers' old 11 Group Boss, Keith Park, caught up with them again in North Africa. Now an Air Marshal and C-in-C Middle East, he arrived at Dekheila to brief them on the current war situation. (74 Squadron)

Below: Courtrai, September 1944: 74 Squadron in front of the camouflaged Wing Operations 'complex'. Wg. Cdr. Crawford Compton's office was on the left, with the Ops office on the right; in between was a raised platform from which briefings were conducted. In the back row, left to right, are Shirkie, Cortis, Church, Morgan, Human, Turner, Peet, Johnston, Davis, Ferris, Hardman, Ivan Butler, Eyre and Kidd; in the front row are Carter, Shanahan, Tooke, Collinson, Davis, Usher, Sqn. Ldr. Spud Hayter, Llewellyn, Alston, Tapley, Bates, Over and Keith Butler. (John Church)

Above: March 1945: Schijndel, Holland. Personnel had changed considerably from those in the Squadron photograph at Courtrai—some had been killed, some taken prisoner and others posted. In the top row, left to right, are de Senneville, Rees, Griffin, Warwick, Turner and Monk; in the middle row are Horn, Eyre, Dalzell, Morgan, Shanahan, Church, Tooke, Agnew, Lambert, Barnes, Racy and Johnston; and in the front row are Davis (Adjutant), Braidwood, Frost, Sqn. Ldr. Tony Reeves, Peet, Davis and Macfarlane (Medical Officer). Also on the Squadron at this time but not in the photograph were Bennett, Murland, Shirkie, Berglund and Eng. Off. Collinson. (John Church/Hugh Murland)

Right: Corporal Tony Blythin, who served with the Squadron through its days in the Middle East, North Africa and Europe and on to Meteors at Colerne. (Hugh Murland)

a metal replica of the Squadron crest, somewhat distorted in shape and sporting a bullet hole or two from a Smith and Wesson!

There was a waggish rumour circulating amongst the ground crews at this time that 74 had been sent to Llanbedr for training in overseas desert conditions. This rumour was not the result of any presentiment as to where the Squadron might end up but arose directly from local experiences involving a lot of time on the cold windswept expanses of sand along the mid-Wales coast—such as at Criccieth, where Ian Shand force-landed after an air test. Before taking off, he had endorsed the necessary forms which signified that the ground crew had completed all maintenance and checks. However, as he was returning to Llanbedr the engine cut out and Ian found that he was out of fuel. He called control, informed them of the situation and chose his spot to come down. All the beaches in the area were protected by anti-invasion poles but even so they provided the best bet. He selected the most favourable line and landed, hitting five poles and seriously damaging the aircraft. His experiences as a consequence of this incident are well remembered:

We had been having a number of accidents and they were looking for a scapegoat. A Board of Inquiry was held and I was asked if I had put a dipstick into the top fuel tank. I said no (at that time there was only a fuel gauge for the lower tank) but went on to say that I knew of no other pilot who had ever done so as we depended on the ground crew to check. That did not go down too well. I was given a Red Endorsement and the sacrificial goat got very tight that night!

During November a programme of air-to-air firing was started, some of the Spitfires being employed on drogue-towing. This task was not without its dangers for the armourers. The drogue and its towing lines had to be laid out in an 'S' shape at the end of the runway and hooked on to the attachment under the tail of the towing aircraft—and there was more than one instance of the armourer not clearing the lines before eager pilots started their take-off runs. At the end of the month 74 lost two men in the space of four days: in the only contact made with the enemy whilst at Llanbedr, Arthur Williams disappeared whilst chasing a Junkers; and the Canadian, Brown, perished when he crashed into the river estuary at Barmouth with such force that the Merlin engine was buried twenty feet deep in the sand. Within a month Sergeant Stuart had been lost too, but in different circumstances. Christmas Eve seemed like an appropriate occasion to beat up the airfield. It had been a pretty depressing time of late, the Squadron essentially having been relegated to training duties, and with the festive season upon them the Tigers were determined to make the best of it. Stuart had decided to celebrate by putting on a show for the ground crews and, returning from formation practice, he peeled off and dived towards Llanbedr. He then pulled out and started a climbing roll. Sadly, the newly delivered Spitfire Vb he was flying (the Squadron had started to re-equip on this mark) suffered a massive structural failure: a wing came off outboard of the cannon, flew back and destroyed the tail assembly. The outcome was inevitable.

Popular figures with the Tigers at the time included the Adjutant, Sandy Powell, who was older than other personnel but managed to stay young in spirit and was adept at combining undoubted efficiency at his job with an ever-ready willingness to help others, and in particular the new pilots. By this time the Tigers had acquired a new CO, the fourth in twelve months. Twenty-two-year-old Peter Matthews DFC took command on the departure of Richey. A charming Irish story involving Matthews relates how he went out to his Spitfire after lunch one day to find that a labourer had dug a trench right under the fuselage! The Squadron had moved on 24 January to Long Kesh in Northern Ireland, where they were given the use of a huge, empty Short and Harland hangar. Their task was now to provide air cover for the convoys sailing from America around the northern Irish coast, and to this end scarcely a day passed by without a scramble to intercept high-flying reconnaissance aircraft. None was ever intercepted, although the exercise seemed to have the required deterrent effect as the Germans retreated as soon as they got a scent of the Tigers and squadrons from other sectors and were thus denied sightings of the convoys. Indeed, direct contact with the enemy was recorded only on one occasion, when Cedric Hesketh and B Flight Commander Peter Cannam chased a Ju 88 from the Mull of Kintyre down towards Eire but were unable to catch it. Meanwhile the Spitfire Vs were fitted with long-range tanks and were flown far out over the Atlantic to provide air cover for the ships as they approached Britain—long, boring patrols in that long, bleak winter when the sun never seemed to shine. At least the scrambles provided some relief from the routines of training. Sergeant Matthews was lost whilst on a routine patrol and Sergeant Brookes cartwheeled his aircraft at Bellyherbert as he attempted a night landing. Brookes survived; the Spitfire did not. Then, almost without warning, the Tigers were on the move again. Sergeant Stan Greeves' log book for 25 March 1942 holds a very significant entry. It reads:

Squadron flew to Atcham. Goodbye to flying in England.

At Atcham, 74 handed its Spitfires (and its Belgian pilots Bobby Laumans and Steve Winterbeek) over to a newly forming Belgian unit. It was now a squadron without aircraft, and this led to an intense bout of rumours about the future. These rumours crystallized a little with the issue of tropical kit and giving of yellow fever inoculations; and they intensified when everyone was sent on leave with instructions to report to Liverpool in a week's time.

CHAPTER 5

Near East Tigers

ON 10 APRIL 1942, 74 Squadron boarded the SS *Rangitata*, a New Zealand refrigerator vessel which was used as a troopship for the duration of the war. Sailing on the 15th to Greenock, the Squadron joined a convoy before making a wide sweep out into the Atlantic en route to its first port of call, Freetown in Sierra Leone, two weeks later. No one was allowed ashore here for fear of contracting any of the tropical diseases. Anchored at a buoy inside the harbour as the water and fuel were taken on, the ship was a very uncomfortable place to be for the hundreds of men aboard her. After the bleak conditions in Wales and Northern Ireland, the heat was oppressive, and, in an attempt to make it a little more bearable, sleeping on deck was authorized. As a precaution against being bitten, however, all had to button shirtsleeves around the wrist, stick trouser bottoms into socks and cover all exposed skin with anti-mosquito cream.

Three weeks later the *Rangitata* reached Durban. There was still no official confirmation as to where the Squadron was ultimately going. Off Cape Aghulas another ship in the convoy, P&O's *Sudan*, hit a mine and sank. She was carrying the Squadron's complement of Spitfires and her loss was to consign the Tigers to many weary months in the desert awaiting replacement aircraft. Shortly afterwards HMS *Hecla*, the escorting destroyer depot ship, was also sunk. All ranks shared a magnificent reception at Durban and the presents of fruit, bananas and cigarettes showered upon the troops were especially welcome after the latter had endured uncomfortable conditions for so long. Within a week everyone boarded the RMS *Mauretania* and they sailed alone for Port Taufik, Egypt. This voyage was, happily, uneventful, with the exception of the death of LAC Henham from typhus. This meant that, on disembarkation, 74 Squadron were taken by rail to a large transit camp at Gineifa near the Bitter Lakes and placed under quarantine for fourteen days. Then 74's men were moved by rail to Helwan, to what was ironically called 'Desert Camp', on 21 June. Members of the advance party went on ahead to erect forty tents as the Squadron's living quarters, but the following morning eight of them had gone missing. No doubt they would be seen in the weeks to come, converted to sails for feluccas sailing up and down the Nile! This was an early introduction to a security problem which all units in the Middle East had to cope with.

It was at Helwan that the Tigers were introduced to their new Adjutant, Flight Lieutenant Grahame Jenkins, who was promptly christened

'Jumpin' Jack' in deference to his ability to come out with some 'crackers' every now and again! Jenkins was a kindly man who was always immaculately dressed, his beautifully creased trousers tucked into leather gaiters and his boots always perfectly polished. It was also at Helwan that Doug Tidy, who thirty years later was to write *I Fear No Man*, joined the Tigers from attachment to the Trans-Jordan Frontier Force. Doug served in the Signals Section, trying with his colleagues to get decent radio telephonic communications ground-to-air and air-to-air when the Squadron finally got its aircraft—not too easy a task given that it would still be equipped with the old TR9 apparatus.

There now began a long period of uncertainty which was compounded by the fact that no aircraft arrived for the Tigers. Crews were informed of the original intention to form a Spitfire Wing comprising 74, 92 and 601 Squadrons, but with the loss of the aircraft *en route* these plans had to be revised. In the interim, 74's CO, Flight Commanders and six pilots were sent to 73 Squadron for duties allied with the defence of the Suez Canal. Pete Matthews was very soon leading 73, although at that stage he and his Tiger colleagues had not been disestablished from 74. This added further to the uncertainty about the Tigers' future. At the end of August Matthews and the pilots joined 145 Squadron at Landing Ground (LG) 154 a few miles east of the Alamein line and Matthews became CO of the incongruously designated 145/74 Squadron. This situation was not to last long and by November 1942 145 became a squadron in its own right.

When Matthews and fellow Tigers were transferred to fly with 73 Squadron, the remainder were allocated to the Middle East Pool in Cairo, whence they were sent out on various flying duties: Clive Hesketh, for instance, went to the Test Flight at Aboukir and Ian Shand was assigned to the Repair and Service Unit (RSU) there. Amongst the other Tigers sent to the Pool were Paul Brickhill, who was to become so well known after the war for his books *Escape to Danger* and *The Dambusters*. Ground crews were employed at Helwan servicing Kittyhawks and Tomahawks from other squadrons in the desert. At the beginning of July they were ordered to Palestine. The advance party travelled via Ismailia and Bethlehem, on towards the Dead Sea, over the River Jordan and up to Salt and Amman before camping in the desert beyond Zerqa. On 8 July the party arrived at Ramat David, about five miles from Nazareth, eighteen from the Mediterranean port of Haifa and situated in a reclaimed swamp which twenty years previously had been one of the worst malarial zones in Palestine. That particular problem had been all but eradicated, but a new one had arisen by virtue of the sudden influx of great numbers of American air crews and then British personnel, which resulted in overcrowding and less than desirable standards of hygiene and sanitation.

There are not many who fail to remember the Squadron's Warrant Officer who joined them at Ramat David. One of his first tasks was to assemble all corporals on the runway for drill, his philosophy being that if he knocked them into shape they in turn would knock the other ranks into shape! He introduced himself to them all as they stood stiffly to

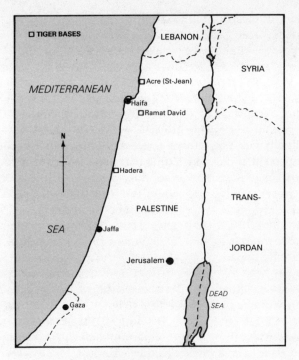

PALESTINE, 1942–1943

attention: 'I'm Billy the Bastard,' he bawled at them. 'Billy by name and Bastard by nature!' At Ramat David the Tigers were seconded to the United States Army Air Corps and were initially employed in pitching camp for the men of the 98th Heavy Bomber Group due in from the States. The first of thirty-six B-24s arrived on 25 July and 74's ground crews were immediately engaged in servicing and bombing up the aircraft under the supervision of the few key personnel the Americans had sent. Within two days the remaining Liberators arrived and, with the support of the Tigers, they were soon operational, engaged in bombing targets at Tobruk, Piraeus and Benghazi. The fuel and bomb dumps were located in the orange groves of a kibbutz some three hundred yards from the airfield. Some of the ground crews were involved in the ferrying of thousands of four-gallon petrol tins from Haifa harbour to the cache, whilst in the bomb dump the armourers had the task of manhandling 1,000lb bombs on to the trolleys and loading up to sixteen aircraft a day. There was no doubting that Ramat David provided extremely hard work, but everyone enjoyed it and the Americans certainly appreciated 74's presence.

Meanwhile moves were afoot to reconstitute the Tigers. Squadron Leader Addison had been posted in to take command on 10 July, although nobody had thought to tell Pete Matthews, still flying with 73, that he was no longer Boss! However, 74 was to remain a squadron of no aircraft and no pilots for several months yet. From Ramat David the men moved the short distance to the rest camp at Hadera on the shores of the Mediterranean. Here they collected some motor transport and all Squadron personnel underwent a weapons training course. Hadera was a popular stop, and 'Doc' Ferris, the Tigers' MO, was far happier with conditions here. The Squadron was on the move again on 3 October, this time *en route* to Teheran in Persia. The first stage of this gruelling journey was completed at 1800 hrs that evening at Mafraq, when everyone slept in the rough under one of the twenty-eight vehicles in the convoy. Such was to be the pattern for the next fortnight, for no tented accommodation had been supplied and consequently there was no cover at night—which resulted in frequent soakings in the heavy rains and thunderstorms that were encountered. Travelling via H4 and Rutbah, the Tigers reached RAF Habbaniyah four days later. Bivouacking outside the camp, they formed into a circle, with armed guards posted as a precaution against any attack by the local inhabitants who may have imagined that rich pickings could be had from the convoy.

Habbaniyah was the Jewel in the Desert, so called because of the amenities and facilities on offer there—shops, recreation, cinema and other entertainments, all specifically designed to combat the stifling and arid conditions. Designated Air HQ Iraq, it far surpassed anything the other stations under the AHQ umbrella could offer. The Tigers only stayed at Habbaniyah for three days, but that was time enough for a new contingent of pilots to join them—which augured well for the prospect of some aircraft arriving in the short term. In the morning of 11 October they all left for Baghdad where, in an effort to reduce numbers in the vehicles, the new pilots then split away from the convoy and travelled down to Basra and on to the coast, sailed by paddle steamer along the Gulf to Bandar-e-Shapur and then moved on by the Trans-Iranian railway to Teheran. Meanwhile the convoy proper embarked on a demanding six-day schedule as it travelled via Khanaqin, Kermanshah, Hamadan, Qum and finally RAF Doshan Tappeh just outside Teheran. Every two hours or so throughout the journey the convoy would make a 'comfort stop', and the sight of sixty or seventy men charging into the desert to answer the call of nature scarcely before the lorries' wheels had stopped turning was a memorable one indeed! The Squadron was employed at Doshan Tappeh until 30 November, working on the few old biplanes operated by the Persian Air Force, and then transferred to RAF Meherebad (nowadays Teheran International Airport), five miles to the west of the city.

HURRICANES IN MEHEREBAD

Soon after its arrival, it was learnt that at long last the Squadron was to receive its aircraft. Hurricane IIbs they may have been, second-hand and well used, but at least they were *aircraft* and the Squadron would be flying again. The first three arrived on 10 December, with five more on the 23rd. Doc Ferris wrote:

For the first time since coming overseas in June 1942 this squadron was to be equipped with aircraft. Previous to this, for all its fine record in England, 74 had been sent to Palestine and Persia doing all kinds of work except that of an operational unit. Consequently this brought about a corresponding change in outlook to all concerned, particularly the ground crews.

Sergeant Allan Griffin flew in in one of the first Hurricanes. With Pete Lovell leading, four aged IIbs had taken off from Kilo 8, refuelled at LG 224 and two hours later arrived at Aqir. Griffin recalls the experience:

I was amazed at how short the runway seemed, so I did a slow-speed pre-cautionary approach and dropped the Hurricane right on the edge of the white concrete. As the end of the runway was approaching very fast and as there was neither room nor speed to go around again, I cut the switches and braked hard. The poor old brakes were so tired very little happened and I did a slow graceful nose-over on the rough ground. When the ground crew arrived it transpired that they had been camouflaging the runway and had stopped halfway down. The white section I had landed on had been the unpainted part! Everyone thought it all very funny and after some sterling work with large hammers the bent prop was straightened, I did an air test and then, a few days after the other three, flew into Habbaniyah and then on to Meherebad.

It was not only aeroplanes that were required but more men to fly them, and these soon arrived. The CO also changed, Addison being replaced by Peter Illingworth. The Tigers found that their operational role was to help to prevent the Germans from reaching the northern Persian oilfields (should they defeat the Russians in the Caucasus) and as such were designated a component of PAIFORCE (Persia and Iran Forces). However, the German defeat at Stalingrad and the diversion of troops to that theatre was the cause of some relief, for many were convinced that, if the unthinkable had happened and the Germans had broken through, PAIFORCE would have been quickly overrun.

When the Tigers arrived, Meherebad was still undergoing reconstruction to make it compatible with RAF requirements. The camp was built in some measure as a fort, with outer defences, the outside walls of the four hangars forming part of the fortifications. So cold was the Christmas the Squadron spent here—temperatures plummeted to 20 degrees below freezing—that local shepherds were allowed to keep their sheep in one of the hangars which had been filled with straw for the purpose. Initially 74's and other RAF personnel shared the same building as their Persian hosts. Doc Ferris was outraged once again as the standards of hygiene and sanitation were poor, although living quarters were soon transferred to permanent, well-ventilated buildings which proved to be very difficult to heat because of their large size and because of a severe shortage of wood and coal. Improvised oil and water heaters were built but they never worked properly. To enjoy a hot shower or bath, the young airmen had to make a journey into Teheran and pay an ill-afforded 2s. 6d to the supervising aged crones, who took great delight in giving them a complete and often painful massage!

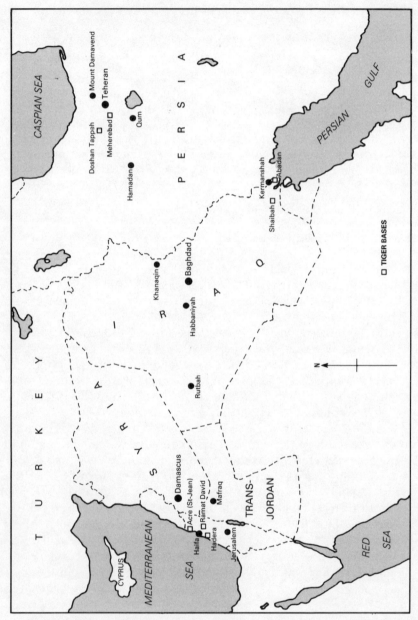

THE MIDDLE EAST, 1942–1943

□ TIGER BASES

Recreational facilities by contrast proved to be quite good, but still time seemed to hang heavily because of the general inactivity and the desire to get into action. Skiing parties made weekly trips into the mountains, and all the pilots and some of the ground crews took advantage of this invigorating sport. Many had their own personal skis. Dharban was the regular venue, and one which was also frequented by the Shah of Persia, who was quite happy to share the slopes with the roughneck and mostly inexperienced and clumsy Tigers! The Canadian 'Speed' Norman was a regular on the skiing parties. Despite his nationality he was not a good skier, but he was certainly a trier. Climbing to the top of the run, he would prepare for the traumas to follow by sitting and imbibing a few glasses of gin before pointing himself in the general direction of 'down', uttering some incredible noises and launching himself forth. Before very many yards had been covered Speed would have his nose in front of the rest of the party and the gap would rapidly widen as the velocity increased. He always ended up in a snow drift beside the approach road, where attempts at snow clearance ensured the presence of eight-foot high banks to cushion the impact for him as he ploughed in, head first, laughing fit to kill. Speed never did hurt himself, ascribing his good fortune to the fact that the Lord always looked after fools and drunkards!

Liberty Runs enabled everyone to visit Teheran frequently and sample its vicarious delights. 74 were fortunate in having a grand bunch of NCOs on strength at this time: the likes of the MT Sergeant Arthur Allen; Warrant Officer Signals, Charlie Scott; former Golden Gloves boxing champion Billy Kendrick, who was with the RAF Regiment detachment attached to 74; Peel and Simmonds, Flight Sergeants of their respective Flights; and Joe Reed the Sergeant Cook, who soon learnt the art of barter in the Teheran market, especially when it came to swapping the squadron-issue dehydrated potatoes for bags of rice. Food was generally not good, partly because of the difficulties in cooking it but also because of the lack of variety and the short supply of vegetables. There was at least one attempt by air crew to improve their diet when they formed a ground party and set off into the forest to the west of Teheran. A Hurricane was loaded with one hundred rounds of ball ammunition and took off; and once the ground party had located a large herd of gazelle, it guided the aircraft in by means of Very lights. The shooting of the deer and, occasionally, largely inedible wild boar by more conventional means became a regular pastime and did lead to some improvement in the menu—a change from oxtail soup and corned beef served in every conceivable variation.

The Squadron began the year 1943 with its few old Hurricanes and no spares or technical equipment, thus making it impossible, for example, to remove the external long-range tanks with which they had been flown in. Nevertheless a limited training programme was formulated, and on 5 January eight pilots completed sector reconnaissances. Seeing Persia from the air for the first time was a chastening experience. Away from Teheran, the landscape was very bleak, alternating between featureless plains and wicked mountain formations. One of the latter, Mount Damavend, stood at 18,000ft, but it was only forty-five miles from Meherebad and it proved to be ideal for homing purposes! Much of the training consisted of firing practice on the salt flats at Qum, where stationed Army personnel laid out targets and then, with 74 acting as simulated targets, themselves indulged in some practice. Other training concentrated on the new 'fours line-abreast' formation that the Squadron had decided to adopt and which was new to most of the pilots. This was an adaptation of the German *schwarm* but the RAF called it 'finger four' because each aircraft flew in a position corresponding to the finger tips seen in plan view. The formation was loose, manoeuvrable and easy to fly and those pilots who were not used to it soon got the hang of things.

On 25 January Bunny de Pass led a section to Qum but, much to his embarrassment, failed to find the firing range which had been blotted out by fresh falls of heavy snow. On subsequent sorties the Squadron concentrated on ground firing at salt marshes in general, but that proved to be less than satisfactory as the pilots could not see their bullets strike home. They also found that they were even more hampered by the substandard TR9 radio, which was particularly frustrating as the new formation they were flying depended on good air-to-air communications. With Qum in operation again, Bill Alston contrived to remove a wireless mast from one of the Army trailers with his wing tip, happily with no damage to him or to his Hurricane. But at the end of the month tragedy struck when the popular Bobby Waugh was killed whilst dogfighting, spinning in off a high-speed stall. His Hurricane burst into flames as it hit the ground and he stood no chance of escape. The night he was killed his colleague Sergeant Pilots had dinner in a Teheran night club and drank his health. The owner of the club had practically adopted those members of the Squadron who regularly visited him, and in return he presented the Tigers with a very small and endearing puppy which was promptly christened Gremlin. He became a great favourite with everyone to the extent that the riggers would take him out to the end of the landing strip as the Hurricanes returned so that the pilots could sit him on their laps as they taxied in. Gremlin was to be killed by a lorry just before the Squadron returned to England in 1944.

Two more Hurricanes arrived on strength on 30 January, together with four more pilots. But still there was no spares package, and Peel and Simmonds continued to work minor miracles. It was testimony to their efforts that the Tigers had actually flown 128 hours during January, against all the odds! John Peel was one of those Squadron characters whom men still remember vividly today. With his long shorts, boots and singularly shaped cap, he was a sight to behold. He was a tall, rugged character who spoke his mind at the slightest provocation and would not stand for any injustice to 'me boys'. His one aim in life was to get more aircraft serviceable in his A Flight than in B—something which he usually achieved despite the efforts of his counterpart, the smart, quiet and efficient Chiefy Simmonds, whom he completely overshadows in terms of

Tiger lore! Between them the two men managed to make the old Hurricanes 'fly like aeroplanes and not like ruptured ducks'. Bob Human has cause to recall John Peel's tippling abilities:

> Officers had been invited to the NCO's Mess for a party. As a South African it was assumed that I had a prodigious capacity for whatever poured, therefore on entering their mess tent I was waylaid by Peel. Imagine my consternation when, after ordering a bottle of gin, he turned to me and said 'Now you order, Sir!' In the traditional fighter pilot manner, and never at a loss to sum up a situation, I asked the barman for two bottles of gin. Psychologically the Chief lost before the first drink was drunk. He staggered away before his bottle was half empty!

On 4 February Sergeant Gibson force-landed at Hamadan on his way to join the Tigers with another Hurricane, bending the propeller in the process. But at least Gibson did have some good news: he had seen the long-awaited Hurricane spares package at Kermanshah—and in the nick of time, for there were just three airworthy Hurricanes remaining. By now the Squadron complement was up to twenty-four pilots, Pete Lovell and Brian Considine commanding A and B Flights, and the number of aircraft was slowly increasing, although Bill Alston tried to reverse the process again when he force-landed, wheels up, twenty miles south of Teheran. The weather continued to be very unsettled, bouts of heavy snow and hail alternating with brilliant blue skies perfect for flying and allowing successful shadow-firing to be practised. This involved two aircraft, with one, the target aircraft, flying at a height which allowed a fairly clear shadow to be projected on to the ground. The attacking aircraft, at a lower level, carried out a series of 'S' turns, firing at the shadow using deflection. Allan Griffin:

> If the pilot of the target Hurricane was feeling so inclined, he would fly all sorts of contortions in an attempt to prevent the attacker from hitting the shadow!

De Wilde ammunition—usually loaded one in six in the belts—contained a small amount of phosphorous which 'flashed' on impact, giving the pilot an idea where (or if!) he was hitting.

On 27 February Pete Illingworth left for Cairo and was replaced as CO by Bill Ogden, but, as with so many of the Squadron's COs around this time, his stay was to be a very short one. By 12 March he was on his way elsewhere and Pete Lovell was detailed to take command until the new Boss arrived. More spares appeared at the beginning of March—'generating much keenness and enthusiasm among personnel', records the Operational Record Book—and by the 7th of the month serviceability was the best yet, with every Hurricane in the air. But despite the new opportunities that this presented for training, morale was still suffering through lack of positive action. The arrival of olive green Spitfires destined for Russia under Lend-Lease agreements only served to rub it in, especially when the Squadron was ordered to service them—brand new Mk Vs standing next to its old, patched-up Hurricanes.

On 17 March 1943, A Flight started a move to Abadan on the Persian Gulf, but of the six aircraft that took off only four arrived, Alston force-landing at Sultanabad and the Canadian Besley disappearing for two days. He, too, had force-landed but was found being looked after by native villagers, fit and well. A Flight's ground crews, under the command of pilot Frank Twitchett, took a fortnight to reach Abadan by road. John Peel was a member of the party, as Twitchett recalls:

> On the first night, when we stopped, he asked permission to borrow the 15cwt truck 'in the interests of everybody' as he put it. He soon returned with beer and cigarettes: it seemed he went to the local bulk NAAFI and explained that, being on the road, we had not been able to collect our rations. Repeating this on each night's stop at the different NAAFIs kept everyone happy en route!

B Flight, who were not moving from Meherebad, were participating in a parade at RAF Doshan Tappeh to mark the twenty-fifth anniversary of the Royal Air Force. At the end of the month they took part in a small exercise involving six Persian aircraft, the latter simulating an attack on the RAF base which the Tigers broke up with considerable ease. Such a break in their training routine, however brief, was a welcome one; but the way in which they dealt with the Persian attack only confirmed them in their belief that they were fully trained and ready to do something rather more exciting. Meanwhile A Flight, having only just arrived at Abadan, now moved on to Shaibah. Their new home was far from popular with the ground crews. Living accommodation was two-thirds below ground and, with only one small window for each room, was consequently constantly gloomy; added to this was infestation by poisonous spiders and other suspect creatures. The working day was a long one—up at 0400, work until 0800 when breakfast was called, then a further stint until 1130, when it was stipulated that a cup of salt water be drunk before the midday meal. When the sun was at its height and the temperature reached 120 degrees in the shade, no work was attempted and crews were instead banished to their subterranean huts. Duties were resumed in the late afternoon.

April 1943 was, administratively, a difficult time for the Tigers, split as they were between Meherebad and Shaibah. At the latter station, patrols were frequently interrupted by sandstorms—rather different conditions from the arctic weather at Meherebad. The sand played havoc with the aircraft and unserviceability continued to affect their capacity for operations. By this time the Tigers' new CO had arrived. Squadron Leader James Hayter, a New Zealander universally known as 'Spud', quickly established himself as a popular commander with most of the air and ground crews. He was a professional who never suffered fools gladly and demanded the best of everyone around him. He was always an ebullient and cheerful man, and one who certainly enjoyed the social side of life too. The commander of A Flight was by this time Tony Reeves. Neither he nor Hayter would allow visiting journalists and correspondents to continue to write the story of 74 Squadron around Sailor Malan as they were still prone to: as glorious a chapter of Tiger history as it had been when he was with the unit, the time was *now*. Having been sent out to the desert theatre, the two men insisted that the humdrum and routine work in which 74 were involved, often in difficult and uncomfortable conditions, should be the focus of any reporting.

By the end of the month the Squadron was able to get in some formation practice at Shaibah and on the 27th was at last engaged in air-to-air firing, the first since it had re-equipped. Frank Twitchett was elected to tow the twelve-foot drogue with one of the Squadron's aircraft which had been fitted with a hook under the tail. After a successful exercise, the procedure by the towing aircraft on its return was to fly low over the runway and release the cable. Needless to say, the opportunities for decorating the Control Tower could rarely be resisted! Anderson and Bates were elected to be the first to fire, but with wry humour it was suggested that the drogue was too small when it was discovered that of 1,200 rounds fired by the two pilots only six had hit the target! However, with perseverance, A Flight's averages gradually improved. But that was all forgotten on 15 May when an 'Ousting the Gremlin' party was hosted by 74, the Gremlin to be ousted in this case not being the Squadron's puppy but the legendary imp that would crawl over the rim of a beer glass after a few pints of the local brew had been disposed of! It was in the middle of this party that a signal was received heralding the Squadron's next move. Would this be a return to the front line at last?

The following day saw concentrated efforts to get all the Hurricanes serviceable ready for a flight to Habbaniyah, although where they would go after that was not yet revealed. The Hurricanes had assembled there by the evening of the 17th whilst Besley prepared to leave Shaibah with the ground crews and light equipment by train and Grahame Jenkins with luggage and heavy gear by road. Having reached Baghdad, some of the ground crews were fortunate enough to transfer to the famous German-built Nairn overland bus. Diesel-powered and extremely comfortable, it had been used before the war for non-stop cross-desert journeys from Basra to Damascus. It was now used wherever it was needed and it was for the moment at 74's disposal. Meanwhile B Flight had also arrived at Habbaniyah from Meherebad, and for the first time in six weeks the Squadron was together again and Hayter had fifteen aircraft under his command. He had only once previously met personnel of B Flight, when he had paid them a flying visit just after being posted in.

On 21 May the Tigers took off *en route* for El Daba in the Western Desert. All the Hurricanes successfully completed the move over the course of two days with the exception of Hayter's, which became unserviceable. He duly arrived in a staff car! Besley, Prendergast and de Pass had already arrived with essential ground crews by DC-3 from Habbaniyah. Cooper was despatched to Helwan with some drivers to collect as much MT as he could find. They soon returned, bringing with them ambulances, water bowsers (water would have to be brought in daily to supply the needs of the Squadron), trucks, starter trollies and enough other types to enable the Squadron to function properly again.

74 arrived at El Daba (which lay to the west of Alamein and nine miles from the Mediterranean coast) a few days after the North African campaign had finally been won by the Allies and immediately began to fly sector recces. Spud Hayter flew over the old El Alamein lines on 29 May, deserted now in human terms but easily identifiable by the great mass of abandoned German and Italian weaponry, tanks and aircraft and the corpses of camels which had strayed into the minefields. (This area proved to be an ideal training ground for the Tigers and other squadrons in the Middle East Air Force as far as air-to-ground firing was concerned, rich as it was in ready-made and realistic targets.) Hayter returned to report what he had seen and then proceeded to give the whole Squadron a pep talk, during which he almost managed to convince everyone that the old Hurricanes they were flying were the best fighters operating with the Desert Air Force and that in the hands of the best squadron they should be almost unbeatable! On 1 June the news came through that they were to take over 237 Squadron's operational duties. Ops at last! Everyone rejoiced!

DESERT OPERATIONS

Operational conditions in the desert presented a whole new set of problems for the Tigers. The bases they used were a vast stretch of dust and stones in the summer and of cheerless boggy marsh in the winter. Personnel lived uncomfortably in tents except when on detachment to the more permanent camps such as Dekheila. Messes were usually in marquees. Caravan-like trailers set up with tables and chairs were used as 'Ops Gharries' or even as instrument and armourers' workshops. A crew room *per se* was rarely provided. Day-to-day servicing was done in the open, although for all major servicing and repairs the aircraft would be flown to an RSU such as that at Aboukir. Nights were very cold in the desert, while the daytime sun roasted the skin. When rain fell it did so in torrents, and when it stopped men foundered in the mud and were badly bitten by insects. Aircraft became stuck in the bog and as ground crews struggled to get them out they sank up to their ankles in layers of thick dust which clung like wet fur. Extremes of temperature, the lack of a varied diet and the prevalence of tropical-like diseases took their toll: it is a wonder that operations could be, and were, sustained by any squadron in such circumstances.

El Daba had been previously used by the Italians and Germans and the tented living areas were infested with fleas. Doc Ferris tried various fumigation procedures but it was found that the most effective way was to remove the contents, seal the tents and soak the ground with petrol. After a while the tents would be reopened and the sides brailed up so that air could circulate through them, thus removing the smell. The whole process worked well until the kit was brought back and everything, fleas included, returned to normal! Pilot Officer Richardson burnt his tent down. Having soaked the ground with fuel, he forgot himself and went back inside whilst smoking. The tent exploded in a fireball and he was badly burnt.

Aircraft, as well as men, suffered in the desert. Often an engine was thoroughly worn out after only thirty hours' use, with valves eroded and cylinders pitted with signs of wear. Cables were rotted by the salt in the air of shore bases: control rods gave way; legs of undercarriages seized up. Tyres had to be specially covered with wet cloths to prevent them bursting in the desert heat, and petrol vaporized in the tanks, making the latter liable to burst at the joints and explode. When de Wilde explosive ammunition was loaded, the aircraft's wings had to be covered with wet sacking to prevent the rounds exploding in the heat. Pilots often took off in clouds of dust which settled on the perspex and obscured all vision. Occasionally they had to land in sandstorms which robbed them of all landmarks. Such a storm could last for up to three days, and once all the aircraft were safely on the ground they would not fly again until it had passed—indeed, there would be very little movement of any kind other than an odd run down to the sea with the lorries picking their way between forty-gallon drums marking the road. It was only when one was a couple of miles from the coast that the sky would suddenly clear. Apart from the coast, the only other recreational possibility for men based at El Daba was Alexandria, and after a while seventy-two-hour passes were issued to air and ground crews. Alexandria was very French in outlook and at the eastern end of the city there were good stretches of beach, with bathing huts and hotels behind. Once again, as with all postings to new areas, a routine quickly evolved. In this case it was to book in to one of the hotels and prepare for the evening's entertainment. There was often a prelude to this in the form of sword-swallowers and jugglers performing outside, and these could be watched in comfort from the balconies which were available in most rooms. As darkness fell the night clubs beckoned.

Convoy duties were listed as being 74's primary task and sorties were flown to protect shipping either moving up from Port Said westwards to Malta to reinforce the invasion of Sicily or on its return to Alexandria. The sorties were usually flown in pairs and lasted $1\frac{1}{2}$ hours, the briefing prior to take-off including the speed, direction and position of the ships together with a frequency and a secret callsign that would be used to establish contact. Radio silence was maintained except for the initial transmission made on sighting the convoy, and once contact had been made the ships were circled at a distance of two or three miles and at a height of 5,000ft for the duration of the sortie, the two aircraft flying in line abreast a couple of miles apart. The relieving aircraft had to be in position before the first pair detached and returned to base for debriefing. Cover was provided from first light until dusk, and pilots often flew these tedious patrols incapacitated by dysentery or some other stomach complaint, although Doc Ferris's chalk and opium powder provided some relief if taken at the right time prior to take-off.

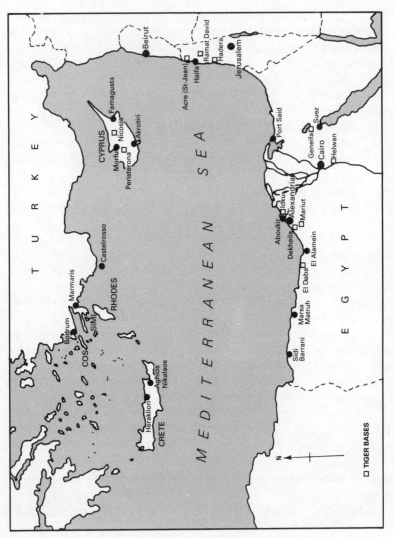

NORTH AFRICA AND THE MEDITERRANEAN, 1942–1944

☐ TIGER BASES

Many a scramble was ordered, too, but most proved to be abortive. Readiness and scramble were operated in the same manner as in Britain, with two aircraft and two pilots drawn up. Immediately a scramble was called (generally in the form of a jangling triangle or by telephone—or both), a Very light was fired to clear the circuit, the engines would fire into life (having been run periodically by ground crews) and the Operations Clerk would brief as to the height, direction and position of the target. The pilots climbed aboard and, taking time only to secure the straps, would take off straightaway and irrespective of wind direction (unless it were particularly gusty) to save taxying into position. At El Daba there were no runways. Once the interception had been completed—usually with no sign of the enemy—the aircraft would return, the Intelligence Officer would debrief and the aircraft would be refuelled, the guns and radios would be checked, the oxygen bottles would be filled and the aircraft would be ready for the next call.

On 8 June Prendergast was forced to bale out during a convoy patrol when his aircraft developed a serious glycol leak. Fortunately he landed in the sea close to a British cruiser, which picked him up and took him to Malta. A few days afterwards, five reportedly new Hurricanes arrived at El Daba for 74 but one glance at the cracked paint and bulging panels instantly gave the lie to the reports, and ground crews were quickly set the task of rectifying the many unserviceabilities found. On 28 June everyone was thrown into a mild state of panic when reports of an imminent attack by enemy parachutists were received. Guards were doubled, the station defence plan was activated and crews slept by the aircraft, but no threat materialized and Station and Squadron soon returned to normal routines. On 3 July twelve aircraft were sent to RNAS Dekheila (HMS *Grebe*), whence intensive convoy patrols were flown during the lead in to the invasion of Sicily. Frank Twitchett was in charge of the arming and refuelling party which travelled by road and with him he had John Peel. Stopping the convoy short of Dekheila to check that all was in order, John asked permission to take the lead in deference to his days with the Fleet Air Arm, with whom he had started his career. Entering the camp, they immediately went to meet the Regulating Petty Officer to arrange for accommodation for the men. He and John stared at each other for some minutes before deciding that they had served together aboard one of the Navy's carriers. Frank was invited to join them in an impromptu reunion liberally lubricated with Pusser's rum issue. Further interest in the proceedings for Frank ceased after they had drunk to every ship in the Home Fleet and the other two were about to start on those in the Med . . .

Twenty-six sorties on convoy patrol were flown by the Tigers from Dekheila and Marsa Matruh before they returned to El Daba on 10 July, the day after the invasion of Sicily, very disappointed that they had not seen a single enemy aircraft. Many hours had been worked by air and ground crews during operations from Dekheila, and the chance was now taken to relax a little, catch up with maintenance and return all aircraft to full readiness. Someone had discovered from Squadron records that 10 July was Allan Griffin's 21st birthday:

> The celebrations continued late into the night with the entire squadron involved. The *pièce de résistance* was organized and executed by 'Gary' Cooper who provided a spectacular display of pyrotechnics which culminated in an enormous explosion when he detonated a vast quantity of German gelignite. He narrowly escaped injury as he had not used a long enough fuse to let him get clear after it had been lit! Then, as each pilot succumbed to the irresistible need for sleep, he was dressed in a Mae West and placed in the Readiness Hut. There were a lot of sore heads the next morning at Doc Ferris's sick parade.

Envy filled the heart of every Squadron pilot when a pair of Typhoons arrived at LG 106 to undergo desert serviceability trials, but Hayter took their minds off things by leading them on one of his now famous Squadron formation practices, this time at night. B Flight imagined that they might actually get to see a German when they were scrambled to intercept an He 111 on the evening of the 17th. Needless to say, nobody saw anything.

On the 19th Hayter flew to Alexandria for a conference at 219 Group. His efforts to get 74 involved in more than just routine patrol work were beginning to pay dividends and the conference was held to put the finishing touches to a plan for a strike on Crete involving fourteen squadrons in all—squadrons which, according to Group, had lost their aggressive spirit whilst languishing on the coast. If that were the case, it was through no fault of their own. Six Tigers had been selected to take part in this Sunday morning operation and they were ordered to prepare for it by practising strafing techniques. The six chosen aircraft were fitted with long-range tanks and were heavily serviced to ensure that they were in tip-top condition, although the general condition of 74's own Hurricanes meant that they had had to borrow three in better fettle from 451 at Idku to make up the number! Hayter, Twitchett, Cooper, Reeves, Bates and Harris left for LG 101 on 22 July to join over one hundred aircraft taking part. Formed into three Wings (and with 74 attached to the Sidi Barrani Wing), each aircraft had approximately fifteen minutes over the island, during which they sought out the briefed targets and also targets of opportunity. 74 had little luck. Frank Twitchett had a go at a German staff car he saw scurrying for cover but otherwise, in common with the other aircraft of the Wing, the Tigers had difficulty in finding the targets and were loath to attack anything other than obvious military installations for fear of injuring civilians. If the object of the exercise were to create pandemonium on the island for a few minutes, then it undoubtedly was achieved, but at a cost when two aircraft of other squadrons crashed. 74 escaped unscathed and returned after their 550-mile, four-hour excursion to land at Gambut in a sandstorm with the feeling that all they had to show for their efforts was sore bottoms!

On 9 August a signal was received from AHQ ordering a detachment of pilots and ground crews to St-Jean (Acre) in Palestine for two weeks of special operations. With the eighty ground crewmen forming the advance party, they set off on the 12th with Frank Twitchett once again in command. This left just two flight crews to service all the Squadron's Hurricanes (none of which was sent to St-Jean), which by dint of long days and hard work they managed. Hayter recorded:

They must receive every credit for they are working like hell from dawn until well after dark.

The advance party to St-Jean was recalled on 27 August. The detachment had been part of a plan to attack the Dodecanese islands, during the execution of which it was also intended to involve aircraft operating from Cyprus, but nothing came of it. Back at El Daba, 74 were flying Wing sweeps led by Hayter which usually concluded with a dummy attack on Alexandria harbour. Spud was never averse to low flying in the vicinity of Alex and flying the flag.

Then came the best news for a long time: the Squadron was to re-equip with Spitfires. Almost everyone, air and ground crews alike, was genuinely excited about getting the beloved Spits back again. The wait was not long. With a permanent move to Idku on the shores of Aboukir Bay between Alexandria and Port Said initiated on the 26th, the first four MK Vcs arrived. All the old Spitfire boys had flown their new charges within twenty-four hours and were like Tigers with two tails after the experience. Those who had not flown the type before had quickly gone solo, and by the month's end the full complement of aircraft (three Vbs and thirteen Vcs) was on strength. There were rumblings of another Cretan operation in the offing, but these were soon superseded by rumours of an even bigger show—raids on the Dodecanese islands. Involvement in these was to lead to a short-lived but significant period in the Squadron's history.

It took a while for the armourers to get used to the cannon-firing Spitfires, although the pilots were soon showing much better results in practice firing. Exercises with other squadrons—one condescendingly referred to as a 'Hurricane mob'!—were carried off successfully. Allan Griffin has some interesting comments on the differences between their old and new charges:

The Hurricane was an absolutely first class gun platform. It was stable and could turn inside any Spitfire and there is no doubting that it was a joy to fly. A Spitfire could outclimb it but there is no doubting that the Hurricane was safer to land, for the Spit tended to 'float' before deciding to stall on the landing approach—which meant that to all intents and purposes it was out of control whilst we fought to get it down! That may be exaggerating it a bit, but we contrasted it with the Hurricane to which we were used and which, once it decided to stall, did so with a vengeance. We took to practising something which was officially frowned upon, that is, flying to the end of the runway at 700 or 800 feet, applying opposite stick and rudder, side-slipping down to about 200 feet and placing it straight down on that lovely wide undercarriage!

On 8 September news of Italy's unconditional surrender was received and the Squadron was put on twelve hours' alert and ordered to be available to move anywhere it was directed. Pilots were instructed to watch for Italian Air Force activity as many officers were surrendering individually by bringing their aircraft into Allied landing grounds, their intentions being divined from the fact that they had been told to complete an anti-clockwise circuit prior to landing. If these instructions were not complied with they were to be considered still hostile and the appropiate action taken. No Italian aircraft attempted to land at Idku. But now the Tigers were sniffing the wind. Would they at long last be striking again? On 13 September two aircraft were scrambled after a Ju 88 and Sergeants Bartlett and Gray made an interception—the first German aircraft the Squadron had seen in the air for many a long month. Bartlett decided to have a go at long range but in the excitement of the moment pressed the wrong button and fired his machine guns instead of his cannon. The Junkers responded by climbing immediately to an enormous altitude, and although Bartlett had missed he entered the record books as being the first member of the current 74 Squadron to have a 'squirt' at a real target.

DODECANESE INTERLUDE

On 15 September six Spitfires flew a first light convoy patrol over units of the Italian Fleet (four battlecruisers, four cruisers and a swarm of destroyers) sailing into Alexandria. At the same time there was increasing activity around the Dodecanese and the general feeling continued to be that the Tigers would shortly be reopening their account with the Luftwaffe. On 22 September orders came for an advance party to move. Totalling forty-five in number, and all under the command of Doc Ferris, the men were taken in a pair of DC-3s to Nicosia Main to join nine Spitfires already there. Over the next five days a state of readiness was maintained at both Idku and in Cyprus until, on the 28th, the remainder of the aircraft and ground crews were ordered from North Africa to Nicosia. Immediately they arrived, nine aircraft equipped with long-range tanks set off for the island of Cos. Cos is one of the smaller Dodecanese islands, but as far as the Allies were concerned its position made it vital to the process of reoccupying Greece, and by the time the Tigers arrived it had been back in British hands for a fortnight. The airfield on nearby German-held Rhodes had been temporarily put out of action by American bombers, and No 7 Squadron of the South African Air Force had moved into Antimachea, the airfield on Cos. Shortly afterwards the Luftwaffe had begun its counter-offensive, which had worn the South Africans down until they had just four serviceable Spitfires remaining. It was to support the defence of Cos that 74 had been ordered in.

Anderson's aircraft developed engine trouble ten miles east of Castelrosso and he was forced to bale out. A high-speed launch and a Wellington air–sea rescue aircraft were alerted and made several unsuccessful searches of the area. The other pilots meanwhile landed safely at Antimachea and within a very short space of time were airborne again on patrol. Later in the afternoon the CO, with John Lewis, Titch Harris and

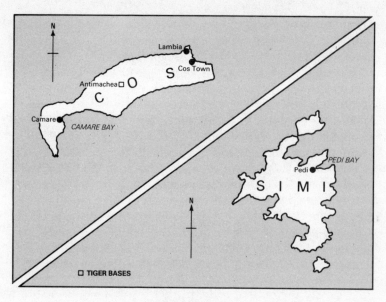

COS AND SIMI, 1943

David Maxwell, encountered five Ju 88s and attacked them, but without scoring. The following morning Bates, Maxwell and Wilson were scrambled, although Trevor Bates was quickly forced to return when his oxygen failed. Willie Wilson became separated from Maxwell and flew the whole of the quite hectic sortie by himself. Meeting three successive waves of Ju 88s, out of the first formation he shot down one, then dived through the second and third and damaged an aircraft in each. Another six Ju 88s came in behind these, and the formation spread as Wilson pressed home another attack. Yet another formation appeared on the scene, and he again went for them single-handedly, but he was almost immediately in turn attacked by five Me 109s although he managed to evade them after a short and very fast dogfight. Enough was enough. Wilson made for home, gratified to see two of the chasing Messerschmitts collide.

On Cos the damage caused by these latest heavy raids was extensive. The landing ground at Antimachea had been cratered, and a second attack by twenty-four Ju 88s later in the day added to the damage, casualties on the ground amounting to two killed and ten injured. It was against this background that all flying from Cos ceased—which, for the moment, prevented the Squadron's ground crews from flying in. Instead, they were diverted to their old haunt at Ramat David in Palestine. Forty were taken to the port at Haifa, whilst the remaining twenty were left behind without further instructions! Those at Haifa were issued with compo rations, two gallons of water per man, mosquito veils, anti-mosquito cream and boiled sweets, and at dusk all were embarked on a destroyer and sailed for Castelrosso, where they transferred to the Greek caique *Panomites*. Space was at a premium, so only a minimum of essential medical and maintenance equipment could be taken on board with them. They left Castelrosso at dead of night and sailed along the Turkish coast, through the German-held Rhodes straits and on to the island of Simi. In consultation with the Greek captain, they decided to put in here for four or five hours so that their arrival on Cos to join their colleagues could be timed to coincide with sunrise the next morning.

Simi was held by thirty Special Boat Squadron men together with a garrison of about one hundred Italians. All were under the command of one Major La Praik, who saw 74's arrival as making a welcome addition to his inadequate force. After a quick meal, ground crews were detailed to reinforce the defensive positions that had been constructed, and any thoughts of moving on to Cos were quickly dispelled with the realization that the Germans were about to invade both islands. After several hours of back-breaking work, Antimachea had meanwhile been made serviceable enough to enable the remaining Spitfires to be flown out to salt flats at Lambia, where a small camp was set up under trees five hundred yards from the landing strip. It soon became obvious that in the face of constant enemy air activity there could be no further flying, and the aircraft were camouflaged with the help of men from the Durham Light Infantry. At midnight the remaining members of 74's ground crews who had been stranded at Ramat David were flown in by DC-3. Tony Blythin was one of those on board:

> We landed in total darkness. There were no runway lights and the pilot showed his landing lights only briefly on the approach due to the proximity of German-held Rhodes. We evacuated the Dakota with engines still running and unloaded the equipment in record time, thereby allowing the transport to take off into the comparative safety of the dark night. As the Squadron Operations Clerk, I carried a suitcase containing not only the famous Form 700s (the aircraft record cards) but also many Squadron comforts such as shaving and washing gear!
>
> Once on Cos we were allocated a billet by the airstrip on the salt pans and, having been reunited with the Boss and the other pilots, we settled in and set about brewing up. But we were not to be left in peace for very long. The alarm went off. We had landed in the jaws of a trap which was about to be sprung. The Germans had arrived!

INVASION AND ESCAPE!

Early in the morning of 3 October a German invasion fleet approached Cos from the south and landed troops on the central northern coast of the island. Troops were also disembarked in Camare Bay to the south, with subsidiary landings elsewhere. These landings were supported by Ju 52s dropping paratroops. By midday it was estimated that 1,500 Germans, with equipment that included armoured cars, were taking up positions. These numbers were to be reinforced throughout the afternoon and evening with more seaborne and parachute landings. There was little the British could do in the face of such odds other than withdraw to positions covering the town, port and airfield. By the following morning the situation was being described as critical. Finally a message was sent from the garrison:

The position in Cos Town is untenable. Intend continuing to fight elsewhere.

With that the troops retired into the surrounding hills—or were captured.

The Tigers acquitted themselves exceptionally well in the aftermath of the invasion. Immediately the alarm had been sounded, the newly flown-in ground party dispersed into adjoining olive groves, where previously prepared ditches at least offered some form of protection. 74's party quickly realized that, after so long consigned to the doldrums, they had now been thrust to the very forefront of the war! After a while, with the enemy still not far away, the detachment was split up and positioned at various locations around the grove.

*

Bunny de Pass awoke at about 0430 hrs in the morning of the invasion and heard the sound of aircraft above him:

I didn't take much notice as the Germans were often sending Ju 88s over. The aircraft continued to fly around and I heard in the distance the sound of a motor launch. By this time I was becoming apprehensive. Shots were coming from the direction of the landing strip. We rushed out of the tents and saw Germans coming up the beaches three or four hundred yards away, and David Maxwell, Titch Harris and I ran off in the general direction of the road. The Germans were spraying the area with tommy-gun fire and were using a lot of tracers. There was little we could do except run and I don't think we've ever moved so fast in our lives. We grabbed our few belongings and made for a jeep driven by a South African. They managed to get in one burst at us and we shed our bundles as we ran! I dumped some clothing near a farmhouse and lost a tin of fifty precious cigarettes but we did all manage to hang on to our log books. The firing became more persistent, flares were being fired and mortar fire could be heard. It was still fairly dark with plenty of cloud. We saw Bates and Norman, joined up with them and headed straight for Cos Town. There was little that could have been achieved in staying—the landing ground was out of action and we were of insufficient numbers to stand and defend our positions. In the event we reckoned the best policy was to try and join up with other British troops.

*

Meanwhile Tony Blythin and his colleagues, having seen the situation developing around them, decided on retreat too, this time into the hills to their rear. A quick discussion of tactics resulted in an initial determination to find a secure hiding place:

Loaded up with tins of fruit and other food which we had had time to hurriedly grab from the store in the mêlée of our retreat, the two dozen or so in our party, which included members of the Durham Light Infantry, embarked on a long march through the hills, trying to get away from the area of intense enemy activity. At night we could see the flares fired off by the Germans as they advanced, approaching the interior in a typical pincer movement. And by day the Stukas had free range of the skies. Flying from their base in Rhodes, they would drop their bombs unopposed and then indulge in aerobatics over the island to demonstrate in no uncertain fashion that they were masters of the sky at that time. Bombing apart, there was little gunfire. Most of the contingent based on the island had been captured; locals were keeping a very low profile. The idea as far as this party was concerned was to keep moving and not get caught!

At one stage the party did stumble across a group of Germans who, showing supreme confidence, were not keeping a proper look-out. During the exchange of fire that followed, the British retreated, joining up shortly afterwards with another group of Durham's under the command of Second Lieutenant Monty Banks:

We continued on our walk through the hills—not sure of the position of the enemy and not sure whether we were in fact advancing or retreating! We could see the coastline from our elevated position, and when we stumbled across a large cave, which was evidently occasionally used by local shepherds, we decided to make camp there whilst a reconnaissance was made. From the mouth of the cave a ravine led down to the sea. An occasional swastika-flagged motor boat would cross our field of vision, and in the air we began to see Spitfires. This excited us at first, but then we realized they were our own Spits being flown by German pilots. There had been no time to destroy or immobilize the aircraft in the suddenness of the attack.

On the following morning a local twelve-year-old shepherd boy approached the cave and we decided to risk talking to him. He could not speak any English but we managed to convey to him the fact that we were hungry by using sign language—there are certain actions which mean the same in any tongue!—and after his initial wide-eyed surprise at finding the British in his cave he agreed to go down to the village to see what he could find. This was something of a worrying time as we could not be sure that the boy would be trustworthy and also we were concerned that the Germans might be in his village and become suspicious if he was seen carrying food into the hills. But it was a risk we all decided was worth taking—a risk justified in the event when he did return some hours later with bread and eggs and no signs of German suspicion.

Recce patrols continued. On one of these regular forays Banks came across more fugitives in the hills—none other than Spud Hayter with some of 74's pilots. They all returned to the cave and a council of war followed, the priority obviously being to get off the island. Tony Blythin recalls the CO's appearance very well:

He was wearing an old trilby hat and with several days' growth of beard almost looked the part of an islander, he and the others all having ripped insignia from their uniforms and having doctored the cloth with mud and by tearing it in a few places. He had managed by some means to contact the SBS, who were operating at that time from a base in Turkey. As he explained to us, his priority was to get the pilots off the island and back to resume operations; this done, he would arrange for the rest of us to be taken off too. A rendezvous had already been made to collect the air crew. Sailing first to the Turkish coast, they picked up a group of Commandos and over the following couple of days they moved along the Turkish coast to Marmaris and Andifli before reaching Castelrosso.

*

Bunny de Pass and his party had reached Cos Town during the morning of the invasion, only to find everyone in a state of utter confusion. Realizing that the only course of action now open to them was to try and get off the island, they moved down to the harbour, boarded an Italian boat and set off for Leros with German shells exploding in the water all around them. *En route* they encountered some enemy patrol boats and so altered course for Bodrum on the Turkish coast. From Bodrum they too eventually reached Castelrosso, where Bates and Norman found a Cant 506 flying boat to take them to Aboukir, where they reported directly to 219 Group HQ. De Pass and the others carried on to Paphos by high-speed launch and from there they flew to Nicosia by DC-3.

*

LACs Simms and Smith had been the first of 74's complement to get off the island by launch. Now, four days later, Tony Blythin and his colleagues also made the seven-mile crossing to Turkey safely, courtesy of the SBS whose position there, it must be said, was something of a delicate one. The Turks were well aware of their presence, but only unofficially. So those rescued from Cos had to be moved on as quickly as possible, and they also sailed down to Castelrosso and disembarked. Tony Blythin and Freddie Fox met up again with Spud Hayter and his party as well as another contingent of ground crewmen which by now had been evacuated from Simi.

*

Whilst Hayter, Blythin, de Pass and company were busily evading the Germans on Cos, those on Simi were encountering their own problems. Simi, much smaller than its neighbour, is an island which lends itself naturally to defence on account of its high mountains overlooking all possible approaches from the sea. 74's men were quickly dispersed around the island on the orders of Major La Praik and soon found themselves in action when Germans landed in Pedi Bay. Doc Ferris gave an account of subsequent events:

> It was just before dawn when our guard on a hill overlooking the town and harbour shouted that the invasion was coming, and, sure enough, a German schooner was sailing into the bay. In half a minute we were ready for them. The airmen had rifles but they weren't content with these. If they had to fight Jerry Commandos then they would be Commandos too. Those who could find knives—the bigger the better—grabbed them and stuck them in their belts. They also got hold of hand grenades. About a hundred Germans landed, armed with Mauser automatics, grenades and two-inch mortars. They didn't try a frontal attack on the town but came round by the hills. And in the hills our lads were waiting for them. Our armourers had gone to help the army gun crews. Others joined the soldiers in defensive positions among the rocks. The whole lot fought heroically all day. By evening Jerry decided he was licked and withdrew. Thirty wounded were taken aboard the schooner and he left behind sixteen dead and six prisoners.

Set against this figure, British casualties were three killed and one wounded—none from 74.

The following day, air attacks continued intermittently. Defensive fire from the ground was enough to cause considerable concern to the German pilots. One Stuka was destroyed by 74's Flight Sergeant Schofield, who had been detailed to man an Italian Breda gun. Schofield's story is one of considerable heroism. He was short-sighted and his spectacles were shattered by the vibration of the gun. He was wounded in the arm but he continued at his post until the wound turned septic and he had to be hospitalized. On the first day of the invasion some Germans were detected below his gun position and he helped rout these out. As an armourer, Schofield was also perfectly qualified to keep his gun going despite the fact that the flash eliminator was burnt off and the sights had come away owing to the heat of the gun. As a result of his actions, Schofield was awarded the Military Medal. A Tiger indeed!

During the German bombing of Simi a direct hit was scored on the General Headquarters of the island, killing one of the SBS contingent and 74's LAC Gray. During the same raid two other SBS men were trapped and rescue parties worked ceaselessly to free them despite continued air attacks and the dangerous condition of the building. The rescue party, which included Doc Ferris, found that it was not possible to free both men at once so it was decided to make an airway to the more deeply buried of the two, then concentrate initially on the other. Work continued overnight, but by next morning it became obvious that the amputation of a leg was necessary if either man were to stand a chance of being saved. Ferris's instruments had been lost so he borrowed some from the island's civilian doctor. These consisted of a few forceps, tourniquets and scalpels, some scissors and a small carpenter's saw. He decided to amputate just above the knee as the lower part of the leg was firmly trapped. It was only with considerable difficulty that the soldier could be reached and the position for working was, to say the least, an awkward one. Nevertheless, the patient was brought out from the debris, but sadly the effects of shock, bomb blast, crushing injuries and finally the amputation itself were too much and the soldier died. And despite the attentions of the rescue team, injections of morphine and the passing of water by rubber tube, his colleague also died before he could be pulled free. The details of this rescue have been drawn from a report made shortly afterwards by Ferris himself. He neglects to mention that the awkward position in which he had to operate involved being held upside down by the legs so that he could reach his patients. As a direct result of his efforts here, and indeed on the island for the duration of the stay, Doc Ferris was awarded the Military Cross.

On 8 October Major La Praik decided that all the British wounded, together with the more serious of the Italian and civilian casualties, should be evacuated, and to this end they boarded a caique bound for Castelrosso, where they arrived safely the following day and met up with the survivors from Cos. A further boat was commandeered and the reunited party set off for Cyprus, always in sight of land and always keeping a sharp eye open for German MTBs. Back on Cyprus, everyone was debriefed and underwent a thorough medical examination. Most were found to be reasonably fit but some were showing signs of shock and had been somewhat disorientated by the speed of events. Finally, everyone was issued with new kit and sent on a few days' survivors' leave to Alexandria and Cairo. They could hardly believe their luck considering their situation just a week previously.

PRISONERS OF WAR

Seventeen of 74's ground crew were trapped on Cos and taken prisoner by the Germans. Len Leake:

It was not a very pleasant place to be! We had no idea exactly where we were on the island. We each had a rifle but only five rounds of ammunition. We played cat-and-mouse for three days, being bombed by Stukas and strafed by Messerschmitts. Eventually we found ourselves trapped on the beach with nowhere to go.

Joe Tombling recalls that after the invasion they linked up with the Durham Light Infantry (DLI):

We were almost on the point of getting a cup of tea when Stukas arrived. Everyone had to lie doggo and not move a muscle. They dropped their load a short way off and we moved back to Cos town. An RAF man told us: 'It's every man for himself.' We made our way to the nearest point to Turkey four miles away and a few of us tried to make a small raft but didn't like the results of our efforts, abandoned the idea and moved inland.

Tom Fawcett:

After the initial bombardment had ceased, Sergeant Lowndes sent a couple of the lads to find out what the score was. They arrived back in a jeep with a load of rifles and a box of compo rations and these were shared out. Anderson and I were given a Very pistol, taken a couple of miles down the road and told by an Army officer to keep our eyes skinned for anything untoward. For a while we did not see another soul but had a grandstand view of the shelling and mortaring of Cos harbour. Then we began to hear increasingly loud machine-gun fire, followed by the DLIs retreating towards us. They came along our trench and told us that if we valued our lives now was the time to move out. This we started to do but an officer had a different idea. He ordered us into a shell hole to watch for German armour. A pair of Ju 88s chose to bomb our position half an hour later. Anderson and I survived but the Army were not so lucky. That was enough for us. We upped and ran towards the sea. Andy was a very good swimmer and he decided to make for Turkey, which was so tantalizingly close. He was about two hundred yards offshore when a bomb or a shell exploded in the water close to where he was. I didn't see him again.

Joe Tombling:

Towards evening we made our way towards Cos harbour, just in time to see a launch leaving port. On board, as we learnt after the war, were de Pass and his pilot colleagues. They were too far away for us to make contact. So we spent the night in an Italian concrete blockhouse. In here we found piles of clothing and, not really thinking about possible consequences, we put on some additional underclothes beneath our light shirts and slacks and also donned a heavy-duty jacket. This additional clothing was to stand us in very good stead as we were moved through a bitterly cold and frosty Germany to our eventual prison camp. It also proved to be very awkward to explain when we were interrogated.

There was no question now that they could do anything but surrender as there was no possible means of escape and they could see German armour and infantry approaching. The Durham Light Infantry were reluctant to be the ones to carry the white flag out, so LAC Charlie Lavers grabbed a mosquito net and led the way with it held high over his head:

All our lads were proud of Charlie that day: he probably saved our lives. We walked up to the tanks and the German troops rounded us up and took us to Cos Castle.

After four days we were marched down to the prison ship which took us to Piraeus. The voyage was very uncomfortable, with the prisoners below the waterline in the ship's stuffy hold and not being allowed up on deck. The coal bunkers were the other side of the bulkhead and the coal slipped constantly, the sound as it did so reverberating through the cavernous hold. The first time it did this panic set in below decks with everyone believing the ship had been torpedoed. From Piraeus we were taken to Athens. Red Cross representatives arrived and registered us all, after which we felt much safer. We were then marched through Athens to the rail station where we boarded overflowing cattle trucks ready for the journey into Germany.

Before boarding the train, all the prisoners were shown a pile of aluminium-lined wooden boxes and were told to clean them out. Two boxes were allocated to each truck, one to be used for drinking water and the other as a toilet. Forty men were packed into each truck and the conditions and sanitation, with just straw on the floor, became intolerable: many men quickly became ill and had to be taken off. This at least ensured that there was more room for those remaining. Jim Twitty:

Some of the lads had dysentery and I can tell you it wasn't very nice. We had to cope the best we could with the disgusting conditions into which we had been put. Once the latrine box was full we took to urinating into our tin helmets and throwing the contents out of the wire grill at Germans on the platforms of stations we passed through. That helped a bit.

Occasionally the train would be halted and the prisoners let out into fields after guards had been posted. The offending latrine boxes would be emptied and the water supply replenished from natural sources.

At Thessalonika, whilst the track ahead was being repaired in the wake of partisan attacks, the train was pushed into sidings for two days in hot sun, but the men were not allowed to leave the trucks and they suffered further terrible privations. Eventually they were on the move again, *en route* for Budapest, and from the Hungarian capital the train took them on to Vienna, where they were marched through the city as a propaganda exercise before being herded back into the railway trucks again. Next stop was Stalag VIIA at Moosberg. They only stayed for six days in the miserable surroundings of this camp before being taken on to Frankfurt-am-Main and finally Dulag Luft, where the men were kept in unheated solitary confinement for four days and fingerprinted, photographed and interrogated.

Joe Tombling encountered some particular problems here:

Most of the other lads were still in tropical kit, which, given the temperature, caused a lot of suffering, although we were soon given an issue of army battledress. I was still wearing the Italian clothing I had picked up on Cos and my Luftwaffe interrogator opened the proceedings by telling me that I would have to prove I was British and to remember that, wearing the uniform I was, I could be shot, although he did not push that particular point any further. Instead, he reeled off all the names of the RAF units on Cos and asked which one I was in. It seemed he knew more than I did. I only knew about 74 Squadron and was not aware of others, although I had my suspicions that much of what they were telling me was supposition on their part anyway. Finally he dismissed me. After a few days I was moved to another compound and met up with the rest of the chaps.

Tom Fawcett had a similar experience:

I was grilled for three days but the only thing they wanted to fill in concerned the time we went up to Teheran in Persia. They knew very little about the Squadron's movements after that and wondered where we had got to.

Two days later the majority of 74's POWs were transferred by train to Stalag IVB at Muhlberg-am-Elbe midway between Leipzig and Dresden, in temperatures which were down to minus 10° Centigrade. A thick frost clung to all the trees and the land was covered in a hoary white rime. The only hot food available was dished out at an occasional food kitchen in some of the towns the POWs passed through. Finally they reached their destination and the interminable admission procedures began—more photographing, fingerprinting, delousing and a haircut, although no one was shaved bald. This done, the men were bundled into already overfull huts without being fed: those already in residence conjured up a hot drink and shared their meagre rations.

The compound for RAF personnel was initially isolated from the rest of the camp. Quarters were very spartan and cold. There was never enough fuel for cooking or heating, and this led to the formation of night raiding parties to steal extra supplies for the coal brickette stoves which were established in most huts—usually in a pit dug under a bottom bunk bed with a false floor covering it. The allocation of Red Cross parcels was initially one per man but this was later reduced. The situation deteriorated still further after the D-Day landings in June 1944, as did the German rations, although there were sometimes opportunities for the men to barter for additional food from other nationalities: many an RAF cap badge was swapped for a few slices of bread.

The chief entertainment in the camp was football—RAF v. Army; England v. Scotland, v. France, v. Holland; hut v. hut; Cockney v. Geordie. The game, with all the endless variations of teams, was played morning, noon and, in the summer, night. On top of that, everybody seemed to argue about it until the lights went out. As a result, many ultimately left the camps with an aversion to the national game! Others sought different means of recreation. Educational classes were started, satisfying those who wanted to occupy their minds productively. Mathematics, Engineering, Radio Communication (theory only!) and Psychology were amongst the subjects on offer. The Red Cross were instrumental in securing notebooks and textbooks.

All of 74's ground crew who spent the rest of their war at Muhlberg have their own memories. Some are humorous, others tragic—such as that concerning Ju 88 pilots who took to beating up the camp once it was known that there were RAF air crews in residence. It seems that the Germans were competing to see who could fly through at the lowest altitude, a game which stopped after one of the Junkers' tailwheels caught the top of the surrounding wire fence. The aircraft survived but a Canadian was killed as wire meshing crushed him. The German guards were rough with the prisoners to start with. There was one in particular who was promptly christened 'Blondie' by the inmates—the archetypal arrogant bully who was found in every prison camp. Jim Twitty enjoyed the baiting of Blondie:

> He was the one who took us for roll call. As the Germans always counted in fives we used to move up one or two places and mess him about. For doing that he used to take our bed boards. Then he started frantically looking for the wireless on which we secretly received news from the BBC. Having saved all the keys from sardine tins which we had received in Red Cross parcels, we strung them together and trailed them out of the window. It looked just like an aerial and Blondie had a triumphant look on his face as he burst into our hut. That look turned to one of fury when he found a note tied to the end of our keyring decoration which simply stated *'Wo ist der Luftwaffe?'* We lost more bed boards after that little escapade. Needless to say, we were never without bed boards for long—we had our own supply.

The guards changed as 1944 wore on and the able-bodied men were transferred to the Russian Front, to be replaced by kindlier old soldiers who had served in the First World War and who hated the Nazis and all they stood for.

Not all of 74's captured ground crew were transferred to Muhlberg. Tom Fawcett and Bernard Harker ended up at Heydakrug in East Prussia. Here they were put into 'K' compound to join a thousand air crew. They immediately became celebrities of sorts, for the pilots found it very difficult to understand how ground crewmen from a Spitfire squadron could get themselves captured at that stage of the war! Life was, in the early stages, bearable, with weekly Red Cross parcels and a steady supply of potatoes to supplement a typical camp diet. Cigarettes were in short supply, although the Canadians always used to have plenty—thousands in fact! As at Muhlberg, football was the main recreation, and a league system was devised, the top six teams taking their names from the English Football League. Players for these teams were taken from those who played for the lesser 'hut' league. Tom Fawcett:

> I was sitting quietly on my bunk one afternoon when a Canadian came in and asked whether I would like to play for Preston North End. Terms were negotiated and eventually I joined them for 500 cigarettes! Obviously my worth

improved after playing six games for Preston for I was then transferred to Aston Villa and my part of the transaction was 750 cigarettes!

*

74's captured ground crew spent the remainder of the war in POW camps and the men all tell similar stories of the hardship, the frustration and the anger of imprisonment as well as the ingenuity applied to making their existence as comfortable as possible when the weather was wickedly cold, when the rains fell incessantly, when they were forced on to working parties on farms or coal dumps, when they fell ill or when Red Cross parcels were promised but did not materialize. They tell of the news of the Allied and Russian advances which filtered through to them and which led them for many weeks to believe that their liberation was imminent. Liberation did finally come, and all made their way back to England by various means. Those times of shared experience have led to lifelong friendships and frequent reunions. Although none rejoined the Squadron after the war, all undoubtedly displayed the tenacious Tiger qualities that Squadron life had bred in them and which enabled them to survive their ordeal.

BACK TO THE OLD ROUTINE

During the Cos and Simi detachments there had been a few aircraft and pilots left at Nicosia. Squadron Leader Bradley of 127 Squadron had temporarily taken charge of 74's affairs and, indeed, had flown four sorties in the Tigers' Spitfires. As soon as he heard of Hayter's return he personally drove down to Limassol to pick him and Doc Ferris up. The rest of the crews were taken by truck to Peristerona, where they were now to be based. On 15 October Hayter and Lewis went to Cairo to report. Since the end of the Cos operation, signals had been flying back and forth, all highly complimentary, and Air Vice-Marshal Saul particularly asked for his congratulations to be passed on to all squadrons' members.

When 74 Squadron started to reassemble at Peristerona after leave, the rains came in an incessant deluge which swamped everything and everyone. Hasty preparations were made to move back to Idku, and two DC-3s flew the main party across on the 23rd. Most of the surviving Spitfires followed, with the exception of those retained to fly sweeps from Cyprus. In North Africa replacements for those aircraft lost on Cos arrived in the shape of Spitfire Mk IXs. By the month's end 74 were again flying convoy patrols and training from Idku. However, the death of Sergeant Gray, who crashed a Spitfire IX, was not an auspicious beginning to November. On the 7th Wooton and Butler were fired on whilst patrolling supposedly friendly ships off Alexandria. On the 13th Titch Harris suffered engine problems at 16,000ft. Coming down to land at Mariut, his engine caught fire. He did well to make a near-normal landing, although the undercarriage collapsed shortly after touch-down. Harris suffered slight burns but that did not keep him away from duty for very long. Flight Sergeant Wilson of the Cyprus detachment force-landed on the

Turkish coast whilst on one of the regular sweeps across Rhodes and Simi and was promptly interned. Prendergast completed November's tale of woe when he burst a tyre on landing at Idku and ended up off the runway and upside down. He was unhurt.

November had proved to be a restless time for the Tigers, with a large proportion of the ground and air crew being sent off on meanderings around the Sinai and Western Deserts which, it was rumoured, had all been devised to confuse the enemy. It certainly confused the Squadron! The Great Trek, as it became known, lasted three weeks, took them across many hundreds of dusty miles and ended with fifteen pilots at Dekheila, two at Cairo West, three at Idku, six in Cyprus and none anywhere near their original destination! Dekheila was a popular detachment. The pilots had initially been a little wary of it because the runway was a relatively small one (it was used by the Navy for practising carrier landings) and they initially found it tight getting in and out of the tarmacadamed runways. Much appreciated by 74 was the use of the station's Magister, not only for flying between Idku and Dekheila but also to give the ground crew some 'jollies' as a way of compensating for their recent fruitless treks around the deserts of North Africa. But the greatest attraction (as may be imagined) was the abundant supply of cheap beer, duty-free cigarettes and chocolate available in the Mess. Navy rules stipulated, however, that the maximum amount officers were allowed to spend was £5 per month; many Tigers had spent that in the first few days of their detachment and were thereafter peremptorily denied further supplies! There is an underlying current of pride amongst the Tigers who remember those days:

> We were a little bit too wild for the Navy. We weren't actually kicked out of Dekheila but they were certainly glad to see us go and probably viewed with some trepidation our occasional returns!

The Anglo-American Conference at Cairo resulted in the Squadron's going on to a higher alert status at the beginning of December, but once all the VIPs had departed this was relaxed. 74 were directly involved twice, the first time on 7 December when seven aircraft flew to El Daba ready to escort three DC-4s from Marsa Matruh to El Adem in concert with a squadron of P-47 Thunderbolts. The following day four Spitfires went to Marsa Matruh to escort a York. This part of the operation went smoothly, but things started to go wrong when Thompson was grounded at El Adem with hydraulic problems. Things went very wrong when Leeke and Parker collided in mid-air on the return. Leeke was killed but Parker baled out uninjured. Of the four who had left earlier that morning, only Rex Froud returned safely.

The Squadron moved back to Idku on 12 December. On the 14th it formed part of a flypast in honour of the Air Officer Commanding-in-Chief at Alexandria, Air Chief Marshal Sholto Douglas, and de Pass led a party of thirty airmen in a march-past at 219 Group. One of Bunny's jobs at this time was that of salvage—rescuing any piece of material which might be of use in another quarter, an extension of the 'waste not want not' philosophy. Bunny was very keen at his job, so much so that if something was found not to be bolted down, he would have 'it', whatever 'it' might be! Many an excursion was made to his private store to retrieve items he had spirited away!

No sooner was the Squadron back at Idku than the rains started again, with a repeat of the Peristerona experience—flooded tents and soaked belongings. By Christmas the Cyprus detachment had finished and consequently the Tigers found themselves totally reunited at long last—and in time to celebrate Christmas too. This was done in the traditional manner, with officers serving Christmas lunch to the airmen and, in the evening, going over to the airmen's canteen for a concert. A borrowed piano and violin, both very ably performed upon, set the seal on an enjoyable day. Boxing Day did not quite match it: a practice scramble was called! Then, in the final week leading up to the New Year, some welcome drogue-firing was possible, with reasonable results and no problems other than the drogue-towing Spitfire suffering damage when, once again, an undercarriage problem manifested itself. Such problems were becoming all too frequent, so much so that a directive was issued stating that once pilots had lowered their wheels they should rock their wings emphatically to ensure that the locking pins had not stuck.

Only on one occasion during the next three months was 74 Squadron to have sight of the enemy, and that was on 14 January 1944 when four Spitfires were scrambled. Froud and Maxwell tally-ho'd a Ju 88, attacked, saw no result and then lost it in cloud. Apart from this brief diversion, it was a case of back to the old routine of training and patrols. Wilson unexpectedly returned from his Turkish internment in the New Year and found a promotion to Warrant Officer awaiting him. At the end of January a distinguished visitor arrived when the Tigers' old 11 Group boss, Keith Park, now an Air Marshal and the Commander-in-Chief of RAF Middle East, flew himself in to see them. Park and Group Captain Max Aitken were to visit again on a later occasion. More heavy rains meant that 74 moved back to Dekheila, the majority of the ground crew included. Not that Dekheila was exempt from the problem: there was more than one instance of an aircraft having to be diverted to Mariut when deep puddles of water formed on the Navy's runway. The weather led directly to two accidents. Butler ran off the runway with another collapsed undercarriage, whilst Shirkie contrived to be even more spectacular. He ran off and overturned, but escaped apparently uninjured, although after a few days he began to complain of back problems and was hospitalized. Worrall and Griffin were sent on detachment to St-Jean to try and intercept a Ju 88 that had been making regular flights over the Eastern Mediterranean. News of their arrival must have been passed on, for the German did not appear while they were there. Otherwise formation practice, interceptions, more drogue firing, scrambles and naval co-operation exercises continued. Two weeks of affiliation with Baltimores of 263 Wing gave scope for more practice attacks.

Idku returned to operational status again. A flurry of activity on 11

March involved six aircraft being fitted with long-range ranks and setting off at dawn for Cyprus. The panic subsided as quickly as it had started and the aircraft returned, having done nothing, two days later. But at the end of the month things moved on with almost electrifying speed. On the 24th the Squadron was released from its readiness states, in preparation, it was thought, to do a job with other squadrons. All personnel were told to pack up and Hayter called everyone together, warned them against discussion of rumours and reminded them of the need for the closest security. They had still been told nothing officially, but nobody was fooled on 1 April when the Squadron received its sailing orders—they were going back home! After a hectic night of preparation, the road convoy set off and arrived the following day at Suez at the southern end of the Canal. The Squadron's Spitfire Vs had been flown to Helwan whilst the IXs remained at Idku with cockpit covers in place and armed guards posted, ready for the next squadron to move in. Last-minute marking of kit, changing of money and the like was attended to and the Squadron embarked on HMT *Devonshire* at Port Said on 7 April. The officers' quarters were found to be quite comfortable for a troopship but those of the NCOs and other ranks were, as usual, not so well appointed. Allan Griffin:

> In fact it was not a particularly happy voyage home for us. The ship was run entirely by the Army and we did not take very kindly to the way we were treated.

Leaving Port Said, the Tigers sailed in convoy along the North African coast, past Idku, El Daba and Dekheila and into Gibraltar. Here they left the protection of the escorts and sailed on alone through the Bay of Biscay. The long days were spent walking the decks, playing Housey Housey, holding concert parties. They were shadowed by a Focke-Wulf Condor for a considerable part of the voyage; and because of the proximity of the French coast they remained on alert. But nothing happened, and two weeks after leaving Egypt they anchored off New Brighton and on St George's Day sailed into Liverpool to the sound of a military band and an emotional welcome from the local people. Disembarkation followed and, according to the ORB, many of the Squadron 'touched the ground affectionately' as they reached the end of the gangway. By this time, and taking into account the voyage out, many of them had actually circumnavigated Africa by sea.

From the *Devonshire* the men were immediately put on to a train and sent off to North Weald in Essex. Such was the urgency, just one week's disembarkation leave was allocated instead of the usual two or three, and that was to only three-quarters of the Squadron. The remainder were immediately involved in taking delivery of brand new Mk IX Spitfires (flown in by some very attractive female ferry pilots), checking them over and harmonizing the cannon and machine guns. This latter task was done by pushing the aircraft to the back of an empty hangar, raising the tail on to a trestle to simulate the flying position and erecting the harmonization board outside the open doors at the opposite end. Tragically an airman was killed when the cannon were fired before the area had been cleared.

By 1 May all personnel were returning to their new home. The Spitfires were marked with a brand new identification code, '4D', and 74 learnt that it was to be part of the North Weald Wing with 33 and 127 Squadrons under Ray Harries. The Tigers also knew by now what the urgency was. They had returned to help prepare for the impending Second Front in Europe.

CHAPTER 6

Return to the Continent

WHEN THE MEN of 74 Squadron reassembled at North Weald they learnt that a new establishment had come into force: with the exception of several specialists (Medical Officer and Intelligence Officer included), administrative staff and ground crew were being assigned to No 6074 Servicing Echelon. Rex Froud was appointed Squadron Adjutant. Tony Blythin, as Operations Clerk, remained attached directly to the Squadron. Holding such a pivotal position, he was a constant factor wherever the Tigers went, working in the Ops Office, signing aircraft in and out, completing record cards and doing all the other administrative work squadron operations demanded. Otherwise the familiar fitters, riggers and armourers for the most part moved on and a new set of faces appeared to service and maintain the Tigers' aircraft. The family spirit which had been so conspicuous throughout the Middle East tour was diluted, and although there were some good men amongst the newcomers it took a while for them to settle down. There was little doubt that this was to be a difficult time for the Tigers, coming to terms with the new working arrangements, coping with a shortage of ancillary equipment (much of which had been left in the Middle East and was not immediately replaced) and preparing for forthcoming operations.

THE LYMPNE WING

Within a fortnight the Squadron was on the move to the all-grass airfield with its scattering of wooden huts and blast pens at Lympne. Although set in the beautiful Kent countryside, this was no compensation for the fact that its comparative isolation meant that it lacked the recreational facilities that North Weald had seemed to offer. The Mess at Lympne was in a large country house, complete with extensive and ornate gardens, owned by the Sassoon family. There was an attractive lounge and bar but generally the men found that they were too tired for carousing. Don Llewellyn recalls:

> Daylight readiness in June 1944 was from 4.10 a.m. until about 10.30 p.m. and so we were not getting to bed until 11.00 p.m. Just four and a half hours later the WAAF who used to wake us would creep into the room and then run out banging our feet as she went. I don't think she realized how tired we were and she often had to come back to repeat the procedure when we didn't wake up! Our aircraft were kept outside whatever the weather—there was nowhere else to put them—and when we walked out to them in the mornings to don parachutes and complete the cockpit checks they had already been run up by

the ground crew who may have worked all night to ensure there were twelve aircraft on the line.

On 19 May, shortly after the RAF had commenced an all-out assault on trains, railway and road bridges, radar installations, wireless and navigation stations, coastal batteries and airfields, the Lympne Wing flew the first of many sweeps. 74 was called into action during the afternoon when the pilots patrolled the Lille area of northern France. They sighted nothing. In the evening they repeated the exercise, this time over Creil, but once again did not encounter the enemy. In fact little was seen of the Luftwaffe in the days before D-Day—or indeed afterwards. Many hundreds of German aircraft had been destroyed in the first few weeks of the Allied assault and the net result was a minimum of enemy interference over the battlefields and so a lack of sightings of enemy Messerschmitts and Focke Wulfs.

Operations on the 20th led to the first blood for 74. After escorting Mitchells which successfully bombed the runway at Creil, Wing Leader Harries took seven Tigers on a sweep against road targets which left at least five lorries in flames beneath the poplar trees of a French road. On the 22nd there was more success when they destroyed five more lorries, two trailers, two railway engines and two wagons, a flak post and a German staff car. Added to this list were canal barges which were damaged together with, in the words of the Operations Record Book, 'various members of the Reich'. The day's success was tempered by the loss of Titch Harris, who hit a tree while strafing German traffic along a Belgian road just south of Brussels, although he escaped with just cuts and bruises. Allan Griffin (who by this time had been commissioned) recalls Harris's later return to the Squadron:

There was a story circulating that Titch had been captured after taking refuge in a supposed safe house in Brussels and being looked after by a most attractive young lady. Titch was known for his prowess with members of the fair sex and it would seem that he was in his element! But the lady in question was not averse to entertaining members of the local German garrison as well and when one appeared Titch would go and sit in the wardrobe and only come out after the German had departed!

But the lady's allegiances were obviously suspect, as Titch woke up one morning to find the Gestapo on both sides of his bed:

I thought I was having a bad dream. They tried to give me the third degree while I was in bed but they got nothing out of me so they hauled me out and took me to Brussels where I was thrown into a prison cell.

Titch was later able to escape and make his way back to England with the help of the local Resistance.

The Tigers undertook their first bombing sortie alongside other aircraft of the Lympne Wing on 24 May. Their target was the Douai marshalling yard and a 500lb bomb with instantaneous fusing and mounted on a rack beneath the fuselage was carried by each Spitfire. Some members of the

Squadron were involved in shipping recces on the same day. These were not amongst the pilots' favourite sorties, involving as they did a cross-Channel flight at wave-top height to a predetermined sector off the European coast, along which the aircraft flew, reporting back dispositions of shipping. These sorties were not offensive in nature, their sole object being to update Intelligence. Their unpopularity was due to the heavy flak barrage that was thrown up as soon as the enemy realized that Spitfires were in the vicinity.

On 25 May twelve aircraft attacked the railway sheds at Formerie, again with 500-pounders. Griffin's log book shows that this was a 1hr 35min mission and that the Squadron effected 'very good bombing'. Don Llewellyn clearly remembers these early sorties:

> Spud told us that we were to approach the target roughly in line astern at 8,000ft—dive, aim and press the bomb release tit at 4,000ft. He described two possible methods of aiming. The first involved pointing the aircraft at the target, pulling up slowly whilst counting off so many seconds and then releasing the bombs. The second required the pointing of the gunsight bead at the target, moving it up a short way, holding steady and then pressing the tit. Most of us adopted the second option. From 8,000 to 4,000ft I would grip my nose with my left hand and blow to clear my ears, letting go briefly to press the tit then blowing down again to about 1,500ft when we levelled off. At first we dived at an angle of 45 to 50 degrees and this was not at all effective. When we were later operating from France, Spud and Tony Reeves allowed me, when I was junior Flight Commander, to lead a dive-bombing attack. I had decided that a steeper angle would reduce the margin of error—and tried it. It seemed to work. But I think we had all come to that conclusion at the same time and the steeper angle became normal practice.

The weapons fit on the Spitfire largely depended on the length of sortie. If additional fuel were required, this would be carried under the fuselage in a ninety-gallon tank, with a 250lb bomb under each wing.

Bombing, strafing and escort duties continued, although not all sweeps resulted in positive results: several sorties yielded no targets. On the 27th Bunny de Pass had his aircraft holed while flying a shipping reconnaissance with Keith Butler near Calais (which had some of the most accurate anti-aircraft defences in the region); the following day the Tigers flew with 33 Squadron on escort duties with Marauders which successfully bombed bridges at Nantes and Gassicourt. 74 was in action again later the same day on an offensive sweep around the Beauvais area which left a lorry and a staff car in flames, several Germans dead and five railway wagons damaged in a siding. Two 'noball' targets were hit on the 29th, 'noball' being a codename for a wide-ranging series of targets including rocket and flying bomb sites and storage and manufacturing centres. Other coded operations included 'cab ranks'. These were flown regularly once the Squadron had moved to France and involved pairs of aircraft supporting Army operations. A typical sortie would involve call-up by a ground observer to assist in the removal of enemy firepower. Allan Griffin:

I remember an instance where a platoon was pinned down by a Tiger tank. Whenever anyone moved the tank would throw a shell in his direction. So the observer gave us a map reference. We went to investigate and found the tank backed into a semi-detached house, one wall of which had been blasted away. All that was protruding was the tank's gun barrel. It was perfectly camouflaged and we only saw it by virtue of the fact that my No 2 and I flew down the adjacent road at zero feet to the map co-ordinates we had been given, which also enabled us to deliver an accurate attack on the house and to silence the tank.

Other patrols included 'rhubarbs', armed reconnaissances over enemy territory (the same as those in which 74 had been involved immediately after the Battle of Britain), and 'anti-diver' patrols, flown against incoming V-1s once they had been launched against the United Kingdom. The bomber-escort duties which the Tigers flew were codenamed 'ramrod'.

In the days immediately prior to D-Day the Tigers patrolled ships in the Thames Estuary that formed part of the invasion fleet. Llewellyn, newly promoted to Flight Lieutenant and in command of B Flight, flew on one of these on 4 June, after which the Wing pilots were all assembled and briefed that the invasion was on. On 5 and 6 June the Tigers were ordered to patrol specific numbers of vessels with specific naval escorts at particular points. But this task proved to be impractical as below them all they could see was an endless line of ships moving westwards across the Channel. All 74 could do was patrol in the designated area, keeping a good, if nervous, watch for the Luftwaffe—which once again did not appear.

D-DAY

D-Day and Operation 'Overlord' were relatively uneventful for the Tigers, flying as they did a series of unopposed sorties in concert with many other squadrons over the 'Utah', 'Omaha', 'Gold', 'Juno' and 'Sword' beaches. Overnight the riggers had painted the aircraft with their glossy black and white invasion stripes as a means of identification for Allied troops. Patrols over the beach-heads continued for several days, some of them lasting for such a length of time that they led to at least one Tiger (Jackson) force-landing due to lack of fuel. He flew back to England after coming down on an emergency strip and being refuelled by the Commandos. Paddy Dalzell, meanwhile, was hit by flak while on a sortie to provide cover for friendly troops over Caen. He managed to glide back over the Allied lines and crash-landed between posts set up to stop glider landings. The Spitfire was written off, and after a few days Dalzell was taken to the beach-head for a return to England by American LST.

Immediately after 'Overlord' the tasks allotted the Squadron were many and various. On one occasion they escorted Stirlings dropping supplies to the troops on the beaches and the hinterland; on another they were involved with two air–sea rescue Warwicks on a search for a downed aircraft. On the 11th, whilst patrolling the eastern beaches, the

Tigers were distant spectators to a fierce tank battle to the south-east of Caen. Enough progress had now been made by the ground forces to allow 74 to carry out a sweep over Evreux, land at ALG (Allied Landing Ground) B3 to refuel, conduct another sweep over the same area and return to Lympne on the 12th. This landing at B3 was the first in France for the Tigers since the days prior to Dunkirk in 1940. B3, as was the case with most landing strips in the British sector, was nothing more than a hastily prepared field which was very dry beneath the Spitfires' wheels, resulting in great clouds of dust being thrown skywards as the aircraft taxied. As they landed and pulled their canopies back, they found Allied soldiers rushing towards them and shouting at the pilots to keep their heads down as there was a sniper in the church tower which overlooked the strip. Nobody was hit and the sniper was soon silenced.

The Tigers moved to Tangmere for a few days as the tempo of sorties was increased. On 15 June they escorted Lancasters bombing the docks at Boulogne, whilst on the following day the whole Squadron was airborne to cover the cruiser carrying King George VI back from the French coast, where he had been visiting the beaches. Hayter went off solo on an 'anti-diver' patrol as the Germans stepped up their offensive using their fearsome V-weapons. Some members of the Squadron had seen their first example a couple of days previously as it had crossed over Lympne on its way to London, although the airfield defences were ordered not to fire at it in case they scored a hit and the V-1 fell on dispersal. Lancasters were escorted again on three successive days from the 20th to the 22nd, this time to bomb V-1 sites in the Pas de Calais. Arras, Caen and Rouen witnessed some particularly vicious fighting as the Allies progressed, and the Tigers acted as escorts to bombers attacking troop concentrations here too. Towards the end of the month they participated in a further series of sweeps against 'noball' targets and on 'anti-diver' patrols. A few V-1s were seen in the air heading for the English coast, but none was within range.

At the beginning of July the Tigers became a component of the 2nd Tactical Air Force (TAF) and moved down to Tangmere on a permanent basis (or so they thought), to join 134 Wing as part of 84 Group. They were delighted to find that their old boss Sailor Malan, now a Group Captain, was the CO and that the Wing Commander Flying was Al Deere. Allan Griffin has good cause to remember Tangmere:

I, together with Johnny Wooton, had been given the afternoon off and we decided to go into Pagham. Dressed in our best blue, we broke all the rules by walking across the airfield, a short cut to the main gate and exit from the camp. This was safe provided we kept away from the main runway. As luck would have it the three squadrons of the Wing were getting airborne at the time. The procedure was for the Wing Commander to take off first and execute a slow turn to port at the end of the runway, with each succeeding aircraft taking a slightly sharper turn. When the last of the aircraft got airborne he would be pulling a very tight turn so that he could take up position with the rest of the formation. Johnny and I were watching all this as we walked, wishing them all luck in what they were about to do but secretly pleased that we were not involved when we suddenly became aware of a high-pitched whistle which had us temporarily foxed until there was an almighty bang right beside us and we were drenched from head to foot in high-octane petrol. The long-range tank had become detached from the last Spitfire as it pulled tightly above us. That was the end of our jolly and we found ourselves instead explaining what we were doing in the middle of the aerodrome.

In the short time the Tigers were at Tangmere, they were visited by the King and Queen:

We were told to assemble outside but, once there, nobody knew what to do. None of us had drilled for months and so we shuffled inexpertly into three ranks. Sailor came across as we were attempting this with an 'Oh my God! Don't stand like that. He hates it when he sees people on parade!' He promptly bent down, arms stretched, as if about to form a rugby scrum and herded us into a less formal mess!

The visit was a great success. Within a fortnight 74 was on the move again, this time to Selsey, with its single, water-to-water runway, to become a component of 145 'Cross of Lorraine' Wing alongside three Free French squadrons, Nos 329, 340 and 341. The Tigers were to strike up a very good relationship with the French, who looked on 74's early attempts at speaking their language with some amusement! As time went by, the Squadron's expertise in this improved and the French in turn lowered their reserve and helped with French lessons. English, and only English, was used over the radio during operations.

For the last week of July and the first of August the Tigers were withdrawn from the offensive and sent to RAF Southend for a fortnight's Armament Practice Camp, the syllabus of which embraced the arts of air fighting, air-to-ground work and close escort duty. Everyone welcomed the chance to hone their skills in an environment other than the front line and by the end of the course all had without exception reached a high standard of efficiency. The Tigers were quick learners and were soon priding themselves on the accuracy of their bombing in pairs. The pilots and eighteen Spitfires returned to join 145 Wing (which had meanwhile moved back from Selsey to Tangmere) on 7 August. They had barely resettled when six aircraft were detailed to Northolt for special duty, the escorting of Prime Minister Winston Churchill in a DC-3 to ALG A9 in France for a conference and his subsequent return to Northolt. New Zealander Johnnie Johnston remembers the occasion:

Some of the boys' remarks on landing after $2\frac{1}{2}$ to 3 hours airborne escorting Winston had to be heard to be believed. Our bladders were not meant to be so distended! His old Dakota, flying at 120mph, was a bit hard to keep station on and our IXs were oiling up badly. Every now and then we had to pull out, increase speed and fly a broad circle to clear the system, emitting clouds of black smoke in the process. Then when he arrived at his destination he would insist on an inspection, still puffing away on his cigar, and we were forced to hold off until he had cleared the airfield!

Another six of the Squadron's aircraft escorted a Marauder with General Eisenhower, Supreme Commander of the Allied Forces, to the same conference. Indeed, escorting VIPs (in particular Churchill) became an almost regular part of 74's duties up to the end of the war.

In the days after APC, the continuing escort of heavy bombers remained the main thrust of the Tigers' operations. There was sometimes the opportunity to break away after the escort had been completed and seek targets of opportunity, as happened on the occasion they swept Amiens with some success. Four trucks were strafed, but Tookey Tooke was hit by flak and force-landed with his engine on fire. He was seen to get out of the burning aircraft—apparently unhurt—and indeed rejoined the Squadron a month later. The technique to strafing was relatively straightforward—a shallow dive, aim and fire. Don Llewellyn:

> By 1944 there were complicated ways of harmonizing the wing guns—two 20mm cannon and two 0.5 machine guns—and the most effective range was 250 yards. Even in a shallow dive (30 degrees or so—it couldn't be too shallow otherwise you would not see the target) a Spitfire would quickly pick up speed to well over 300mph. It was rule-of-thumb judgement as to when one fired, but bearing in mind we were firing directly at a usually stationary target on the ground, you had about two seconds in which to make up your mind to fire, then fire and pull up. It was actually very close-range work, almost point-blank, and was most effective. I never liked it when we encountered return fire, but then I had been shot down on my first day's strafing with my previous squadron at Alamein!

The advance proceeded, with Allied ground forces continuing to fight their way out of Normandy and towards the Seine. The Tigers patrolled Argentan on 15 August while 670 Lancasters bombed targets in the Falaise gap where the Germans were virtually surrounded, creating an incredible spectacle as smoke and dust rose to 6,000ft and causing extensive fires over a huge area. Another offensive was launched in the late afternoon as Marauders bombed a bridge at Fontoise. Before taking off, Llewellyn had asked Tony Reeves, who was leading, whether he could take a Section to look for opportunist targets on the ground on the way back. Reeves said no initially, but, escort completed, he called Llew on the radio and said quietly 'Okay! Off you go!' Blue Section went down and found a convoy of eight trucks moving slowly through a sparsely wooded area:

> Seven of them were carrying gasoline and exploded at a touch. I'm damned if we could get the eighth to burn, although we damaged it.

They returned to English shores, landing at Manston to refuel, and found a quite remarkable gathering of aircraft doing the same thing:

> We were told that seventeen squadrons landed there that evening and night. What a wizard show!

That evening the RAF bombed an enemy night fighter airfield at St-Trono:

We met a seemingly endless procession of heavy bombers out to sea, using their night-time stream technique in daylight. All we could do was attach ourselves to the stream when we got to the rendezvous point and when it broke up into groups near the French coast we followed the nearest to us. Their bombing completely flattened St-Trono.

Afterwards the Tigers strafed in the Ghent–Lens–Ypres triangle and the next day they swept Cambrai and its environs, encountering intense and accurate light flak in the process. A staff car, four trucks and three barges were destroyed or damaged, but Burman was hit by German machine-gun fire and was seen by his colleagues to bale out after climbing to a safe height to do so. Nothing more was heard of him until, some weeks later, it was learnt that he had landed in the village of Rouex. He was wounded and had surrendered to the Germans, but such was their state of mind in the face of the continuous Allied onslaught that they did not trouble with any of the conventions of war and unceremoniously shot him on the spot.

SOMMERVIEUX

The escorting of Lancasters to the Pas de Calais on 18 August marked the end of the sometimes tiresome bomber escort duties for the Tigers, and the next day they returned once more to French soil with eighteen aircraft, landing at ALG B8 Sommervieux, just outside Bayeux in Normandy. Ground crews and administration staff followed by sea, sailing from Southampton on an uncomfortable Channel crossing in a landing craft and docking at a Mulberry harbour in Arromanches and then transferring by lorry to B8. In the ensuing months the Tigers would find themselves back at some of the same airfields they had used twenty-six years previously. The Tigers were now, as then, a squadron of several nationalities, led by a New Zealander. They were to spend the rest of the war in Europe—France, Belgium, Holland and Germany—and would operate from a variety of airfields, some makeshift, some well established, and from a variety of surfaces—asphalt, PST (Pierced Steel Tracking) or grass. Ground crews would follow them in convoy, the advance party having already gone on ahead so as to be *in situ* when the aircraft landed. Accommodation would range from tented encampments to requisitioned boarding schools. They would find the local people helpful, friendly and generous. Food was always either scarce or mundane (or both), and opportunities to supplement the diet were always eagerly grasped, such as at Schijndel in early 1945 when the Wing catering staff were offered sheep to augment the food stocks. The sheep were indeed plain to see, tethered near to some of the Squadron's allocated huts, and the purchase was quickly completed. Only afterwards was a problem revealed: they were grazing in an area sown with German mines!

The Squadron would always help the local people whenever it could by giving them items of clothing and shoes, which were always very gratefully received. There was rarely much opportunity for recreational pursuits, the routine being one of flying day in, day out, with time for just a few beers in the evenings and very occasionally a short spell of home leave. Soon after arriving in France, Spud Hayter acquired an American Chevrolet—nobody was quite sure whence it came—which followed the Squadron around on its European travels and was used by 74's officers. It became a familiar sight on the local roads wherever they went. Also, not long after arriving at Sommervieux all pilots were docked £3 by the Mess. The 'contribution' was given to the Wing's French Roman Catholic padre, who set off to see what he could do with it on the black market. Amongst his purchases was a remarkable quantity of champagne: for a few days there was not much else to drink and an attempt was made to swap a few bottles! One of the 2nd TAF's Austers was requisitioned, loaded with three cases of the champagne and despatched across the Channel to Tangmere. A few days later the Auster returned with a case of gin and a case of scotch in exchange!

During the Squadron's first sortie from Sommervieux, a late afternoon armed reconnaissance in the Bernay area, twelve pilots shared in the destruction of eight trucks and an armoured car, with a tank and seven other vehicles damaged. This really was an excellent start to operations from French soil and nobody could now doubt that the war was being won. Ground crews worked long and hard hours, often all night, with little recognition other than their own satisfaction at a job well done. Hayter was extremely conscious of the need to keep their morale up and helped this along by insisting on slick flying within sight of the airfield, smooth take-offs and closing up quickly into tight formation before opening up into battle formation—all of which the tradesmen watched with a feeling of considerable pride. The same applied to their return from a sortie in close formation, whereupon they would break and land rapidly within three minutes—an exercise which took careful timing, with the Section leaders completing sliding turns on the approach. The idea was that the ground crews would be able to recognize them by the way they flew. It was the mark of a first class squadron. Don Llewellyn expands on this:

> An indication of good morale in both air and ground crew is when there are very few occasions when less than twelve aircraft take off and even fewer occasions when pilots return early from a sortie with minor problems. It took a lot of hard work and organization to keep twelve out of seventeen Spitfires serviceable, at all times, in all weathers and in often atrocious conditions.

If the German Army were forced to keep moving during the day by the Allied advance, the Squadron's tally was certain to increase considerably. On the 22nd the pilots again participated in a sweep in the Bernay area and two trucks were destroyed by Trevor Bates. Three days later they launched thirty-five sorties, including twelve aircraft which were involved in an armed reconnaissance around Rouen. Sparks Parker was hit by flak and tried to force-land west of Buchy. Unfortunately his aircraft hit some trees, the wings were torn off and the fuselage rolled

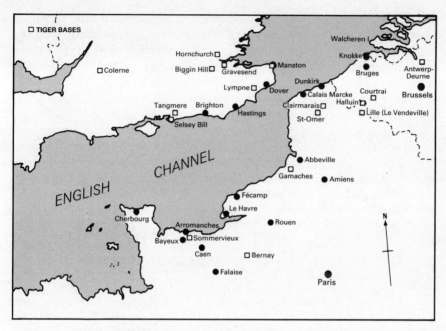

TIGER BASES

FRANCE, BELGIUM AND SOUTHERN ENGLAND, 1918 AND 1944—1945

several times. Parker was killed. Of the enemy traffic attacked, two trucks were destroyed with one probable.

There is a contentious entry in the ORB for this day:

> Two westbound ambulances were also attacked. One destroyed and one damaged.

Attempts to ascertain that the Squadron was actually authorized to attack such targets has met with vehement denial—unless the ambulances were a recognized subterfuge on the part of the enemy and the vehicles had been identified as something other than they seemed. The Tigers came across many such instances on a larger scale. On one occasion they were briefed for a sortie and it was stressed that great accuracy would be required and that they must press home their attack whatever it was they seemed to see in their sights at the co-ordinates given. When they arrived overhead they saw that the target was smothered in Red Cross flags but, mindful of the briefing, they pressed on and destroyed the ammunition dump which the subterfuge was hiding. The Germans were also masters of the decoy, large derelict sites often being surrounded by a lethal ring of AA emplacements on which many an Allied bomb was wasted.

The impetus was continued on the 26th. The almost mandatory twelve aircraft again performed an armed reconnaissance north of Rouen. This was an early-morning show, and four trucks and a staff car were destroyed, two trucks and a pair of tanks being damaged. In the afternoon the sweep moved towards Paris, encountering heavy flak as the aircraft neared the capital. The Tigers destroyed a truck and damaged several others in return for one aircraft being slightly damaged. Jackson was shot down but escaped injury as he crash-landed. Climbing from the wrecked Spitfire, he ran for cover, pulled a sweater over his RAF tunic, pulled his trouser bottoms out over his flying boots, found a farm and was hidden by four brave French women who were prepared to accept the ever-present possibility of being found out by the retreating Germans. Jackson was subsequently captured and taken to Brussels:

> One morning, and without warning, I was taken from my cell and bundled on to a train. The Germans were in a confused and chaotic state. It was an absolute shambles. Monty had really caught them on the hop. They heard that the British were very close, so they grabbed bicycles and horses and carts and competed in a hectic scramble to get out. The attitude of the guards in the train changed very quickly in the final few hours. They offered us cigarettes and sweets. At the very end I had the impression that they were frightened of us, we who were supposed to be their prisoners. The officers were dashing around giving orders one minute and contradicting them the next, squabbling amongst themselves and trying to decide who should be taken to Germany and who should be left behind.

Jackson was one of forty British and American airmen who escaped from this, the last German train to pull out of Brussels as Allied tanks and infantry were moving into the suburbs. He was rescued by the advancing Canadians and rejoined the Tigers on 3 September.

During a further early-morning reconnaissance of Rouen on 27 August (the city would fall a few days later), Jock Malcolm was shot down as the Squadron encountered a barrage of flak. He survived the ensuing crash although badly injured and was only found, barely alive, when advancing Canadians came across his wrecked Spitfire. He was sent back to England for hospitalization, confined to a wheelchair. Then, briefly, there was a change of emphasis when Spitfires took off having been briefed to bomb a concentration of forty or so barges ten miles north-west of Le Havre. Thick haze over the target prevented a good search and no barges were found at the co-ordinates they had been given, so Reeves elected to drop the bombs on flak positions instead. Don Llewellyn remembers the operation vividly:

> Tony Reeves was leading and I had the last section of four. The 88mm was on the go as we approached and for the first couple of thousand feet of the dive. Then the 'pale' tracer (40mm) took over, followed by the myriad white puffs of the 20mm cannon. Sensibly Tony did not level out and pull up but kept on in a shallow dive out to sea, levelling off very low down. This was the first and only time I recall seeing all three kinds of flak at one time.

Flak was a constant source of worry:

> It was incredible. The heavy stuff burst up to 20,000ft with the rest at 10 or 12,000ft, although a lot of it had proximity fusing which in itself caused problems. It was also rumoured at the time that the Germans had special machines for throwing up empty shell cases at us! It is certainly true to say that not many pilots who were caught in a flak trap survived to tell the tale. We certainly didn't fly straight and level for very long—those that did usually paid

the price—for few gunlayers could keep up with a weaving Spitfire. When there were twelve of us in echelon starboard, going down to bomb from 8,000ft with flak bursting all around, there was not much you could do other than turn over and go down as near vertically as possible, release your bombs and then pull out and come up just hoping and praying you were going fast enough for them to miss you. Then, having bombed, we would re-form and come home all together. If anybody had been hit or were suffering engine problems, we would try and return in pairs: if we got separated it would be a matter of getting down low and coming home as fast as possible on the deck, hoping that nothing would catch us!

THE ALLIED ADVANCE

On 1 September the Squadron moved forward to ALG B29 at Bernay. Then came a new problem. Owing to the rate at which the Allied armies were advancing, there were difficulties organizing operations as there were hardly any targets in the vicinity for bombing. It did not seem worthwhile sending off the Squadron to the rapidly moving front line for a five- or ten-minute patrol. A further move forwards would have solved the problem, but the lack of serviceable airfields precluded this from happening immediately—although when they were given the go-ahead the Tigers found themselves occupying three bases in two weeks. In the meantime a few new tasks were allotted to the Squadron, leaflet-dropping amongst them. On the 6th, eight Spitfires paper-raided Le Havre after being briefed by the Psychological Warfare Officer at SHAEF.

How well informed was the Squadron about the progress of the Allied advance? The men could see for themselves that considerable progress was being made, but official communication regarding the current position was non-existent. Allan Griffin:

Each of us fought our own war and we all knew it was a life or death situation. The only means we had of seeing how things were progressing was by the fact that every morning the bomb line was revised on the map kept by the Intelligence Officer. The limit of our forward troops was marked in crayon and we knew that we were not to attack anything our side of that line: if you got close to it you had to be very sure that whatever you were going at was theirs and not ours! The situation could be quite fluid and fast moving.

Don Llewellyn also remembers the bomb line on the Ops Room maps:

Actually we did not really need the map to know the disposition of the troops on the ground. On our side there was incessant bustling activity, on theirs virtually no movement at all. It was often very hard to find a mobile target. During the long daylight hours of summer the enemy had to be stopped from moving supplies to his front line or moving reserves. Our philosophy was one of staying over the enemy territory as long as possible and constantly harrying them on the deck. Maybe it was not as glamorous as shooting down enemy aircraft—but it was sure as hell effective!

Fighter sweeps were prepared for individual squadrons. Allan Griffin again:

There was little co-ordination between us and the other units in the Wing or indeed other Wings. When the Form D came in in the morning detailing attack requirements, each outfit was given its own task. A sweep was usually organized, with the Boss running Red Section in the middle, with his No 2 on his starboard wing and Nos 3 and 4 on the port, each aircraft about a mile apart. B Flight, flying in a similar configuration, would fly to the port of Red Section with A Flight to starboard. All twelve aircraft would be flying in an extended line abreast. Any opportunity targets would be dealt with by individual sections going down to attack, then coming back up to rejoin the formation. All instructions would come from the Boss or whoever was leading.

By the beginning of September the Allied advance was moving towards Holland to the north and to Luxembourg and the Franco-German border to the east. Brussels was totally in Allied hands by 3 September and Antwerp by the 4th. The Tigers mounted fighter sweeps into Holland in support of the offensive there, moving up to ALG B37 at Gamaches to the south-west of Abbeville on 10 September. Their first operation from the new airfield was an armed recce by twelve aircraft over the Dutch islands and Dutch western mainland. Further sorties were flown over south-west Holland on the 12th, following which the Tigers bade farewell to Gamaches and moved to Le Vendeville—'a genuine airfield', as the ORB delightedly states; it had, after all, been Lille's airport during peacetime. They stayed at Le Vendeville for three days, time enough to fly in support of the Army against targets in the Dunkirk area, where they were somewhat surprised to find that German flak positions were still functioning. A similar operation the following day incorporated the bombing and strafing of a gun position to the south-east of Boulogne. The target was a small one and looked like earthworks on top of a hill. The Tigers had been briefed to bomb no earlier and no later than during a specific five-minute period and the first aircraft went into the dive at precisely the start of that period; three minutes later the last aircraft pulled out of its attack. With two minutes remaining of the briefed period, Red Section went back again and strafed, doing further damage. Eight direct hits and four near-misses were scored altogether—ample evidence of their skills. The Intelligence Officer was often sceptical of the Tigers' claims—as was Hayter, too, if he had not been taking part himself. On this occasion Tony Reeves put in the claim and this was backed up by a message from the Army congratulating 74 on some fine work!

Don Llewellyn describes the format of a typical ground-attack mission:

We would be given a specific time at which to start engines and then three minutes later commence take off. Once airborne we would set course on the pre-briefed heading. We had excellent maps and would have been able to find most targets without the photographs our own Wing Ops provided for formation leaders. Later in the campaign the Army would attempt to indicate targets with red smoke shells, but these tended to be less accurate than we were at map reading. Like most pilots I got into the habit of carrying the maps in my flying boot at all times, even on the ground, and wrote briefing details in ink on my wrist—which was not as likely to get mislaid as a slip of paper!

On 16 September thirty-six Army support sorties were flown to Fort Perle north of Antwerp. Reports were received that German troops were evacuating across the River Scheldt and consequently the Squadron was briefed to attack barges, beached and afloat, on the northern tip of the mainland west of Jerneuken. The Tigers roared in, but owing to mist and approaching darkness it was impossible to give the exact position of bomb hits to the Intelligence Officer when they returned. The Squadron had some very effective IOs attached to it during the course of the war, each skilled in the art of extracting coherent information whilst debriefing pilots who were still often on an excitable 'high' after returning from a mission.

September 17 was the day on which Montgomery mounted a big thrust to the Rhine at Arnhem. 74 moved to the single strip at Courtrai (ALG 55) in Belgium, whose most recent incumbents had been Me 109s. The quarters here were extremely cramped, the billets being wooden huts and the Tigers being allocated just a few large rooms into which everyone —Hayter included—was crowded. As soon as they had settled they were in the air on more Army support sorties. There were still stubborn pockets of resistance on the Belgian coast to the east and north of Bruges which the Squadron would be instrumental in helping to clear over the ensuing six weeks while the main Allied thrust to the west of Belgium was progressing further towards the Rhine. 74's first targets from Courtrai were an active gun site at Cape Gris Nez and another at Calais, and while attacking these Frank Hardman's aircraft was hit by flak, although he returned safely. Four machine-gun placements were bombed in a village east of Antwerp on the 22nd and eleven hits were counted on the target. In the evening of the same day twelve aircraft took off to bomb a garrison at Flushing, and after scoring two direct hits and five near-misses the Tigers went down and strafed, reducing many buildings to smoking ruins and killing a number of the enemy into the bargain. More Army support demands streamed in. Then, as the situation of the British First Airborne Division at Arnhem became critical, fighter sweeps were changed into continuous standing patrols. Over the next few days the Tigers carried out a series of such patrols, all of which passed without incident while the battle raged beneath them. On one such sortie Jackson, only recently returned from his brief capture by the Germans, suffered an engine failure just after take-off. He tried to get back to Courtrai but undershot and hit the top of the local church steeple, crashing on the Photographic Section's lorry and tent. He was severely burnt and his Spitfire burst into flames on hitting the ground. He died in hospital a few hours later.

Between October and December, when Hitler launched his Ardennes offensive, the Squadron maintained relentless pressure on the enemy's positions, probing the rear of their lines towards the German border, supporting the Army and providing escorts for bombers. Returning to Courtrai after a sortie, the aircraft would be bombed up immediately and the Tigers would take to the air again. A typical day was 10 October, when they hit Schoondyke village and crossroads, where the enemy had dug in. Pairs of aircraft were sent in at ten-minute intervals to keep the Germans' heads down and disrupt any thought of retreat. Bombs were dropped from low level, each with an eleven-second delay to allow the Spitfires to clear the area before they exploded. The following morning the Squadron continued to harass the German troops: they succeeded in blocking the road from Costburg to Schoondyke as well, destroying more houses within the village itself. Moving transport to the north of Schoondyke was also attacked, and two trucks were destroyed and four damaged. The same operation was repeated at midday with six bombs hitting the village, one the road and one a slit trench to the north-west. Another accurate delivery blew up a farm. Bombs expended, the Tigers then moved away to look for opportunity targets in the surrounding area and strafe horse-drawn traffic requisitioned by the Germans.

The Tigers were back at Schoondyke on the 12th. On the way, Keith Butler saw an enemy vehicle and went down for a kill but as he was on the point of pressing the button the vehicle slipped behind a convenient haystack. Butler pressed home his attack and the haystack erupted in flames; it was probably concealing a fuel dump. On the same day, the Squadron were briefed to bomb a large gun on a farm at Borsellen in Holland. Initially failing to find any sign of it, the Tigers then went on to prove themselves good spotters by identifying their target between the farm and a little wood nearby. The farmhouse was set on fire and the gun was hit; the latter's ammunition exploded and a few hits in the woods also caused explosions, presumably also where ammunition was stored.

Dennis Usher's colleagues were delighted to hear of the award of a DFC to add to his DFM, for 'zealous leadership and a high percentage of successful actions against heavily fortified enemy positions'. At the same time he was promoted to Flight Lieutenant and appointed A Flight Commander in place of Tony Reeves, who was posted out. At this juncture the Senior Flight Commander (now Llewellyn) was leading about 50 per cent of Squadron sorties: the other 50 per cent were shared by Hayter, the Junior Flight Commander (Usher) and occasionally the Wing Commander Flying (Bill Crawford-Compton). And so the process continued. Johnnie Johnston was hit by light flak but returned safely to base on 14 October. On the 15th twelve aircraft led by Hayter took off to bomb a train moving south of Meteren. It was not found, but an alternative at Breda was attacked instead. On the following day the Tigers got themselves airborne just fifteen minutes after an order was received to bomb a stationary train south of Dodrecht. On the 17th the Squadron was back, successfully hitting gun positions north of Schoondyke. German troops were also attacked in a series of operations codenamed 'Winkle', which involved the concentrated bombing and strafing of roads, hedges and trenches and gun emplacements in the area—a strategy which was designed to winkle out the Hun from his holes and enable the Allied troops to advance.

Flying during the latter half of October was hampered by days of low cloud and rain, and it was not until the end of the month that the Tigers were back in continuous action again when Hayter and then Llewellyn led the Squadron to guns firing from Walcheren Island and silenced them. Guns were again the target the following day. The artillery on Walcheren commanded the passage up the Scheldt Estuary to Antwerp and was thus blocking the use of the port. Clearing this pocket of German resistance was taking a long time. Its existence had prevented Montgomery's use of Antwerp at the time of his push to Arnhem over a month previously, and the advance was not completed until early November, after a concerted effort by amphibious and air forces, including 74, during which the RAF's heavy bombers breached dykes which caused flooding to a large part of the island. Concurrently with the operations against Walcheren, the Tigers had been ordered into another area of resistance. Knokke and its neighbouring ports on the Belgian coast to the south of Walcheren had proved to be as difficult to clear. Llewellyn led twelve aircraft there on the

THE NETHERLANDS, 1944—1945

30th, strafing German positions and trenches alongside dykes and setting houses on fire.

November began with sorties against enemy positions alongside a canal to the north of Breda, a concentration of enemy troops in the village of Noordhoek and anti-tank gun emplacements south-east of Willemstadt. Infantry positions around Bovensiuis and twenty-five machine guns in emplacements along a road east of Klundert were attacked on subsequent sorties. Laurie Turner was hit by return fire and crash-landed on the Allied side. He was uninjured and, having hitched a lift from a passing Army vehicle, was soon back at Courtrai, shaken but otherwise uninjured. Fireworks were most certainly provided by the Squadron on 5 November, when ten aircraft, led by Usher, were despatched to bomb and strafe a section of the road seven miles north-west of Breda. White smoke laid by Army spotters was supposed to indicate the boundary line for strafing, but, as the aircraft approached, the pilots could see that it was well to the north of the position that had been briefed. Rather than risk any possibility of strafing the wrong target, or at worst their own men, Usher chose instead to divert to an alternative target at Klundert. Ten days of rain and fog then kept the Tigers firmly at bay until the 18th, when Hayter led his men on an Army close-support operation to Cuijk, close to the Maas River and just three miles from the German border. The Tigers' Spitfires wreaked considerable damage with at least five direct hits on houses.

Now operating so close to Germany itself, the Squadron really felt that the war's end must be in sight, and this feeling was strengthened next day when 74 actually crossed the border and flew over the Third Reich as escort to twenty-four Bostons and eighteen Mitchells bombing Viersen in the face of heavy flak. Later the same day the Tigers provided area cover over Venlo at 15,000ft while a similar combination of Mitchells and Bostons bombed the marshalling yards below them.

ANTWERP-DEURNE

The Tigers flew their final sortie from Courtrai on 25 November and, after escorting Mitchells and Bostons to Rheydt, they landed at their new base, in a rather more forward position. Deurne (ALG 70) was Antwerp's airport and had dual and cross runways, although only one was serviceable when 74 first arrived. Almost immediately a new hazard presented itself in the shape of V-1s and V-2s, which the Germans were launching in the general direction of Antwerp port: a greater weight of V-2s was to fall on Antwerp than on London during the course of the war. Just after 74's arrival one landed near the airmen's billets, the blast completely disrupting their living and washing arrangements, although with the ground crews' usual talents for improvisation everything returned to a working basis within a very short space of time.

Many of the V-weapons were destroyed on the way in by anti-aircraft fire using proximity fuses, but there were regularly a few that got through. The Tigers did manage to destroy some in the air themselves: Paddy Dalzell, for example, claimed three while he was operating from Deurne. The missiles were very successful psychologically and were certainly a conversation-stopper. Everybody paused to listen as the distinctive noise of the V-1 got louder and louder, and if it stopped each man threw himself to the floor. Bill Crawford-Compton was as averse to doodlebugs as everyone else, as several surviving stories testify. On one occasion he was walking across the aerodrome in a brand new barathea uniform. Halfway across, a V-1 approached and then cut out immediately overhead. With an anguished cry of 'Oh my God, my new uniform!', Crawford-Compton got down on to his hands and toes on the wet, muddy tarmac in the 'push up' position, assiduously trying to keep his uniform out of contact with the ground. He stayed that way until the V-1 exploded some distance off!

The opportunities for recreation were as scarce in Antwerp as they had been elsewhere and the Tigers' routine of eat, sleep and fly hardly faltered. Officers slept in beds in requisitioned houses close by. Llewellyn recalls that

> In our house there was running water and gas. In the bathroom someone had removed the hot water geyser and had suspended a Messerschmitt 109 radiator over the open gas pipe and connected it to the water taps. We turned on the gas, lit it and the open flames heated the radiator. It worked very efficiently and there was always plenty of hot water!

Nobody now believed that the war could last for more than a further few weeks, particularly as the Germans were in full retreat again, having pushed too far forward too quickly through the Ardennes and paying the penalty when their supply lines failed. 74's assigned missions continued to be armed reconnaissance sorties as well as interdiction and concentrated close support work. But the enemy still occasionally hit back. January 1, 1945, dawned bright, clear and frosty. All the squadrons in the Wing were on sixty-minute availability, as, with temperature now dropping towards 20 degrees of frost, the runway was unserviceable thanks to a thick coating of ice which ground crews were attempting to clear by the application of hundredweights of salt. Taking advantage of the problems this presented, the Luftwaffe launched a strafing attack on Deurne, with up to thirty Me 109s screaming low across the airfield, cannons blazing. There had been no warning of their arrival and surprise was complete. Amazingly, 74 escaped virtually unscathed: there was damage to buildings and equipment, but the Spitfires were not touched. Colleagues on the French squadrons were not so fortunate, neither were the Typhoons of 146 Wing which also shared the airfield at this time. The attack was part of a well-coordinated plan by the German Command with all TAF airfields targeted as part of a concerted show of force and a desperate attempt to destroy as many Allied aircraft on the ground as possible. Total Allied losses were indeed considerable.

Runway damage was soon repaired, but icing gave way to a new menace—fog. Visibility was often down to twenty-five yards, which precluded any sorties but which did not stop the Germans launching their usual V-1s and V-2s. Flying recommenced on 5 January, although, in a winter when all the elements were contriving to show their very worst aspects, there was now snow to contend with. The newly promoted Tony Reeves, having returned to 74 to replace the long-serving Hayter as CO on 30 December, led his first sweep as Boss to bomb the village of Renesse on Schojen Island in a snowstorm. A popular choice, particularly as he was well known to most of the Tigers from his recent days as Flight Commander, Reeves was rather less outgoing than Hayter; indeed, he was positively quiet, studious, steady, reliable, experienced and therefore effective. He was a good listener and there were few people who ever disagreed with his running of the Squadron.

Poor weather did not prevent 74 from getting airborne on the 6th, but conditions by the end of the trip had deteriorated considerably and it was only with the aid of a fine pyrotechnic display by Flying Control that all the aircraft landed successfully in visibility that extended no further than half the length of the runway. After the ice, fog and snow came blizzards and more miserably low temperatures. It was not long before a white blanket, inches deep, overlaid everything, and in places the wind had caused drifts several feet thick. Once again, various jobs were found to fill the time. Some chose to go to church when the Church of England chaplain held a rare service at dispersal. A Canadian Concert Party got through by road to entertain the men and were afterwards entertained themselves in the Officers' Mess. Non-operational weather continued until the 13th, although the Tigers had managed to get two aircraft, flown by John Church and Frank Hardman, airborne on the 9th to investigate reports of a roving Ju 88 playing hide-and-seek in the snowstorms near Bergen-Op-Zoom: they scrambled in eight minutes—which, considering the conditions, was impressive. Unfortunately the effort was wasted as they saw nothing. More heavy snow soon closed the runway again, so there was nothing for it but to throw a party! Nobody was quite sure what was being celebrated, but everybody who attended undoubtedly enjoyed himself!

When flying did restart, Reeves led his men on a sweep over Rheine. Keith Butler and Paddy Dalzell later investigated a German-held airfield and pressed home a strafing attack. Armed reconnaissances uncovered the fact that the austere weather was having its effect on enemy movements as well as on the Allies' progress, and very little attackable traffic was seen. Enemy airfields were also apparently closed, allowing the squadrons to relax for a short while. When the skies temporarily turned blue again—a welcome sight for spirits depressed by weeks of gloom—an armed recce was flown over Leeuwarden. But with those blue skies quickly deteriorating back to grey at base, the Squadron was recalled. Bombs were dropped on the railway east of Utrecht and the lines cut in a couple of places. Bennett did not escape damage from defending flak. He force-landed, successfully, at B77 with fuel pouring from a severed line.

On 29 January the Squadron's ground crews started a move to ALG B85 at Schijndel. The aircraft could not follow for days afterwards, as a long period of heavy rain had flooded the newly laid runway there, so the pilots all moved into the Officers' Mess, the NCOs' Club or the Hotel Century in Antwerp, where all their personal needs were met, their kit having been packed and sent ahead with the ground crews in anticipation of an early move. Those at the Century, with a grandstand view from their eleventh-floor rooms, witnessed a V-weapons attack against the docks, the rockets flying by *below* them as they watched from their vantage point! With the ground and air elements now split and Antwerp-Deurne still operable, 74 continued to fly from there with support from the other resident squadrons and by the end of January they had clocked up a total of 227 sorties in a month during which there were just eleven days on which operations could take place.

Frank Hardman led an attack on an Army HQ west of Zaltbommel on 2 February but came to grief when he was hit by flak over the very heavily defended target and crashed in flames behind enemy lines. Flight Lieutenant Keith Butler took over the lead, although by now his charges numbered just two aircraft as Laurie Turner had also been hit by flak. The following day, 74 and the two French squadrons operated as a Wing, the latter's CO, Sampson, leading the thirty-six aircraft against railway sidings used for the unloading of V-1 supplies at Nijverdal. The Tigers finally moved their Spitfires to Schijndel on the 6th after an early mission led by Reeves to bomb and successfully cut a pontoon bridge at Doesberg. There was still plenty of water covering the new PSP runway which had been laid across the cornfields, but it was not as deep as it had been. One of the first visitors at the new location was Air Chief Marshal Tedder, who told the Squadron of Operation 'Veritable', an attempt to clear an area between the Meuse and the Rhine, which was to be launched the following day. 74 opened the account on this when they took twelve aircraft to bomb another German Army HQ. After the first days' operations, Allied ground forces began to move in, although the Army was soon calling for help as Me 109s appeared overhead to harass them. 74 sent aircraft off in pairs to look for the intruders: they found none, and a system of continuous patrols thereafter appeared to keep the Luftwaffe away.

Other sorties flown by 74 included the bombing of the village of Hassum, which was held by a battalion of Germans who were in turn holding up the Allied infantry's advance south from the Reichswald Forest. Buildings were destroyed or damaged and German soldiers running into the church for safety were strafed. The Squadron returned later and repeated the exercise, thus clearing the way for the Army to enter the village. When they did, they found the Germans quite demoralized by the Tigers' offensive and quite willing to surrender. Meanwhile Reeves and Bennett were dropping safe-conduct leaflets on Goch in a more peaceful attempt at persuading the enemy to surrender. Interdiction on the railway system continued. In the final analysis, all the objectives of 'Veritable' were met. It had been, as the Record Book stated, a 'pretty big do!'

The Tigers now returned to armed reconnaissance and bombing duties, dodging the flak, destroying ground targets and making the best of the still unfavourable weather. Lambert was shot up by flak which burst one of his aircraft tyres. He landed at Eindhoven with his colleagues but was unable to hold his Spitfire on the runway and it had to be retrieved from the mud alongside. Joe Eyre meanwhile was separated from his wingman and was bounced by half a dozen Me 109s near Arnhem but was glad, for once, of the amount of cloud cover available and made full use of it to escape. Nick Carter's aircraft was damaged by ground fire. There was a period in the middle of the month when fog returned for several days, grounding everything except the V-weapons, which could be heard passing overhead and occasionally falling nearby, causing a few Tigers' hearts to flutter again! The Squadron was instructed to keep two aircraft on readiness and the pair were called into action on the 21st in minimal conditions when a German jet was reported circling the base. They climbed to 33,000ft but found nothing. A pair were scrambled again on the 22nd, getting airborne in a very impressive 2½ minutes, and set course for Antwerp to intercept inbound enemy aircraft. Once again they saw nothing.

On the 24th the clag lifted and uncharacteristically beautiful weather briefly took its place. 74 seized the chance to fly fifty-two sorties. It attempted to beat this record number the following day, but after thirty had been flown the bad weather rolled in again and curtailed operations —but not before Bill Cortis and Ivan Butler had been lost on an armed reconnaissance. Cortis was shot down, taken prisoner and admitted to a hospital in a POW camp suffering from spinal injuries and a fractured knee but received only a minimum of medical attention. He returned to the Squadron when the Americans liberated the camp at the beginning of April and was immediately sent back to England. Warrant Officer Butler was also badly injured when he crash-landed; he died the following day.

From February 1945, 74 Squadron started using rockets, the only Spitfire squadron to do so. One 60-pounder was attached to a rail under each wing in place of the usual 250lb bombs, and a 500-pounder was retained under the fuselage. With such a varied selection of weaponry, the Tigers were certainly ringing the changes, although, during the last couple of months of the war, rockets were only employed perhaps a couple of dozen times, their main users being Typhoons with updated gunsights—far more stable platforms. Techniques for rocket delivery varied. On interdiction sorties the Squadron would fly high and individual aircraft would turn on their backs, pull round and fly straight through on to the target. Otherwise it was simply a matter of diving, aiming the aircraft at the intended target and loosing off the rocket. This was a very hit-and-miss affair—one reason why the pilots always preferred cannon and bombs. Hugh Murland recalls incidents with rockets when they were fitted:

... such as the occasion when suddenly, from the back of formation, a rocket would launch itself spontaneously (or so the offending pilot would have us believe!) and you would undergo the unnerving experience of seeing a missile whistling past your ear! Any spontaneous launchings were actually caused by electrical faults.

Operation 'Blockbuster' commenced on 26 February. As with 'Veritable', this was an area-clearance offensive as part of the preparation for the launching of the Battle of the Rhine. Initially air support was limited by the plague of bad weather, and it could not really get under way until the 28th, when the Tiger's contribution took the form of a close-support operation against Weeze led by Reeves. Interdictions and armed reconnaissances occupied the rest of the day as the Americans moved forward through western Germany below them. The gap between Allies and the Germans was a narrow one and for their close-support missions the Tigers were often asked to attack targets literally yards in advance of the troops, which called for very disciplined bombing. This pattern continued into March. On the 5th, by way of a change, Reeves led fourteen Spitfires to A68 at Juvincourt near Rheims to escort a C-54 Skymaster carrying Winston Churchill to Northolt. Having successfully completed the mission, and pleased at the opportunity of setting foot on English soil again (albeit briefly), the Tigers returned to the Continent the next day but had to divert to Grimbergen (Brussels) in deteriorating weather. Allan Griffin's log book shows 10/10ths cloud at 300ft! Not all the Squadron went into B60 however: Red Morgan ended up at Lille and Bob Human must have had urgent business in London as he did not leave Northolt at all! The Squadron was stuck at Grimbergen for three days and returned to Schijndel to find that re-equipment with Spitfire XVIs had started. Johnny Bennett did not make it; his Spitfire's engine burst into flames in the air. He managed to land near Dienst but could do nothing to contain the fire and the aircraft burnt out. He was later awarded a Green Endorsement for his skill in getting his stricken aircraft down.

The Spitfire XVIs arrived in threes and fours over a period of days until 16 March, by which date the Squadron was fully re-equipped and at least one example of a teardrop-canopied Spitfire XVIb had arrived. The Tigers were not completely happy with the change, the problem being that the Mk XVI was powered by the American-built Packard Merlin 266 engine, which gave the aircraft a poorer performance than the British-powered Spitfire IX. Considerable trouble was also experienced by the ground crews in relation to the poor workmanship of the engines, which gave rise to many glycol and oil leaks. However, careful maintenance remedied most of the faults.

Interdiction missions followed. An armed recce accounted for seventeen barges and one lorry on 16 March, whilst thirty-two sorties on the 20th resulted in three lorries destroyed and eighteen damaged, one tug damaged, eight barges damaged, one fuel storage depot strafed and two rail trucks destroyed and one damaged with eight Germans killed. 74 suffered two casualties. Taffy Rees had to land at B89 with engine trouble and Jock Agnew's aircraft was hit by flak, although fortuitously he was not himself injured. This was followed with a big score of barges damaged on attacks on the Rhine at Zwolle. On the 24th an operation designed to afford a crossing of the river by the British Second Army in the Wesel–Emmerich sector (Operation 'Eclipse') started. 74 was airborne early on patrols and armed reconnaissances, and these lasted throughout the day. During one a V-2 caused considerable panic when it passed *through* the Squadron formation!

On the 25th another considerable tally of motor transport damaged or destroyed was recorded. This was followed by another call to escort the Prime Minister's Dakota from Venlo (A55) to Northolt on completion of his tour of the Rhine crossing. Escorting a slower flying transport aircraft was no easy job. Allan Griffin:

> It was very difficult trying to keep behind the PM's aircraft. What we in fact did was a kind of convoy patrol, flying round and round 4 or 5,000ft above him, always keeping him in sight.

Hugh Murland has memories of the escort too:

> We lined up near Churchill's Dakota at Venlo and as the VIPs arrived we started up. As each Spitfire turned to taxi down the runway clouds of dust blew back over our charges!

There were no problems with the escort, other than the fact that the twelve aircraft involved were subsequently weatherbound in the UK and were not able to return to the Continent until the 30th. Hugh Murland again:

> At Northolt we went into a local pub, where there was also a bunch of lads from the Parachute Regiment. One of our lot rashly asked: 'What are you all doing this side of the Rhine?' The mildness of their response was obviously tempered by the likely consequences of striking an officer! However, at closing time we filed out of the pub and the innocent last member of our party—Cam Davis—was thumped extremely hard by unseen assailants, although Army boots were plainly heard clattering off into the night. . .

The six aircraft left at Schijndel meanwhile joined the other Wing squadrons, continuing operations amidst a renewed V-2 assault on the area around the airfield (although none landed on the aerodrome itself). As soon as the full Squadron complement was together again, 74 mounted an attack on transport in the Aimelo area and forty vehicles were either destroyed or damaged.

INTO GERMANY

By 1 April 1945 the defeat of Germany was all but complete. Montgomery, with the Canadian First, British Second and US Ninth Armies under his command, had been given the main striking role across the Rhine. His grand plan was to launch a massive attack during the night of 23 March. Over 3,000 guns, and waves of bombers, preceded the crossing by boat, barge, amphibious tank and armoured vehicle. Two airborne divisions were dropped ahead of the ground troops to help clear the way. Behind them, bridges were rapidly built for the passage of reinforcing units. As the advance developed, the Tigers continued their close support, during which Racy force-landed in enemy-held territory but managed to reach friendly troops. Other sorties were thwarted in part by low cloud, although transport was seen and attacked in the area west of Bremen and for a few days this remained the Tigers' hunting ground. Braidwood was leading a section of eight when he suddenly saw a pair of Me 262s. Allan Griffin:

> It took a while to identify the unusual shape of the swastika-carrying aircraft below us. We turned over and went down for them. They obviously saw us coming for they opened everything up and off they shot. Warwick had a go from beyond the effective range of his cannon. They didn't come back.

The following day a section of three from 74 Squadron attacked Rotenburg aerodrome, where a dozen Me 109s and Fw 190s parked on the dispersal were caught: five were destroyed and four damaged. As ground crews ran for cover they too were strafed. Flak was heavy and Bill Warwick was hit, but he nursed his Spitfire safely back to Schijndel with a jammed aileron. The rest of the Squadron were busy on the same day destroying and damaging motor transport around Emden, Gronigen and Varel.

Friday the 13th heralded a move to ALG B105 at Drope in Germany. The fact that the Tigers had finally crossed the border was of course itself a reason for some celebration. Ground crews saw plenty of evidence of the war's progress when they moved up by road and passed train loads of liberated Belgians and French travelling homewards. The initial impressions of 74's new home were quite favourable, although the first night was an uncomfortable and wet one, with personnel sleeping in tents. For added security everyone was armed and carried their revolvers everywhere they went, on camp and off.

The Tigers' first operation from Drope involved the successful bombing of troop concentrations at Delfzyl, evading a heavy flak barrage in the process. Over subsequent days armed recces revealed He 177s and Ju 88s at Nordholz airfield and Me 109s and Ju 88s at Arduff. Piearce joined 74 just after the move and was very lucky to escape with his life when he got stuck in sand beside the airstrip after landing and was run into by a Typhoon whose propeller very quickly and easily demolished the Spitfire's fuselage. Providentially, it stopped short of the cockpit. Bennett had a lucky escape, too, whilst attacking Arduff: shrapnel from the flak barrage burst behind the armour plating and passed out through the side of the cockpit, just missing him. Barnes was not so fortunate. He crashlanded near Oldendorf north-east of Bremen: his aircraft burst into flames and skidded three hundred yards into a wood.

On 20 April eight aircraft were sent off to deal with a German strongpoint in houses south of Lake Zwischenahner and seven of the Squadron bombed a stationary train south of Wilhelmshaven. Part of the train caught fire and, since it was carrying petrol, the ensuing explosion was quite spectacular. Later in the day eleven Spitfires bombed and strafed a gun position at Edewich. Once again the target was successfully hit and the Squadron suffered no damage other than that caused by small-arms fire to Griffin's aircraft. On the 22nd, sections led by Morgan and Griffin destroyed three locomotives by the Kaiser Wilhelm Canal. Several bomber escorts were flown before a return to Army support on the 24th with sections bombing gun positions and SS troop concentrations in houses south-west of Arnhem. Griffin was hit again, on this occasion four times by flak, and he was forced to land at Twente where he spent the night.

April 25 was a busy day. Forty operational sorties were flown against oil storage tanks at Brake, woods containing German troops, a windmill used as an observation post, 88mm guns near Emden and houses containing enemy infantry. The momentum was carried into the next day when only slightly fewer sorties were mounted. Tony Reeves led a dozen aircraft to bomb coastal defence guns and Pat Peet a dozen which attacked targets near Leer. The last sorties of the day included the bombing of troop and mortar positions near Delmenhorst. The Polish Armoured Division was impressed with the efforts of 74 and its fellow squadrons, as was the Canadian Fourth Armoured Brigade.

With more atrocious weather effectively grounding the Tigers at the beginning of May, news of the surrender of all German forces in Italy and the fall of Berlin was cause for celebration. Then news came in of the collapse of the German forces throughout Europe, a signal being received by all Allied units on the morning of 5 May:

SECRET

Special Announcement, issued by Supreme HQ...

German Forces in NW Germany, Denmark—including Heligoland and the Frisian Islands—have surrendered to Field Marshal Montgomery...

Cancel all offensive ops forthwith. Ceasefire 0800.

This effectively put 74 outside the range of any operational area and marked the end of their war, although on the 8th flying did resume for a while with Red Morgan and Jock Agnew getting airborne. It fell to New Zealander Shan Shanahan and Mauritian Des de Senneville on 9 May to complete the Tigers' last operational flight of the Second World War.

Following their return from the Middle East in April 1944, the Tigers had been in action for twelve months without respite. There is no doubt that the 2nd Tactical Air Force played a very significant part in the defeat of the German war machine and that as a component of that force the Tigers' record was as fine as any. Indeed, wherever 74 served during the Second World War it was with pride in their achievements and in the desire to emulate the success of their forbears. By the end of the war they had added 'France and the Low Countries 1940', 'Dunkirk', 'Battle of Britain 1940', 'Fortress Europe 1940, 1941, 1944', 'Mediterranean 1943', 'Normandy 1944' and 'France and Germany 1944–1945' to their Battle Standard.

CHAPTER 7

Jets!

A S SOON AS hostilities had ceased, Tony Reeves announced that the Squadron was to move off immediately *en route* for Colerne in Wiltshire to convert to the Gloster Meteor. Accordingly, ground crews and administration staff were up and about early in the morning of 11 May to strike all tents and prepare for the first leg of the road journey to England. From Drope the convoy drove to Deventer, and from there to the much battered and bombed Arnhem and down through the war-ravaged countryside to Nijmegen. In the evening the Tigers arrived at Antwerp-Deurne, now a much happier place than it was a few months previously. The convoy was under way again early the following morning, bound for Ostend, where men and machines embarked on an American LST. They steamed out of harbour on a sunny spring evening for the crossing to England, although there was quite a sea running and the ship developed a vicious roll which ensured that most of 74 became rather sea-sick Tigers! Delayed for a further eight hours at Tilbury when a merchant ship jammed the locks leading into the docks, 74 earned a word of praise as they finally cleared the ship of all men, equipment and transport in twelve minutes! Whether this was a demonstration of organized efficiency for the benefit of the Americans or whether it was merely the Tigers anxious to see the back of a thoroughly uncomfortable voyage is a matter for conjecture! The final leg of the journey across the peaceful and poignantly beautiful southern English countryside to Colerne in Wiltshire was savoured by all.

Meanwhile the pilots had flown back to Colerne, having exchanged their Spitfires for older examples from 485 Squadron. They left most of their New Zealand and Australian colleagues behind—they would be sent back to their homelands separately—but, recalls Hugh Murland,

> ... for a reason best known to some equipment officer, it was deemed that the tents they were occupying should be taken down as well as ours. So they slept on a corner of the airfield, their camp beds surrounded by their possessions —folding chairs, canvas wash basins and all—open to the skies!

Not all flights home were uneventful. Murland's Spitfire developed engine trouble and he left the formation to land at Bruges. For a couple of hours mechanics tinkered with the engine whilst bottles of champagne stowed under the metal covers of the ammunition bays in each wing got warmer by the minute, threatening to explode. Eventually he was told he could continue, although the engine was still running roughly:

I headed for Calais and the narrowest piece of sea. At the coast I spiralled upwards, gaining altitude so that I could glide to land if the engine stopped over the water.

But he had no need to resort to such measures, and he, and his colleagues, landed safely in England.

At Colerne, twenty-three Tiger pilots joined 1335 Conversion Flight, under whose auspices they would remain until July. The conversion to the Meteor started with ground school, a lecture on the development of jets and flying in the base's Oxfords to learn how to handle two engines. Lambert and Adams had the distinction of becoming the first-ever jet-propelled Tigers when they flew Meteor F.1s on 18 May. By the 23rd of the month every pilot on the Squadron had made at least one trip on the jet, and the general consensus was that, once its size had been come to terms with, the big, solid Meteor was a fine aircraft, though noticeably heavier on the controls than the Squadron's previous mount and not so manoeuvrable. The pilots nevertheless appreciated the speed (particularly that of Derwent-powered Meteor F.3) and the fact that the aircraft had two engines which, as the ORB succinctly states, 'we single-engine pilots have found no difficulty in coping with at all.' A later entry alludes to the fact that the pilots found their first attempts at single-engine approaches straightforward to cope with:

> They are very easy in the Meteor. At cruising speeds the failure of one engine makes very little difference and handling is almost as easy as with two. Landings can be made either by turning on finals into the dead engine or otherwise.

This statement proved to be at odds with the RAF's experience over the ensuing years, many unwary pilots falling prey to the problems of asymmetry thrown up by two wing-mounted turbojets.

The interest and excitement of the change from propeller to jet outweighed the apprehension and nervousness felt by the pilots on their first flights, which always turned out to be exhilarating affairs. Hugh Murland recalls the transition:

> The advantages with the Meteor were greatly improved forward vision—after the huge nose of the Spit you could suddenly see everything! Almost too much in fact. In the Spitfire, when airborne, you could tell you were flying straight and level by the nose in relation to the horizon. Now suddenly there was no nose, and flying it for the first time you were confronted with the problem of knowing how you were flying level without constant reference to the instruments. We overcame the problem by switching on the gunsight—and bingo! There was a ready-made horizon reference. Visibility all round was so much better. It was a bigger cockpit in which you could turn your head comfortably, and with the Meteor there was far less noise, and no engine in front meant there was no oil being sprayed back on to the windscreen! Other memorable differences included the easier engine control and, not least, the ability to climb like a homesick angel! Initial acceleration with the Meteor was slower than the Spitfire by virtue of the characteristics of the early jet engines. In those early marks of Meteor duration was very limited, with the maximum permitted sortie length being twenty minutes and a maximum of fifty miles

from base. After fifteen minutes, Flying Control routinely called up to remind us it was time we were back in the circuit. For some came the chance to get lost! When Jim Cooksey flew a Meteor for the second time he eventually landed some 105 miles from Colerne!

At the end of May 1945, Wing Commander Hugh Kennard DFC arrived to lead the Tigers at the same time as they became a component of the first Meteor Wing with 245 Squadron. 74's first Meteor F.3 arrived at the beginning of June, this new airframe having the same engines as the F.1 for a while, simply because production of the aircraft was at this time outstripping that of engines. The Welland was a considerably less powerful engine than the new Derwent (it took twenty minutes to take a Welland-powered Meteor to 25,000ft) and it tended to blow out a lot of black smoke. It was also a matter of considerable resentment to the pilots that they were constantly being overtaken by piston-engined Tempests! The Squadron's engine fitters had been sent to RAF Locking on a jet conversion course. Aubrey Ping was amongst them:

The theory and course officer was a Squadron Leader who had been with Sir Frank Whittle Power Units. I teamed up with Ernie Hardwick and we soon got to know the ins and outs of a Welland. There was a detachment of Fleet Air Arm air crew on the camp at the time and with typical Naval profanity they soon christened us the Blow Lamp Fitters! But such disparagement made no difference to us, for we all thought the aircraft and its engines were out of this world. There were teething troubles of course, particularly with lubrication oils. The oil companies were constantly taking samples for analysis.

With the onset of a dismal summer, the cancellation of all flying for considerable periods was necessary; indeed, the situation became so critical that crews would be called in on Sundays to fly if conditions became favourable. Weather handicaps notwithstanding, by the third week in June the Squadron had managed to finish its preparations for its first air firing practice, during which pilots found that, as a gun platform, the Meteor proved to be ideal. Firing completed, they were immediately pronounced fully operational and this was marked by their leaving 1335 Conversion Unit's dispersal and taking up residence on their own. The state of rivalry which had grown between the Tigers and the Mustang OTU at nearby RAF Keevil was intensifying now that the Meteors, as part of 74's training, were authorized to bounce their propeller-driven colleagues whenever the opportunity arose—although the Mustangs, perhaps to avoid the embarrassment of being beaten, did not always respond!

Almost inevitably, there were accidents. Taffy Rees hit a tree during a low-level flypast, wrote off his aircraft and killed himself instantly. Operations apart, the Squadron found that it had aerial social duties to fulfil too. A small air display was given for the benefit of Royal Navy officers and Wrens visiting Colerne, and later three aircraft flew over the neighbouring city of Bath in support of a British Legion meeting. This straightforward flypast was described on the leader page of the following day's

Above: The Tigers were detailed to escort Winston Churchill from Venlo to Northolt in March 1945. Here Tony Reeves, Geoff Lambert, Taffy Rees, Des de Senneville, Pat Peet, Johnny Johnston and Paddy Dalzell await the Prime Minister's aircraft as it arrives to collect him. (Hugh Murland)

Below: 74's dispersal at Schijndel, next to the railway line which carried guns eastwards and POWs westwards! The Spitfire XVIs are standing on recently laid PSP. (Hugh Murland)

Far left, top: LAC Evans and colleagues undertake daily inspection on one of the Tigers' Spitfires at Schijndel. The LF Mk XVIE had the American-built Packard Merlin engine which proved to be considerably less reliable than its British counterpart. (Hugh Murland)

Far left, bottom: 74 Squadron was the only rocket-firing Spitfire unit in the RAF but pilots were not greatly enamoured with the accuracy of the weapons. Two 60lb rockets and a 500lb bomb are shown on this Mk IX. (Hugh Murland)

Left: Hugh Murland sits on the cockpit sill of a Spitfire XVI at Drope in Germany. 74 received several aircraft of this mark with the bubble canopy shown here. (Hugh Murland)

Below: 74's dispersal at Drope, with another example of a bubble-canopied Mk XVI (TB695 '4D-V') in the foreground. (Allan Griffin)

Left: Once the Squadron had moved to Drope, the business of pitching the tented accommodation and then equipping it began. Here the Squadron Adjutant Cam Davis gets down to business as he unpacks his Orderly Room! (Hugh Murland)

Below: 74's Commanding Officer, Sqn. Ldr. John Lapsley (on the right of the picture), and Flt. Lt. Bob Baelz, who himself commanded the Tigers, brief Squadron pilots prior to a sortie against USAF B-29s. There are some interesting aircraft silhouettes used for identification exercises behind them! (74 Squadron)

Right: In November 1946 long-serving Tiger Flight Sergeant John Peel, who had been with the Squadron for six years and had certainly stamped a very individual presence on it, bade farewell. (74 Squadron)

Below: A line of silver Meteor F.4s at Horsham St Faith, resplendent in their natural metal finish and devoid of any Squadron markings other than a tiger's head on the side of the nose. (74 Squadron)

Left: From September 1950, 74 began conversion to the superior Meteor F.8 with its revised tail, the provision of an ejection seat for the first time in an operational RAF aeroplane and an improved canopy. (74 Squadron)

Below left: Arming up: the Squadron's armament NCO, Flt. Sgt. Blake, checks the contents of the ammunition box. (74 Squadron)

Right: Since the inauguration of the programme in the early 1950s whereby officers of the Royal Air Force exchange places with their counterparts in the United States Air Force or Marine Corps (and indeed other air forces too), 74 Squadron has enjoyed strong links with US personnel. In September 1951 the programme got off to an impressive start when Major George Milholland was appointed Commanding Officer. Seen here being strapped in by LAC Turner, he was the first at Horsham St Faith to wear the soon-to-be-universal 'bone-dome'. (74 Squadron)

Below right: CO Bill Johnson succumbs to the tedium of sitting on readiness for long periods during an English summer exercise! (Neil Robertson)

Above: The Tigers built a fine tradition of formation aerobatics in the 1950s and early 1960s. In 1951 Eddie Edmonds (left), Tug Wilson, Bertie Beard and Al Nisbett flew several displays. (74 Squadron)

Right: Many hours were spent practising air-to-air and air-to-ground firing and 74 regularly topped the scores at APC at Acklington, Squadron averages climbing regularly. In December 1956 Sgt. Bernie McParlin (left) and Fg. Offs. Pete Rayner, Ken Hunt and Wally Taylor produced a record flag (seen hanging behind them) with an average of 39.2 per cent. (Bernie McParlin)

Right: Chuck Sewell was another very popular American exchange officer. He came to the Tigers in 1955 after serving in Korea and stayed for two years. Chuck later became Chief Test Pilot for Grumman Aerospace. (74 Squadron)

Below: Sqn. Ldr. Keith Haselwood assumed command of 74 Squadron in January 1956. During the war he flew Mustangs with 26 Squadron and then went to Burma and operated with one of Wingate's Chindit columns until hit by a sack of supplies during an air drop and casevacked back to the UK. After recovery he was posted to a Typhoon squadron. He came to 74 from the Day Fighter Leader School. (74 Squadron)

Left: In 1956 the Tigers (seen here over Great Yarmouth) won the Fighter Command Inter-Squadron Meteor Formation Aerobatic Competition with a team comprising Haselwood, Sewell, Allison and Walpole (the last-named later replaced by Lewis). (74 Squadron)

Below left: An air-to-air study of Ian Cadwallader's Meteor 8, by John Whitehead, Christmas 1956. John was 74's exchange officer from the Royal Australian Air Force. (John Whitehead)

Right: The Tigers' first Hunter F.4, with Chuck Sewell, Ian Cadwallader, Tony Hilton, Pete Rayner, Mike Norman and Geoff Holden. (Ian Cadwallader)

Right: Tony Hilton keeps a wary eye on Begum, the Sumatran tigress who was brought by trainer Alex Kerr to Horsham St Faith to meet the Tigers. All concerned were pleased that Begum behaved herself on the day! (74 Squadron)

Below: Showing the familiar lines of a Hunter F.6, XE559/'D' lifts off the St Faith runway in the hands of Fg. Off. C. Wallis. (Ian Cadwallader)

Above: A publicity photograph taken to show all the trades involved in the support of Hunter operations. Boz Robinson is the pilot and the Chief Technician standing to the right of the aircraft is Frank Kyme. Trades represented are fitter, rigger, instrument, electrical, armourer and motor transport, and a WAAF from the photographic section completes the picture. (John Drewell)

Above right: 'Trog' Bennett waits in the cockpit as ground crewmen undertake a speedy operational turnround, April 1959. (Arthur Bennett)

Below: Hunter F.6s XE589/'Q' and XF502/'R' form a backdrop to a September 1958 Squadron photograph with Sqn. Ldr. Chris Curtis flanked by Flight Commanders Mike Norman and Arthur Bennett. Between them and the assembled Tiger personnel are, from left to right, pilots Roddy Mundy, Tim Nelson, Pete Budd, Bernie Brennan, Roy Booth, Ian Sheppard, Boz Robinson, Jerry Cohu, Captain Jack Martin (USMC), Tony Dean, Henry Riley (Eng. Off.), Guy Thrower, Glynn Roberts, John Atkinson, Ian Cadwallader, Mike Ginn, Mike Cooke and Ted Nance. (John Drewell)

Above: Sailor Malan visited his old squadron shortly after it had moved to Coltishall in 1959. A Spitfire was flown in from Martlesham Heath for the occasion and Sailor is seen here with Arthur Bennett and Sqn. Ldr. Peter Carr, the Tiger Boss at the time. (Arthur Bennett)

Below: Hunter F.6 XK142, seen here at Hawker Siddeley's factory at Kingston undergoing conversion to FGA.9 standard, still bears 74's tiger's head and asymmetric dicing and a facsimile of Sailor Malan's signature. (British Aerospace)

Above: 'Tim Nelson aborted take-off and entered the barrier. The lower steel cable rode up over the wheel and cut into the starboard drop tank, spilling fuel over the red hot brakes, causing a fire which burnt out the aircraft. Tim was unhurt.' (74 Squadron)

Below: The Tigers used Hunter T.7s as instrument trainers between 1958 and 1966. All were sorry to see them go: Hunters have always been a favourite aircraft among pilots in terms of handling and looks. The swept-back fin flash adorning XL620/'Z' was a legacy of its previous days with 66 Squadron. (David Jones)

Above: Enter the Lightning—a huge step forward into the supersonic age for the RAF. Here 74 proudly displays its prestigious new mount at Coltishall in early 1961. (David Jones)

Left: Sqn. Ldr. John Howe, who was tasked with the responsibility of bringing the Lightning F.1 into operational service with 74 Squadron. Despite major serviceability problems and time-consuming commitments to display the aircraft at Paris and Farnborough, he succeeded. (74 Squadron)

evening paper as 'spectacular aerobatics over the City'! Some public relations work was aimed at, influencing the possible purchase of the Meteor by foreign governments. A Swiss delegation arrived at Colerne looking for an opportunity to see at first-hand an aircraft they *might* buy, but on this occasion the Meteor was completely upstaged. For some reason the demonstration was confined to a staid and unambitious flyby. As the aircraft landed, a Vampire suddenly appeared in the sky overhead and put on a display of scintillating aerobatics. This helped De Havilland win an order from the Swiss for Venoms and Vampires.

On 10 August 1945 the Japanese capitulation was announced, and this was followed four days later by the signing of the surrender document itself. At long last the world was at peace, and the relief was evident in the universal celebrations to mark VJ-Day. The RAF virtually stood down for a week, and the Tigers, along with the rest of the United Kingdom, celebrated too. At the end of August, 74 said farewell to Hugh Kennard, his place being taken by B Flight Commander Llewellyn (not the Don Llewellyn of 1944), amongst whose first duties was the organization of a four-ship formation and flypast over the liner *Queen Elizabeth*, which had a large complement of Americans on board. 74 was later to escort the *Andes*, carrying home Australians and New Zealanders (including the Squadron's erstwhile colleagues). The weather on that occasion was bad, and as the Meteors flew into a thunderstorm over the ship, lightning leapt dramatically through the formation from wing tip to wing tip.

For participation in the Battle of Britain commemoration, the Squadron deployed to Andrews Field near Chelmsford. Three days of intensive rehearsal preceded the flypast itself on 15 September. 74 was but one of twenty-three squadrons involved, although one of only two flying jets. October, November and December 1945 were devoted to the honing of the Tigers' new-found Meteor skills. Within a month of the New Year, 74 was to have yet another CO when Jim Cooksey was given command after his promotion to Squadron Leader. Otherwise 1946 got off to a particularly inauspicious start when Spud Miller was killed whilst 'beating up' Warmwell aerodrome. The Squadron lost another pilot a few weeks later when Bamjee (who had been attached to the Tigers for jet conversion from the Indian Air Force) was killed when he crashed near Chippenham with such an impact that the wreckage was spread over three fields. The Squadron spent most of January and February at Fairwood Common on a successful Armament Practice Camp.

Back at Colerne, the year developed into one of routine training with very little to break it other than a few Fighter Command exercises such as 'Jim Crow' and 'Big Bull' and some Army co-operation work at Manorbier in South Wales. There continued to be a high turnover of personnel, many men leaving the Royal Air Force in the aftermath of the war and their replacements, straight from Meteor conversion, lacking in operational experience. During June 1946 several sorties were made to Bentwaters on pre-detachment visits prior to the Squadron's participation in the V-Day Flypast over London on 8 June. When the crews were briefed for this they were warned of a bad weather front approaching from the west, but the Met boys forecast that it would not reach central London until the afternoon. Until the last moment, this prediction promised to be accurate, for up to the rendezvous point over Fairlop aerodrome near Romford the rain held off, the cloud base was no lower than 3,000ft and visibility was reasonably good. But in the short distance between the eastern suburbs of the capital and the centre there was a sudden change. As the leading aircraft approached the City, the rain started in earnest, an almost unbroken curtain of clouds started to descend and before Admiralty Arch (the aim point) was reached visibility was reduced to about half a mile. The conditions imposed a severe strain on the crews of the aircraft flying in close formation and it was only with the utmost concentration that they managed to adhere to the strict timing of the programme and maintain the prearranged order.

TO NORFOLK SKIES

On 12 August, 74, together with its sister-squadron at Colerne, 245, received a signal ordering a move to RAF Horsham St Faith in Norfolk. By the following day final preparations had been made and, on the 14th, the transfer of aircraft began, the first nine Meteors arriving at Horsham and making an impressive run over the airfield. So began a long and happy association with St Faith—an association which was to last almost thirteen years. There are few tangible reminders these days of 74's occupation of the camp other than a magnificent tiger's head painted on the wall of a store in their old hangar, which is now occupied by Air UK.

74 did little flying from St Faith during the remainder of August as air crew and airmen were concerned mainly with settling in. Sorties increased during September as pilots familiarized themselves with their new aerial environment, and, once established at its new home, the Squadron set about the serious business of air-to-air firing at No 2 Armament Practice Camp at Acklington. For a month the Squadron worked hard at the live gunnery sessions, and by the end of the Camp it had achieved averages in air-to-air firing of 41.6 per cent and in air-to-ground of 27.3 per cent. Back at St Faith, the pilots were able to continue practising their marksmanship against drogues and banner targets towed off the Norfolk coast by the locally based Martinet tugs of 34 Squadron. The Tigers were granted ten days' leave in November and then found that bad weather delayed the resumption of flying when they returned. This hiatus allowed energies to be concentrated on a most significant social event—the farewell party for 'Chiefy' Peel, who had been a Tiger for six years.

A feature of the 1947 winter was the heavy and prolonged snow falls which were to last for many weeks and which would severely disrupt not only Horsham St Faith's flying programme but life in general in the Eastern Counties. There were often periods, lasting days at a time, when no aircraft could get off the ground and others when, after the prolonged and back-breaking efforts of all station personnel (air crew included) to clear the runways and taxiways of snow, a heavy overnight fall would mean that the job would have to start all over again. Indeed, conditions during February became so difficult that the Squadron was sent on ten days' privilege leave. When the men returned they were promptly sent away again for a further week when heating fuel ran out. The situation did not improve during March. The Tigers should have gone to Lübeck in Germany on detachment, but this was first postponed and then cancelled when it became evident that there was to be no let-up in the snow. By this time the airfield (and indeed Norfolk) was buried under drifts many feet deep. By 17 March Horsham had been effectively grounded for seven weeks and it was with considerable relief that 74 were able to recommence flying during April.

Horsham St Faith was at this time the proud possessor of one of the early models of mobile GCA units, which on one particular occasion during the spring of 1947 was parked at the south-east corner of the intersection of runways 28 and 22 on a day when there was a very strong crosswind. Tiger pilots were sometimes seconded to 34 Squadron to fly their Martinets. An anonymous Tiger had been granted this rather dubious privilege and took off with the usual airman in the back to operate the winch, but once airborne the wind picked up speed significantly and the Martinet was recalled to base. This type of aircraft was not the easiest to land in a severe crosswind, and it made several unsuccessful attempts to get down. On the final attempt the pilot gritted his teeth and planted his unco-operative aircraft somewhere near the runway and bounced—straight into the GCA, demolishing the entire outfit. Luckily, most of the radar crew were at lunch at the time, with the exception of a very neat and proper Flight Sergeant who had been in the support trailer. Hearing the racket of the approaching Bristol Mercury with the Martinet following, he threw himself flat on to the wall-mounted bench. The Mercury tore its way underneath the bench, which fell off the wall, allowing room for the mainplane to pass over the top of the new panic-stricken Flight Sergeant. The winch-operator broke his leg in the accident whilst the pilot suffered a broken nose; the latter did not fly Martinets again.

Jim Cooksey retired on 22 April and the equally popular Squadron Leader Bob Baelz DFC took command. Shortly afterwards the detachment to Lübeck—a regular feature for Fighter Command squadrons in the postwar years—finally went ahead. This was to be a useful and successful stay not only from the point of view of training and operations, but also in terms of social and sporting activities. John Drinkwater remembers the detachment well:

We ground crew went by train to Harwich and sailed on the *Empire Wansbeck* to Holland, where we were put on a bullet-scarred train. *En route* I remember we were given food in paper bags on which was inscribed 'Do not throw food to the children'. Apparently many were getting hurt scrambling for it. The city of Lübeck on the Baltic coast I remember as being very like York with its old walls. Our accommodation close to the ex-Luftwaffe camp was excellent and recreational facilities first class. In fact those three months in that beautiful summer were amongst the most enjoyable of my life!

Back in the Norfolk skies for September, formation training was once again possible. Four aircraft flew to Duxford to practice for, and take part in, the Battle of Britain Flypast over London on the 15th, whilst five days later Horsham St Faith held its own Open Day, during the course of which 74 provided the leading section of four aircraft in a formation of twelve Meteors which went on to overfly the principal towns and aerodromes of East Anglia. A short trial running a pair of Meteors on petrol led to some interesting moments, with start-up invariably leading to a loud bang, tongues of flame and scorched grass! The trials did not continue for long. Tragedy struck at the end of September when Flying Officer Dennis was killed after his aircraft spun and crashed close to the runway's end while carrying out simulated single-engine approaches. He had only been posted to the Squadron a few days previously, and his lack of experience with the asymmetric characteristics of the Meteor had led him to turn into the dead engine. The Tiger's early optimism that dealing with such problems was to be straightforward did not always prove to be well-founded.

During October, night flying was introduced for the first time, and by the end of November all pilots with over fifty hours' experience on the Meteor had completed at least one period of this. The training routine was briefly interrupted by 'Landit One', a Group exercise which for 74 involved the interception of Hornets attacking targets in Lincolnshire. This was one of the last exercises on which the Meteor F.3 was flown, for in early 1948 the Tigers became the first squadron of the Horsham Wing to begin the transition to the superior F.4.

The F.4 was in essence a re-engined (Derwent V) F.3 with a much strengthened airframe to cope with the extra power and performance. In addition it featured a slightly lengthened fuselage, clipped wings and cabin pressurization. Bob Baelz collected the first F.4 on 21 December from Glosters; the last arrived during March, just before Squadron Leader John Lapsley DFC assumed command of the Tigers. One of Lapsley's first jobs, in common with the commanders of the other Horsham squadrons, was to play host to a large visiting press corps and they produced an account of Squadron and Station activity as well as addressing the question of high-level interception:

The first duty of the Royal Air Force today is to defend this country against attack. That responsibility has to be carried in the first instance by Fighter Command, of which 12 Group and RAF Horsham St Faith are a component... The AOC 12 Group is faced with the usual peacetime dilemma. The RAF has to be at the peak of efficiency (as the first attack on this country would come from the air), yet there is no indication of the type of warfare which would mark the opening phase of another conflict. Since the war it has been assumed that in the Meteor, and with squadrons strategically placed around the country, we have an aircraft capable of destroying effectively attacks by all types of enemy bombers—at any rate those fitted with piston engines, although it should not be thought that all piston-engined bombers are necessarily easy to destroy . . . and the Russians may by now have a bomber fleet of Superfortress copies of considerable dimensions. This is the sort of thing that 12 Group is up against. Indications are that the exceptional performance at altitude of the Meteor F.4 does guarantee a degree of real security.

Attacks are carried out at speed—elapsed times of four minutes have been recorded from the take-off to the kill at 15,000 feet. Some very fast scrambles can be made—the starting operations taking 30 seconds—and the aircraft can be hurriedly trundled along to the downwind end of the runway without the usual ignition and power checks and without warming up. If the aircraft happen to be dispersed near the downwind end (as they would in an emergency), it will be evident how quickly they could be flown away.

INTERCEPTORS!

When John Lapsley had taken command of the Tigers he had done so accepting a reduction in rank from Wing Commander to Squadron Leader. Bob Baelz stepped down to Flight Lieutenant at the same time. The reason for this unprecedented shuffle was the choice by Fighter Command of 74 Squadron to carry out trials on the practicability of high-level collision interception, Lapsley being brought in specifically to lead these trials. Lapsley came to 74 with an already distinguished career, although latterly he had not had a great deal of opportunity to fly and so jumped at the chance of an operational command:

I must say that I personally found the Meteor 'child's play' after the later mark of Spitfire and Typhoon which had been my previous types. My conversion to it at Horsham took the form of Bob Baelz buckling me into one of the last F.3s and showing me what and what not to do. Having mastered the F.3 with no problem, I then went down to Bentwaters, where the OCU was at that time situated, to convert to the F.4. The intrinsic difference between the F.3 and F.4 was that the latter was a faster aeroplane—but had less fuel. Until the drop tanks were adopted, F.4s only had forty minutes' endurance. Forty minutes in the winter in England is a very short period of time in which to do something useful and get back again! Actually, many pilots found flying the Meteor a fairly dangerous occupation in the early stages, particularly prior to the introduction of the two-seater. Coming from single-engined aircraft, their experience in relation to the problems of asymmetric flying was fairly low. The early Derwents were very prone to complete failure due to rotating guide vane trouble and to flame out at altitude on rapid throttle movement and at low level at idling revs. The pilots were also unused to the slow acceleration and response of early jet engines in comparison to piston engines. The air bag-operated drum brakes were also inadequate and very prone to failure due to overheating on landing.

The worst flying times I had with the Meteor on the Squadron concerned icing. Having been operating at 40,000 feet, the great slab of glass which acted as a windscreen would severely ice up on descent. The number of times that pilots were put at risk in these situations without any sensible navigation aids was quite disgraceful. The only way icing could perhaps be avoided was to take great trouble in interpreting the forecast to see whether it was likely to happen on that particular day and then, if practicable, spending the last ten minutes or so of any exercise at 8–10,000 feet. Otherwise you just learned to live with it! Later, when I was commanding the Air Fighting Development Squadron at West Raynham, this problem was one which I was determined to solve, and eventually, after extensive research and trials, a system was implemented of heating the screen.

The perfecting of a high-level homing system designed to bring the aircraft back to base was part of the Tigers' remit under Lapsley. The existing method had been evolved for piston-engined aircraft and was optimized for heights of no more than 3,000ft in cloud. It was not altogether reliable, and being picked up by GCA and brought in was not guaranteed. To bring an aircraft that operated at 30,000ft down to low level, amidst the attendant problems of icing and weather, to pick up an unreliable homing system seemed to Lapsley to be something of an anomaly:

> I asked myself the simple question—why not stay at height as long as possible before descending into the murk? 74 showed the way, and it very quickly became standard operating procedure for Fighter Command. It was aided and abetted by the fact that at this time radar stations were better served with new equipment which gave those on the ground much more accurate information as to the height and bearing of individual aircraft.

The other important development with which Lapsley and the Tigers were involved was the validation of head-on attacks against large formations of bombers, and to this end they worked extensively with American B-29s and B-50s during the summer of 1948. In those days the Central Fighter Establishment (CFE) was advocating a stereotyped attack profile which dated back to the days of the war but which, with the new generation of high-performance aircraft, needed to be greatly modified:

> It was very apparent to me that the fighters were out of range when they started their attack. During Exercise 'Dagger', the Horsham Wing tried a new method under my direction, one of simply ensuring that just the two inboard engines of the bombers were contained within the deflector sight of the Meteor and not the whole aircraft as they pressed home their head-on attack. We produced a film for CFE showing that we got extremely close into the B-29s, as close as one hundred yards, thereby ensuring a far greater rate of success in shooting them down. CFE studied the pictures—as did Basil Embry, for this was the sort of thing he loved to be involved in himself—and gradually the new tactic came to be adopted universally. The Tigers initially (and then the Horsham Wing) were involved with this for some time, to see just how close we could get to the opposing aircraft before breaking away!

On 19 April Lapsley led Todd, Burge and Bradley in two highly successful interceptions of B-29s after being scrambled by Neatishead (and getting airborne within 2min 10sec of the alarm). A week later the Tigers and 257 Squadron intercepted seventy naval aircraft. Considerable confusion characterized the ensuing dogfight with such large numbers of aircraft involved! Actually these exercises served to heighten morale in all of Horsham's squadrons, their pilots competing keenly to fly on the intercepts. The Squadron diary records similar interceptions during the ensuing months, mainly against American formations. On 23 May B-29s were again the target, and by this time the new procedures for high-level interception were beginning to be tested not only in the air but in the manner of scrambling at ten-second intervals and then climbing to height at optimum speed. All this was very good training for Neatishead's controllers too, and although the trials were tending to dominate all else and the normal training regime was beginning to suffer, the pilots were quite enjoying themselves!

On 10 August Lapsley was re-promoted and took command of the Horsham Wing. When, in later years, the 74 Squadron Association was formed, Sir John Lapsley was asked to become its President, a position he accepted without hesitation. With Bob Baelz now leading again, the Tigers prepared for one of the large-scale exercises of the period. With the onset of the Cold War and the perception of a new threat to Britain, the country's air defence capability was regularly tested. In Operation 'Dagger', 'Northland' (the Midlands, East Anglia and South-East England) were the defenders and were mainly pitted against long-range attacks from 'Southland' bombers which, based in England, flew outside the early-warning screen before returning to attack. 'Northland' had at its disposal all Fighter Command's forces plus sixteen squadrons of the Royal Auxiliary Air Force, Anti-Aircraft Command, the Royal Observer Corps and Civil Defence units. The attacking 'Southland' forces included most of Bomber, Coastal, Reserve and Training Commands, plus elements from RAF Germany and the US Air Force. Many hundreds of aircraft were involved, and the underground Operations Room at Fighter Command, the nerve centre of the Battle of Britain, returned to its former intense activity.

'Dagger' started at 1300 hrs on 3 September with the Horsham squadrons either at immediate or five-minutes' readiness. At 1415 the first scramble was ordered and Baelz and Bradley took off. They intercepted one aircraft at 10,000ft over the North Sea but on identification this was found to be a Swedish airliner that had strayed into the exercise area! Bardman and Todd were the next to get airborne: they found legitimate targets, intercepting three B-29s. By this time the order to scramble was coming through every few minutes. Cottam was vectored to intercept low-level 'attacks', perhaps the most difficult to deal with. Some aircraft got through the defensive screen and St Faith was 'strafed' by a pair of Hornets which would have caused havoc amongst the closely parked aircraft had they been doing it for real. Black Section had been briefed specifically to deal with this type of 'attack' but had received no warning of the Hornets' approach so stayed firmly on the ground and were themselves 'shot up', and by the time the survivors got airborne the 'attackers' had disappeared. The second day was taken up almost exclusively with continuous B-29 'raids', most of which were successfully intercepted. But the strain of the exercise was beginning to tell on the crews, and in between sorties pilots were grabbing brief snatches of sleep, although they enjoyed something of a respite in the morning of the third day as the first scramble did not come until 1015 and then it was only against a lone Mosquito, which was dealt with by Hickson and Cottam. The same pair were airborne again, this time in company with Todd and Batchelor, when they were scrambled with aircraft from the other Horsham squadrons to intercept a large force of 'Southland' bombers consisting of Wellingtons, Mosquitos and Lincolns. Returning to Horsham, they found Mosquitos bombing the aerodrome from low level and dived to the attack.

Extensive debriefing of all involved once the exercise was over threw up some disparate conclusions. As far as Lapsley and the Horsham Wing were concerned, it seemed that Bomber Command was not adapting to the new generation of air defence aircraft:

> They still retained the concept of mass formation attacks. Actually such exercises used to do both sides a lot of good, with much co-operation and contact between the different Commands. Also very important was the involvement of the Auxiliary squadrons with their Spitfires. The later disbandment of the Auxiliaries was a great loss to the RAF.

RATS AND TERRIERS

After 'Dagger', the Tigers not only resumed their training programme in their own right but also participated in a significant deployment as a component of the Horsham Wing when Meteor F.4s, including several of 74's machines and one Tiger pilot, Den Todd, under Group Captain Lewis, the Station Commander, flew to Copenhagen on a flag-waving exercise organized in conjunction with the British Exhibition being held there. The jets left St Faith on 16 September on the first leg of the journey to Eindhoven in Holland, subsequently staging through Lübeck. The final leg, the flight to Kastrup the following day, proved to be an eventful one with Todd and Bertie Wootten, CO of 245 Squadron, reporting that their belly tanks were not feeding fuel. This would not have presented so much of a problem had they been flying at high altitude, but at the transit height of 6,000ft fuel consumption was rather heavy and the offending tanks could not be jettisoned because there were no more available to replace them when they returned to Horsham.

The formation's callsign, 'British Meteor Squadron', also led to some confusion within Danish ATC, as did the latter's contention that the flight was an hour early, no allowance having been made for the time difference! By the time the formation was in sight of its destination, Todd and Wootten estimated that they had just five minutes' fuel to spare. Lewis attempted to inform ATC of this and requested emergency landing clearance. But this too proved to be difficult since, apart from the evident language problems, Kastrup was a joint-user airfield with frequent airliner movements and ATC were preoccupied with an incoming flight. Wootten decided that he had to make a straight-in approach and landing. Den Todd also left the formation, with the intention of following him, but at 1,500ft the pilots heard control say, 'Military aircraft landing at Kastrup—you are landing downwind!' Wootten had little option: he was by now making a dead-stick landing with dry tanks. Todd responded to the controller by making a very tight circuit on to the runway in use, only to find a DC-6 on approach in front of him. With insufficient fuel to go round again, he also had no alternative but to land on the right of the runway, overtaking the DC-6 to his left as he did so!

The final weeks of 1948 were routine by comparison but were enlivened towards Christmas with a sustained period of night flying, which included a navigation exercise to London and the aerial identification of Piccadilly Circus and the Windmill Theatre from 25,000ft—not an easy task, as those concerned were quick to find out, but all did agree that London at night was a quite magnificent sight from the air!

The Squadron still carried the coding '4D' on its aircraft. Other markings changed over a period of time, and there was considerable debate within Air Force circles about the need for camouflaging fighters. The Tigers' F.3s had been camouflaged dark green and medium sea grey above, with light sea grey undersurfaces. They also carried sky blue rear fuselage bands and codes, and the individual aircraft codes were repeated in black on the nosewheel door. At this stage there were no Tiger markings. The F.4s, on the other hand, retained an overall silver finish, with black codes flanking the fuselage roundels and nosewheel door. This was the beginning of one of the most colourful periods of Fighter Command markings. Towards the end of the Meteor F.4's front-line service, and in the following years, aircraft in general and the Meteor in particular adopted a dazzling variety of squadron colours. Each unit had its own combinations, usually presented in horizontal bars on either side of the fuselage roundel, and the Squadron Commander's aircraft would often have additional decoration in the form of a multi-coloured fin and rudder. As far as 74 was concerned, colours began with a small tiger's head on the nose, the engine nacelles and later the fin and then developed into full-scale black and yellow asymmetric dicing either side of the fuselage roundel (which had last been worn on the prewar Gauntlets) when aircraft coding was finally abandoned.

More night flying was completed during January 1949, including one sortie where Baelz, Lynes, Cottam and Bradley landed in the dark at Acklington, refuelled and returned to Horsham at an average speed of 540mph from brakes off to a point over base by Bradley and Lynes and an average 580mph by Baelz and Cottam, who were favoured by a tailwind at the height they flew. The Meteor was no slouch! There were two B-29 exercises during February, although the second of these could not be considered an unqualified success when the Wing was vectored to a spot off the mouth of the Thames by mistake—the controllers should have sent them to a point off the north East Anglian coast where the bombers were orbiting! Much of March was spent on the ground, fog causing great problems. When flying did take place, B-29s 'invaded' Britain's shores once again and Baelz, Higson and Bradley found twenty-nine of them eighty-five miles out over the North Sea and in the process achieved the fastest controlled intercept that had yet taken place.

Bob Baelz received permission during April to form the Squadron's own four-aircraft aerobatic team, and this duly worked up with Glen Lynes in command. The Tigers at this time could not be compared with the other squadrons of the Horsham Wing (particularly 245) in this respect, largely because they did not fully appreciate the need for team-work when it came to this type of flying. Glen Lynes was a brilliant pilot but was also very much an individual, and under his control the team had little chance to develop. His solo display was very much in demand, consisting as it did of a spectacular take off:

> ... As the wheels were retracted he gently turned the Meteor on its back in a half roll and climbed away upside down. A steep inverted climb from take-off demands the utmost from both man and machine and must surely be the ultimate expression of mutual quality. Low-altitude loops were followed by a rocket climb and three vertical rolls and the Meteor then went over the top and dived vertically, still rolling ...

During May Horsham hosted a number of visitors and saw the commencement of the arrival of contingents of F-80s which deployed from Europe at regular intervals to spend a fortnight at a time working with the Meteors. Squadrons were always pleased to be involved in such programmes, especially as meeting their American counterparts offered the chance to study alternative methods as well as different aircraft. 'Foil', the next in the series of large-scale air defence exercises, took place at the end of June. The first phase of this saw few scrambles but plenty of 'enemy' Hornets attacking St Faith and the sight of the occasional Tiger chasing the De Havilland aircraft across Norwich at low level! This was the early manifestation of the 'Rats and Terriers' concept, which became a recognized inter-squadron and inter-sector training regime over the ensuing years, with the Tigers the acknowledged experts. The 'Terriers' (defenders) generally flew in pairs with the leader low so that the intruder could more easily be seen against the sky's background, with his number two above, waiting for the interception. Radar controllers broadcast the given height and position of a 'Rat' (attacker), but it would then be down to the individual 'Terrier' to plot his own interception course. Tiger pilots quickly came to know the Norfolk and Suffolk countryside intimately as these techniques were practised regularly, flying at high speed at altitudes below one hundred feet.

The second phase of 'Foil' took place during some of the hottest and finest days of the year. Large numbers of scrambles were called and interceptions made, whilst the final phase was also a busy one. On the last afternoon the 'enemy' had their final fling when the Horsham Wing intercepted large boxes of B-29s at 28,000ft. In the crystal-clear weather the ground crews were able to watch the air battles over the Great Yarmouth area, the Meteors' small, weaving vapour trails intertwining with the long, broad trails of the bombers. The Tigers' score for the exercise was ninety-three aircraft confirmed as 'kills'.

EXERCISES AND TRIALS

Shortly after the first two-seat Meteor T.7 was delivered to the Tigers, Bob Baelz left for HQ 12 Group and Squadron Leader A. R. de L. Inniss DFC—popularly known as 'Sinbad'—assumed command. His arrival marked a temporary change in the role of the Horsham Wing to that of high-speed, high-level bombing for the duration of Exercise 'Bulldog', which took them across to the Continent:

74 Squadron along with other Fighter Command squadrons co-operated with the bomber force in an exercise designed to prove Britain's strike capability. This focused upon the capabilities of the Meteor as a defender and also included the use of F.4s to simulate high-flying bombers (the only aircraft in the RAF inventory capable of doing so). Despite American claims to the contrary, defending Meteors were able to successfully intercept the USAF's new B-50.

74 themselves were rarely intercepted, and they attributed this success to the evasive tactics they employed. A few pilots later had the opportunity to fly in B-50s from Lakenheath and they were as impressed with the big Boeing bomber as were the Americans who flew in the two-seater Meteor in return.

On 12 November a Squadron reunion was held in the Cock Tavern, Fleet Street, London, and guests included Ira Jones and Captains Hunt and Clements from 1918 and 'Tinky' Measures and Bunny de Pass from the second conflict. Also at the reunion were members of the West India Circular Committee. Privately, the Ministry of Defence was reluctant to allow the link between 74 and Trinidad to be maintained after the war—although it had been happy enough during hostilities to accept the money for the purchase of Spitfires—and it also wanted the title '74 (Trinidad) Squadron' dropped. Despite this, the latter lingered on for some years, partly because the Committee continued to send an annual gift of a keg of Trinidadian rum with which the celebrated 'Tiger's Blood' cocktail was made and partly because the Tigers felt a sense of obligation and made the effort themselves to maintain the link—which did, however, finally disappear in the early 1960s.*

Meanwhile another major exercise, 'Victor', got under way, and this included a mock Army battle in the Thetford Forest area of Norfolk, with 74 acting in the armed reconnaissance role in concert with 245 Squadron. There were, unfortunately, a number of accidents and incidents throughout the week of the exercise. In all, six Meteor F.4s were written off and five pilots killed throughout the Command—a sad record indeed and one which would have justified the cancellation of the exercise before those figures were reached. 74's participation was not without incident either. Peet and Priestly struck a flock of birds during a formation take-off: the aircraft were damaged and the pilots were forced to land immediately with full tanks. Peet managed this successfully but Priestly

*There has been occasional contact since, the most recent being at the time of the Squadron's 74th Anniversary in 1991.

stalled and struck the ground two hundred yards short of the runway, the aircraft ground-looping and injuring the pilot. Jerka was another Squadron casualty during a routine take-off a few days later. His port engine lost power as he climbed away so he returned to land, under-shooting in the process and coming down in the same field as Priestly had done earlier in the month.

As the new decade arrived, inter-squadron and inter-Group exercises appeared on the monthly flying schedules with increasing regularity, and in the first six months of 1950 the Tigers participated in Exercise 'New Year', Exercise 'Pancake', Operation 'Twelve Bore', Operation 'Easter Offering' and Operation 'Stardust' as well as a plethora of interception tasks against other RAF units and those of the USAF. A large engine-change programme was initiated in June, and, with the remaining available aircraft, practising for the RAF Display at Farnborough (the only postwar RAF Display *per se*) dominated training for the month. After Farnborough the Squadron relocated to Acklington for the APC and then, returning to St Faith, the commencement of Exercise 'Fabulous'—the 1950s equivalent of Quick Reaction Alert (QRA). Over the ensuing years, 74, alongside all other Fighter Command squadrons, had regular commitments to 'Fabulous' (and later 'Halyard') and the interception of threats to British air space by unidentified aircraft.

The most important aspect of the autumn from the Squadron's point of view, however, was the changeover from Meteor F.4s to F.8s. The F.8 was produced in greater numbers than any other mark of Meteor and the basis for its development had been a realization that the F.4 was beginning to be outclassed by more modern aircraft. Refinements included the provision of an ejection seat for the first time in an operational RAF aircraft: gone were the days of reducing speed, jettisoning the hood and diving over the inboard trailing edge of the wing! There was an improved canopy too, which greatly increased the field of vision to the sides and rear. As a combat aeroplane, the F.8 had good handling characteristics, but the asymmetry problem still manifested itself. Pilots took little time converting to the new aircraft. The F.8 was good to handle from the ground crews' point of view too, being fairly simple in construction and having good access to all major components, including the engines, which themselves were easy to change.

On 4 September 1950 the Duncan Trophy, awarded annually to the day fighter squadron achieving the best all-weather flying record during the previous twelve months, was presented to the Tigers, largely as a legacy of the work they had done on high-level homing under Lapsley. Captain Klibbe USAF was posted in, the first in a long line of United States exchange officers to serve with the Squadron. Lord Tedder had started off the exchange scheme immediately after the war. It was worth its weight in gold to the RAF, fostering as it did knowledge of, belief in and trust between the two air forces. The same precepts apply to the NATO exchange system today. October was dominated by Exercise 'Emperor', but this turned out to be a disappointment to the Squadron, which had expected to work hard but actually worked very little, a direct result of the fact that the intensity of raids over the Eastern Sector was too small for the number of fighters involved—four squadrons of sixteen aircraft at Horsham as well as other squadrons at Honiley and West Raynham.

After 'Emperor', 257 and 263 Squadrons bade farewell to St Faith for their new base at Wattisham, leaving just 74 and 245 in residence and the latter to begin its pioneering work on air-to-air refuelling. 74 began its involvement with the 'many v. many' high-level interception exercises, carried out in conjunction with the AFDS at West Raynham. Neatishead and 74 did a great deal of work on this 'many v. many' concept, taking it up to the point where more aircraft were required than the Tigers could supply. The essence of the concept was that at heights of 40,000ft it was very difficult for pilots to pick out other formations visually (only in later years were the reasons for this fully understood and air crews taught how to use their eyes correctly) and the techniques for working with GCI at these altitudes required perfecting.

In a period of continuing involvement with trials, the Squadron also tested new engine relight procedures and participated in high-altitude firing. During one such firing sortie, Wilson's canopy blew off at 40,000ft. He managed to bring the aircraft back to base, having made an emergency descent to 6,000ft, and then, staying at that height to avoid a weather front for a considerable distance, he finally landed safely despite suffering from the effects of extreme cold. Wilson was unfortunate enough to experience a repeat of this within a matter of days, although this time at low level, when, after a few bursts of fire, his canopy shattered. He again landed safely at Horsham. But Bill Slater was not so fortunate. At the year's end he crashed and was killed as he was returning after a night cross-country exercise.

DACRE AND DUNCAN

Dave Cullen joined the Tigers in early 1951:

I, with about a dozen others who arrived at the same time, came straight from Cosford to be trained as an engine and airframe mechanic by the Squadron as all trades courses were full. A proper syllabus was set out—practical and theory—instructors provided and a classroom allocated in a spare office in 74's hangar. Making use of the facilities made available by the engineering workshops and the Station Education Officer, we were passed as proficient after weekly and monthly tests and a final examination. I was accordingly promoted to Aircraftman First Class and with it my pay rose to eight shillings a day as a regular. After a stint cleaning engine drip trays and sweeping the hangar floor, I went on to gain experience working with the seasoned staff on the Meteor F.8s and soon became familiar with such things as pre-flight, minor and intermediate inspections. With the Squadron came detachments, operational standbys and air exercises. Abiding memories are those of the smell of kerosene and the sudden blast of searing heat from the Meteor's jet pipes as, when taxying out from the concrete apron and turning sharply, it would catch you unawares. Then it would be a matter of turning your back on the aircraft and whipping up your overall collar as far up the neck as you could. And then there were moments such as that on the day most of the Squadron were airborne and the hangar almost devoid of aircraft when a couple of the lads decided to 'borrow' Squadron Leader de Inniss's two-stroke to do a quick burst around the building, weaving around the few remaining aircraft. What happened next was inevitable: drawn by the din created in a nearly empty hangar, our Chiefy rushed in from his office. It was of course a case of all hands to the sweeping brushes—double quick—before the Boss returned and spotted the criss-cross of tyre marks that in no way could be passed off as those of a Meteor! Talking of hangars reminds me of hangar doors, in particular the heavy armour plated design with a winding handle and the seemingly constant cry of 'Two Six . . .' that came from the NCO i/c servicing every time human power was needed to move aircraft or to open or close the hangar.

Late one evening, after night flying, a colleague and I went down to the unit. What we saw when we entered that ultra bright interior after emerging from the darkness outside could well have been the epitome of all Fighter Command stations and squadrons of the period. There, ranged against both sides of the hangar and precisely spaced, were the Squadron's Meteors, each with its polished drip tray and proudly displaying the tiger's head badge and black and yellow bars. The scene was a mass of wings, fuselages and tails from which was reflected a silvery sheen of breathtaking intensity. A stirring sight.

In this age of the anonymous Hardened Aircraft Shelter, these are evocative words indeed.

Participation in the 'many v. many' exercises continued into 1951. More emphasis was now being placed on rapid turnrounds between sorties, on reducing the reaction time for scrambles and on the constant practising of air-to-air firing and interceptions. Price became the envy of his colleagues when he had the distinction of being the first and only member of the Squadron to attack one of the massive USAF Convair B-36s during their training visit to Britain during January, but delight at this opportunity was tempered by the loss of Pilot Officer Corn, whose aircraft inexplicably crashed into the sea off the Dutch coast while he was on a navigation exercise. The Tigers spent most of February at Acklington for the annual APC, where the weather was poor and there were many non-flying days. Conversely, during March the Squadron broke all records for the Horsham Wing by attaining over 400 hours of flying for the month. Exercise 'Fabulous' continued, the Tigers having two one-week stints at readiness, with two aircraft at the end of the runway armed with live ammunition in contact with Sector Operations and ready to scramble in thirty seconds.

During June the Tigers' new aerobatic team was scheduled to appear at the Paris Salon. Initially under Bertie Beard's leadership, this was a team in the real sense of the word, and one which would carve a deserved reputation for itself over the following few years. After Paris the Tigers went on to fly at other European venues during the course of the year. But 74 lost its third pilot in six months when Turner unaccountably dropped out of a practice formation of four and crashed into Barton Broad on 19 June. There were considerable problems recovering his body from the water, and the rescue parties had to commandeer a number of pleasure boats on the Broad to do so. Turner was a National Service pilot and only had a few weeks of his service left to do.

Squadron Leader de Inniss was posted at the beginning of September and in his place came Major George W. Milholland of the US Air Force, attached to the RAF under the exchange scheme. He would prove to be an extremely popular Boss. One of his early claims to fame was that he was the first pilot at Horsham to wear a 'bone dome' on operations—the RAF were still doggedly soldiering on with the leather flying helmets. During his first few months as tenant of 74's hot seat he presided over the continuing training programme, night flying and participation in the *Daily Express* '50 Years of Flying' display at Hendon. The major exercise of the year was 'Pinnacle' in late September. Shortly afterwards the Squadron discovered that it had been chosen to carry out yet another trial in which the main aim was to determine the maximum aircraft utilization possible with the numbers of pilots and ground crews available—almost a time and motion study, in conjunction with the Scientific Advisory Branch of the Air Ministry whose main task was the accurate recording for statistical purposes of all the problems which confronted the running of a jet fighter squadron. Following the delivery of further Meteor F.8s, some aircraft were camouflaged for trials purposes. Up to this time the F.8 had retained the overall silver scheme of the F.4, but the success of the camouflaging saw all Squadron aircraft later reverting to dark green and medium sea grey paintwork with individual codes in yellow on the fin and in black on the nosewheel door and the Squadron crest on the nacelles.

On a series of bright and brilliant midwinter days at the beginning of 1952, 74 was able to devote time to the continuing series of interceptions of high-flying B-29s and Washingtons, but the early promise of uninterrupted flying soon disappeared as the English winter once again took its predictable course. February was a foggy month, and 74 failed to reach its flying target. A pilot shortage did not help, although, on the positive side, aircraft serviceability greatly improved. As George Milholland said a little bitterly at the time:

> The continuous requirement for the small number of assigned pilots to participate in secondary duties places an additional limitation on the amount of flying possible. Squadron commanders are responsible for training pilots and maintaining their proficiency at a high level. However, nearly every other activity now takes precedence over flying duties.

The spring heralded better weather, and during April five hundred hours were flown. Interception work against Belgian Meteors was indicative of the continuing and indeed increasing involvement with European air forces as far as training was concerned. A sustained period of preparation for the APC continued during June, the Squadron obviously bent on coming away from Acklington with top marks and a real chance of the Dacre Trophy (awarded to the squadron with the highest scores in air-to-air drogue firing), and to this end Milholland flew dual sorties in the T.7 in an attempt to improve some of the lower-averaged pilots. The APC finally came on 14 July and lasted for three weeks. All the hard work and long hours of practice paid off, for the Squadron achieved the scores that ultimately enabled it to win! By this time the Squadron already knew that it had won the Duncan Trophy for the second time in three years as well (2 Squadron having stepped in and taken it in 1951). So, despite Milholland's misgivings about 74's being unnecessarily diverted from its task, operational efficiency and expertise had demonstrably not been compromised.

The exigencies of Acklington over, it was the impending major autumn exercises that again influenced Squadron operations, and both flying and servicing were directed towards maintaining 74's peak of efficiency for the first two weeks in October. Telescramble equipment had been installed on the ORPs in readiness for the exercises, and the Tigers were the first to test it on 16 September. The Battle of Britain Open Day at St Faith followed four days later, and the highlight for many was the interception of four USAF B-45 Tornados over the airfield during a mock attack. 74 flew formations under the clear blue skies, and Beard (who would shortly be posted on to command 19 Squadron) gave an inspired individual display. Bertie Beard had enjoyed at least one memorable incident whilst with 74—returning from a sortie with both engines trailing thick black smoke and landing wheels-up on the grass beside the runway. The aircraft was liberally doused by the Fire Section and later lifted by crane and taken to the hangar, where inspection revealed scarcely a dent! Engines attended to, it was back on the line within days.

Exercise 'Ardent' was planned in the customary three phases and 74 was involved in the first and last. Both these were at weekends, and they included dawn-to-dusk operations against a variety of targets ranging from bomber streams to Vampire Rats. It was during 'Ardent' that one pilot filed an operations report where the height of intercept read 'nine feet'. When this was queried, the pilot concerned responded with: 'I pulled up to go over a hedge!' As the year came to an end, a continuing modifications workload finally caught up with the engineers which necessitated a restriction in flying as aircraft became unserviceable. What flying was done resulted in a nasty incident for Alan Colman, who was No 2 in a section of four at 27,000ft on a cine exercise: his canopy shattered around him in a manner similar to the two incidents the previous year. He landed safely and on this occasion the cause was discovered—a blocked air vent, which was traced black to Glosters. A plug of Bostik which had carelessly not been cleared up by one of the manufacturer's employees had almost caused a disaster.

ACCOMPLISHING THE TASK

Sergeant Pilot Mercer made an inauspicious start to the New Year while engaged in a Rats and Terriers exercise when a bird struck the starboard mainplane and caused considerable damage, necessitating a wing change. Later the same month his colleague Sergeant McCue was acting as safety pilot for Pilot Officer Morter, took over the controls at 400ft for a GCA, touched down on the runway, rolled and started an overshoot. The aircraft lifted off the ground and McCue selected 'undercarriage up', but the Meteor sank back for a fraction of a second. An ominous grating sound and a shower of sparks spelt potential disaster, but the aircraft struggled into the air again. McCue climbed to 6,000ft, tested the Meteor for undercarriage and flap operations and also to judge whether its stalling speed had been affected. He found no indication of a problem and landed successfully. The ventral tank had borne the brunt of the impact and had indeed split open. Fuselage ribs had also been distorted and the flaps and the starboard engine nacelle damaged.

February 1953 will long be remembered by the residents of Norfolk, Suffolk, Essex and beyond for the tragic East Coast floods which inundated mile upon mile of the countryside, with considerable loss of life. Horsham St Faith immediately committed men to the disaster areas until, by 7 February, every available man was engaged in helping with the repair of the broken sea defences—urgent work, as more high tides were due and it was feared that the sea would break through once again. The operation, appropriately codenamed 'Canute', was carried out in conjunction with the Army and other RAF units. The defences held, and by the 16th St Faith personnel had been withdrawn, so that the station could resume flying. Towards the end of the month, seven days of clear skies and sun allowed superlative airborne views of the massive area that had been flooded but, whilst spectacular, they were tempered by the knowledge that the clearing up operation by the civil authorities would take many months and that, whilst the disaster had been faced with considerable stoicism by those whose homes, and indeed lives, had been devastated, it would take far longer to return to any semblance of normality.

Nairn enlivened operations at Horsham when he made the mistake of starting up with a petrol bowser behind his starboard engine, spilt fuel on the ground beneath the bowser immediately bursting into flames. The Fire Section were very quick to react, and although the cab was wrecked the tank itself mercifully did not catch fire and explode. Australian Geoff Boord arrived on an exchange, taking the place of Chunky Ball, who went to serve in Korea with the RAAF for a few months. Another Tiger, Murphy, went to the United States to convert to the F-86 and then on to Korea as a USAF exchange officer. Considerable excitement was engendered amongst Tiger pilots when the Defence White Paper for 1953 contained news that 74 would be re-equipping on the Supermarine Swift at 'some time in the future' when the aircraft's development was complete. In the event, 56 Squadron were to receive the new aircraft instead and 74's initial disappointment at being seemingly passed over turned to relief when the Swift proved itself to be a disaster operationally. For the moment, then, the faithful Meteor remained the Tigers' charge, and during March they took it to Jever in Germany on a visit to the 2nd TAF. On their return Sir Basil Embry, C-in-C Fighter Command, presented the

Dacre Trophy to the Squadron (as so often happens, the presentation took place months after the actual winning!). It was a proud squadron that was able to display both the Dacre and Duncan Trophies at the presentation dinner.

The year 1953 really was a great one for ceremonial, starting with the Squadron's participation in a flypast over Manchester to celebrate the RAF's 35th birthday. 74 and 245 next joined their former St Faith colleagues (257 and 263 Squadrons) at Wattisham to practice for the Coronation Flypast that June, which was dogged by the poor conditions that seemed to accompany most London flypasts in those days. A month later the Tigers sent twelve aircraft to the Royal Review at Odiham, which with 639 aircraft in the air and 318 on static display proved to be a masterpiece of planning. But in the meantime there had been two fatal accidents. Tacchi crashed and was killed at RAF Leconfield whilst on a course there, and then Margetts, who had been with 74 for barely a fortnight, was killed when he hit the ground during an attack on a disused airfield. Lloyd was rather more fortunate when he caught his leader's jetwash during a formation landing and dug his wing tip into the ground. Lloyd survived but his aircraft's mainplane was badly damaged.

During April 1953, 660 hours were flown, with an average of just thirteen airframes available for use throughout the month. The price paid for such an achievement was that the ground crews were on duty $10\frac{1}{2}$ hours a day for twenty-seven days. George Milholland was concerned: three days off was too few, and $10\frac{1}{2}$ hours a day was too much. The problem was the continuing inability of engineering staff to keep up with the constant modification instructions issued in respect of the F.8s. 'If sixteen aircraft could be made available, the flying task could be achieved by working normal duty hours,' recorded the Tigers' Boss wistfully. The summer months continued to be busy, and during Exercise 'Momentum' in August everyone lived from dawn to dusk in tents at the Wood Farm dispersal at St Faith. A large marquee was used as a Mess, and mobile kitchens were used by the cooks to feed the men. Neil Robertson:

The large-scale summer exercises invariably seemed to have their share of wet overcast days. On one particular day I remember that we were grounded because of zero-zero conditions and then we were unceremoniously put out of action by a Dutch Thunderjet which loomed out of the murk at nought feet much to our embarrassment!

Horsham St Faith lost its Wing Commander, R. D. Yule, during rehearsals for the Battle of Britain Flypast over London when on 11 September he and a Meteor from 245 Squadron collided. In the immediate aftermath of the accident, Milholland took over the duties of Wing Commander Flying at Horsham and Joe Maddison assumed temporary command of 74. A crowd of 30,000 attended the Horsham St Faith Open Day, during which 74 despatched pilots to other venues too. Rus Ward went to Coningsby and Geoff Boord to North Luffenham to give solo demonstrations. Sadly, Ward became the Squadron's third fatality in

1953 when his aircraft disintegrated during a fast run over the airfield shortly after take-off. All Meteors were grounded as a consequence, and problems caused by skin wrinkling were detected, although it was not suggested these had contributed directly to Ward's crash.

An American Marine joined 74 as part of the exchange programme during September—Captain Hal Berge, who had been flying Grumman Panthers from a carrier off Korea. Also joining the Squadron was Dennis Brennan:

The Tigers were my first-choice squadron after OCU. Horsham was certainly the showpiece of RAF Fighter Command, and in many respects 74 was the showpiece squadron. A tremendous spirit of teamwork was prevalent when I joined, and everyone was extremely aware of the Squadron's past and its traditions. Everyone passionately believed that the Tigers were the best in the RAF and worked hard to maintain that position.

Flying was regular and involved all sorts of regimes:

All take-offs were in formation. Battle formation exercises were regularly flown. Tail-chasing featured often; aerobatics were practised; air-to-ground and air-to-air firing formed a large part of Squadron ops, with the banner 'towline' being along the coast from Yarmouth to Blakeney Point. Interceptions continued to be another major part of the training programme. Wing tanks were rarely fitted as they caused considerable deterioration in performance, although without them endurance was still a reasonable sixty minutes. Indeed, once we had taken off and climbed to operational levels, the remaining fuel was such that the Meteor was at an ideal fighting weight. Army co-operation work was regularly participated in. Low flying was the essence here, 250 feet minimum officially, but Meteors used to return with twigs and leaves from tree tops adorning them! Other disciplines practised were within the framework of exercises—base exercises, Group exercises and full-scale air defence exercises. It sometimes seemed as if there was an exercise on almost every week and we were all well versed in the three states of readiness —Hangar 30 minutes, ASP 10 minutes and ORP 2 minutes. RAF-issue bikes (complete with roundel on the rear mudguard) were always used to get to the flight line from the crew room and were often left in vulnerable positions with pilots regularly returning from sorties to find that their steeds had been flattened by fuel bowsers!

Overall, it is true to say that, as a Flying Officer earning the princely sum of £32 a month, I was very happy with my lot!

Neil Robertson remembers his year with the Tigers fondly too:

This was my apprenticeship as a pilot—fresh and green. There was a lot of experience on 74 then—ex-World War 2, Korea etc. I learned in a good school. Joe Maddison was my mentor as my Flight Commander. He, and many other Tigers, I would have followed anywhere, and did, when we lurched into the overcast at 400ft and emerged at 30,000ft in a section of four. I learned a lot and fast. Two other stalwarts were Pickering and Wickman, known to us all as Pickens and Wickens—public school boys like Wayne and Radford. Grand chaps all.

Squadron rivalry as far as we and 245 were concerned was intense, and pranks and jokes were for ever being perpetrated by one side or the other. I remember them taking up temporary residence in our hangar with an adjoining crew room. On our side was the squadron crest of a tiger's head and 'I Fear No Man'. On the reverse side of the door was a similar plaque of a tiger's backside with 'No Man Fears Me'. On another occasion, 245 Squadron launched an attack on our hangar walls and crests with white paint and uncomplimentary signs! This called for retaliation, and it was not too long before the lawns before 245's hangars withered and died in places so that from the air the figures '74' stood out bright and green against a yellow background!

The popular George Milholland was wined and dined prior to his return to the USA at the end of a very fruitful exchange posting. His place as CO was taken by Squadron Leader Bill Johnson DFC, with Ian Worby taking B Flight and Joe Maddison resuming command of A Flight. The Armament Practice Camp for 1953 took place in December, and 74 approached it with some confidence. This was Dennis Brennan's first of three APCs with the Tigers, and on this occasion he averaged seven per cent:

> Acklington had its own towing flight of Meteor F.8s. There were always two squadrons at the camp at the same time, which served to enhance the competitive edge when it came to firing. Acklington also strengthened the spirit of teamwork which existed within squadrons. It was a much-looked-forward-to three weeks of satisfying hard work. But tragically the 1953 camp was marred by the death of five armourers of the Squadron in an Anson crash at RAF Newton. Another was seriously injured.

AGEING METEORS

The emphasis during the first two months of 1954 was placed on the tactical training of the Squadron's new, young pilots. This was put to the test when the Tigers climbed from their beds at 0400 on 1 March to participate in the week-long Exercise 'Magnaflux', only to be greeted by another season of deep snow which had settled overnight and a temperature that was so low that the snow froze solid. The cold spell was doubly unwelcome as the Squadron was operating from a tented dispersal again—which became extremely uncomfortable. By contrast, excellent April and May weather enabled a great deal of flying to take place after paintbrushes and brooms had replaced joysticks and throttles in anticipation of the AOC's inspection. And the first two days of the month saw the majority of the pilots, with feet firmly on the ground, dodging the arm of the law in the escape and evasion Exercise 'Rabbit Trek'. The summer Exercise 'Dividend', plagued by low stratus and rain, confirmed what the Squadron already knew—that the Meteor's performance was by this time becoming decidedly outclassed and that although Bomber Command's Canberras could occasionally be caught, all too often they sailed past at 40,000ft while the Meteors were still struggling to get to their level. Encounters with Canadian or USAF F-86s were even more depressing, and the Tigers' eyes were turning more and more in the direction of the developing Hawker Hunter, which had made its début during 'Dividend' in the hands of the Central Fighter Establishment.

Captain Walt Panchesan USMC was welcomed to the Squadron to replace Hal Berge in August. Pancho was a typical American, always smoking (or chewing) a big cigar which he would never relinquish until he was strapped into his Meteor and then only handing it over to his crew man with the instruction 'Keep hold of this until I return'. Also welcomed was Sergeant Bernie McParlin, a significant Tiger as he was the last NCO pilot to join the Squadron. Bernie remembers his first few weeks vividly:

I was 'converted' to the Meteor by Bill Farrer, not having flown the type for three years, and then flew my final acceptance check with Joe Maddison. As an NCO pilot, I soon came to appreciate the Tigers' way of doing things. The Boss was 'sir', but everyone else tended to be on Christian-name terms whatever their rank whilst within the Squadron, a policy which led to a seemingly relaxed approach but the benefits of which included the encouragement of frank and open discussion on all matters flying or otherwise. Serving with the Tigers, you led by ability; and it was not unusual to find a four-ship with the Squadron Commander or a Flight Commander in its number led by a Flight Sergeant.

By this time all 74's Meteors were having their canopies replaced with the new bubble type which allowed for a greatly improved field of vision to the sides and the rear. The aircraft were also being repainted in a new day fighter camouflage scheme on the instructions of Fighter Command. Although many initially looked on the new colour scheme with disfavour, it was considered to be operationally advisable and in fact provided an even better backcloth for 74's tiger stripes than the previous scheme had done! There was one exception, Aircraft 'M' had had an experimental finish applied, and the standard cellulose finish of the new camouflage would not stick to it. Even the roundels flaked off, and for a while 'M' was the most conspicuous Meteor at St Faith. The problem was eventually solved by sandblasting the experimental paintwork off.

Late summer and autumn were spent in long-term preparation for the forthcoming APC. As was usual in these periods of intense activity, the Squadron's averages increased as the days went by, but, as Bill Johnson reported, 'whilst averages are improving, they will have to improve even more if the Squadron is to retain the Dacre Trophy'. He also took the opportunity to remark again that the F.8 was now showing signs of age as well as incapability. Indeed, there was growing frustration on the part of the Squadron as a whole at the fact that they were being passed by as far as re-equipment was concerned. Fighter Command was rapidly becoming swept-winged, but there was still no word of the Tigers' relinquishing their Meteors.

Little could be done at APC in February 1955 because of the recurring problem, heavy snow. The aircraft had no sooner been shut down after their arrival than they were armed up, the radios recrystallized, and flown off for gun tests prior to starting the flying programme. Then it started. The Station Commander, who took to riding his horse to get around the camp during the bad weather, had everybody out on the runways and taxiways with spade and shovel from time to time but soon realized that they were fighting a losing battle. Crews retired to their cold and bleak wooden barracks. After two weeks the weather cleared again and each pilot fired a thousand rounds. The average 19.01 per cent (compared with the Fighter Command average of 13.2) was the highest ever recorded, but this was beaten by the narrowest of margins by another squadron later in the year and so the Dacre Trophy was lost.

During the summer of 1955, 245 Squadron moved *en bloc* to Stradishall, leaving 74 as the sole permanent incumbents of St Faith. The Tigers moved all their own equipment, aircraft and belongings into the hangar 245 had vacated, completely obliterating that squadron's markings and superimposing the tiger's head where necessary! Re-equipment gripes aside, morale on the Squadron was good and the men were proud of the fact that they were now the only day fighter squadron in their Sector. The Tigers' aerobatic team for the year (Johnson, Martin, Pickering and Walpole) rehearsed almost daily in readiness for their assigned display commitments. Panchesan left on 28 July and in his place came the most famous of 74's exchange officers, Captain Chuck Sewell USMC, a native of Fort Worth who had flown ninety-seven missions in Korea. Boz Robinson:

> He was a typical gung-ho Texan, a go-getter in every sense of the word, who lived for air-to-air firing, and a larger-than-life character who could fit in anywhere. He proved himself to be a fine leader of men, was extremely popular and we all very quickly warmed to him.

In later years Chuck became Chief Test Pilot for the Grumman Corporation and, sadly, was killed on 4 August 1986 whilst flying a TBM Avenger which he was ferrying for a friend from a small field in Connecticut to Florida.

August produced seven hundred hours in the air. The Tigers displayed regularly and continued with their training, once again concentrating on improving still further the air-to-air averages and then with the coming Exercise 'Beware' in mind. 74 entered the fray with continuing apprehension as to the capabilities of their aircraft in the contemporary environment, but they did successfully achieve a limited number of interceptions which did something to maintain some confidence in the F.8. Unfortunately, however, the Squadron spent many hours on standby and all too few hours in the air, largely because Sector Controllers preferred to use the Hunters from the DFLS which had been detached to St Faith for the exercise. If the Tigers were aware of the inequalities between their Meteors and the attacking Canberras, they were even more conscious of the superior performance of the visiting Hunters which they so dearly wanted to be flying themselves. There was another exericse later in the year—'Sunbeam'—in which a force of four hundred attacking aircraft (USAF B-47s, B-66s and F-100s and Belgian and Dutch F-84s, together with CF-100s and F-86s of the RCAF and three Vulcans of 617 Squadron) were ranged against Fighter Command's Hunters, Javelins and Meteors. The exercise also included Bloodhounds from North Coates, but a major deficiency which was increasingly causing concern was the absence of air-to-air missiles with which to equip the defending aircraft.

At Christmas the annual party was held in the hangar and the Tiger's Blood rum punch concocted from such fine brands as those of the houses of Fernandes and Siegert (courtesy of their West Indian friends who once again donated £100 to Squadron funds) was as popular as ever. There was talk from time to time of the Tigers taking a detachment of aircraft across to Trinidad and at one stage a short list was drawn up of pilots who would actually take part. Unfortunately the deployment, which would have taken the Tigers along the northern route via Scotland, Iceland, Greenland and Newfoundland and down the eastern seaboard to the West Indies—thus making their aircraft amongst the most travelled of RAF Meteors—never materialized.

Bill Johnson left the Squadron in mid-January 1956 and his place was taken by Squadron Leader Keith Haselwood. He was a gentle giant of a man who, while he may not have been the world's best aviator, was a first class CO. As he arrived, a new rumour that the Squadron was shortly to convert to the night fighter role was circulating. During March contractors were busy on Horsham's runways and 74 moved over to Coltishall for a few days, where they spent much of their time practising GCAs (with the equipment Coltishall had but Horsham lacked) in simulated conditions of bad weather and poor visibility. Shortly afterwards A Flight, commanded by John Granville White, won the Morse Trophy, which was presented every six months to the squadron Flight with the best scores in air-to-air firing. At the end of April the AOC approved another Tigers display team for the season in which the places were taken by Keith Haselwood, Brian Walpole, Chuck Sewell, Duncan Allison and, later, replacing Walpole, Dick Lewis. The team won the Fighter Command Inter-Squadron Meteor Formation Aerobatic Competition and ironically, in a year of still diminishing numbers of squadrons still flying the day Meteor, became the official display team for Fighter Command. It is perhaps significant that 74 were to be upstaged somewhat when Princess Margaret came to Horsham St Faith on an official visit. 43 Squadron came down from their Scottish base and displayed for her, leaving the Tigers on the sidelines. 43 flew Hunters. However, when the Tigers participated in Exercise 'Stronghold' in September (during which they acquitted themselves very well), little did they realize that this would be the last occasion on which they would be asked to commit Meteors against massed invading forces.

November was notable for the restriction in flying designed to conserve fuel in the wake of the Suez Crisis. Chuck Sewell turned in an individual record of 66.7 per cent amongst an overall Squadron average of 38.6 on air-to-air firing, but the record flag for this session was that achieved by the quartet of McParlin, Rayner, Hunt and Taylor, who averaged 39.2 per cent on one shoot. This was a fitting end to a year in which the air-to-air scores achieved by the Squadron continued to rise. The biggest relief of the year was the news that the threatened change to the all-weather and night role had been cancelled and that 74 was to remain the only day fighter unit in the Group. The best news of all was that the Tigers were at long last to re-equip with Hunter F. Mk 4s. The fact that the aircraft were to be second-hand did not matter at all.

CHAPTER 8

Tiger Hunters

I T IS A SAD IRONY that, at the very time 74 were to begin their conversion to the Hunter, Squadron life should be marred by the deaths of two Tigers in a Meteor mid-air collision. The pilots concerned were Jock Baillie and Wally Taylor, who had been engaged in mock dogfights, their aircraft coming down a few hundred yards apart and scattering wreckage amongst farm workers in the fields. Two days later a working party from HQ Fighter Command arrived to give instruction to the ground crews on the Hunter, and six pilots went down to Chivenor for a three-day course on the type. Other pilots followed throughout the month. Bernie McParlin flew Keith Haselwood up to Leuchars in the T.7 to collect the Squadron's first ex-111 Squadron Hunter F. Mk 4 on 16 January; three more from Leuchars followed shortly afterwards, and three from Odiham at the end of the month. The programme accelerated during February as Meteor operations wound down, until, on 12 February, the Squadron was withdrawn from the line and pilot conversion could begin in earnest. Chuck Sewell had been the first to go solo, pleased to have had the opportunity of flying the type before his posting came to an end a few weeks later, and the subsequent rate of conversion was governed only by the number of aircraft available. By the end of February seventeen aircraft had been delivered but, with ground crews unfamiliar with the type and having a large number of acceptance checks and modifications to carry out as they arrived, only six of these were initially available for flying.

Whilst the pilots praised the qualities of the Hunter F.4, the ground crews (which would shortly include the first girls to join the Squadron) were often not so ready to do so as the aircraft did have a few idiosyncrasies which did not endear it to them. Engine changes necessitated the removal of the rear fuselage, and ailerons tended to be a problem as they were only thin-skinned and pop-riveted on to the ribs. Refuelling was very difficult because of the thin wings. The Hunters had to be watched when being started up, too, as sometimes they would 'wet start', with excess fuel spilling from the jetpipe and the exhaust setting fire to it. Ground crews would use sheets of asbestos in an effort to shield the rear ends of the aircraft from the effects of these fires.

The Tigers' conversion to type was completed by the end of March and the Squadron reassumed its operational role on the 25th when it rejoined the line after just $5\frac{1}{2}$ weeks. On individual sorties, emergency procedures were practised assiduously, including those following engine flame-out —which proved to be particularly useful for Boz Robinson:

All our second-hand Hunters made funny noises! We did not really know what they were, although we did not realize that they were signs of age and wear and should not have been there at all. WV269 made such noises. I was in a battle pair with Tony Dean over Cambridge at 35,000ft when there was an enormous bang and the aircraft started to vibrate. Almost instinctively I shut the engine down, which stopped all the bangs and thumps. Full of the confidence of youth, I decided to take the aircraft home. Everything was fine until I turned on to finals at Horsham and found I was too high. I applied full opposite rudder and full aileron, so much so that the aircraft almost rolled over on to its back (at which point those watching on the airfield below doffed their caps!), but it had the desired effect and I lost height quite dramatically! I put it down on the runway rather fast at about 180 knots but the brakes worked well and I stopped the Hunter before the runway's end and turned off on to the ORP, relieved and pleased at getting down safely. But, instead of congratulations, I was told off for not inserting the pin in the ejection seat when I left the aircraft!

Robinson was subsequently awarded a Green Endorsement and the Hunter was re-engined and was soon flying again.

Eight Hunters left Horsham for Chièvres on 10 May on an exchange with the Belgian Air Force, but before they did so Alex Kerr from Bertram Mills' Circus brought his tiger, Begum, to the Squadron, to be photographed with men and aircraft. There were certainly some reservations about this event, but on the day both tiger and men behaved well! Keith Haselwood was told by Alex to give Begum a sharp rap over the ears with a whip if she misbehaved! The Boss was understandably relieved that he had no need to resort to such measures, and in retrospect the resultant pictures were considered to be well worth the bravado! Begum was adopted as the Squadron's mascot, and at the end of the year 74 were invited to Olympia to see Begum perform. Sadly, she was to die a few weeks later.

During Exercise 'Vigilant', held between 25 and 27 May, the famous 'Horsham Triple' occurred. At dawn on the first day, Boz Robinson and Tony Hilton were scrambled. One of the Hunter 4's great weaknesses was that it was underpowered, and at height and in a tight turn the engine would tend to surge. This is exactly what happened to Tony over the North Sea. He shut the engine down and set course for a return to Horsham, not realizing that, with the reduction in his angle of attack and the reduced power setting he had applied, he did have a perfectly serviceable engine. Meanwhile a Javelin of 141 Squadron, which was based at St Faith for the duration of 'Vigilant', had been scrambled too. It was fitted with two 'bosom' tanks, and as it started to move the front attachment of one of them failed, allowing the tank to swing down about its rear mounting. Because of the large delta wing the tank failure was hidden from the sight of the crew, and the pilot taxied on, unaware of the problem, pushing the nose of the tank along the ground, the noise unnoticed because of the scream of the engines. The rough surface of the taxiway quickly wore a hole in the tank, there were sparks and the fuel caught fire but mercifully did not explode. The Javelin continued to taxi, trailing flame and black smoke.

Meanwhile Tony Davies in another Tiger Hunter was in the process of taking off when he heard Air Traffic's urgent call—'You are on fire!'—on the station frequency. Thinking the warning was directed at him, Davies aborted the take-off and overshot the runway, smashed through the fence on the edge of the airfield, skimmed across the main road which runs alongside its western boundary and pancaked in a ploughed field opposite with the aircraft's tail overhanging the grass verge. Fortunately there was no public traffic about at the time. The Station's emergency crews roared off towards the incident, although thankfully Davies had escaped unscathed. The shouted 'on fire' message was also heard by Tony Hilton, and he thought the message was directed at *him*. He decided to get down as quickly as he could, turned in short, blew the wheels down and without ceremony force-landed across the airfield. He put the Hunter down hard. It bounced and broke up, the impact fracturing the fuselage behind the cockpit and simultaneously firing the primary charge of the ejection seat. As he shot upwards, his elbow partly severed in the process, the aircraft continued to slide along the ground. The wing sliced through an airmen's hut, providentially missing all the occupants. It went on to demolish several bicycles. Tony Hilton's parachute had deployed meanwhile and he floated back to earth, landing in front of the bemused ambulance and fire crews who were rushing to the assistance of Tony Davies.

The Javelin pilot watched all this going on, saw red Very flares being fired and people jumping up and down gesticulating but still did not associate the activity with anything that was happening to his aircraft. He continued to taxi, but by now the navigator was complaining about feeling hot. The pilot confirmed that the temperature control was at 'full cool' but then noticed an orange tinge to the edges of the canopy. Realization dawned and the crew hastily evacuated, climbing along the nose and dropping the fourteen feet to the ground. The only injury sustained was to the pilot's feet 'through landing in the running position'. The aircraft burned, without exploding, to a pile of ash, leaving a conspicuous delta outline on the ground. Horsham St Faith was closed for two hours.

Boz Robinson could not believe what he saw:

When I returned to St Faith there was the most extraordinary sight of smoke, wreckage and devastation. There were still a lot of us in the air in our exercise-marked, white-finned Hunters. We had all found plenty of targets and had pushed our fuel to the absolute limits. Coltishall was out of action: its runways were being resurfaced and we could get nothing out of a shell shocked ATC at St Faith so we went to West Raynham, praying that our fuel would last, but found that here Air Traffic were totally preoccupied with something like sixteen aircraft waiting to land. The fuel situation demanded that we find a suitable gap amongst the Meteors, Meteor night fighters, Javelins and Hunters and get down. Having landed, it was literally a case of steering amongst aircraft that had rolled to a halt out of fuel.

Four hundred and fifty raiding aircraft, V-Bombers included, were ranged against the defences of Fighter Command during 'Vigilant'. The Tigers achieved a high interception rate during the exercise and they were particularly pleased with a turnround time of twelve minutes for each aircraft under the stringent conditions imposed. Normal practice was for two aircraft to be constantly on standby to scramble or to replace those aircraft already in the air and whose fuel was getting low. Based squadrons would take turns at filling this very short notice alert. For those taking the opportunity of resting from the busy schedule imposed by the exercise, disturbance would come again all too soon:

> And so it came to pass, as the first hour before the night approacheth, into the land of Norfolk an airman goeth forth to the rooms of the birdmen and he speaketh unto each saying 'Verily, arise and don thy garments and go forth to the gathering place for the Boss hath decreed that it shall be thus'. The birdmen, staring and muttering, saith that his mother hath not morals and his father knoweth him not and they arise and seek out their friends and go forth . . .

After the exercise, an air-to-air firing programme started on the Trimingham ranges off the north Norfolk coast. This was the Tigers' first firing since they had re-equipped with the Hunter, and they found that the technique differed considerably from that employed with the Meteor. The scores were not initially so high, but they improved considerably as the programme progressed. In September, 74 was detached to Aldergrove for the NATO Exercise 'Strikeback', at the end of which the Squadron set a speed record for the return to St Faith. Keith Haselwood and Duncan Allison completed the journey in 28 minutes at an average speed of 724mph over the 338 miles, somewhat faster than the 717.5mph set in a Hunter by Squadron Leader R. L. Topp on a flight between Farnborough and Edinburgh two years earlier. Over the ensuing years the Tigers were to set their sights successfully on other speed records both in Britain and abroad.

Keith Haselwood left during October and his replacement was Squadron Leader Chris Curtis. Almost immediately it was learned that 74 was to relinquish its Hunter 4s in favour of the F. Mk 6, a far superior aircraft, particularly in terms of available power. The aircraft the Tigers received were amongst the last examples of the type to be bought by the RAF, although for a while the Squadron was equipped with a complete cross-section of Hunter modification states, ranging from the earliest F. Mk 4 to the latest F. Mk 6. Chris Curtis and his Flight Commanders were concerned at this as the mixture was, they felt, conducive to accidents.

There were shades of things to come when 74 hosted the 79th Fighter Bomber Squadron from USAF Woodbridge. Invitations had been issued to the Americans after Boz Robinson and his colleagues had seen an F-86 at Sculthorpe the previous year with a tiger's head emblazoned on its fin. Robinson recalls the memory:

We were highly incensed at the time as we thought that *we* were the only Tiger Squadron. We went back to St Faith and told Haselwood about this American squadron which was using *our* emblem. His immediate reaction was to invite them to a Dining-In Night—which they accepted, but unfortunately after Keith had left us. This was without doubt the first of the Tiger Meets.

The weather during March 1958 was particularly severe, a blizzard blowing on the first day of spring, but, in spite of the intense cold, during the rest of the month flying conditions were very good and over five hundred hours were clocked up—the best month so far on Hunters. Daily flying included dogfighting—one v. one and two v. two—which was legal if briefed (that is not to say that it did not happen otherwise!) and would start at high level and finish at a minimum of 5,000ft. Chris Curtis and later Pete Carr, together with the USAF's Jack Martin (the latest American exchange officer), spent a lot of time working on tactics and impressed the Day Fighter Leader School with some of the results! The 'sliding attack', for example, was evolved for use against the Russian 'Bears' and 'Bisons' with their rearward-facing guns. It was discovered that there was a blind spot which the bombers' guns could not reach without damaging their own tails, so the attacking aircraft would position itself 2,000yds ahead and to one side of the aircraft, flying in the same direction. It would turn in twenty degrees and drift towards it in its blind spot, opening fire at two to three hundred yards, raking the wing with fire from the Aden gun. The tactic, practised frequently in Hunter v. Hunter exercises, was considered far preferable to creeping up behind the enemy in the vulnerable position.

Exercises as the year progressed included 'Halyard' (which had succeeded 'Fabulous') and the combined Army, Navy and Air Force 'Parahandy'. The latter was particularly enjoyable, as Robinson remembers:

It involved simulated attacks against the Royal Navy off the East Coast. It all happened at low level, during the course of which they fired break-up shot in opposite sectors so that we actually had flak appearing in the sky, which was great fun!

The year 1958 also saw the introduction of the long-running series of 'Kingpin' air defence exercises. Then the Squadron was placed on short-notice alert for transfer overseas as a direct result of the increased tension in Lebanon and were on standby to fly to Cyprus as part of the RAF's strategy of rapid reinforcement of its overseas bases. But in the meantime 74 was to lose another pilot. On 21 August a report came in that Nick Tester was missing and almost simultaneously that an aircraft had been seen to crash into the sea off the Norfolk coast. A full air and sea search was initiated, in what was one of the biggest rescue operations mounted locally for many years. Tester's colleagues themselves flew until dusk, but apart from oil slicks nothing was sighted. Diving operations were subsequently started at the marked position of one of the slicks but, again, nothing was found. Nick Tester, who had been practising interceptions with two other Hunters, was presumed killed.

FROM CYPRUS TO COLTISHALL

The Tigers finally moved to Cyprus on 8 September, at a time when almost half the RAF's day fighter force was in the volatile Middle East. They transited to Nicosia via Malta, the ground party being flown out by Beverley transports. After the Squadron had settled in (not without difficulty, for, with three others already in residence, the accommodation problem was acute and many personnel had to resort to tents), based transport was commandeered and painted up with tiger stripes and flying began—a twelve-day cycle comprising four days on battle flight, four days on Squadron training, three days on stand-down and one day 'at the Squadron Commander's disposal'. On one particular exercise, 'Dragon', the squadrons were divided into two sides, 'attackers' and 'defenders', and 74 were assigned to the latter. The attackers took off at dawn to position themselves, ready to 'attack' Nicosia at various levels and in different formations from different directions.

The first 'attack' was picked up on radar and 74 were scrambled. Once the incoming aircraft had been intercepted, a series of 'dogfights' developed over the base with apparently no height or speed restrictions in evidence to the watching ground crews. They saw one Hunter pursue an 'attacking' aircraft at tree-top height, trying even at that stage to get below his adversary. Suddenly disappearing from view, the 'attacker' reappeared and climbed away, but 74's aircraft did not immediately show itself. Fearful that he had crashed but having heard no explosion, the spectators raised a cheer of relief when it eventually came into view, emerging with wire embedded firmly in its radome—wire which had also travelled across the top of the cockpit and sliced the aerial off the spine of the aircraft and then sawn through the tail as far as one of the main spars. When the aircraft landed, wire was also found embedded in one of the wing tank pylons!

Other Squadron training continued, with a large number of low-level strike sorties often using 2in rockets as well as the Aden gun. Army co-operation work was always interesting, and other disciplines practised included air-to-air firing on the Larnaka range. Later in October, 74 provided aircraft to protect a daily supply convoy travelling between Famagusta and the GCA station at Cape Greco. This convoy had suffered many ambushes by Eoka terrorists. Arthur Bennett:

> We flew figures of eight at one hundred feet as slowly as possible just ahead of the convoy, with the aim of spotting anyone who might be setting up an ambush. As it happened, a suspect was caught on the very first morning, having been seen by Chris Curtis. That was the only incident, and the flights were discontinued after two or three days anyway as they were potentially quite hazardous, both from the point of view of presenting an easy target for ground fire as well as the risks of flying low and slow.

A detachment of five aircraft went to El Adem for four days:

> This was also interesting as it provided a useful opportunity to do some low flying over the Libyan desert. However, the main purpose of the detachment

was to deter the Egyptians from sending I1-28 Beagle reconnaissance flights over Libyan territory. In the event we did have one scramble and interception, but the target turned out to be a civilian aircraft of the I1-14 type. The pilot was most unhappy about the interception and complained bitterly to all and sundry over the distress frequency when our aircraft drew up alongside.

Returning to Nicosia, those who had been on the detachment found that the rest of the Squadron were on readiness to provide air cover for transport aircraft airlifting troops and equipment from Amman; but they were not called upon to do so, for at the beginning of November 74 were instead preparing to return home. They had been in Cyprus just a few weeks short of the qualifying period for a campaign medal.

With the Squadron's establishment now having been reduced in line with all others to just twelve aircraft, and with the first of the Squadron's two-seat Hunter T.7s now *in situ* (having been collected from Kemble by Geoff Steggall and 74's Engineer, Norman Riley), 74's pilots started the month of January 1959 back at Horsham St Faith, waiting for the dangerously icy runways to clear and reading the pilot's notes for their new two-seater. As spring approached, so the exercise season intensified again and a maximum effort was made during 'Kingpin ADEX'. April's flying included Dacre Trophy work and low-level strikes in support of the Army in the Stanford Battle Area. There was a similar pattern to June, which also included high-speed, low-level interception trials, on one occasion interception being made just $1\frac{1}{2}$ minutes after scramble instructions had been received. Then nine Hunter F. Mk 6s and the T.7 deployed to Acklington on the last detachment to be flown from Horsham St Faith.

St Faith had for long been under mounting criticism from the residents of Norwich. The advent of the jet over a decade earlier and its attendant increase in noise was an unacceptable intrusion into the life of the city, the camp surrounded as it was by the northern suburbs. Norwich City Council was interested in purchasing the airfield for use as a civil airport, and the Ministry of Defence were sympathetic to the idea and agreed —which meant that the Tigers had to end their long association with St Faith and find a new home. Changes at Coltishall meant that there was now room for them to move in there, and on 6 June the Tigers took up residence. Chris Curtis left the Squadron immediately afterwards, to be replaced by Squadron Leader Peter Carr, although the latter would not arrive for a month: in the interim, Arthur Bennett took on the CO's duties.

The Squadron's QFI, Geoff Steggall, was selected to be part of the RAF team for the London to Paris Air Race of 1959, organized by the *Daily Mail* to celebrate the fiftieth anniversary of the crossing of the Channel by Blériot. The course was from the Arc de Triomphe to Marble Arch. Geoff was based, as the spare Hunter pilot, at Villacoublay near Paris. Shortly afterwards the Tigers were delighted to welcome Sailor Malan, who had come to Britain from South Africa for a few months, when he visited the Squadron on 17 July. Ted Nance flew a solo aerobatic display for his benefit, and a Spitfire arrived from Martlesham Heath to commemorate the occasion. Hunter and Spitfire were placed side by side and Sailor signed the fuselages of both. That evening an informal dinner was held in his honour and Malan made a short speech, during which he said that he had expected the visit to be 'full of memories and dead leaves' but that it had been completely different and he felt that 'the Squadron was as fresh and new as it had ever been'. This was to be 74's last personal contact with their wartime CO as he died a few years later in South Africa of Parkinson's Disease.

Four Hunters were provided for more displays during the year, Ted Nance continuing to perform most of the solo aerobatics. More firing work at Acklington saw the Squadron average rise to 21.8 per cent, Mike Cooke being the top scorer with 40.3 per cent. Then, on 25 August 1959, the Squadron was in the middle of a night flying programme when, at ten minutes before midnight, two Hunters collided shortly after take-off. Pete Rayner ejected successfully from his aircraft, but Pete Budd had no time to do so and lost his life. Eye witnesses afterwards described the accident in terms of hearing a sound like a thunderclap and the sky brightening as though daylight. However, accidents notwithstanding, Squadron life had to go on. September was certainly a busy month, with weekend aerobatic commitments and a large number of visitors in addition to normal Squadron training. Indeed, it seemed as though 74 was, not for the first time, being diverted from its prime purpose. As Pete Carr said, it could only be hoped that the Squadron would soon be allowed to settle down and become a fighter organization once more.

Tigers have fond memories of 10 September 1959, when nearly every pilot on the Squadron had a short flight in a single-seat Vampire 5. The previous day a Vampire from the AFS at Valley had called in with an instructor on board, and whilst waiting for his aircraft to be refuelled he had asked if there was any possibility of flying one of 74's Hunters. 'Only if we can fly your Vampire,' was Arthur Bennett's response! The following morning three Vampires buzzed Coltishall in tight formation and then landed and parked on 74's flight line:

> The leader was our friend of the previous day and he greeted me with the words 'My Boss says it's OK.' So there was nothing for it other than to set up a briefing system for each of our pilots to fly a Vampire and the three Valley instructors to fly a Hunter. There were fortunately no mishaps, but several of our people who had not previously flown the single-seat Vampire, including our USAF Flight Commander Jack Martin, were caught out by the massive nose-up trim change which occurred when full flaps were lowered for landing. In fact he crossed the threshold so high that he had to go around again. This was only one aspect of the 'first-generation jets' which we accepted as a matter of course in those days.

The rest of the year was fairly routine and culminated with the Army exercise 'Winged Coachman' in Northern Ireland in December. But training and exercises were overshadowed by some tremendous news. All eyes in the RAF had been cast for some time towards English Electric and the brand new Lightning production line. The first three pre-production examples had already been built and delivered to the Air Fighting Development Squadron at Coltishall for initial operational evaluation by the Service. Shortly afterwards, the Tigers were informed that they would be the first squadron to equip with the type. With the AFDS next door to them, the pilots of 74 had a grandstand preview of what was in store. However, Pete Carr would not see the new aircraft into service. Finding the attractions of speed on the ground and water comparable to the potential of the high speeds the Lightning offered, he left the RAF to join Donald Campbell as manager of the CN7 project at Lake Windermere and to be first reserve driver in his new attempt on the land speed record. His place as the Tigers' Boss was taken by the South African John Howe.

CHAPTER 9

Lightning Tigers

IN BRINGING a new generation of twin-engined, supersonic aircraft into front-line service, John Howe was to face one of his greatest challenges. He was certainly under no illusions about the difficulty of his task. The eyes of the Service, the country and indeed the world were upon him and his team. One of the first things he took on board as new CO was a visit by staff of the Day Fighter Combat School, who arrived to assess the Squadron's tactical flying skills. Their report proved to be the very thing Howe wanted to hear and gave him an almost immediate insight into the capabilities of the men he would be working with. 'This is the best Squadron we have yet assessed in the United Kingdom,' quoted the DFCS men—an opinion echoed by the AOC on his annual inspection on 20 March.

At the end of March, 74 returned to its old home at Horsham St Faith whilst Coltishall's runways were resurfaced and strengthened ready for the advent of the Lightning. In the meantime, Squadron commitments continued, and, with a major air defence exercise looming in May, efforts were directed towards working up for that. In the event, 'Yeoman' was relatively inactive as far as 74 was concerned, pilots generally flying only a single sortie during each of the three days the exercise lasted. Things did get off to a rather dramatic start on 17 May, however, when Tim Nelson aborted his take-off. The lower steel cable of the barrier rode up and over the wheels of his Hunter and cut into a drop tank, spilling fuel over the red-hot brakes and immediately causing a fire. Tim escaped unscathed, but the aircraft was severely damaged. In many respects 'Yeoman' was the swansong for the redoubtable Hunter from the Tigers' point of view, for at the end of June 1960 the first of the Squadron's initial batch of twelve Lightning F.1s was delivered to join those already being operated at Coltishall by the AFDS (who were to play a big part in 74's working up on the type).

By this time conversion from Hunter to Lightning was well under way. There was no OCU and no twin-seat Lightning, so conversion was undertaken by the Lightning Conversion Unit, a team from the Central Flying Establishment. The programme started with a five-day aviation medicine course, during which pilots were fitted out with their new flying clothes and Taylor pressure helmet (à la Canberra PR.9 crews) and underwent physiological tests at an aeromedical centre. These tests determined whether they would be able to cope with problems which could be encountered during high-level flight. John Howe was on the first of these courses at RAF Upwood. Of the Taylor helmet, he recalls:

I didn't like it and I didn't wear it—it wasn't mandatory to do so in the early days at least. I used to tease the aviation medics by suggesting to them that by trying to save our heads we would get our arses shot off. The fact is, with the Taylor helmet, you couldn't see. When turning your head to look back, you should be able to see down the spine of the aeroplane. With that big helmet you couldn't. Other special flying gear was the *g*-suit tied in to the pressure jerkin, both of which inflated. There was an air-conditioned suit which could be either hot or cold depending on conditions but I didn't fancy that one either. The environment of the cockpit was actually good—no problems with demisting, excess heat or cold (as was later to be suffered in the very different climatic conditions in Cyprus and the Far East). However, I was actually surprised that the big guys flew it as well they did for there is no doubt that the cockpit was built for a man of average build. It fitted me perfectly. But the big chaps needed a shoe horn!

After the return of the pilots from Upwood, the next stage encompassed seven days of lectures from members of the LCU covering the aircraft systems, emergency drills, performance and so on before starting simulator training which consisted of ten one-hour sorties in the General Precision Systems Mk 1 Lightning simulator. During the tenth such sortie, 'we had absolutely everything thrown at us.'

The first solo trip in the Lightning included flying away from the airfield circuit, during which the pilots had their first experience of the aircraft's phenomenal acceleration and rate of climb. Rejoining the circuit, they completed a couple of ground-controlled approaches, which were followed by either a GCA or a visual approach and landing. On his first familiarization trips in the Lightning, the pilot was accompanied by an instructor in a Hunter. For the pair to form up at operational height, the pupil had to give his 'chase' aircraft a 28,000ft start! John Howe still recalls his first solo vividly, as do all those who went through the conversion without the benefit of a two-seater:

> You were confident enough until you actually started down the runway, and then you had your doubts! But of course you *were* ready, and it was all tremendously exciting. The Lightning was such a step up. The Hunter could almost fit underneath the Lightning as a drop tank! It was *big*. Taxying out for the first time, you had to keep putting the brakes on because to get the generators and other systems to run you had a system known as 'Idle Fast Idle', which meant that for one engine the throttle was at idling revs of 30 per cent and the other was at 50 per cent. If you didn't keep the brakes on, you would be belting round at 60 or 70 miles an hour! That was idling! And the *power*! It was right there. You could feel it. And the first take-off and climb I don't think anyone will ever forget. However, it was not as you might suppose such a daunting prospect to climb into the machine and go solo for the first time. We could hardly wait. Which is not to say that we weren't nervous. The old snakes in the tummy were working overtime! But everybody I think went supersonic at about 18,000ft, still trying to get the nose high enough to get the speed right! And that was in cold power. We didn't use reheat. Cold power from brakes off to 35,000ft was 3½ minutes. It was one of the most exhilarating aeroplanes, even by today's standards. There is no wonder that it was considered the most desirable aeroplane in the Air Force inventory to fly, and that competition to get on to a Lightning Squadron was fierce!

Mike Cooke:

The conversion from Hunter to Lightning was less traumatic than the Vampire to Hunter which I had undergone earlier. The Lightning was a fine aeroplane to fly, with very similar qualities to the Hunter but with that much more power. It had to be *flown* off the deck but was easier to land. In the early days it tended to be used subsonically, and I suppose it took fully eighteen months to get used to the aeroplane and do the sort of things that had been done with the Hunter. The threat at the time was still that of the subsonic bomber, although in time this would be replaced by the high-flying reconnaissance aircraft and bomber, in anticipation of which the Lightning had been designed and against which it really came into its own.

Once flying conversion had been completed, weapons training commenced. The F.1 was armed with two 30mm cannon in the nose either side of the cockpit and two De Havilland Firestreak heat-seeking missiles on pylons either side of the nose, just forward of the wing leading edge. There was also provision for a removable pack under the fuselage which could carry either forty-eight 2in rockets or two more Aden cannon. In any armament configuration, the ground crews soon found that they could achieve a ten-minute turnround time for refuelling and rearming after a sortie.

John Howe had flown the first Squadron sortie in a Lightning on 14 July and other pilots followed him rapidly (Mike Cooke becoming, on the 16th, the first Flying Officer in the RAF to go supersonic). The Tigers were expecting three more deliveries before the end of the month but they did not materialize and all but one of those aircraft that they possessed were grounded because of a shortage of spares. August saw little relief. Seven Lightnings were now on strength, but still the Squadron was down to using just one at times, with the rest grounded because of unserviceability. Around this time a signal was received requiring the Squadron to do flypasts at Farnborough in September, and so any Lightning flying that was done tended to be devoted to close-formation practice. AFDS helped extensively with the work-up for this. For a while it seemed as though there would not be enough aircraft to fulfil the Farnborough requirement—a requirement that was extended when it was decreed that solo aircraft should appear at air displays all over the country during September too! John Howe:

> When we received the signal to put four over Farnborough each day, we didn't even have four aircraft! But arrive they did—just in time! We operated from Boscombe Down for the week, having taken six of our seven aircraft down with us, and basically our display consisted of four-ship flybys and steep turns. There was certainly an inherent sales drive in this as well as the publicity angle, a sales drive which sadly came to little, of course, other than the later Saudi Arabian order. As far as the solo displays at other shows were concerned, the brief was a simple one—keep low and make plenty of noise!

John Howe, Alan Wright, Ted Nance and Jerry Cohu formed the Farnborough team and they flew every day except one when bad weather prevailed.

Returning to Coltishall, the aircraft were immediately taken into the hangars in preparation for Battle of Britain commitments. But much as the Squadron appreciated being in the limelight, the showmanship had to stop and the serious business of attaining operational status take priority. Howe again:

We used to have a lot of technical snags. Our main problem was constant AC failure. It was always happening and was tremendously frustrating. But, that said, remember that the Lightning was a radical new design and was indeed the first modern aeroplane introduced to Squadron service that had not suffered a loss in its early operational flying. Support from English Electric and Rolls-Royce was outstanding. We used to visit Warton and Derby regularly—and they us, from the Chief Designer downwards . . . Frank Page, Roland Beamont, Jimmy Dell, Johnny Squier, Ralph Hooper. After the first few months of enduring the no-spares situation, I used to regularly speak to Beamont at Warton when we had a spares snag and somehow the system would be speeded up (or, dare I say, bypassed), which offended and upset quite a few people. I stuck to my guns, saying that if I could get the spares quicker my way I would continue to do so, often flying the Station Meteor up to Warton to collect them. In 1961 the Early Bird spares replacement procedure was introduced, possibly as a direct result of the pressure we as a Squadron were able to bring with our commitment to displaying the aircraft and to working up on it. Rolls-Royce were similarly tremendously supportive. I well remember at the 1961 Farnborough display something happened to one of the aircraft which necessitated an engine change. We didn't have an engine. We got one. We put it in in the morning and then ran it, calibrated it and flew it the same afternoon. Some going, especially in an aircraft with a unique engine configuration which meant that engine changes were not easy. The Squadron engineers were fantastic, invariably working all hours to meet my demands on them. As they gained experience they became the best to be found anywhere, having in effect undergone a conversion programme just as daunting for them as for air crew converting from the Hunter.

Chief Tech 'Red' Kyte was with 74 through its early Lightning years:

At times the going was extremely tough. Modifications apart, the Squadron was going flat out to become an operational unit again and the demand was for six of the twelve aircraft to be on the line at one time. That meant the working of a day-and-night shift system. With the added requirements caused by a sustained programme of aerobatics and demonstrations during the first couple of years, this led to an increased requirement of nine out of twelve on the line. Inevitably, with the problems we faced, this meant working all hours. The edges of the shift system became blurred at times, with crews overlapping to enhance manpower: the complexity of the Lightning as opposed to the Hunter meant that our complement of servicing personnel had already doubled. Weekends would often disappear completely, particularly if there were shows on! And leave? Everyone by necessity seemed to be saving that for Christmas! All the effort paid off though. We usually managed to achieve our target, and the only things that beat us were grounding orders brought about by the need for emergency modifications. An important side effect, too, was the speeding up of the climb along the learning curve by all the engineers in whatever trade they were. Manuals were gradually replaced by experience, and most of those on the Squadron saw the whole episode as a challenge to be overcome in order to make the Lightning a reliable aeroplane and rightly claim its place as the best interceptor in service. Morale remained pretty good throughout, although there were times when we all wondered whether the aeroplane would ever work properly.

There is no doubting that, by necessity, Howe was a hard taskmaster. He wanted aeroplanes, and whenever it was humanly possible, as 'Red' Kyte reaffirms, he got them. His dedication to the job in hand transmitted itself to the ground troops, and, whilst he was not always popular, he was a highly respected leader of men: this and the unit's high morale were instrumental in the success of the Squadron in reaching operational status, despite the problems, within ten months of the first Lightning being delivered.

OPERATIONAL LIGHTNINGS?

A three-day publicity exercise had been arranged by the Air Ministry for February 1961, the world's media being invited to Coltishall to watch the Lightning in action. With this event coming closer, the desperately needed spares started to arrive and serviceability rates took a temporary turn for the better. The New Year had started with over one hundred hours being flown, Coltishall being able to put 23 Squadron's Javelins to very good use as snow clearing machines by taxying them up and down the runways, their nose-up attitude allowing the engines' heat to melt the snow and regular tots of Tiger's Blood fortifying the manual snow-clearing parties! With the advent of the New Year it was officially confirmed that 74 was to be a day and night all-weather squadron. Clearly, however, there was much still to do to reach that status.

Some of the sorties were not without incident. Jim Burns was part of a close-formation finger-four practising a high-speed, low-level pass along Coltishall's runway when his aircraft started to yaw badly. Observers on the ground initially thought that he had suffered a birdstrike but were alarmed to see pieces of aeroplane floating down to the ground in front of them. It was Alan Wright who first raised the alarm when he realized that most of the fin and rudder of Burns' aircraft was missing, as well as the radio aerial on the spine, which effectively prevented any communication. Jim pulled away from the formation, not realizing the extent of the damage, and brought the Lightning in on a long straight approach using aileron control, landing safely. An investigation by English Electric concluded that it was the effects of the aerodynamic pressure which had built up during the course of the high-speed, low-level manoeuvre by four aircraft in close proximity which had exposed a structural weakness and caused the fin to shear off. All Lightnings were subsequently strengthened. Ever afterwards Jim Burns was known as 'Finless Jim' to the Squadron! On another occasion, Tim Nelson's drag 'chute failed to deploy on landing. Mindful of the restrictions on braking, he put the throttles through the gate, intending to go round again. As he rotated, the 'chute extended and was immediately incinerated by the reheat! Braking without a 'chute often led to the brakes burning out, and Nelson used every inch of Coltishall's runway with the Fire Section in close attendance when he touched down for a second time. Another point which pilots did have to watch closely was their take-off speed—not for any aerodynamic reason, but because if they remained on the runway after the appropriate speed has been reached there was a risk that the mainwheel tyres might throw their treads.

Less than a week after the press visit, a serious fire hazard was detected in the area between the ventral tanks and No 1 engine and jetpipe of the Lightnings. A temporary solution to this problem was to remove the ventral tank completely, and this modification was carried out on all aircraft, which meant that the latter were at least flyable but that, of course, their endurance, already limited, was curtailed even further. A manufacturer's modification was quickly authorized, and by the 18th the Tigers were grateful to have their Lightnings cleared to fly with tanks again and to make rather more realistic sorties (which on the F.1 averaged forty-five minutes in duration). By the end of April all the pilots had completed their conversion to fly the Lightning by both day and night. Against the odds, and despite the unserviceabilities, the lack of aircraft to fly and the display commitments, all of which diverted it from its primary task at one time or another, 74 Squadron was declared fully operational on the Lightning F. Mk 1.

As the months slid by, the silver aircraft of 74 Squadron, with their large tiger's head in a white circle on the fin, their black codes and their black and yellow nose dicing, became an increasingly familiar sight in the Norfolk skies. John Howe and his team became more and more enthusiastic about their mounts with each sortie they flew. Here was a weapons system, designed as such from the outset, which could outfight anything in the American 'Century Series' of fighters. Apart from being the RAF's first single-seat night fighter for many years, the aircraft was also the first integrated weapons system capable of accurately identifying, tracking and destroying enemy aircraft without visual contact; the first capable of Mach 0.9 in level flight at operational altitude within $2\frac{1}{2}$ minutes from brakes release; and the first that could fly above 60,000ft. In considerably less than $3\frac{1}{2}$ minutes it could accelerate from the speed of sound to Mach 2.

But it was to be a fact of 1961 that, once again, 'prestige commitments' were to take priority and training was effectively relegated to second place until after the autumn. The first big date on the calendar for the Tigers' display programme was the Paris Air Show. Joining them for this was Ken Goodwin of the AFDS, who is recognized as being probably the all-time best of the Lightning display pilots. Demonstrations were flown at Sculthorpe and Mildenhall for the American Armed Forces Shows, at Coltishall on a NATO press day, at RAF Woodbridge on the occasion of the first Tiger Meet and then at Farnborough again. The complete display sequence involved the mandatory noisy reheat take-off and a 70-degree climb to formation at 3,000ft, then a return to the airfield to execute a rolling box with all nine aircraft and other manoeuvres before breaking off for a stream landing. An impressive sight indeed! 92 Squadron, who provided the RAF's official aerobatic team, were also at Farnborough with their Hunters. An overheard conversation, repeated in one form or another many times over the week no doubt, commented on the sleek Hawker thoroughbreds: 'Pretty aeroplanes, those, but old stuff now compared with the Lightning!' By the end of September, 74 were preparing to revert to a programme of full operational training, starting with a full night dual check of all pilots in the Hunter. But no sooner had this been done than they were appointed to display before the Queen Mother at Leconfield. It was November before 74 could finally try and get on with the normal business of a Fighter Command squadron again, and it proved to be the best month in terms of the number of hours flown since the unit had re-equipped, raising hopes that, at last, major engineering problems were over. However, the failure of the tailplane motor of one aircraft dashed any such hopes as it led to a $2\frac{1}{2}$-day grounding of the rest for a full inspection and subsequent motor replacement. Added to this was the fact that seven of the Squadron's aircraft had reached two hundred hours, which necessitated a nine-day inspection on each. Hangar space was at a premium, and ground crews returned to routines of long, exhausting hours.

Just prior to Christmas 1962 John Howe moved on to HQ Fighter Command and was awarded the Air Force Cross for his work with the Lightning. Howe, whose amazing Zulu war dance would be sorely missed at Squadron parties, was dined out in memorable fashion. The Squadron's tiger skin was hung in the 'snarling' position from the window behind Howe's seat at the top table in the Officer's Mess and then hidden by a remotely controlled curtain. Suitable arrangements were then made by the Squadron's pyrotechnic expert, David Jones. As John Howe stood up for his farewell speech, the dimly lit hall burst into light and through clouds of white smoke appeared the now unveiled squadron mascot in the very best pantomime tradition! In John's place, Squadron Leader Peter Botterill was welcomed. Botterill, together with the new SEngO, Neville Hartwell, who had replaced Pete Stevenson, was to start his term by leading the Squadron through another period of operational inactivity as the F.1 was grounded yet again, this time for major hydraulic work to be carried out.

By 26 January 1962 there was not a single F.1 available for flying: they were all in the hangar being modified by the English Electric Contractors' Working Party. The Tigers' roar was to be muted for over two months. 'Red' Kyte remembers well those long weeks of toil to get the Squadron back into the air:

It had been found that the aircraft were suffering increasingly from hydraulic leaks. The pipes were aluminium instead of high-tensile steel and took a lot of vibration, but they were not flexible and were prone to cracking, particularly in the wings. Inevitably there were many failures which led to fire problems. The Lightning was not an easy aircraft to work on; every available internal inch was used, and the pipes around the engine touched it and each other too. To prevent chafing and cracking, the Squadron developed a kind of fibreglass tape to bind the pipes where there was room to do so. But this was not a total nor a lasting solution. English Electric eventually decided upon a complete re-piping programme for the hydraulic system on each aircraft. 74's aircraft were grounded and one of the Coltishall hangars was given over exclusively to this modification work. Each aircraft was stripped of engines, canopies, ejection seats, control surfaces . . . in effect, leaving just the aircraft shell. Teams were sent down from Preston to complete the re-piping, assisted by 74's engineering officers and men. Once the job was finished I and the other Chief Techs made the pre-acceptance checks for the Squadron. Once this and the air testing was done, they came back on to 74's strength and training continued. We didn't let the opportunity slip by to fit in some progressive servicing whilst the aircraft were grounded, for we knew what the demands would be when they started flying again!

Once all the Lightnings had been swallowed by the CWP's hangar, alternatives had to be found. Pilots made good use of the Squadron's Hunter T.7, as they did of the simulator. And, as always during such periods, those jobs for which there is never normally time finally got done—such as painting the crew room! The whole episode gave the Squadron poet the chance to indulge in a wistful sonnet, dedicated perhaps to English Electric:

> Hangar filled with chaos,
> Hearts filled with pathos,
> Whispers to the world at large,
> 'Wot about the French Mirage?'
> Heard in the coffee bar too,
> 'Is it the same with the Phantom 2?'

The first aircraft re-emerged on 26 March, although subsequent recovery from the programme did not proceed as quickly as expected and it was not until the end of May that all F.1s were deemed serviceable after the completion of air-testing. There having been such a long lay off from Lightning operations, each member of the Squadron had to undergo a reconversion programme of at least three preparatory sorties before being permitted to take the Lightning on an operational mission again.

AEROBATIC TIGERS

By the time the Lightnings were operational again, 74 had learnt of two more major commitments. The first was a visit to Scandinavia, and this got under way on 24 May when eight Lightnings left for Vasteras in Sweden. The deployment was to serve several purposes: it was a goodwill visit, a sales drive and a training exercise all in one, with the usual round of parties and entertainment thrown in as well! An aerobatic display over Stockholm and an eight-ship flypast of the British Trades Fair then in progress were the highlights of the week. At the beginning of June the

Squadron bade Sweden farewell and flew to Gardemoen in Norway to take part in a display commemorating fifty years of aviation in that country.

Meanwhile HQ Fighter Command had announced that 74 Squadron would form the official aerobatic team for the 1962 season. With such a radically new and complex aircraft as the Lightning, there was a corresponding change in the technique of formation flying compared with that employed by the Hunters which had been the mainstay of RAF teams since 1956 when 43 (The Fighting Cocks), 54 (The Black Knights) and 111 (The Black Arrows) Squadrons had used them. The physical and mental strains imposed on pilots flying high-speed aircraft in close-formation aerobatics proved, predictably, to be intense. The Lightnings were flown five to six feet apart at 450mph, and, despite their size and weight, were extremely manoeuvrable and capable of astonishing slow-speed turns. The impressive, near-vertical take-off was always a show-stopper and was the ideal way of demonstrating the climb potential for a scramble interception. The tight-turning qualities of the aircraft permitted displays to be given in a small area of sky, so that the public had no difficulty in keeping the formation in view. John Howe had always considered the F.1 to be a superlative aerobatic machine: flying it as such taught pilots very quickly a lot about its capabilities and its handling.

Immediately after the return from Scandinavia, the Squadron began working up its display routine, work up which was disrupted when one of the Lightnings experienced stick-jamming in conditions of high-g loading. On investigation, it was found that balance weights attached to the lower end of the control column could foul the structure beneath the cockpit flooring when the aircraft was pulling in excess of $2g$. Following this discovery, all aircraft were restricted to $2g$ as a maximum, and further formation practice was abandoned until the beginning of July when all the aircraft had been modified. With their third Farnborough commitment fast approaching once again, 74 was withdrawn from its operational duties so that all efforts could be concentrated on preparing for that event. At the same time the Tigers were informed of an ambitious scheme for synchronized aerobatics with Hunters of 92 Squadron, The Blue Diamonds. Accordingly, nineteen of the latter arrived at Coltishall to participate in rehearsals as early as 7 August. At the end of the month they flew down to Woodbridge, where a Tiger Meet was in progress, and displayed before the critical eyes of the assembled crews there. A week later 74 and 92 were in Hampshire for the final pre-Farnborough practices and then came the culmination of many hours of unremitting effort for both squadrons. Farnborough was an unqualified success. The seven gleaming, glistening Lightnings and sixteen all-blue Hunters earned special commendations from the SBAC Flying Commander, the Secretary of State for Air and the C-in-C Fighter Command. And if for some inexplicable reason the Lightning had not caught the imagination of some members of the British public hitherto, it had certainly done so now as complimentary letters cascaded through the Tigers' letterbox, although to keep things in perspective it must be reported that there were a few less than complimentary letters too. Said one:

> It is obvious to all but a few Air Marshals that these toys are no use for defence. Their only function is entertainment. But at what cost and annoyance to a long suffering population! Are we really made safer from enemy attack because half a dozen aeroplanes can fly in assorted formations and roll over from time to time?

After Farnborough, the Squadron returned to Coltishall in classic style, arriving over its home base in a new formation of thirteen, delivery having recently been taken of the two-seat T.4. Battle of Britain displays at Biggin Hill, Wyton and at Coltishall itself followed, the last concluding the Squadron's commitments for the year. This heralded a return to operational status, which was quickly realized when 'Matador', the summer exercise for 1962, commenced. For several days the Tigers were at a high state of readiness but they were not scrambled once for any intercepts—viewed at the time as a dubious record for any unit! The reasons for this are not clear: perhaps it was simply a recognition of a supposed operational rustiness. After 'Matador', the T.4 flew long hours as all pilots were checked out on the two-seater. For the first time the Squadron now operated under the manpower and equipment restrictions of Quick Reaction Alert (QRA). On the engineering side, things at long last seemed to have settled down to a routine of scheduled servicing, with no prospect of major modifications or Contractors' Working Parties invading the hangars. SEngO Neville Hartwell bid adieu to the Squadron during October and Pete Webb arrived to replace him. Also saying farewell to Coltishall during the month was the Air Fighting Development Squadron: its members were dined out in style, and 74 were sad to see many good friends move away to Middleton St George, where the AFDS was to form the nucleus of 226 OCU. This left just 74 with its Lightnings and 23 with its Javelins on the Station.

The New Year brought good news with the announcement of the award of the British Empire Medal for Chief Tech Thurlow. Everybody saw this as an award for the Squadron as a whole for its dedication and hard work in a year which had, after all, seen them allotted many and various tasks and duties, some glamorous, others not so. 74 rose to the challenge of continuing the gunfiring trials which had been previously conducted by AFDS, and Pete Botterill was kept busy welcoming the many new visitors to Tiger Ops who came to observe the Squadron's progress. March 12, 1963, was a red-letter day as it marked the end of the work-up phase and target banners were hit by live ammunition from an F.1 of 74 Squadron for the first time. Ferranti and English Electric had good cause for celebration, for the subsequent run of high scores on the banners (which was in contrast to the hitherto somewhat dismal experience of air firing on the Lightning) exceeded all expectations and, in all probability, saved the gun installation for the time being on the aircraft. After the cessation of the firing trials, 74 was released to normal operational standing again and participated in a round of Fighter Command and NATO exercises and alerts – 'Barrage', 'Kingpin', 'Tophat', 'Quicktrain' and, of course, QRA. Fighter Command's famous 12 Group, under whose auspices 74 operated, ceased to exist on 1 April 1963 and control was subsequently exercised by No 12 East Anglian Sector.

April was also the month in which 74 lost its first Lightning. Jim Burns was forced to bale out of XM142/'B' off the Norfolk coast near Overstrand whilst on an air test following a 400-hour servicing. After rolling out of a ten-second inverted run, the hydraulic warning indicated the failure of both control systems. At that time the aircraft was over land and pointing out to sea, and, as circumstances were ideal for ejection, Jim abandoned the aircraft. He was credited with one of the cleanest ejections ever, suffering no after-effects at all (he was back on duty within 24 hours), and was picked up from a field eight miles inland by a helicopter of 228 Squadron. Asked afterwards about the incident, he is quoted as saying, 'Once I was out it was most pleasant and most enjoyable', but one suspects that the pleasure and enjoyment were largely brought on by relief at such a successful escape and by the fact that he missed 33,000-volt electricity cables by just thirty yards as he landed!

On 7 May the Tigers were involved in hosting a royal visit when HRH Princess Margaret asked to see Coltishall at work. On a fine spring day she was able to enjoy a five-hour programme arranged for her, 74's contribution including Martin Bee's solo display, a four-ship flypast and a full-reheat stream scramble by the whole Squadron. Exercise 'Mystic' was Fighter Command's summer exercise for the year, and also participating in this were West German F-86s at Coltishall on a ten-day detachment, following in the footsteps of Dutch and Belgian Hunters which had visited earlier. August saw the completion of two more exchanges, to Norway and Holland. Pete Botterill, Martin Bee, Ed Durham and Peter Phillips took aircraft to the 3rd Annual Tiger Meet at Kleine Brogel, the first time that the Meet had been held outside Britain and an indication of its development into a major annual event.

SCOTLAND, THE F.3 AND THE IFT

From November 1963, the thoughts of everyone were on an impending move to Leuchars which had first been announced during the summer as part of the RAF's rationalization of its defence commitments. 23 Squadron had already gone. The administrators were now hard at work preparing inventories and planning the intricacies of a move which would demand that the Tigers be operational again within twenty-four hours of the change of location. Botterill went up to Scotland himself to sort out the many hangarage and accommodation problems that were becoming apparent. These were not easily soluble, however, and once the move was completed in February of the following year the Squadron engineers were, for example, forced to convert engine crates into servicing control cabins until the building programme had been completed! The

Lightning needed far more in the way of support than any previous aircraft that had been stationed at Leuchars and the facilities were simply not adequate.

In February 1964 came Missile Practise Camp (MPC) at Valley. The Camp, the first to involve Lightnings, proved to be a detachment which had more than its fair share of adverse weather, and of missile, missile system and target troubles. Those aircraft and crews participating flew straight on to Leuchars from Valley whilst, at Coltishall, all flying ceased on 26 February; two days later an eight-ship formation of six Lightnings and two Hunters departed for Scotland. It was to be expected that 23 Squadron would attempt some form of sabotage prior to the Tigers' arrival, and painters who, the day before, had arrived to decorate the Squadron's hangar wall with a large tiger's head found that a red eagle had been put there overnight by 'intruders'! An advance party under the command of Roger Chick had been at Leuchars for almost two weeks to pave the way: the result was that, in effect, the Squadron had been declared non-operational at the end of one week and declared operational again at the beginning of the next—quite a logistical achievement. However, 74 were rather surprised to find themselves grounded for the first few days because of crosswinds. The main weather problem was to be the famous local haar, the mist which would creep up unexpectedly from the sea and quickly blanket the airfield. Experienced officers soon became quite adept at predicting the arrival of this hazard whilst on duty in the tower and were universally successful in recalling aircraft with split-second timing to land just yards in front of the advancing fog! Even so, aircraft often landed at the clear end of the runway and taxied straight into a wall of fog that was encroaching at the other!

The hard flying of the Lightning F.1s (much of it on aerobatic and display work) was beginning to tell and was becoming very noticeable in terms of serviceability. Pete Webb and his team found it more and more difficult to patch up and mend the wearing systems. Many faults were occurring with monotonous regularity, but there was no underlying trend other than that to be expected of well-used aircraft. Despite many hours put in by the long-suffering ground crews, the number of flying hours achieved was low:

> Ten shiny Lightnings standing on the line,
> One must have a wheel change, now there are nine.
> Nine costly aircraft, looking simply great,
> One needs a bullet change, now we have eight.
> Eight eager Lightnings wait to soar to heaven,
> One is put on QRA so now we're left with seven.
> Seven potent monsters which fly like powered bricks,
> But one has sprung a fuel leak, leaving us with six.
> Six high speed fighters must scramble to survive,
> One can't start an engine, so taxying are five.
> Five Tiger warplanes running up full bore,
> One's AC comes off line, leaving only four.
> Four remaining aircraft, straining to get free,

One has a fuel light on, for take-off we have three.
Three noisy Lightnings, streaking for the blue,
One aborts with bird strike, and now we're down to two.
Two lift off successfully, as all ten should have done,
The leader cannot raise his wheels, climbing there is one.
The one roars off to sea to chase the wily Hun,
But his AI blows every fuse and targets he finds none.
The costly interceptors lie on the hangar floor,
This surely cannot happen here . . . it can to 74!

It was the advent of the Lightning F. Mk 3 which constituted the light on the horizon, and the first of these shiny new aeroplanes arrived on 14 April. A second followed at the end of the month, and by August a full complement of aircraft had been taken on charge. As Henry Ploszek recalls,

The Lightning F.3 had a more powerful engine than the F.1 and could take enhanced-range Red Top as well as Firestreak missiles. We considered it the all-singing, all-dancing aeroplane. It was a straight conversion for pilots with a team coming up from the OCU. We did our ground school at Leuchars then climbed aboard and away we went. The differences were in the radar and the much more sophisticated weaponry which had head-on capability and meant we had to learn all about attacks other than the line astern variety! Better range was not one of the attributes of the F.3, the thirstier engines and no increased fuel capacity ensuring average sortie times were reduced to a meagre thirty-five minutes. The better thrust-to-weight ratio made it a formidable interceptor with a rate of acceleration and climb to over 60,000ft which would be unsurpassed among Western fighters for several years to come. Distinguishing features were the square-topped fin and the deletion of the nose-mounted 30mm cannon which had been standard fit on the earlier marks, a controversial deletion which we operational pilots were critical of.

The F.3 showed early promise. The first two aircraft to be delivered completed forty sorties between them during the first month that they were on charge. Then, in June, 74 was suddenly declared non operational. The purpose of this rather drastic change in status was to free the Tigers to conduct an Intensive Flying Trial (IFT). 74 had been the first squadron to receive the F.3, and the intention was to put three hundred hours on to each of six aircraft as quickly as possible so that an accurate measure of component serviceability and servicing schedules could be taken. The theory was that such a trial would help smooth the type's entry into service with other squadrons, but in practice its value was doubtful. Henry Ploszek explains:

We split the Squadron into a Day and Night Flight. The idea was not to have an aircraft on the ground serviceable—it would be in the air flying if it was capable! The day shift would fly as much as they could then the aircraft would be repaired and maintained as they were recovered to the airfield. As the night shift came on, whatever was serviceable they would fly; if nothing was serviceable they would wait until an aeroplane was produced and this was sometimes not until the early hours of the morning. Then up it would go, ready to break it again and put it back into the hangar! It wasn't a very happy time on the Squadron because of the pressure on all ground and air crews to keep the aircraft flying. The ground crews were bushwhacked as they were working round the clock, week in week out. I don't think it all proved very much as in the final analysis we *didn't* achieve much more flying overall and the available spares could not support the programme. The IFT only served to lower morale considerably: the air crew because it was a non-operational, burning-holes-in-the-sky activity, and the ground crew because they seemed not to be able to keep the aircraft flying no matter how hard they worked. It didn't help either that the F.3 was a new aeroplane with significant changes from the F.1, and consequently the engineers were at the bottom of the learning curve again. They didn't have the experience to fix faults quickly and had to go by the book, which obviously took a considerably longer time until experience built up and short cuts were found.

By September there were eight F.3s dedicated to the trial as opposed to the previous six, but the news that 74 would be declared fully operational again from 1 December was very welcome, although there would be an overlap on the IFT which would not close formally until the end of January 1965.

By far the saddest moment during the year had been the death of Glyn Owen, killed while practising low-level aerobatics. The tragedy cast a gloom over the whole Station, and particularly difficult was the fact that a large contingent of personnel from 74 and some of his relatives, including his wife, had been watching the routine. Not having flown aerobatically for a month, Glyn had been briefed to carry out two practice sequences, one above 1,500ft and the second above 500ft, which he completed successfully. As the loop from the first sequence had been deleted because of a low cloud base, he had requested permission to carry out one more loop at the lower level before landing. He ran in at 500ft and 320 knots, engaged reheat and initiated the loop at a speed of around 180 knots over the top. It was at this point that the nose dropped rather sharply and, after descending almost normally for a moment, the aircraft entered a spin from which Glyn did not recover. He tried to eject by pulling the face blind: the canopy left the aircraft cleanly but the aircraft crashed before the seat cartridges had fired.

NEW STANDARDS

The operational task of a Lightning squadron in the 1960s was to conduct the air defence of the United Kingdom. The threat was perceived to be that of an all-out nuclear war, consisting of a pre-emptive ballistic missile attack followed, some sixty to ninety minutes later, by a bomber raid. The Air Defence Concept of Operations relied on a preliminary intelligence warning of the heightened preparedness of Warsaw Pact forces, which in turn triggered an immediate response by bringing the air defences to full wartime readiness as soon as possible. A maximum period of twelve hours was allowed to achieve 75 per cent readiness of squadron unit establishment. One of the advantages of the F.3 was that it could be armed and prepared very quickly, and the ground crews took pride in the fact that they could often achieve the goal in half the allotted time.

Shortly after returning to operational status on 1 December 1964, the Tigers were plunged into the deep end when Exercise 'Quicktrain' was called, a no-notice alert which required the generation of the maximum number of aircraft in the shortest possible time. Standard Operating Procedure (SOP) was that once the aircraft were generated and crewed up, there was then a pause whilst the attack materialized. The Ballistic Missile Early Warning System (BMEWS) could detect the missile launch and gave fifteen to twenty-five minutes' warning, which allowed a high proportion of the fighter force to scramble for survival (as it was called). At Leuchars sixteen aircraft (eight from each squadron) took off. The lead aircraft flew a set pattern, climbing to a predetermined height, flying outbound and returning to land twenty-five minutes after take-off. Each subsequent aircraft climbed 1,000ft higher than its predecessor and added thirty seconds to the outbound leg before returning to land a minute later than the previous aircraft. Having landed after the ballistic missile attack, always assuming that Leuchars had escaped unscathed, the aircraft were refuelled, the pilots remaining strapped in to launch on the blind scramble to meet the postulated follow-up bomber raid. Each pilot had previously been allotted a patrol lane which he now flew to, turning to an easterly heading to meet the as yet unseen enemy head on. Both the survival scramble and the battle scramble were flown in R/T silence so as not to alert the enemy, and only minimum assistance from the ground radar sites was anticipated as they may have suffered battle damage.

Bill Maish, who arrived from 111 Squadron to replace Botterill as CO on 11 December, remembers these scrambles clearly:

> In exercises it could be quite awe-inspiring as a host of aircraft winged their way in the darkness, seeking the unseen enemy. Then to find a blip on the B-scope, make a successful attack, turn outbound again and simulate firing your second Red Top at another target before returning to base. Sadly the complacency was often shattered when, on closing in on the target, one found a 23 Squadron Lightning or, worse still, another Tiger returning out of lane—or were you yourself out of lane? Similarly, the helter-skelter return of all the Leuchars Wing aircraft, often short of fuel—and when was the F.3 not short of fuel?—in the dark and often in poor weather, led to a rise of blood pressure and was the source of many an interesting story told in the bar afterwards!

With Bill Maish now at the helm, the first and ever-present implication of the return to operational status was QRA, a particularly onerous task for the squadrons at Leuchars because they were the only two available to share the duty for the whole Northern Sector. One real hazard of the winter was that the two QRA aircraft were parked out in the open. A QRA shelter was being built, but it was not completed until the late summer of 1965 and so, in all the snow, frost, rain and wind, the aircraft stood prey to the elements. On one night, in the midst of winter, a Force 11 storm blew up very quickly, so quickly in fact that there was no time to move the Lightnings into cover. SEngO Fred Buick (who had replaced Boscombe Down-bound Peter Webb) devised a measure of protection by placing fuel tankers on three sides of the aircraft. Even so, the Lightnings swung and shuddered as each blast hit them. The tip of the pitot boom, which protruded some four feet forward of the leading edge of the engine air intake, swung a foot from side to side in the furious wind. Fortunately the storm was short-lived and by morning all was calmer, but the need to change all the tyres on the aircraft proved that the overnight happenings had not been a dream.

The Tigers greeted the New Year with some optimism. The emphasis was for the moment on essential procedures using the F.3's new mark of radar. There was also a series of exercises (codenamed 'Profit') against electronic countermeasures (ECM) Canberras, exercises which had always been part of the training syllabus but which had rarely been practised and which constituted the first attempt by many of the Squadron's pilots to work with such techniques. Also in the New Year came the adoption of new immersion suits, full pressure suits and partial pressure helmets.

On 26 March Bill Maish took an F.3 to Upper Heyford to initiate an in-flight refuelling trial (codenamed 'Billy Boy') with USAF KC-135 tankers. The necessity for verifying the compatibility between the two types had arisen with the demise of the RAF's Valiant tanker fleet after a problem with the former bomber's main wing spar had materialized.

The replacement Victors were not to be ready for several months and so an interim solution was necessary. With increasing intrusion into British airspace by Soviet long-range reconnaissance aircraft attempting to gather electronic intelligence and testing the British defences in areas north of Scotland, 74 and 23 Squadrons aimed to intercept the visitors two hundred and fifty miles off the coast. The poor endurance of the F.3 made flight refuelling essential, and when the Victors did come on line it became common practice for them to be available at predetermined rendezvous points so that the Lightnings could be replenished regularly. The KC-135 trial was interesting in that there were no established procedures for refuelling from the American aircraft's hose and drogue, the normal USAF method being to use the manually operated boom only. The six-foot long hose with drogue attached was fixed to the end of the boom for the Lightning, and after some trial and error the optimum angle for trailing the boom, drogue and hose was arrived at. One problem never totally overcome was that the hose, being so short, did not have much 'give', but, provided good station could be kept and the receiver could maintain some slack during the transfer, everything went well. However, if there were excessive movement, causing the slack to be used up, because of the rigidity of the boom and the shortness of the hose there was a tendency for the probe to shear. If it did, the American crews took great delight in sending the probe head back to the Squadron, having recovered it from the drogue! They also, on occasion, gave out Green Shield stamps after a successful transfer of fuel!

What made April 1965 doubly interesting from the point of view of training was the ten-day detachment for six aircraft and eight pilots to the German Air Force base at Wittmundhaven, famous as the HQ of the

Richthofen Wing during the First World War. The Tigers took their own ground crews with them, a party of sixty flown out in three Beverleys of Transport Command. The weather during this period was unfortunately not as good as the hospitality, with the result that a few days were lost to fog and low stratus. Nevertheless, fifty-two sorties were still achieved and a few of the trips were flown as mixed formations with the home-based Starfighters of JG 71. During the course of the detachment the number of serviceable F-104s declined steadily until at the end the Tigers' six Lightnings, which for once held up, outnumbered them. It is true to say that it had been a matter of pride for air and ground crews to keep the aircraft going. On the last day of the detachment the German crews began to congregate around the pan to watch the Lightnings' start-up procedure, no doubt quietly hoping that the 100 per cent serviceability so far enjoyed would not last! Ian McBride takes up the story:

> They nearly had their wish, for Bob Turbin was in his aircraft trying to start it but to no avail. Then out of the crowd strode big, swarthy Chief Tech Trussler, who wandered across the pan to the offending Lightning, climbed up on the back, flipped one of the spine panels open, came back down, shared a few hand signals with Bob, climbed back up and when the starting sequence was initiated again thumped the offending component as hard as he could! It worked! The aircraft started! Trussler closed the panel, slid back down to the ground and wandered back into the admiring crowd of onlookers to a round of unreserved applause. 74's record had been maintained.

Back home in Scotland, two press days were held to publicize Leuchars as the first fully operational Lightning F.3 station. Leuchars' role was described as that of one of 'the key stations in Britain's eight-mile high fighter defence wall'. It was during this visit that Desmond Morris, C-in-C Fighter Command, caused some disquiet in Fleet Air Arm circles by saying that he could 'see no reason why, with the defence emphasis switching to the Far East and aircraft carriers assuming a new importance, the RAF could not operate off their decks.' Actually there were times when the Tigers were not averse to having some fun with the Royal Navy. During an exercise which involved HMS *Ark Royal*, a pair of Lightnings led by Terry Maddern had called up the carrier for a homing to the overhead, a let-down and a carrier controlled approach (CCA). Although puzzled, the controllers aboard the 'Ark' obliged, only to be rewarded by the two Lightnings engaging full reheat on the CCA and passing one each side of the carrier's island going rather quickly! As the Tigers climbed away, a message was received from *Ark Royal*'s captain to the effect that they should go away and *not* come back! The return of the *Tiger* to Rosyth and to northern waters after an extensive refit in the early spring gave 74 another opportunity of repartee with the Navy. *Tiger* was an air defence cruiser fully equipped with search radar and an extensive command suite. Henry Ploszek spotted the report of her departure from Portsmouth in the press and he and Bill Maish thought up a suitable signal both welcoming the ship and challenging the Captain and crew to anything, anytime, any place! Little did they know that the ship carried the flag of the Flag Officer

Home Fleet and that the Rear Admiral, his staff and the ship's complement accounted for over five hundred souls! In retrospect, and in view of the imbalance in numbers, they were somewhat relieved that the Royal Navy did not, on this occasion, respond!

The next item on the Squadron's busy agenda was the visit during June by HRH Princess Margaret to present the new Squadron Standard. Rather than prolong the pain of preparation, Bill Maish decided to make a late start, with a concentrated effort on the complexities of a full ceremonial parade only beginning four weeks prior to 3 June, the big day. So, during May, three parades a week were planned for all ranks. Jim Throgmorton, the United States Marines exchange officer whose drill was somewhat different to say the least, was made safe by placing him in static position as the point guard for the dais. He was only placated after the event because in this position he was strategically placed for being photographed resplendent in his magnificent dress uniform, even during the actual presentation by Princess Margaret to Standard bearer Rich Rhodes. On the day everything went according to schedule and, with an AOC's inspection prior to HRH's visit, two very big birds were killed with one stone! Both the AOC and HRH were treated to a formation flypast as was customary on such occasions. This commenced with the Spitfire and Hurricane of the Battle of Britain Memorial Flight from Coltishall, contrasting with a two-Lightning scramble from the brand new QRA sheds. Twelve Lightnings drawn from both squadrons did a spectacular reheat rotation take-off and were joined by two Javelins and two Hunter T.7s. Dave Mitchell flew his newly rehearsed solo display before the composite formation of sixteen aircraft joined up to fly past, the Tigers displaying a four-ship, six-minute aerobatic sequence to conclude the event.

During July the first of the Victor K.1 two-point tankers became available for Lightning refuelling operations to commence. Most of the Squadron had only refuelled from the KC-135 and thus had no experience of the RAF system of probe and drogue refuelling, but it was soon deemed to be a straightforward exercise—although not before one or two of the less experienced Squadron members had endured some sticky moments. Briefing for refuelling, usually carried out by Dave Liggit, was short and to the point: 'There's the basket! There's the probe! Go for it!' Most of 74's pilots had never aimed for anything in the air before, and it was an acquired art to approach the basket without weaving and without overshooting, causing the hose to whip along the fuselage. Several Lightnings returned from their first AAR sorties with black rubber grazing up the fin! The reason for this urgent training was that in August the Squadron was due to detach four aircraft to RAF Akrotiri in Cyprus. 55 Squadron was responsible for the planning of the flight, the first time the Victor had been used on an operational overseas deployment and, indeed, the first time the Lightning F.3 had operated from that most popular of bases. The time in Cyprus was to be an active one operationally, the resident Javelins of 29 Squadron having flown down to Rhodesia in response to the emergency there.

Back home, Dave Mitchell flew several solo aerobatic displays during the Battle of Britain season and on Battle of Britain Day itself the Boss and Terry Maddern flew at low level over Leuchars, demonstrating flight refuelling behind a Victor. Unfortunately, as the formation crossed the coast, the convection off the hot sand produced an up-gust which showed both Lightnings a plan view of the Victor from above! This caused Terry to lose contact between his aircraft's probe and the tanker's drogue but he was able, by desperate methods, to plug in again as the formation flew over the airfield. Later he was congratulated by a spectator on his excellent timing in making contact right in front of the crowd! MoD were not similarly impressed: from that day, low-level refuelling demonstrations were banned. Another incident involved a Chipmunk of a visiting Air Experience Flight which took off with one of the Tiger's brake chutes which had just been blown clear by a landing aircraft wrapped around its tail. The Chippie got airborne and completed a circuit before coming in to make one of the shortest landings Leuchars had ever seen, with no harm done to man or machine!

FIRST-TOURISTS

A further quartet of F.3s was tanked to Cyprus (leaving just four and the T.4 on home ground), allowing the 'Tiger Black' team to clock up another record during October, when they became the furthest travelled of any Lightnings by deploying to Teheran/Meherebad to display with the Imperial Iranian Air Force in commemoration of the Shah's birthday. Unfortunately Meherebad was, at that time of the year, hot, high and very dry, and problems with evaporating AVPIN and the high-energy igniters led to Tim Cohu's aircraft failing to start on the day of the display, despite thirty minutes of trying. A less than satisfactory three-ship display resulted. However, an introduction to the Shah was an honour for all concerned, whilst the evening out, by courtesy of an Iranian F.5 squadron commander, was an enjoyable bonus (*real* belly dancers included), as was the trip to the very old city of Isfahan aboard an Iranian Hercules the next day.

Returning to Cyprus, Bill Maish found Jim Throgmorton waiting anxiously for him with a tale to tell. Apparently, at a dawn sortie, Jim had asked for a reheat rotation take-off, which had been granted by ATC. Unfortunately a Canberra flying over at about 4,000ft to the nearby range, and above the ATC zone, saw, heard and felt the slipstream of Jim's Lightning in its near vertical climb as it shot past! The subsequent airmiss report led to some unpleasant and unfounded accusations of indiscipline, which were dropped only when the OC Strike Wing intervened. Shortly afterwards four of the Lightnings returned to Britain, the final four following some weeks later. Terry Maddern and Gerry Crumbie set a new record for the longest Lightning flight to date by flying direct to Leuchars from Akrotiri in five hours and forty minutes.

Scotland in November came as a nasty shock after Cyprus, but in truth the Squadron relished their being home again after a busy summer. They were soon to take over the duties of Northern QRA, demonstrating that, from pilot and ground crew being at a sitting start in their crew rooms, an aircraft could be on the runway, rolling for take-off, within five minutes. The Squadron almost met the Russians 'for real' for the first time on 6 December 1965. A series of scrambles after intruders failed to establish visual contact, although at the extreme of the F.3's range Bill Maish got a positive AI lock on what was said to be a pair of Naval Aviation 'Bears'. This first contact led directly to the increased emphasis on Victor tanker deployment to Leuchars when 'activity' was anticipated.

A Lightning T.5 replaced the T.4 during November, whilst the work-horses of the Squadron, the much-loved Hunter T.7As, with their Light-ning instrumentation for check rides, were soon to go. At the same time the MoD issued a directive 'that all highly coloured fin markings carried by the Lightning squadrons must be erased forthwith'. Squadron badges were to be presented within an eighteen-inch diameter circle on the fin, and nose markings were to conform to a strict geometrical pattern. It was said at the time that it was the red and white chequerboard markings that suddenly appeared on the fin of Hank Martin's 56 Squadron Lightning, making it look like a flying GCA hut, that finally pushed MoD into this unpopular directive!

The main event of early 1966 was the detachment to the Missile Prac-tice Camp at Valley to fire five Firestreaks. Henry Ploszek had never launched a missile in his six years on Lightnings, so he was keen to grasp the opportunity now offered him:

> Planning for the MPC was a detailed affair, with the lectures for the crews involved on specific procedures and launch profiles flown in the simulator. The aircraft to be detached to Valley were rigorously checked, for if the firing system didn't work properly once there it was counted as a very black mark against the Squadron. All the rounds themselves had to be inspected and test-flown to make sure that good acquisition was obtained. The experts at Valley would immediately be able to spot anything that wasn't up to scratch. In fact air crew were always quite worried about MPC. Profiles had to be flown absolutely correctly, and if an aircraft became unserviceable so that a firing slot was missed—that was a heinous crime! Timings were worked out to the second and all firings were photographed by a chase aircraft. In short, every-thing was done by the book.

The Squadron finally launched its last missile on 31 January, having had to extend the stay by a day to do so. As compensation, it was gratify-ing to note that not a sortie was wasted as a result of Lightning unservice-ability or poor attack patterns. But the detachment did little to improve confidence in Firestreak, because two out of the five missiles did not explode correctly and there was subsequently considerable disappoint-ment in the fact that the simple task of firing five live missiles in three weeks could not be accomplished successfully. The net result of the failures was an instruction to carry out an investigation into the effects of age on stored missiles.

74 was the first Lightning unit to take first-tourists on their aircraft; at the same time, the experienced air crew were being posted out to help with the training on the new squadrons. The remaining 'old hands' were a little suspicious of the capabilities of the new boys, who in turn felt that they were under the microscope when they first arrived. Within eighteen months the situation had changed and first-tourists predominated. But in the meantime the Flying Officers' Union, headed by Heinz Frick, was a hard school to contend with. Henry Lether recalls his indoctrination vividly:

It was a most embarrassing episode. There I was, coming as a fighter pilot to a squadron that I had always wanted to join and flying the acroplane that I had always wanted to fly. Full of enthusiasm, feeling that the world was my oyster, I was met by Bob Lightfoot in the bar on the first night: after a few beers my enthusiasm just couldn't be restrained and I told all—how great it was to be there, dreams come true ... and all the rest of it! Next morning was the Boss's interview and, unbeknown to me, the Flying Officers' Union stepped in and rigged it. Heinz Frick and Bill Maish swapped uniforms and when I walked in I saw this imposing, slightly silver haired gentleman behind the desk whom I immediately and quite understandably took to be the Boss.

After the briefest of introductions he launched into a strong condemnation of the policy which allowed first-tourists on to front-line squadrons. He let it be known to me in no uncertain terms that he had fought my posting strongly on the grounds that I would be a liability in a Lightning. But his objections had been overruled and my posting had gone ahead.

'I am not convinced that you can do the job, Lether, and I will need a lot of convincing that you can ...'

This tirade went on for several minutes. In my anxiousness to please I was ready to agree to anything and to take anything thrown at me.

'I distrust your loyalty to the Squadron, Lether. I hear what you say about always wanting to be a Tiger but how can you have any loyalty when you have only been in the RAF two minutes? Why did you want to join the Tigers anyway?'

Heinz knew very well what my answer to this would be, having been fully briefed by Bob Lightfoot after the previous evening in the bar! I gave it all I had got—my lifelong ambitions, the best squadron in the Air Force ... I dug a deeper and deeper hole for myself, blissfully unaware of the audience clustered outside the door listening to every sickening word and hardly able to contain themselves!

'I am sending you to Iceland, Lether, as Ops Officer to liaise with the American Q Squadron at Keflavik. What do you think of that?'

'Very good, Sir! Just what I need, Sir!'

'And then when you come back you will spend three weeks in the simulator before you fly any of my aeroplanes! What do you think of that?'

'Very wise, Sir! Very wise!'

Interview over, I meandered off to the bar, wondering just what I had let myself in for. By this time all the boys who had been listening at the door were studiously map-reading, drinking coffee or discussing tactics for a forthcoming sortie. Bob was there again.

'Firm but fair, the Boss, eh?' observed Bob.

'Oh yes! Very firm but very fair,' I ventured. 'Just how I found him!'

This, of course, was enough to set all the rest of the boys off.

I stood and watched them, wondering just what was so funny! Then in walked Heinz and the Boss, having changed back into their own uniforms. I had been well and truly taken in—as in fact were Chris Mullan and Clive Mitchell, who went through the same ordeal, Clive with the added stigma of not only being a 'first bloody tourist' but a newly married one at that!

During the spring of 1966 the Defence Minister, Lord Shackleton, made mention of a possible move for the Tigers to the Far East during the following year. There was even talk that the Lightning might be used in the ground-attack role, and in a season of rumours the British Government was understood to be on the verge of ordering the General Dynamics F-111 in the wake of the controversial cancellation of TSR.2, with 74 supposedly listed as being the first recipients of the big, trouble-torn, American jet. More immediately came the beginning of fighter-versus-fighter combat with Hunters from West Raynham, training that the pilots were short of and which they found to be of great value in sharpening up their tactics, particularly against dissimilar types. Unfortunately, after the anticipation, came disappointment when two of the Hunters were involved in a mid-air collision in the early afternoon of the second day. Bill Maish, who was working with them at the time, had completed one attack against a Hunter four-ship and had descended. The Hunters were re-forming and trailing white contrails in the clear blue sky when, to Bill's horror, two converged and the aircraft collided, dropping fuel tanks and other debris. Fortunately both aircraft were able to land safely.

During May, Tiger ground crews had an opportunity to show their skills to the new AOC-in-C, Air Marshal Sir Frederick Rozier. By now the F.3 had become renowned for the speed with which an Operational Turn Round (OTR) could be performed. On AOC's inspection, the Tigers flew four aircraft in the display and then demonstrated the OTR under the AOC's watchful eye. Jim Throgmorton should have commanded B Flight on the parade but during rehearsals his 'Forward ho!', delivered in true US Cavalry fashion when he wanted to get things moving, did not get the reaction he wanted, the flight dissolving into laughter instead! Even when Jim had mastered 'By the left! Quick March!' he could never master the about-turn which, in the Marines, is a totally different action. Much to his annoyance, he was forced to watch the parade from the sidelines.

June was enlivened by several potentially serious accidents. The first involved eight of the Squadron's aircraft, and in particular Henry Ploszek, on a day when cloud extended from near ground level up to 23,000ft. Henry was scrambling on an Exercise 'Kingpin'. Leuchars was 'Red' for the purposes of the exercise and so the sortie was planned with the sixteen aircraft from both the Tigers and 23 Squadron diverting into Binbrook. However, soon after take-off, Henry was confronted with a No 2 engine fire warning. He immediately took the correct fire drill, called Scottish Centre on emergency frequency and at the same time tried to ascertain whether or not there was indeed a fire. As other indications on the panel were normal, he elected to divert and began a descent towards the 2,000-yard-long Turnhouse runway. The airport was very wet from continuous rain, but, with precise judgement, Henry was able to land his overweight aircraft without incurring any damage. The fire warning had been a false one. Shortly afterwards he was awarded a Green Endorsement in recognition of his courage and professional skill.

There was drama, too, for the fifteen remaining aircraft as Binbrook's weather was atrocious as well. Nevertheless the Lincolnshire station seemed to be the only option available, not only to the fifteen aircraft from Leuchars but to others from the Wattisham Wing also! Binbrook had only recently been reopened, and few of the Leuchars pilots were familiar with it. Ian McBride recalls the situation:

> We didn't know how to get in to the base or even where the dive circle was. We were all out over the North Sea when eventually somebody calculated that we were not far away. We then saw a lone Lightning circling. It was a 5 Squadron machine with Kevin Mace flying, and we immediately latched on to him and followed him down to Binbrook. Imagine the picture—this young first-tourist letting down with a great gaggle from the Leuchars Wing hanging on behind! I remember vividly calling up and being told I was number eleven to land and that there were over thirty drag 'chutes already dropped on the taxiway leading off the runway!

As a consequence of the large number of unscheduled visitors, Binbrook ran out of fuel and it had to be ferried in by road from Waddington and Scampton! The Leuchars Wing, having put their aircraft to bed around the airfield, were anticipating a great reunion in the bar when the unwelcome message came through that Leuchars was clearing and they were to return!

The following day the Tigers had a lucky escape from what could have been a double disaster. Mike Laughlin, who was completing an ILS on Runway 27, found to his horror that, after touch-down and with his brake 'chute deployed, he was being approached head-on by another Lightning taking off. Chris Mullan, who was on his first stint of QRA, had been scrambled and in turn found that, taking off in reheat on 09, he was confronted by a Lightning landing. Both pilots saved the day by following the standard operating procedures which required aircraft to move to the north side of the centreline. It transpired that Terry Maddern on 74's Ops desk had obtained clearance from ATC for a QRA scramble against the traffic pattern and had transmitted this to Chris over the telebrief. However, the local controller had not warned approach (who were working Laughlin) and, when Chris scrambled, his radio had not warmed up sufficiently for him to get final take-off clearance and in his excitement at his first QRA scramble he had pressed on regardless! The F.3 had a very rapid start and taxying capability, so fast in fact that often the master reference gyro had not erected fully nor were the radios fully warmed up by the time take-off commenced—exactly what had happened to Chris. An enduring postscript to the incident was the story freely circulating in the bars for weeks afterwards that the controller had instructed the landing Lightning to move to the left of the runway and the other to move to the right to avoid a collision . . .

TIGER MEET

When 74 first re-equipped with the Lightning in 1960, John Howe had been well aware of the US Air Force Tigers at Woodbridge, the 79th Tactical Fighter Squadron of the 20th Tactical Fighter Wing. Correspondence between the two units had been going on since the first contacts had been established during Keith Haselwood's time, and occasionally a social meeting was arranged. On impulse one day, John picked up the phone to speak to his counterpart at the Suffolk base, perhaps with a subconscious idea to set the ball rolling on some sort of operational exchange rather than a purely social one so that 74 could show off their new mount. What he was not aware of at the time was that an old friend of his, Ed Rackham, had just taken command of the 79th TFS. Their meeting again after almost ten years prompted the idea of the two squadrons getting together on a regular operational basis.

At around the same time, the French Minister of Defence was writing to all his commanders emphasizing the importance of Franco-American military co-operation, and as a response to this the C-in-C of the United States European Command suggested that every opportunity should be taken to further professional and social relationships between the two countries. Ed Rackham approached his Boss for permission to go ahead with the proposed Tigers meeting, and it became plain for all to see that, if a French Tiger Squadron could be found, here was a way of promoting the ideals expounded by the C-in-C and the French Minister. Captain Mike Duggan of the 79th TFS was entrusted with the search and he soon found that EC 1/12 at Cambrai had been christened a Tiger Squadron. Contact was made and the idea greeted enthusiastically, the first Meet being held on 19 July 1961 at Woodbridge. The following year the Meet was a much bigger affair and eight squadrons were represented; the credit for this goes again to Mike Duggan, who had spent a large part of his time identifying Tiger Squadrons in all the European and European-based air forces. 74 was heavily involved in the work-up for Farnborough at the time and, sadly, this commitment allowed the Squadron to send only officers to observe and to participate in the social activities, although, as we have seen, it was able to display the Lightning at the end of the Meet.

Activity was not confined to the air, for, apart from a full flying programme, a series of conferences was held which dealt with a variety of problems and activities within the sphere of NATO operations. Neither were social aspects overlooked. Receptions and dinners were organized for air as well as ground crews; and at the final banquet the guest of honour was General Anderson, the SHAPE Air Deputy, who by his very presence underlined the importance of the Tiger Meet in the eyes of the highest command. In his speech, General Anderson put into words for perhaps the first time the underlying aims and objectives of the Meet

—the promotion of NATO solidarity, the achievement and maintenance of firmer professional relationships amongst NATO personnel and the creation of a better understanding of NATO military objectives and the problems of NATO partners. These objectives remain as valid today as they did thirty years ago.

In 1963 the Meet moved to Belgium and in 1964 to France, where a new emphasis was placed on the attendant ground crews, an element of cross-training and practical experience on other country's aircraft being introduced. The year 1965 saw the Americans once again taking responsibility for its organization, but this time at Bitburg in West Germany. In 1966, for the first and in fact the only time, it was the turn of 74 Squadron to host the event. Arrangements were protracted and involved with visits by advance parties from the European squadrons to discuss details. Fighter Command was supportive financially and in the provision of manpower to assist. Much sponsorship was obtained from local industry and commerce as well as the aviation world at large. The organization involved not merely the Squadron but all sections at Leuchars. Being such a major event, covering all aspects of operations in the air and on the ground, the gathering of large numbers of air and ground crews necessitated the finding of accommodation for them both on and off camp, room to hangar and service twenty-one participating aircraft and room for the storage of spares and ancillary equipment; transport to and from the flight-line and to and from dinners and parties as well as organized visits outside the base; the feeding of several hundred additional Europeans and Americans, all with varying culinary expectations and tastes; and additional medical facilities, fire and rescue cover and communications.

The participants began to arrive on 5 July and, as the transport aircraft came in carrying technical support personnel and equipment, the nominated teams of liaison officers, SNCOs and airmen of 74 began their first task of clearing the visitors through customs, allocating them to their respective technical areas and helping them to prepare for the arrival of the fighter aircraft—the Belgians with three F-104s, the French with three Super Mystères, the Canadians with two RF-104s and an RF-104D and the Americans with two F-4 Phantoms of the 53rd TFS from Bitburg and three F-100Ds of the 79th TFS from Woodbridge. AKG 52 from West Germany were unable to bring their new Fiat G.91s on to which they were converting but, determined not to miss the Meet, they arrived in a pair of borrowed T-33s! The other Tiger Squadron of the German Air Force, JBG 43, were converting to Starfighters but they, too, were determined to be present and brought four F-86s later in the week.

Throughout the first afternoon, in the midst of parking, refuelling and servicing the visiting aircraft and accommodating the visitors, many old friendships were renewed and many new ones initiated. That evening, after the welcoming addresses and briefings, SNCOs and airmen met again in their respective Messes and talked shop, anticipating the days ahead. The officers of the 53rd TFS were sporting their tiger-striped waistcoats much to everyone's admiration—and to their amusement when the Canadians managed to remove one from the American CO's chest before his troops could rally round! This led to practical jokes throughout the week which in turn saw the application of considerable ingenuity in temporarily removing another squadron's prized possessions (74's 'Battle of Britain' Class engine nameplate being an example). Occasionally things got just a little out of hand and Bill Maish was compelled to call the squadron commanders together and ask for a certain measure of control over their charges!

Wednesday saw the beginning of operations (which Henry Ploszek and a small team had spent many hours organizing and planning) when all the Tiger squadrons took off for a sector reconnaissance and familiarization sortie. In the afternoon, squadron pilots began to fly in each other's two-seaters as a means of acquiring an insight into some of the problems and techniques peculiar to each unit's operational role. Perhaps the most popular ride was that in the RF-104D of the Canadians to sample their low-level photo-reconnaissance task. The 53rd TFS flew many eager aviators in their Phantoms, too, and one American pilot was heard to offer a Phantom trip for only twelve T-33 rides! The F-4 was of particular interest to 74 for they were able to make a direct comparison between it and the Lightning from the point of view of performance, handling characteristics and weapons systems (little thinking that, twenty years later, they would be flying the same aeroplane). A scramble of an F.3 alongside a Phantom produced an interesting spectacle, the Lightning shooting off to an early lead on the climb-out. By 30,000ft the Phantom had caught up!

On Thursday, flying in each other's aircraft continued and the first fighter v. fighter sorties were flown. In the meantime the Canadians were busily continuing their reconnaissance training, as a result of which some excellent photographs of Scottish beauty spots and the Open Golf course at St Andrews were soon on display. They also photographed the various aircraft types in flight and on the ground, and the excellent prints produced excited much comment in the crew rooms and Messes. The Belgian Starfighters and the American Super Sabres were meantime engaged in low-level exercises in the Scottish Highlands, all pilots admitting that the opportunity for aerial sightseeing over some glorious scenery was an added bonus. On the Thursday evening there was an airmen's dance at the Station, an open evening in the Sergeants' Mess and an informal gathering in the Officers' Mess, although pilots participating in the final day's flypasts were excluded from these activities!

The weather on the Friday continued as fine as it had been throughout the week. Some limited operational flying was completed early on but ceased for a rehearsal for the afternoon's displays. At just after 10 o'clock Capitaine Joel Dancel of 1/12 Escadrille took off in a Super Mystère to practise. Minutes later he crashed into a field just outside the airfield boundary and was killed instantly. His death brought all activity to a stunned halt, but it was indicative of the regard in which he was held that it was decided that the afternoon display in which he had been so eager to take part should take place as planned. First off were a Spitfire and Hurricane. As they finished, five Lightning F.3s of 74 climbed near vertically in a stream reheat rotation take-off. As they cleared the circuit the combined formation took off. Led by the Lightning T.5 flown by Jim Throgmorton and Captain Denny Wills of the 53rd TFS, it comprised a Belgian F-104, a Canadian RF-104, an American F-4, a French Super Mystère, an American F-100 and a West German T-33. As the last of the formation rotated, Dave Liggit arrived overhead to give an individual low-level aerobatic display in an F.3 and, as he completed his show, four Lightnings, led by Bill Maish, came in for theirs.

After the flypast each squadron was presented with a model of the Lightning F.3 and Bill Maish presented to each of his opposite numbers an album containing photographs taken throughout the Meet, this in addition to the traditional exchange of squadron plaques and mementos. A Guest Night in the Officers' Mess and a dance in a St Andrews hotel wound up proceedings. Ian McBride had been detailed to play host to the 79th TFS from Woodbridge and amongst their complement were some very good golfers. After the Guest Night four of them decided to play a round on the Royal and Ancient course. Dressed in full Mess kit, they took their clubs down, teed off around midnight and proceeded to play the complete eighteen holes! The first two were a little difficult in the gloomy conditions but, being midsummer and with the nights extremely short, visibility quickly improved: by the time the usual Saturday morning golfers appeared, McBride and friends were completing their round in front of an admiring audience. They paid their green fees and went off to bed for a few hours before transport aircraft flew in to collect equipment and personnel and the fighters flew out. Suddenly Leuchars had a very quiet and empty ramp. The sixth NATO Tiger Meet was a singular success. It was the last in which 74 would participate for twenty years.

KEN GOODWIN

Either side of the week of the Tiger Meet, 74 intercepted more Russian aircraft. The first, on 4 July, came after a series of scrambles against three 'Bears' which, in line astern and several miles apart, flew down the North Sea to a point abreast Boulogne before turning east and then north to fly up the Norwegian coast, dropping chaff and jamming radars in the process. No photographs were taken as no cameras were, at that stage, permitted to be taken aloft: similarly, as the interceptions were deemed to be 'top secret', nothing could be said about them. The second interceptions took place a couple of weeks later. As 1966 progressed a continuance of the increase in Russian activity meant that a pair of Victors were on almost permament detachment to Leuchars. Heinz Frick had a few problems when, as he intercepted two 'Bisons' his air brakes refused to close after he had slowed to match the Russians' speed. He immediately began a diversion into Kinloss, where he landed, brakes still extended, with just five minutes' fuel remaining.

Wing Commander Ken Goodwin arrived to take command of the Tigers on 7 October 1966 after a small ceremonial parade at which the Malan Sword was handed over for his safekeeping. The Sword, recently presented by Doug Tidy and 'Brookie' Brookes and used to this day on ceremonial occasions, had been beautifully crafted by Wilkinsons. Down one side of the blade is the dedication and on the other scrolls in which the names of commanding officers are recorded. The scabbard has a tiger's head embossed on it. Ken generously gave Bill Maish the opportunity of flying the first sortie in the first Lightning F. Mk 6 which had recently been delivered to the Squadron at the start of a programme to replace the F.3s before he left to join the Royal Australian Air Force Staff College. In the New Year's Honours List, Bill was awarded the Queen's Commendation for valuable service in the air.

Ken Goodwin had come from the Far East Air Force (FEAF), with which he had been Flight Safety Officer. He had travelled widely in this capacity, and part of his brief involved advising on the preparation of Tengah on Singapore Island 'to receive an air defence squadron from the UK in the near future'. At the time Goodwin was not aware that he would be commanding that squadron, and he is candid enough to admit that many of the things he recommended and indeed oversaw whilst out there he changed once he arrived in his capacity as Boss of 74! Goodwin had had previous contact with the Tigers, of course, in the early 1960s whilst he was with the AFDS. To the young pilots on the Squadron, he seemed to do the most outrageous things, and there is no doubting that he led a charmed life! The Tigers quickly fell under his spell and willingly followed him wherever he led, although it must be said that there were times when Ken did make the job of his senior officers that much more difficult by virtue of his unorthodox approach. But it cannot be denied that, during the three years he led 74, he had an extremely happy Squadron, with a tremendous spirit permeating all ranks.

By the end of the year all the F.3s had moved on to pastures new and the Tigers were fully operational on their new mount, having been the first squadron to receive full production F.6s (5 Squadron at Binbrook had received the interim model the previous year). The major external difference between the F.3 and F.6 was brought about by a determined effort to improve the Lightning's abysmal endurance — the addition of a new, larger ventral tank fitted with two fins to augment directional stability. Allied to a more efficient wing, this meant that the aircraft's range was increased by 20 per cent. The option of 250-gallon overwing ferry tanks (which could not be fitted underwing because of the position of the undercarriage) further increased the aircraft's range. It was some time before the means of jettisoning full tanks in emergency was authorized, for the initial system involving the use of explosive bolts was found to be dangerous when tested, the bolts disconcertingly blowing themselves through the bottom of the wing! On the debit side, there was still no reinstatement of the Aden gun, although it was included in the ventral tank on later production models. The Squadron appreciated the

**THE LIGHTER SIDE OF SQUADRON LIFE. THESE CARTOONS WERE
A PARTICULAR FEATURE OF THE SQUADRON DIARIES IN THE 1960s.**

advantages of the new aircraft immediately: conversion was straight-forward and very soon pilots were finding ways of burning up all that extra fuel, for a 1hr 10min unrefuelled sortie in a Lightning was a novel event! This time there was no IFT to contend with and the engineers appeared to take the new servicing and technical features in their stride, a cumulative six years of experience of the Lightning in its various marks under their collective belts.

As the F.6 supplanted the F.3, the Squadron sphere of QRA operations extended further and further north and, with tanker support, the Iceland–Faeroes gap became a regular stamping ground. On one of the first intercepts after Goodwin's arrival, Rich Rhodes took some photographs of a 'Bear' with a borrowed camera. The resultant photos were sent off to HQ Fighter Command who were so impressed that they, for the first time, released the photographs for publication. Because of its remote situation, Leuchars was shunned by the press when it came to writing up the story and they went to Wattisham instead and interviewed 56 Squadron, who were promoted nationally as the cameramen respon-sible—much to their delight, of course, but not a situation to be accepted lightly by the Tigers. Ken Goodwin plotted immediate retribution with a raid on the Firebirds' Wattisham eyrie. Arranging for several thousand leaflets to be printed (the contents including aircraft recognition silhouet-tes of 'Bisons' and 'Bears' and a Jim Jewell cartoon depicting a Tiger in the cockpit of an F.6), these were then packed into the airbrake housings of a pair of Lightnings. Arriving at Wattisham, Ken and Henry Lether roared low across the ORP from a GCA overshoot, opened the airbrakes —'Airbrakes! Airbrakes Go!'—and dumped these leaflets over a wide area. Unbeknown to the Boss, a Staff College party was visiting that day, was in the tower at the time and witnessed the whole escapade. Fortunately the affair was taken in good part and little more was heard of the incident—the first of many instances when Ken Goodwin's guardian angel stepped in to prevent an awkward situation from developing!

Just prior to Christmas 1966 four Lightnings deployed to Cyprus and an uncharacteristically wet environment. Although still charged with QRA responsibilities (this time against the Egyptian Air Force in the arena of high tension in the Middle East), these detachments continued to be an ideal training opportunity too. The Tigers enjoyed showing off their new F.6s to the local population in Limassol—not that it could be pretended that anybody could fail to notice they were there. This was not to the liking of the Station Commander, however, who would call Goodwin in regularly to complain that the noise was disturbing the whole camp and 'could not something be done about it?' This sometimes uneasy existence was further exacerbated on Christmas Eve when Henry Lether was on QRA whilst the rest of the Squadron and their wives were enjoying the usual Christmas festivities.

The story went as follows. Goodwin and a large contingent of Tigers were at a party at the house of an old friend in Episcopi. During the course of the evening the conversation turned to Ken's new command

and the F.6, and those present took it into their heads that they would like an impromptu flying display despite the time of day and the location! Never one to shirk a chance of creating an entertaining diversion, Ken got through to QRA radar asking to be put in touch with Henry Lether. Henry meanwhile was himself surrounded by the party spirit, with all the ground crew NCOs and other ranks suitably adorned in party hats and streamers ready for a celebration after their duty had finished!

There was a provision within the regulations which allowed an airborne Q to be flown at the end of any stand-to period, and, having spoken to Goodwin ('Come on Henry! Give it a go!') and having been egged on to comply by his ground crew ('Go on, Sir! You've got to go for it!'), Henry threw all caution to the wind and agreed to launch. Hitting the alarm bells, he declared his intention of scrambling. Completing two low passes over the pan ('to show all those not working that there was still an air force operating, even at Christmas!'), he then set course for Episcopi. Not able to remember exactly where the party was being held, Henry put landing gear and flaps down, descended to 250ft and slowly followed the road towards the married quarters. He knew he was over the right place when everyone suddenly burst out of the party and started cheering and gesticulating wildly on the front lawn! That was the signal to clean up, engage reheat and climb vertically, twinkle-rolling to 30,000ft—'disappearing into the heavens like the Star of Bethlehem,' as Goodwin recalls.

Since Henry Lether had taken off, Akrotiri Radar, unable to see the low-flying Lightning on its 'scopes, had been calling for verification of height and position. His rocket climb suddenly brought him into their view and, with telephones ringing urgently and voices demanding to know 'what the hell is going on?', Henry was instructed to return to base to meet a reception committee which was already assembling. By this time the elation of the incident had gone:

> I began to realize the implications of what I had done. How was I going to talk my way out of this one? As I approached Akrotiri I could see cars converging on the Q sheds. There was nothing for it but to face the situation head-on, so I landed and taxied straight in. The ground crew and NCOs were now all rather subdued: the Station Commander had been and gone and there had been a predictable stream of irate phone calls. By this time, too, the Boss had been located and pulled in, and he and I were ordered to present ourselves before the Station Commander next morning, Christmas Day, in full dress uniform and with a full written report of the incident.

Meanwhile Ken's amazing luck stepped in again to save the day. The post of Commander-in-Chief Near East Forces was held by a Lieutenant General and chance had placed him at a different party in Episcopi at the time of the incident. He had seen Henry's performance and had immediately contacted the C-in-C of the Near East Air Force *congratulating* him on the 'bloody good show from the RAF'. This immediately took the pressure off Ken and Henry, for what could be done other than drop all thoughts of disciplinary action with such a testimony from the Army ringing in the RAF's ears? A mild rebuke was all that was left!

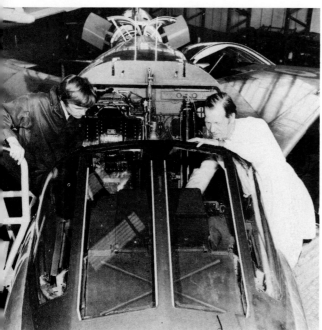

Top: Lightning F.1 XM165/'F' prior to the application of the famous black fin and spine. (Mike Cooke)

Above: XM135/'B' is one of the few Lightnings of any designation to have been preserved. This F.1 has been magnificently restored in full Tigers' colours and can be seen today at the Imperial War Museum at Duxford. (Steve Jefferson)

Left: The Squadron did not receive its two-seat Lightning T.4 XM974/'T' until 1961. Chief Tech. Red Kyte (on the right), together with his fellow-engineers, played a vital part in overcoming the many problems the Lightnings posed. (74 Squadron)

Above: Purposefully striding towards the flight line during the 1962 display season are (left to right) Vaughan Radford, Pete Phillips, Jerry Cohu, Peter Botterill, George Black and Jim Burns. By this time the 'Trinidad' nomenclature was about to be abandoned. (David Jones)

Below: 74 Squadron re-equipped with the Lightning F.3 from April 1964. Here Bob Turbin in XP751/'P' and Terry Maddern in XP702/'C' overfly the new and old Forth Bridges in September of that year. (Terry Maddern)

Above: RAF Akrotiri, October 1965, prior to 74's tanking with Victors to Meherebad to perform on Imperial Iranian Air Force Day on the 17th of the month. From left to right, standing, are Fred Buick (SEngO), Tim Cohu, Bill Maish and Gerry Crumbie and, kneeling, Bob Turbin and Terry Maddern. Note the tiger-striped refuelling probe! (Bill Maish)

Below: Tiger Meet, July 1966: Lightning T.5 XS416/'T' overflies Leuchars and the assembled NATO Tigers. (Henry Lether)

Overleaf: Between 2 and 21 April 1967, 74 deployed to Valley on Missile Practice Camp and became the first squadron to fire the Red Top. The Camp was not without its problems—a subject to which Jim Jewell, one of 74's fine diary cartoonists, applied his talent for caricaturization. (Jim Jewell/74 Squadron)

0829½

IN FACT THE TRANSPORT WAS ORDERED FOR 0845 BUT, EITHER TURNS UP JUST AS OUR HERO GETS HIS NOSH, OR DOESN'T APPEAR AT ALL.

0900

THE ROUTINE RUSH TO STALAG M.P.C. WOULD NORMALLY TAKE ABOUT 7 MINUTES BUT USUALLY LASTS ABOUT HALF AN HOUR DUE TO ALL TRAFFIC LIGHTS ON THE AIRFIELD BEING LEFT AT RED.

(a)　　(b)　　(c)

0900 - 0915

CARRY OUT VITAL DUTIES

0915

CHECK WITH ABERPORTH, LLANBEDR AND AIR TRAFFIC. USUAL ANSWERS:

(A) RANGE FULL OF CORNISH & DRUID FISHERMEN.
(B) LLANBEDR IS BLACK 3, BESIDES WHICH THE MASTER CONTROLLER IS AT HOME NURSING A SICK TOMATO PLANT.
(C) A.T.C. AT VALLEY IS NOT SURE OF SURFACE WIND

0930

INVENTORY CHECK ON BRITISH RAIL REJECT GOODIES THAT HAVEN'T BEEN GOT AT BY THE M.P.C. MOUSE.

0945 - 1045

KEEP STEELY IMAGE ALIVE WITH VITRIOLIC GAME OF UCKERS. MEANWHILE EVERY COMMAND, EXCEPT FIGHTER, HAS A RANGE SLOT AND IS LOOSING OFF ALL MANNER OF HARDWARE. IT IS EVEN RUMOURED THAT A VICTOR IS DISPENSING EMPTY SOUP TINS FOR A NEW E.C.M. TRIAL.

1045-1145

DRAGGED AWAY FROM UCKERS AT A CRUCIAL STAGE IN
THE GAME, UNCOMPREHENDING SQUADRON RECEIVES INCOMPREHENSIBLE
HOT POOP FROM M.P.C. PROFESSOR WHO BULGES WITH KNOWLEDGE
OF STRANGE SYMBOLS AND HAS EVEN STRANGER IDEAS ON WHAT TO DO
WITH THEM. GIVES SIMILAR FEELING TO GOING TO CHURCH ~ NOT SURE
WHAT HAS BEEN GOING ON BUT FEEL IT HAS DONE YOU GOOD

1220

"THE COMPLEAT FIRER"

FIRING LINKS
SANDWICHES
EGON ROMAY'S GUIDE TO EATING IN WALES
WAR RECORDER

1430

...FOLLOWED BY

BEER CALL

THE REPS APOLOGISE
FOR THIS AFTERNOON
AND INVITE 74 SQN
TO ANOTHER BARREL
AT 1700 HRS IN THE BAR

1500-1600

THE USUAL POST MORTEM

IF I'D BEEN CARRYING A
PRACTICE ROUND I BET I'D
HAVE GOT AN ACQUISITION

1200

RE-ENGAGE BRAIN AND THINK
ABOUT GASTRONOMIC DELIGHTS
WAITING IN THE MESS, PREPARED
WITH SUBTLE CARE BY DRUID
CHICKEN-SEXER-TURNED-COOK.

13TH APRIL
LUNCH
RED SOUP
FRIED NASTIES
ON
RICE
4 G PUDDING

1205

PANIC !! WEATHER CLAMPING, ALL AIRCRAFT IN U.K. ARE
GROUNDED, RAPID DETERIORATION EXPECTED IN LOCAL
AREA, RANGE AVAILABLE EXCLUSIVELY FOR M.P.C. SCRUB
LUNCH, ORDER SANDWICHES, GET CHANGED, BRIEF, BLACK
FACE, GO SHOOT LIVE 10 YEAR OLD FIREWORK.

OUT TO THE AIRCRAFT
SMASH OFF - PUNT UP
TO HEIGHT - I'LL DO THE
FIRST RUN - YOU DO
PHOTO CHASE - REST
AS PER S.O.P. - O.K. ?
~ WHERES MY B----Y
LEG RESTRAINERS?

1245 -1400

S.O.P. FIRING SORTIE.........

1700-2359

FORGET DINNER — REPS. BEER AS GOOD AS
ANYONE ELSES — WIPE FLOOR WITH F.T.S. STUDENTS
AT ARROWS ~ BURP HIC ! GOODNIGHT

Above left: On the final day of the 1966 Meet the formation of Tigers was led by Jim Throgmorton (USMC) flying the T.5. He was followed by Belgian and Canadian F-104 and RF-104 Starfighters, a USAF F-4 Phantom, a USAF F-100 Super Sabre, a French Super Mystère and the Germans in a T-33. (Terry Maddern)

Above right: In 1965 Princess Margaret presented a new Squadron Standard to 74. In July 1966 came the presentation of the Malan Memorial Sword, an idea conceived and brought to fruition by Brookie Brookes and Doug Tidy. Amongst those present at the ceremony at Bentley Priory were Tom Rowland, John Lapsley, Doc Ferris and H. M. Stephen. Here Bill Maish holds the magnificent Sword, which is carried on all ceremonial occasions by the Tigers' Commanding Officer, before the equally magnificent new Standard. (Bill Maish)

Left: Once the Squadron had moved to Tengah it found itself working regularly with the Royal Navy and Fleet Air Arm. Here Red Top-armed Lightning F.6 XS895 receives fuel from an 893 Naval Air Squadron Sea Vixen, XP920, the latter flying from HMS *Hermes*. (Trevor MacDonald Bennett)

Above: When Ken Goodwin left 74, the Squadron decided to have an 'unofficial' photograph taken for the Squadron diaries. Amongst the unlikely looking Tigers here are David Pugh (SEngO) and Tony Saw (JEngO) in khaki drill, Ken himself, sixth from the right on the wing, and Pete Carter, swinging from the boom! (David Pugh/Dave Roome)

Right: On the occasion of the Squadron's 50th Birthday in July 1967, Dennis Witham of Rolls-Royce presented CO Ken Goodwin with a silver cigarette box. Amongst those looking on are Frank Whitehouse, Jim Jewell, Ian McBride, Pete Carter, Tony Ellender and Neil Davidson. (Ken Goodwin)

Above: RAF Tengah, looking towards the north-west. The Johore Straits are in the background, with Malaya beyond. (Jim Jewell)

Below: Ian McBride's python, which wound itself around the oleo leg of his Lightning as he was taxying in after a sortie. Ian tentatively holds the python's tail on the right of the picture. To his right is Dennis Caldwell, who replaced Ken Goodwin as CO, and next to him is Ch. Tech. Jock Elphick. SAC Mike Lobb has taken control of the other end of the python, albeit with the help of a local civilian. (David Pugh/Alan Thompson)

Above: Seven thousand hours of Lightning flying: (left to right) Tony Craig (SEngO), Kevin Mace, Barney Bullocke (OC B Flight), Dennis Caldwell (CO), Pete Carter, Tony Ellender and Dave Roome. Above them is the Battle of Britain Class locomotive nameplate '74 Squadron', which has since disappeared. (Tony Craig)

Below: Taken in August 1967, this photograph shows aircraft of the Far East Air Force (FEAF) and includes an RAAF Mirage III of 75 Squadron, with whom the Tigers were to establish a particular accord on Tiger Rag detachments. (Fg. Off. B. Adcock, 75 Sqn. RAAF)

Above: RAAF Butterworth: A Flight detachment, February 1968. (Jim Jewell)

Below: The interesting architecture of the 74 Squadron hangar at RAF Tengah, March 1968. (Jim Jewell)

Right: XS897/'K' lifts off from Gan's runway with Roger Pope at the controls in September 1971 during the deployment to RAF Akrotiri, where it, and 74's other Lightnings, would be handed over to 56 Squadron. (Geoff Parselle)

Below right: One of 74's two-seaters lies derelict at Leconfield with engines removed, panels off, systems gutted—and no future. A sad obituary for a fine aircraft. (Bob Hulls)

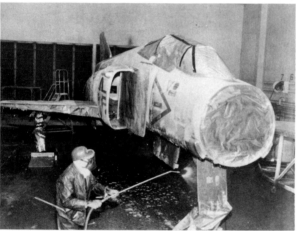

Above: US Navy F-4J 153783 arrives at San Diego direct from storage at MASDC, 30 November 1983. A first flight for '3783 from the McDonnell Douglas facility, St Louis, on 18 March 1967 preceded delivery to VX-4 (one of the Navy's Air Test and Evaluation Squadrons) at Point Mugu in California where she spent her service career and where she was to become one of the most celebrated of the Phantoms which were converted to F-4J(UK) standard by virtue of the fact she was painted in an all-black scheme and nicknamed 'Black Bunny'. When re-work was complete she carried British serial ZE353. (Naval Air Rework)

Centre left: The process through which each of the fifteen Phantoms bought from the United States were put at the Naval Air Rework Facility included the stripping of all paintwork . . . (Naval Air Rework)

Bottom left: . . . the removal of engines . . . (Naval Air Rework)

Right: . . . and the gutting of many systems, including those in the cockpits. (Naval Air Rework)

Below: The end result: pristine F-4J(UK)s finished in a beautiful non-standard colour scheme! (Via Dave Allan)

Bottom: Tiger crews trained and converted with the United States Marine Corps' VMFAT-101 at Yuma, Arizona, on the F-4S as there were no F-4Js remaining in USMC or US Navy service. The F-4S is virtually identical in appearance, although it has the advantage (some would argue) of leading-edge slats. Here ZE352 formates on a shakedown flight from San Diego with F-4S 155542 of VF-301 for a publicity photograph. (Via Dave Allan)

Left: In 1988 the Tiger Meet was held at Cameri in Italy, where 74 and other NATO Tiger Squadrons were hosted by F-104s of 21 Gruppo. 74 applied some tiger-inspired nose art to attending aircraft, including ZE355/'S' shown here. (Kev Wooff)

Centre left: 74 was the proud winner of the Silver Tiger Trophy at the Cameri Tiger Meet. Participating crews included (back row, left to right) Ian Gale, Neil Dedman. Cliff Spink (with the trophy), Kev Wooff and Russ Allchorne; and (kneeling) Ken Moore, Dave Best, Al McSherryt, Steve Noujaim and Louis McQuade. The aircraft is ZE351/'I'. (Cliff Spink)

Below: At the beginning of 1991 the Squadron suddenly lost its F-4J(UK)s and was re-equipped with Phantom FGR.2s (XV433/'E' included) which became available when the Phantom OCU at Leuchars disbanded. (Tony Dixon)

During February 1967 and for the ensuing four months, all Squadron training was directed towards the forthcoming deployment to Tengah. Amidst this activity, three weeks were spent at Valley on MPC. This was a particularly significant event as 74 had been selected to be the first operational squadron to fire Red Top in the wake of a long period of development work elsewhere. Three of these missiles were allocated (as well as two Firestreaks), and six F.6s set off for Anglesey. Hopes were high that, after the frustrations of the previous Camp firings, this occasion would be more successful, although the trials with Red Top during its development had hardly been encouraging. Ken Goodwin takes up the story:

We were ready for live firing by the middle of the first week but attempts to actually do so were continually frustrated by the presence in the range of the Cornish fishing fleet, displaced from its own waters by the Torrey Canyon disaster; by target unserviceability; by the weather at Llanbedr; and by the system of allocating range slots. When we did get on the ranges, our troubles continued because, despite having fully serviceable weapons systems, we could not induce Red Top to leave the aeroplane in the head-on attack profile. Indeed Norman Want, who had carried out the Red Top tactical trial whilst with the AFDS, had no fewer than four attempts before it was finally agreed to try another profile. Meanwhile Pete Frieze actually managed to become the first operational pilot to successfully fire a Red Top from a Lightning. His launch was carried out in textbook style at low level. The missile left the aircraft cleanly but it soon entered a series of violent convolutions, during which it shed all its control surfaces before plunging into a watery grave. Thus began the rumour that Red Top was made out of old torpedo parts by the Min of Ag and Fish!

Morale and confidence in the Lightning's missiles were not improved when a Firestreak fired by Jim Jewell chose to explode shortly after leaving his aircraft. With Chris Mullan as camera ship (the purpose of the camera being to record all firings for debriefing afterwards), the Jindivik target was in its prescribed position towing the flare when Jim pressed the firing button and the left-hand Firestreak was released. The missile's controls were designed to stay locked rigid until a certain speed was reached, but on this occasion they unlocked immediately, the missile curved round in front of Jim and blew itself up. Chris reported back to Ops:– 'The target is okay! Don't know about the firer. Waiting till he comes out of the smoke!' A few days later, in far from ideal weather conditions, Chris launched a Firestreak himself which exploded very close to the flare but which also did considerable damage to the Jindivik. At the very end of the detachment Ian McBride finally fired a Red Top which behaved as designed and hit the target.

OPERATION 'HYDRAULIC'

Towards the end of May 1967, 74 Squadron was declared non-operational prior to its forthcoming flight to Tengah, where it was to assume the air defence role until the emerging Singaporean Air Force was capable of assuming responsibility for the commitment itself. It took eight days to complete Operation 'Hydraulic', the largest in-flight refuelling operation to have been carried out by the RAF to date, the planning having been carried out principally by the Victor tanker crews of 55, 57 and 214 Squadrons from Marham. A few records tumbled in the course of the deployment as this would be the furthest cumulative distance Lightnings had ever flown; the longest sector distances Lightnings had flown (74 were to improve on this whilst in the Far East when four aircraft flew non-stop from Tengah to Darwin in northern Australia); the first time a Lightning had flown south of the Equator; and the furthest a Lightning had been situated from a diversionary airfield.

The advance party (led by JEngO Tony Saw) and the route support parties (led by SEngO David Pugh) left Leuchars on 1 June. The three non-tanker-qualified pilots on the Squadron—Steve Brown, Simon Bostok and Dave Carden—were based at Masirah, Gan and Tengah respectively, in command of engineering detachments which had been established to turn the Lightnings round when they arrived and send them on their way (or, in the case of Tengah, provide engineering support on their arrival). 56 Squadron personnel performed the same function at Akrotiri. The ground crews at each detachment covered all trades, and there was enough spare equipment to cater for all major problems. A 'goalkeeper' tanker circled overhead each staging post to cater for any fuel emergency. Experienced Lightning operators (all ex-74 Squadron, and released especially by their current units) worked in liaison with the tanker controllers along the route. Andy Markell was at Akrotiri, Henry Ploszek at Masirah, Dave Trick at Gan and Heinz Frick at Changi. This quartet were in charge of the flight authorization aspects of the operation and attended a daily teleprinter conference to look at the weather and other criteria before making the decision whether to proceed to the next stage.

The first six Lightnings left Leuchars on 4 June, five left on the 5th and the remaining two left on the 6th; all reached Cyprus safely, with few unserviceabilities. A potentially dangerous aspect of the operation was the concurrent outbreak of the Arab-Israeli conflict. However, it was decided that there should be no change of flight plan from that which took them over Turkey, across Iran and into Masirah as there would be no incursions into sensitive airspace. As the Lightnings flew over, however, their radios were constantly busy with largely unintelligible chatter, and the Arabs in particular, who were very much aware of 74's presence, used the occasion to claim vociferously that the aircraft were in the area to help the Israelis. 'Bombers became airborne followed by their fighter escort,' began Arab media reports. 'The fighters are armed with missiles and a new weapon which we have not been able to identify.' The truth was that the aircraft all carried dummy Red Top rounds and a Red Top pack which contained the aerials for the NDB with which they had been fitted for the deployment. The 'unidentified weapons' were the overwing tanks. And the bombers were, of course, the Victor tankers! Once the aircraft were at Singapore, all authorization papers and clearance documents for the journey were impounded by the authorities and these were sent to the United Nations to verify the purpose of 'Hydraulic'.

The last wave out of Akrotiri, comprising Want, McBride and Rhodes (the 'route sweepers'), became more closely involved with the tense situation than the rest of the Squadron. Ian McBride:

On our way through Turkey somebody had called up in perfect English on the discrete tanker frequency to ask politely where we were from and where we were going. The tanker leader gave a reasonably accurate reply and that was that. We later deduced from D/F bearings taken by the Victors that the call had come from a Russian ground station. Heading south through Iran, we were apparently invited to divert to Teheran, an offer which because of prevailing radio conditions was not received with sufficient clarity for the formation to act upon it. Instead we made best speed to the Gulf, thereby eating into our fuel reserves which also had to accommodate a non-feeding tank on my aircraft and a venting problem that Rich Rhodes was by now experiencing. Norman Want's radio had failed by this stage so he was blissfully unaware of what was going on, although he did wonder why we were going so fast! The tanker leader wanted us to divert to Bahrain but the airfield was closed by sandstorms so on we went. Never was the sight of Henry Ploszek, our man in Masirah, more welcome. We later learned that the Iranian QRA, flying F.5s, had been scrambled from Teheran to intercept us, presumably to reinforce the invitation previously extended to us.

Having already completed this particular leg rather less eventfully, Ken Goodwin had flown into Masirah only to find that he could not open the canopy of his aircraft. Once again Henry was on hand, but he was unwilling to operate the emergency system as that would have meant a considerable delay for the aircraft, so instead there was a twenty-minute wait, Ken suffering the humidity and heat as well as the tantalizing behaviour of those outside who were holding aloft ice-cold cans of beer while a corporal technician fixed a blown fuse and finally released a very hot CO! On 8 June he and Clive Mitchell took off on the last leg from Gan to Tengah. Half way across the Indian Ocean, and coming up for a refuelling bracket in severe turbulence, both pilots had great difficulty in probing the basket. Ken eventually made it but as he did so he saw a great white cloud suddenly appear on the other side of the tanker, followed by an apology. 'I'm terribly sorry Boss, I've broken the probe off!' Goodwin immediately spoke to the tanker captain. 'What happens now? What does the plan say?' After a pause, the reply came: 'We divert to Ceylon'. 'Hang on,' said Goodwin. 'How far is Butterworth?' '723 miles.' Goodwin's mind went back to the leaflet raid on Wattisham and the fact that they had completed the round trip from Leuchars, including a let down, with fuel to spare. Mitchell's internal tanks were full, although the overwings were empty. The decision was made. 'We go for Butterworth.' The Lightnings made it safely, proving that there was endurance in a Lightning after all—provided there was a tanker waiting for it after the climb-out!

Jim Jewell and his No 2, Derek Burrows, almost had to return to Gan on the final leg when the rendezvous with the tankers took place in thick cirrus. Hoses were trailed but the turbulence was such that no probing could take place. It was with just ten minutes to spare that they broke into clear weather and refuelling was possible within the planned bracket. Meanwhile, back at Masirah, Norman Want, Ian McBride and Rich Rhodes had found Tony Doidge, whose aircraft had, initially, resolutely refused to start when required but which was by then serviceable. It was decided that they should proceed in two pairs and Want wisely picked his teams so that each pair contained an aircraft with a fuel problem. For McBride it was a close-run thing. His Lightning was leaking so badly by the time he arrived at Tengah that the fuel was literally flowing straight through and venting out as fast as the tanker was putting it in. Goodwin, who was by now at Tengah, was made aware of the problem. He scrambled the crew of a tanker which had just landed to get back up to assist. This they did extremely quickly (within five minutes of the request), and with the fuel they had left on board helped get Ian safely down. The final four single-seaters arrived at Tengah on schedule on Sunday 11 June. The squadron's new T.5 (XV329—the final Lightning built for the RAF) arrived some weeks later, having been shipped out to Singapore on board the MV *Calchas*. On arrival, the T.5 had to be unloaded from the ship by craning it on to a trailer on a landing craft, sailing to the slipway at Seletar, towing it off and negotiating the narrow camp roads to 390 MU, where it was checked and taken on charge.

In general, the deployment had been an unqualified success. Ground crews at the staging posts had worked under difficult and sometimes extremely trying conditions, especially at Masirah. Their efforts were particularly praiseworthy, especially when one takes into account the fact that they had come directly from the east of Scotland to the weather of the Persian Gulf and the Equator. In recognition of their efforts, the Senior NCOs at each staging post received a commendation from the C-in-C of the Far Eastern Air Force (FEAF).

CHAPTER 10

Tengah

S OON AFTER their arrival, 74 personnel attended a series of lectures by station officers dealing with topics particular to the Far East. The acclimatization process was in some cases to take a considerable time, with the inevitable problems for the individual, the family and the Squadron; but there is no doubting that everyone soon realized the potential of Tengah as a posting, likened to a Squadron detachment that never ended! Arriving as they did during the closing stages of the Indonesian conflict, 74 found that there was something akin to a wartime atmosphere lingering in what was an exciting place anyway. Morale remained high throughout the Tigers' stay, and everyone threw themselves into station life with gusto, sharing all the many activities with a will, wives and children included. The facilities were excellent and the accommodation was of the highest order for the air crew and senior officers. This was not always the case for other ranks, though, and there were initially considerable problems for some. Off camp it was not unknown for families to be allocated one hotel room or small apartment whilst something more suitable was found. This was a bad start for men and their wives who had viewed the chance of sampling life in the Far East with a certain measure of anticipation, but fortunately it was not long before the welfare services stepped in to improve the situation and things began to take on the expected rosy hue.

The climate was not always idyllic, of course, the monsoon season disrupting life for several weeks of the year, but it was in general far from unhealthy; and the overseas allowances and duty-free concessions were an added attraction. Opportunities were taken by all ranks to explore as much as possible the delights of South-East Asia, the whole of the Malayan peninsula and Thailand included, some venturing as far as Japan. Locally, full advantage was taken of the perfect beaches for picnics and swimming expeditions in the warm, clear water around the offshore islands. Mersing on the east coast was a favourite spot, and there was often a Friday night exodus of husbands with wives, two cool boxes and a guitar. It was during one such picnic that the Incident of the Foot occurred. Jim Jewell had been exploring the area around the chosen picnic site. After a while he walked back into the camp and went straight up to Ken Goodwin and thrust a sandal complete with a severed, decaying foot still strapped into it, into his hands. 'What do you make of this, Boss?' It was decided that the nauseous object should be taken to the nearest police station, but here they were surprised to find that the officer on duty appeared less than bothered. He took it, put it under the counter and wished them all a good evening. 'Is that all you wish to know?' 'Have you got the other one?' 'No.' 'Well, if you find it, bring it in!' And with that he carried on with his paperwork. Jim and Ken left, convinced that once they had gone the sandal and contents would either be deposited in the refuse bin or thrown out for the local dogs! The sequel to the story was spotted in the *Straits Times* a few days later when a short report was carried about a body which had been found near a railway line minus its feet. But what really caught the eye was the continuing detail, which quoted the fact that the body also had four bullet wounds in the back. 'Police,' the article concluded, 'have not ruled out the possibility of foul play.'

Forays would be made by the men across the Johore Straits into Malaya, both as tourists and as participants in jungle survival courses which involved one week at Changi with a day in the Mandai Swamp to learn the difficulties of travelling in secondary jungle. Time would be spent learning about signal flares, rudimentary cooking, first aid and how to decapitate chickens. This knowledge was imparted by a Geordie instructor whose accent was almost unintelligible but whose lecture technique was superb. His favourite saying concerned the most dangerous snake in the jungle. 'It is yellow and black', he would intone, 'and about four feet long. If you get hold of one you'll quickly find about fourteen stone of hacked-off tiger on the other end!' The second week of the course was spent in Malayan jungle, where trainees were left to their own devices, drawing on their new-found expertise. Tengah had its own Station Combat and Rescue Survival Officer (SCRSO) and amongst the requirements of the job was that of demonstrating the use of the 'Treescape', a pack containing two hundred feet of nylon rope and a brake unit. This was carried, when flying over jungle, attached to the flying suit under the Mae West. If after ejection the crew member finished up suspended in the jungle canopy, he was meant to tie one end of the rope to the parachute harness and let himself down by the brake unit attached to the lifting points on the Mae West. Dave Roome used to demonstrate the technique by descending from the pan lights in front of the Squadron hangar! Dave will forever be remembered for the incident flying as No 2 to Simon Bostok when he suddenly shouted over the radio, 'My bloody feet have run away!'—then promptly disappeared from sight in the cockpit. The bottom portion of his ejection seat had collapsed, leaving Dave more or less flat on his back (or as flat as one can get in a Lightning cockpit!) and having great difficulty in reaching the rudder pedals! Landing proved to be a tricky business with Dave having to wedge himself into an upright position so that he could both see and reach the controls!

Sharing the station with the Tigers when they arrived were 45, 20, 81, 60 and 64 Squadrons flying Canberra B.15s, Hunter FGA.9s, Canberra PR.7s and Javelin FAW.9s. As on any RAF station, there was the customary rivalry between the squadrons. Indeed, 74's arrival with its new jets on a station with so many different squadrons fulfilling different roles in itself created a measure of animosity. But this is where the likes of Ken Goodwin proved their worth, and it was not long before everyone got on famously, both operationally and socially, although the Tigers did gain a permanent reputation for gatecrashing other people's parties! And not to be forgotten was the special relationship with the Tiger Brewery, a concern which did not hesitate in embracing the arrival of the Tiger Squadron as a marvellous promotional opportunity. Within days every nook and cranny of the Squadron seemed to be stacked out with the potent, fizzy beer. Thus began a long and prosperous understanding! Relationships between the RAF and local people were always very good and everyone made friends amongst them. Chinese, Malays and Indians worked closely together on base as stewards, clerks, security officers, policemen, tanker drivers and so on. And Ken Goodwin could still count amongst his acquaintances many old friends from his previous period of duty with FEAF, including Singapore's Prime Minister, Lee Kwang Yew.

There is no doubt that the years at Tengah were a particularly challenging and rewarding time for all. It made for a marvellous spirit, and Tigers remember it as amongst the most demanding times that they can recall in their service careers. Several factors contributed to this: the Lightning F.6 itself; the new and very different environment, with weather which enabled training programmes to be planned and completed with virtually no disruption; and the effective 'freezing' of postings, so that the Squadron personnel—air crew and ground crews alike—all got to know each other very well. 74 soon established a comprehensive training and operational routine, and by the end of the first full month in Singapore had flown a creditable 317 hours—this despite a spares problem, which reared its head very quickly and was destined to remain throughout the four years at Tengah, largely because of the length of the supply line which relied on the regular VC10 flights from Brize Norton. The immediate problem was partially solved by the consigning of one aircraft to 'hangar queen' status and using her as a spares source. A relaxation of the MoD directive about individualizing squadron aircraft prompted a session of fin painting, and before long the Tigers were proudly resplendent once again with black tails—but not spines, because of the problem of heat dissipation. The initial attempt was not very successful, a couple of newly painted aeroplanes losing all their colour after flying into a storm. The problem was solved by etching the surface to be painted, thereby allowing the paint to adhere. BAC were certainly none too happy about such unsophisticated activity when they found out about it. Nor were 56 Squadron when they took 74's aircraft on charge in Cyprus in 1971: they could not get the black paint off—hardly surprising when cumulo-nimbus (known as 'bumblies') was unable to remove it.

The weather as well as the terrain in the Far East was in great contrast to that left behind in Scotland, but pilots and ground crews soon settled into the new environment of heat and humidity. Adjustment to the superb flying conditions did not take long. It was generally always fine in

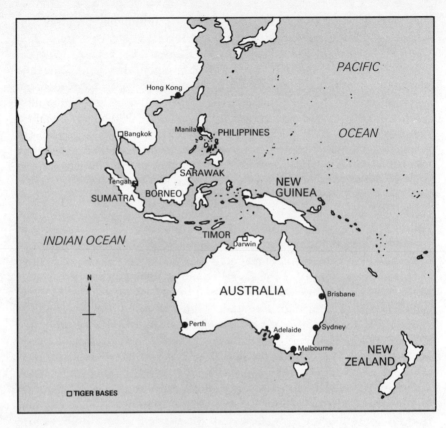

THE FAR EAST, 1967—1971

the mornings, any build-up of towering bumblies and the resultant storms taking place in the late afternoon and evening after the heat of the day had done its work. The exception was the occasional great storm which would brew up over Sumatra and move across to southern Malaya at four or five o'clock in the morning, when Tengah would wake to the sound of wind-blown trees and a feeling of cold even though rooms might not be air-conditioned. Walking outside, people would be confronted by an awesome pale grey mountain of cloud; and when it hit, the noise of the rain and the power of the storm were spectacular.

Under the auspices of 'Cockpit Air Redistribution Trial—Lightning Mod 4336', one aircraft was fitted with a modification to the ventilation system. Six temperature sensors were fitted to the cooling ducts and the pilot, and readings were taken at five-minute intervals at different speeds and heights. The trials were not an unqualified success. On one occasion the pilot of the modified aircraft suffered more from the effects of heat than the one flying the unmodified companion aircraft. This former was Ian McBride, whose air-conditioning turned into hot air-conditioning when the whole system malfunctioned, the metal inside the cockpit becoming too hot to touch! One of the problems of operating the Lightning in the hot and humid conditions of Singapore was the readiness with which the cockpit canopy became opaque with condensation if the pilot forgot to switch on the demist prior to descent after operating at the cooler higher altitudes. But even with demist on and the conditioning working, pilots would arrive soaked in sweat as the descent into the warmer atmosphere very quickly turned the cockpit into a greenhouse, temperatures of 50°C being reached on occasions. It was not unusual for individuals to lose 7lb in weight in the course of a single sortie. On landing, the first job would be to down a couple of glasses of cold orange juice to replace lost fluid. Traditionally, if a pilot reached a milestone in numbers of Lightning hours flown, he would be greeted on the tarmac with a bottle of champagne, but the effect of just a few sips of this before the orange would be one of inducing intoxication very quickly! When the Squadron first arrived at Tengah the men were issued with air-ventilated suits, but there were no walk-round bottles with them, so walking out from the building to the aircraft would leave a pilot drenched and unfit to fly straightaway. The suits were discarded. Thereafter, beneath the *g*-suits, the standard wear was teeshirt and shorts.

At the beginning of August four Mirage IIIOs from the Royal Australian Air Force at Butterworth arrived at Tengah to take part in Exercise 'Cry Havoc'. This was to be the start of a long and fruitful relationship with the Australians both operationally and socially, the Lightnings and Mirages later deploying alternately to Butterworth and Tengah on 'Tiger Rag' detachments. Much of the work they did together was in air combat, and this was undoubtedly highly beneficial to both parties. The Lightning showed considerable advantages over the French design in turns and accelerations, especially over 35,000ft, but often this could not be put to good use because of the lack of a gun, something which gave the Aussie pilots a distinct psychological advantage, knowing that they could not be hurt at close quarters by a gunless fighter. Ken Goodwin:

In truth, the Mirage and the Lightning were fairly evenly matched. The Mirage equalled the power-to-weight ratio of the Lightning and generally had the edge on manoeuvrability. Certainly, if they had the initiative to start with they would maintain it. At lower altitudes the Lightning had that lovely character-istic of square corners! And once the speed dropped we could sit and defy the laws of flight. The Aussies were not quite so keen to get so slow. Before a speed limit imposition we could get down to an amazing 150 knots and sinking! Then a 210 knots minimum was imposed after a couple of Lightnings had been lost in the UK and Tony Doidge confessed to me that he had spun one, falling a long way before recovery. To spin a Lightning was not easy. If a spin was looming you simply let everything go and it would stop almost regardless of your attitude.

The vexed question of an integral gun comes up in every pilot's assess-ment of the Lightning as a fighting machine.

We should never, ever have had an aeroplane without a gun. This was a decision in the aftermath of the Duncan Sandys missiles edict which predicted wars without manned aeroplanes, a statement which lost the UK a lot of ground. The gunpack was not fitted to the Lightning until Dennis Caldwell became CO. Without the gun the Lightning could only be regarded as a bomber interceptor and not a one v. one fighter; with it, the Lightning was superior to any other interceptor in the East or West.

Norman Want enjoyed the regular fighting with the Australians.

Having flown the Mirage as a trials pilot on AFDS, I had a healthy respect for it. However, the Mirage reputation was built on Israeli mythology and I would like to think that we could put up a slightly better fight than some of their opposition. I have often felt that British industry and the Air Force tended to absolute honesty in aircraft and weapons system performance whereas both the French and the Americans made some fairly wild claims about comparable systems. There was no doubt in my mind that the Lightning was an exceptional aircraft. It lacked the range and the firepower of the Mirage III and F-106 and the auto attack system of the latter. Conversely the AI23B was rugged, easy to operate and allowed great flexibility with our training, emphasizing operator skills as opposed to relying on black boxes. I've met a lot of air forces whose world collapses if the kit isn't working properly!

It was not only the Australians that the Tigers were to work with in Singapore. New Zealand Skyhawks and Canberras, RAF squadrons on deployment from the United Kingdom and, most frequently, the Royal Navy were visitors to Tengah during the years the Tigers were there. A few weeks after their arrival, the carrier *Hermes* docked in Singapore and the Lightnings completed a lot of valuable flying with Vixens and Gannets. 74 investigated the possibility of using the Vixen as a tanker and the Navy used the Gannets to control 74 during low-level pilot interceptions. The Tigers in turn provided the Navy with targets in a series of exercises during which the Tigers would 'attack' a ship, giving their gunners aiming practice and allowing the defending fighters to practise interceptions of an incoming threat. Simon Bostok recalls one such exercise:

Ian McBride and I were flying as a pair and had just engaged two Sea Vixens. Closing up after the interception had been completed for a photograph, the Vixens misinterpreted the manoeuvre as another attempted rear quarter attack and immediately broke hard right, one of the aircraft pulling excessive *g* and springing several panels from the fuselage which spiralled down to the sea. Unfortunately, attached to one of these panels were black boxes essential to the operation of the aircraft, the net result being the declaration of a major emergency by the Navy pilot and a very cautious let-down into Tengah. Ian and I chalked this up as 'One damaged!'

TRIALS AND TRIBULATIONS—AND RECORDS

On 7 September Ian McBride was out on an air-to-air training sortie when, at the start of an evasive manoeuvre, he found that the control column could not be moved any further than an inch aft of centre, all his attempts to free it proving futile. With experimentation he established that in the landing configuration at 180 knots he could control the rate of descent by the use of full nose-up trim and by adjusting the engine power. After two very flat practice approaches, he landed the aircraft safely,

> ... although, despite my best efforts, it was little short of a controlled crash which rattled my teeth and dislodged the loose article which had caused the problem in the first place.

McBride was awarded a Green Endorsement for his handling of the situation.

Four aircraft were detached to Butterworth for the first of a series of 'Tinsmith' trials during September, 'Tinsmith' being an early form of Automatic Data Processing (ADP) for intercepts. The trials were conducted in two parts, the first at Butterworth involving the hardware and proof-of-concept of the system and the second with the radar facility at Bukit Gombak which concentrated on the software and on the evaluation of the system. The role of Bukit Gombak in this was the assessment of incoming threats and directing available air defence aircraft on to them. The ADP operation consisted of various profiles being produced by computer after the necessary parameters had been fed in—speed, height, heading and fuel state. A target would be released and the computer would work out the optimum times for the use of reheat, when to climb, when to turn and so forth. As long as the operator passed the commands to the aircraft when they appeared on his console, ADP worked very well. One problem which occurred in the early days was the fact that controllers worked in pairs, one acting as safety officer and the other as data reader, and many a pilot heard two voices telling him to do opposite things simultaneously! Slowly though (and according to Bukit personnel this was the only way a pilot could think!), the ADP system became of more use. It was not always reliable in terms of serviceability, and the cry 'Going manual' would often be heard, which meant that the controller had to revert to conventional means of vectoring aircraft.

Another series of exercises which began in late 1967 was 'Malayan Litex', involving the deployment of Victors from the UK-based tanker squadrons to the Far East to enable 74 to remain current on in-flight refuelling. Night tanking in the conditions prevailing in the Malaysian skies often provided glorious views of St Elmo's Fire, which would enshroud the wing tips and often the forward fuselage, spreading from the nose to split and dance back alongside the cockpit. 'Kitten' was an alert exercise designed to test the Squadron's ability to generate the maximum number of aircraft in a given time and then scramble them against 'enemy' Mirages of 75 Squadron RAAF. Exercise 'Nigella' involved all the air defence units and strike aircraft of FEAF. Exercise 'Hesper' was conceived primarily for strike and PR units and 74 was tasked with intercepting returning Tengah-based aircraft. On Exercise 'Light Rage', six Red Top Lightnings were placed on alert and scrambled, but in the climb out through cloud, three of the Red Top nose cones fractured. This highlighted a problem that 74 had been experiencing for some time and an investigation now showed that the temperature change between the ground and normal operating height, allied with the impact of rain and hail when flying through bumblies (which often seemed like an underwater experience), could not be withstood by the rounds. Firestreak was still carried as well, and following the Red Top problems Exercise 'Fireflash' was called, in which the Tigers were tasked to fire five. Unfortunately, flares manufactured in 1944 were used as the infra-red source and, as may be expected, were totally unreliable! Out of seven firing sorties, only one successful launch was achieved.

During April 1968 the Tigers captured the Tengah-to-Butterworth speed record. Over the previous months, both 74 and 75 Squadrons had set out to complete the transit between the two bases on 'Tiger Rag' deployments as fast as possible, and inevitably, as the times quickened, competition became more intense with the honour of both at stake. During the March exchange the Aussies had reduced the transit time to 27min 30sec. Ken Goodwin immediately retaliated by attempting an unsophisticated full 'burner throttle through the gate run with his fuel disappearing at an alarming rate but failing to regain the record. Obviously a more scientific approach was needed and, as the commander of the April detachment, Norman Want was ordered to retrieve the record for the Tigers. He takes up the story:

I was summoned by the Boss and told to put the time out of reach once and for all! Apart from the environmental factor (by this time Malaya was getting a little tired of having sonic booms dropped across it), there were restrictions on airframe and engine times at very high Mach numbers. We didn't have much information on fuel consumption figures so, given that we were taking four aircraft, I decided to send each individually. Clive Mitchell went first and was told to run at a relatively conservative M1.3 and to call back his fuel states. Ian McBride and then Tony Doidge were to follow, each basing their runs on the results of the former and pushing up the speeds and continuing to call back fuel and distances to me. But the plot got out and the Station Commander —Phil Lageson—told the Boss to 'bin it'! The Boss, being the Boss, accompanied me to my aircraft, patted me on the head, uttered the immortal Goodwinian catchphrase 'Don't worry about a thing' and told me to get on with it. Obviously our devious ways were well known because I received a personal directive from the Station Commander as I taxied out that I was *not* to attempt any records. But I was having all sorts of trouble with my R/T that morning and got airborne and went for it. The aircraft behaved beautifully, no fire warning lights came on, I landed with enough fuel to taxi in—and we had the record. The distance, I remember, was around 330 miles; the date April 18th, 1968; the aircraft XR768; and the time from tower to tower 24 minutes 17 seconds in a run which saw me accelerate initially to M1.6 and then to M1.99, at which the aircraft was far from full throttle.

In the annals of Tiger folklore, it is said to this day that the attempt literally cut a swathe of damage through jungle, felling trees and causing native huts to collapse! The record was truly a team effort and the subsequent rigorously enforced ban on any further attempts obviously suited the Tigers. After all, they had the record in the bag—and, as far as is known, still hold it today.

The record had been achieved with the total co-operation of Singapore ATC and, indeed, in many ways had served to cement a relationship with that facility, a relationship which had been further strengthened by the negotiation of a procedure unique to 74 Squadron. In consultations between Bukit Gombak, Singapore Radar and the other squadrons on the three Singaporean camps, it was agreed that the Tigers could make use of their high rate of climb when departing Tengah bound for the supersonic training area to the east. Instead of staying at low level initially, the Lightnings were now authorized to zoom-climb over Tengah to a height which would clear the airway over Singapore Island in a departure which became known cryptically as the Tigers' Leap. Bearing in mind the fact that Tengah was bordered by controlled airspace to the north and east and by the international boundary with Indonesia to the south, the value of the Leap can be appreciated.

As SEngO, David Pugh had to face up to constant unserviceability problems. A look through the Squadron's 540s for the period shows a series of incidents which, added to a formidable list of modification requirements, made the engineer's lot if not an unhappy one then certainly a busy and demanding one. The spares problem did not improve; and it was not only spares for the aircraft themselves that were lacking but tools with which to do the job too. On the first detachment to Butterworth for the 'Tinsmith' trials, the alternator of one aircraft caught fire on landing. David had decided that the tape around the 'elephant's ears' (the large panels covering the equipment bay just aft of the cockpit) to seal out monsoon weather when on the ground could remain in place when the aircraft flew. It was found that it usually peeled off, but this was thought not to be a problem until it was ingested by the cooling intake of one Lightning at the forward base of the fin, thereby blocking all the filters. All the aircraft had to be checked; and this could only be done by taking out No 2 jetpipe. David could not claim to have been popular with the ground crews or with Command HQ, especially when it was found that there were no jetpipe cradles in Butterworth for the job to be done! This problem, allied with concurrent rudder feel simulator seizures, meant that during September 1967 there were eight Lightnings LOG. Such serviceability problems reached critical proportions with some regularity over the ensuing months, so much so that the T.5 was on more than one occasion pressed into service when it was itself officially grounded with a ruptured ventral tank. The twenty-five minutes' endurance left to her was better than nothing! It was the realization that the Lightning was a highly complex machine and that many of the problems were caused by the necessity for design modifications and were not as a result of maintenance deficiencies that kept morale good.

David Pugh takes a fairly relaxed view of the period that he and Tony Saw were with the Tigers:

It is difficult to know where to start when it comes to experiences on the engineering side. Perhaps they were best put into perspective by the old adage,

'The only thing that you can do with the Lightning without taking out the engine is to wipe the windscreen!' My time at Tengah was largely a tale of the usual scramble for hours with overmuch work caused by the need for engine and jetpipe removals. Having noted the pilots' frequent celebrations of 1,000 hours on type, we in turn celebrated Chief Tech Sharp's 1,000th jetpipe removal. But most of the time there was the routine struggle to reach the flying target. The demise of 81 Squadron helped us, for this meant that there was more hangar space available in which to work; and it also meant that all of 74's Lightnings could be put away every night and at weekends, which in turn meant fewer starting and electrical problems caused by the humidity. Although we were never flush with aircraft for the flying programme, we used to scrape home most of the time. And despite all the problems there was one great success. This was down to Tony Saw, who devised a way of cleaning the space between the inner and outer layers of the canopy glass. After much consultation with BAC and the failure of many ideas as to how it could be kept clean, he solved it by filling the space with Fairy Liquid, swilling out and drying in the sun!

DOWN UNDER

Most of the air crew experienced airborne problems at one time or another. Rick Lea landed safely after declaring an emergency with a double hydraulic failure on only his second solo F.6 trip. Tony Doidge was up to practise short-field landings when, three quarters of the way through a morning sortie, his arrester hook released. Tony asked for the RHAG to be de-rigged. This was done and a normal landing was made. The same aircraft flew again uneventfully during the day, but on a further sortie in the evening, with Tony once more at the controls, the hook fell again. Short of fuel, the pilot had no time for the RHAG to be de-rigged on this occasion and Tony had no option but to come straight in. He failed to miss the wire and the aircraft was brought to rest from 160 knots in 330 yds—surely amongst the shortest Lightning landings ever—with only minor damage sustained. Squadron wags talked in terms of Tony's going for HMS *Hermes* when she was next in port!

Within a few weeks Steve Brown was forced into an arrester situation too, but this time with the barrier as opposed to the wire. His brake 'chute had deployed normally on landing, but the brakes then failed. By the time the runway's end was reached, the speed of the aircraft was relatively slow, but, even so, entry into the barrier caused serious damage to the spine. And Trevor MacDonald Bennett suffered a disastrous engine fire whilst on three-mile finals to Changi on his first sortie after returning from a spell back in Britain recovering from a broken hip sustained in a car crash. Brian Kneen was in charge of the party tasked with the repairs to the aircraft which T. MacD. B. had managed to get down safely:

The fire not only did considerable damage to the engine but to aircraft systems as well. We were sent to Changi to start work on the Lightning. First the damaged engine was removed and then the aircraft was jacked and trestled and supported. It was to be in this state for six months. We had a mammoth task ahead of us, not helped by the necessity of travelling from Seletar airfield

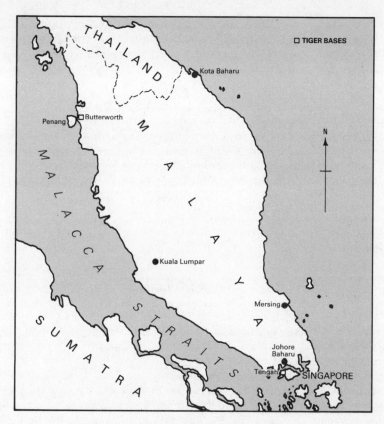

SINGAPORE AND MALAYA, 1967–1971

(where 390 MU were based). And all the time the aircraft was in our hands we had to keep up to date with all modifications as if the aircraft was operational and on line. But the job was done and it eventually went home. We had grown quite attached to her!

Shortly afterwards Jim Jewell reacted quickly when a No 1 Reheat Fire Warning illuminated. He put out a Mayday call and played a hunch by shutting down No 2 engine. The fire went out—which was just as well, for there was no extinguisher in the Lightning for reheat fires. A fuel leak from No 2 engine had ignited and caused the problem, and the incident subsequently led to the examination of all Lightnings, the removal of their engines and the coating of the engine bays with a special sealant. Jim's 'chute failed during his emergency landing and, the aircraft at an all-up weight of 37,000lb, the brakes were unable to bring it to rest. The subsequent engagement of the RHAG was entirely 'text-book', with no damage—the first *intentional* RHAG engagement for the Tigers!

This incident had taken place at exactly the same place as Pete Thompson's fatal accident a few weeks previously. Pete had joined the Squadron during August 1968 but within the month he had been killed. Returning to the circuit in close formation on his leader (Pete Carter) prior to a pairs landing, he was overshooting from a GCA when he called an emergency. A double reheat fire had broken out in the jetpipe area of his aircraft. With undercarriage and flaps down, and just about to turn finals, the aircraft pitched up and spun. Pete ejected too late and was killed when he hit the ground a mile north of the airfield. The Squadron was particularly saddened and angry about this accident when it was discovered that a similar fire had occurred in Britain when one of English Electric's test pilots had suffered an identical problem and had survived. Pete Thompson caught fire with the runway under his wing; had the Squadron been made aware of the previous incident then he would have climbed or been instructed to climb so that he could have ejected with a far better chance of survival rather than when trying to bring the aircraft in. Thinking about this incident and the cause of Pete's death led Jim Jewell to the fuel leak theory which had caused the fire in his aircraft. David Pugh:

> The subsequent 'Leaks' programme was designed to prevent leaks of fuel in the top (No 2) bay of the aircraft and therefore fire penetrating to the bottom (No 1) bay. We had splendid help from the BAC man who had come out to oversee the programme and who promised us that he would make our Lightnings as 'tight as a tiger's arse'. When he left he was given a tankard made from sheet aluminium, riveted together and with the cracks stopped with all the various 'gunges' used in hangar!

74 Squadron celebrated its 50th Anniversary in March 1968. It should of course have been celebrated in the July of the previous year, but 'Hydraulic' had put paid to that. After a month of practising, the Tigers' display team, led by Jim Jewell and christened 'Jim's Frantic Five', performed on the day. The Squadron's First World War CO, Keith Caldwell, remembered the 50th Anniversary by writing to Ken Goodwin from his home in Papatoetoe in New Zealand, regretting that he could not attend the celebrations but sending his best wishes to all serving Tigers and advising that everyone 'keep watch for ghosts of the past' as festivities commenced.

During October 1968 the Americans came to Tengah, bringing with them an RB-57F. The Royal Aircraft Establishment from Bedford arrived, too, with a Canberra PR.7, both aircraft being employed on research into high-altitude meteorological conditions with a view to future supersonic transport operations, Concorde and the Boeing SST being exciting concepts on the world's aeronautical horizon at the time. There were occasions when 74 were able to make use of these high-flyers, and they took great pleasure in reminding the Americans in particular that the stratosphere was not entirely their own domain when pairs of Lightnings intercepted and carried out simulated attacks on the RB-57 at 60,000ft, an altitude at which the American crew had every reason to believe they were safe from manned interceptors.

Before Christmas at Tengah it was the usual practice for each squadron to build a bar which would be entered in a competition to be judged by a team headed by the Station Commander. The features looked for included originality, ingenuity, decor, theme, atmosphere and hospitality. 74's 1967 entry had been an Austrian ski lodge named 'Das Tigerhaus' and had come complete with expanded-polystyrene snow and an Oompah Band. It had been constructed in one of the Squadron offices and was awarded second place. In 1968 the Squadron built the winning entry, an African native compound with a circular bar in the middle. In 1969 attention was turned to the United States of America, a Mississippi river boat being built, and in an effort to achieve complete authenticity a brass bell was borrowed from Shell. Unfortunately the 'Wheelhouse' was raided and the bell was purloined, never to be seen again.

In the New Year of 1969 the Tigers were joined at Tengah by 11 Squadron, who brought ten aircraft to Singapore on Exercise 'Piscator Plus'. Escorted in by the Tigers after a seventeen-hour flight, the UK-based Lightnings stayed for three weeks and participated in several exercises, including 'Mulse', during which 74 and 11 provided the 'air defence' for Singapore. The 'attackers' were 20, 45 and 81 Squadrons as well as aircraft from HMS *Hermes* and the Australians from Butterworth. The Victors which had brought 11 Squadron from England participated as well. The 'Battle of Singapore' ended only after fifty 'strikes' had been made on Singapore's civil airport in the course of 4½ hours, during which time international and domestic flights had had to be rescheduled. Another exercise involving both squadrons was 'Enchanter', in which high-level CAP for *Hermes* was provided. On the first day the runway at Tengah was blocked for three hours by a Hercules after the first two pairs of Lightnings had got airborne. Using a tanker launched for the purpose, 74's aircraft remained airborne for 4hr 40min and were then diverted to Changi to allow two very sore pilots to land and escape the confines of the cockpit.

After 11 Squadron had returned to the UK and Ken Goodwin had been dined out prior to his posting to the Joint Services College (during which he was presented with a pewter tankard inscribed with his catchphrase 'Don't Worry About a Thing'), A Flight Commander Pete Carter took up the reigns pending Dennis Caldwell's arrival from Britain to lead the Tigers. Dennis was a scrupulously fair Commanding Officer who was full of fun too. He was very much a pilot's pilot and a leader's leader, respected by air and ground crews alike, very supportive of his men and quickly defensive of his Squadron. There is a lovely story of the day Dennis was escorting a Chinese delegation around the Squadron shortly after his arrival. He started by showing them the Honours Board on which the names of all the Squadron's COs are inscribed with his own at the bottom. The keen eye of one of the delegation quickly picked out the same name of the Tiger's first CO at the top: 'Ah so! Still here I see!' Operationally, close liaison with 75 Squadron RAAF continued, particularly in early 1969 when the Australians deployed to Tengah for several weeks while Butterworth's runways were being resurfaced, and a new friendship was struck with another Mirage-flying Aussie squadron, No 3, which shared the ramp as well. Both the Australians and the British were deeply saddened when 75's CO, Wing Commander Myers, was killed when his Mirage crashed into the Malacca Straits fifty miles west of Singapore while conducting low-level interceptions at night.

On 16 June 1969 two Lightnings, flown by Dennis Caldwell and Neil Davidson, left Tengah on the 2,000-mile journey to Darwin in North Australia as a component of Exercise 'Silver Swallow'; a second pair, with Chris Peile and Ian McBride, followed two days later. Four Victors had flown out from Britain to tank 74 across the archipelagos of Indonesia, Sumatra and Java. The deployment had been organized to enable 74 to participate in 'Townhouse', which had been conceived to test the defence of RAAF Darwin from both air and ground attack and was one of the biggest exercises yet staged in Australia's Northern Territories. Working in conjunction with RAAF Mirages, the Tigers' four aircraft flew eighty sorties over the eight days of the exercise against attacking Canberras (of the RAF, RAAF and RNZAF) and Vulcans of Waddington-based 50 Squadron which had also deployed to Australia. The Tigers mounted QRA for the duration, keeping one aircraft on two-minute alert (the pilot *in situ*), and the fastest time from scramble instructions being passed to getting airborne was a very snappy thirty-five seconds.

Darwin's airport remained open to civilian traffic throughout, and this required the close supervision and timing of incoming raids, fighter scrambles and movements of civil aircraft. In the process many airline pilots were reminded of their earlier flying days, and passengers in the terminal certainly saw flying from a different angle! In one instance an attacking Canberra evaded *around* a departing BOAC 707 which had ignored the ATC instruction to stay low! The Australian Mirage and Dave Roome's Lightning, who were both chasing the Canberra, passed each side of the 707, whose Captain promptly tried to file an airmiss: this was refused on the grounds that the civil pilot had brought it upon himself!

While at Darwin the Squadron used a stretch of taxiway for servicing. The advance party had requested a hangar in case it rained: 'This is the dry season mate! It *doesn't* rain!' True enough. But it was very, very warm—warm enough in fact for the taxiway to start melting. It was fortunate that an alert airman spotted the Lightnings sinking through the tarmac in time to tow them out of the dents their wheels were making! Whilst 'Townhouse' was still in progress, the telephone rang in 74 Squadron Ops at Tengah and a voice asked to speak to Flying Officer Dave Roome. 'Ah, but he's in Australia.' 'Okay, I'll ring back in ten minutes!' Which serves to give some idea to the uninitiated of just how fast the Lightning could fly!

Lightning serviceability improved enough during July for a considerable number of sorties to be flown against the Vulcans (which, after 'Townhouse', had flown to Butterworth from Darwin) operating in the electronic countermeasures role. The chance was also taken to fly some one v. one sorties against a pair of A-4 Skyhawks from the carrier HMAS *Melbourne* which was undergoing repairs in Singapore at the time. July was a month of small-scale exercises—'Agnostic', 'Fragrant' and 'Julex'. For the benefit of newcomers, overwing tanks were fitted to two aircraft to enable cross-country exercises to be flown up to the Thai border. For the experienced crews, the 'Tiger Rags' continued, although sorties suffered because of more unserviceability, largely brought about by the need to keep the Lightnings outside in torrential rain for the period of the detachments to Butterworth. Unserviceability back at Tengah could not be attributed to the weather, with the aircraft parked overnight in dry hangars; rather, there was now a large turnover in engineering staff as first-tours in the Far East came to an end and the learning curve of the newcomers climbed only slowly. During December alone, for example, forty airframe and engine fitters were replaced.

Tony Craig arrived to take on the SEngO's mantle. He was a rare breed amongst engineers in the RAF, being the only one at the time who was also a fully fledged Lightning pilot. Throughout his stay with 74 he kept himself current, mainly by carrying out personally most of the air testing of aircraft emerging from deep maintenance or modification. He also flew a few operational sorties when time permitted. As with his predecessors, his time with 74 was not an easy one, and the constant flow of modifications and problems with fuel leakage remained. In respect of the latter, Tony and his JEngO, Jim Bates, devised a stainless steel and titanium casing to fit around the wing where it blended into the fuselage, thereby allowing the leakage to be contained. This was not immediately sanctioned as details of the official modification programme were due and work could not commence until they had arrived. When they did come they took the form of a stainless steel titanium box to fit around the wing where it blended into the fuselage . . .

There was a decidedly offbeat incident during the autumn of 1969. Ian McBride was taxying his Lightning after a night sortie when, in the glare of his landing light, he saw a mysterious moving object. He stopped, looked and reported a very large snake on the taxiway which slithered towards him and disappeared from view underneath the aircraft. When it failed to reappear Ian rapidly closed the canopy and taxied to dispersal. Back at the Squadron he warned the ground crew that somewhere on the aircraft they might find a large reptile and, on inspection, sure enough, they found a python, 14½ft long, wrapped tightly around the oleo leg in the nose wheel well. Getting it out was no easy matter because it was in an ugly mood and had made a really professional job of tying itself in. But eventually the snake was doped by squirting it with a fire extinguisher and out it came, alive and well. The python was given a new home in the Station Hygiene Flight, which was actually a small zoo that took in animal pets presented by RAF families returning to Britain, but the following night, obviously resenting its rejection by 74 Squadron, it decided to desert and was last seen by a police patrol slithering off into the undergrowth!

The Tigers were back on the Australian subcontinent again shortly afterwards on Exercise 'High Swallow'. The logistics were essentially the same as for the summer 'Silver Swallow', with 214 Squadron Victors tanking the four Lightnings across in two waves and ground crews and equipment following in a Hercules from Changi. There was no exercise participation this time, the idea being simply to give the rest of the Squadron experience of operating from Darwin and to give Australian controllers experience of handling Lightnings. In total, thirty-seven sorties were flown on the detachment, considerably fewer than hoped for and not helped by serious damage to one of the aircraft when an AVPIN explosion frightened the life out of T. MacD. B. while he was in the midst of his starting cycle. AVPIN was a continuous problem in the Far East because its flashpoint was only 26°C and the ambient temperature was higher than that! This explosion and its cause, followed by other AVPIN explosions and a serious fire at Tengah, eventually brought about a directive that Lightnings be attended by station fire appliances during the start-up sequence, and indeed it became a common sight to see taxying Lightnings escorted by fire crews to the runway threshold itself.

'COMPLETE UNITY'

The run-in to Christmas 1969 was dominated by further, largely unsuccessful attempts by the Squadron to fire its air-to-air missiles and by its continuing involvement in exercises, including 'Anther', a large-scale affair involving all the Tengah and Butterworth squadrons, Meteors from the Target Facilities Flight at Changi and the Lightnings of Binbrook-based 5 Squadron which had arrived from Britain at the beginning of December on the Exercise 'Ultimacy' detachment. 5 Squadron took four of the Tigers' Lightnings back to the UK when it returned (leaving four of its aircraft in Singapore), which placed additional responsibilities on the hard-pressed Squadron engineers as those departing needed a thorough check since they were to go straight into squadron service on arrival back home. It should have been an exchange of six aircraft, but two of those arriving were so far behind in the 'mods' programme that FEAF refused to accept them. As it was, the remaining aircraft needed considerable attention. When the leading edge of one of these Lightnings was removed during the course of acceptance checks, out fell two bottles of gin, obviously forgotten after being placed there during the course of some European deployment!

Tengah bowed to the inevitable as the new decade arrived. The Javelins had already gone, and now 81 (PR) Squadron disbanded, followed later by 20 and 45 Squadrons, leaving the Tigers as the sole tenants of the base for the last eighteen months of their Far East sojourn. But the Royal Navy still patrolled the surrounding seas, the Australians were still at Butterworth and the fledgeling Singaporean and Malaysian Air Forces were involving themselves to a limited degree in exercises. Aircraft continued to be deployed from Britain, too, although the 'Malayan Litex' series of Victor flights ceased in March, all such future training being completed as the opportunity arose when tankers accompanied deployments to the Far

East. Exercise 'Janex' found the Tigers performing a new role, that of simulating SS-N-3 and 'Kelt' missiles for the benefit of participating Commonwealth navies! During the exercise Frank Whitehouse and Mike Rigg were seconded to the Fleet, learning all about wardroom etiquette as well as advising on operational matters!

Exercises 'Light Rage', 'Bukit Timah' and 'Crackshot' also kept the Squadron busy, while grounding orders and modifications kept the engineering team at its usual full stretch and the number of available aircraft at a low level. The 'Trappers' arrived from CFS to evaluate the Squadron and a Families' Day was held, during which much time was taken up protecting equipment from the attention of small children! But then tragedy struck. On 25 May Dave Roome was leading John Webster on a night low-level interception exercise over the Straits of Malacca. While acting as target, John hit the sea. Dave, three miles behind him, saw nothing and heard no call. A full-scale search was mounted, but the only thing that was ever recovered was the rear portion of an overwing tank. John was a young, almost boyish Scot who, although only with the Tigers for a few months, had endeared himself to all with his ready smile and pleasant manner. He delighted in wearing garish kipper ties at Squadron functions and after a while others accepted the challenge of trying to outdo him.

Paul Adams almost had a very nasty accident when his aircraft caught fire during start-up. Fuel leaking from a jammed overwing vent valve ran down the top surface of the wing and ignited on the No 2 engine starter exhaust under the port flap. The fire engulfed the aircraft very quickly and burnt fiercely for ten minutes. Paul escaped smartly over the front windscreen and down the right-hand side of the nose, his fifteen-foot drop culminating in a pool of burning fuel after he had collided with the missile on the way down and bruised himself in the process. Several officers and many airmen, at considerable risk to themselves, rushed out and pushed the adjacent Lightnings away, and the crash crews eventually put out the fire, but the starboard side was badly rippled from the heat and the undercarriage doors had melted. However, it was decided to repair the aircraft back in Britain (at an ultimate cost of 25,000 man-hours). It eventually flew again and was in service at Binbrook when the Lightning was finally retired. Interestingly, the replacement aircraft was flown out to Tengah by Flying Officer Graham Clarke of 11 Squadron: Graham assumed command of 74 at Wattisham in April 1989.

The most spectacular item in the Lightning's repertoire was without doubt the rotation take-off. The seemingly almost vertical climb was an unforgettable sight and was achieved by holding the aircraft down until the last possible moment and then pulling the stick fully back. This manoeuvre intrigued the pilots themselves, and on 27 July Frank Whitehouse arranged for a film cameraman to record his take-off. Frank and his leader, Roger Pope, entered the runway and lined up in echelon port. Roger was away first, accelerating rapidly. Getting safely airborne, he waited for a call from his No 2; Frank had taken off just five seconds behind his leader. While still some 300ft short of the runway barrier, he rotated. Spectators saw the Lightning snap into the vertical without apparently climbing and mush along before staggering to 400ft. The air-craft autorotated, coming down like a falling leaf, and after what looked like an attempt at recovery, disappeared behind a screen of trees, a pall of black smoke confirming the crash in which Frank Whitehouse, and Chinese farmer Cheong Say Wai, lost their lives. Frank did in fact eject at a very late stage but was only just separating from the seat when he hit the ground. The subsequent investigation revealed that the safe limit of $3g$ had been exceeded on take-off, witnesses confirming that the rotation was the fastest and most abrupt they had ever seen. Frank's aircraft had passed rapidly through the pre-stall buffer zone into a flick manoeuvre, the aircraft rolling and yawing. Another contributory factor was a new procedure which had been adopted after Paul Adams' fire on the ramp a few weeks previously. Starting, taxying and taking off were all accom-plished with 'Flight Refuel' set. This stopped the pump in the central tank from running—in Paul Adams's case the pump had caused the fuel spill-age leading to the fire. What nobody realized at the time was that not using the pump caused a rearward movement of the centre of gravity as fuel was drained from the wings. Frank had been held on the ground for some time and had had a long taxi. He was then overzealous in his handling of the controls, causing the permitted g to be exceeded. He was not aware of the potential hazard and so did not compensate for it. With a cameraman poised to film the take-off, one can imagine his determina-tion to ensure that he provided a rotation to remember, but his eagerness to do so cost him his life. The whole issue of the aircraft's centre of gravity was subsequently investigated by the manufacturer and the RAF.

The third aircraft to be written off in 1970 did not, fortunately, involve further loss of life. On 12 August Mike Rigg found that he was unable to lower his port mainwheel during normal recovery to Tengah. All efforts to release the malfunctioning undercarriage failed, so he was instructed to head for the sea and eject in the designated area to the east of Changi. Over the area, but at only 12,000ft, his aircraft ran out of fuel. This was 4,000ft below the barometric capsule setting of 5,000 metres on the seat, so consequently the main 'chute deployed instantly when he ejected, the deceleration being sufficient to rip the stitching from the harness in the crutch loop. Very severely bruised, Mike managed to stay in the remains of his harness and he landed safely in the sea and successfully climbed aboard his dinghy, although one of his emergency flares for use in the jungle went off in the process, causing him some further alarm. Within half an hour he had been recovered by a Whirlwind and taken to the military hospital at Changi. It was only after this incident, when the Navy refused to attempt a salvage of the aircraft, that the designated ejection area was found to be also a Navy ammunition dumping ground!

Designed to test the air defences of Singapore Island and Western Malaya, 'Bersatu Padu' ('Complete Unity') was a particularly significant exercise because it involved a scenario projected five years forward when there would be no British presence in Singapore. It would test the ability of those nations taking part to reinforce and defend the Far East in times of crisis. The real question was, could it be done quickly enough as required by the treaty obligations of the United Kingdom in particular, which lay 12,000 miles from the area, to help save what might be a rapidly deteriorating situation? In spite of some serious unrealities in the assumptions behind the exercise, it did, within limits, provide a satisfactory demonstration of British capabilities. Those unrealities included the fact that any British troops flown out from the UK would find their lack of acclimatization a serious threat to their effectiveness; that the airlift capability as far as heavy supplies were concerned could not be handled by Transport Command, the alternatives being sea passage (lasting a month) or help from the Americans; and that projections indicated that, after the withdrawal from the Far East, there would be no aircraft carriers in the Royal Navy and that local air supremacy would have to be won by the other powers.

Aircraft from four nations participated—Britain, Australia, Malaysia and New Zealand. The Singapore Defence Force itself was not involved as its air force was in too embryonic a state, but its ground troops and air defence controllers did take part. The RAAF contributed Mirages and Neptunes; the RMAF S.61 helicopters and Tebuans (CL-41s); the RNZAF Canberras, Iroquois, C-130s and Bristol Freighters; and the RAF Canberras, Phantoms, Victors, Vulcans, Wessexes, C-130s and 74's Lightnings. The main part of the exercise began in mid-June when 40 Commando made an amphibious landing from the carrier HMS *Bulwark* off the east coast of Malaysia, supported by Wessex helicopters of 848 Squadron. The Australian carrier *Melbourne* with its Skyhawks, Trackers and Wessexes, the helicopter cruiser HMS *Blake* with Wessexes and the 'County' Class guided missile destroyer HMS *Fife* with one Wessex also formed part of the invasion force. The aim of the landing was to secure the airfield at Penerak which then formed an airhead for the supply by Hercules of the multi-national ground forces advancing from the south. Troops were supported in the jungle by RMAF S.61s and Wessexes of 72 Squadron which had been airlifted out to Malaya by Belfast. Phantoms of 54 Squadron had flown non-stop from the United Kingdom to participate, and also at Tengah were the Vulcans of 44 Squadron, Victor tankers from 57 Squadron, 14 Squadron RNZAF with its Canberras, and Mirages of Nos 3 and 75 Squadrons—a total of forty-three aircraft operating from the ramps in addition to the Tigers.

'Bersatu Padu' was divided into five phases. The first, codenamed 'Crackshot', was the work-up phase during which the average sortie for 74 consisted of a rendezvous with a tanker about twenty minutes after take-off, then descending to a low-level combat air patrol over the Fleet. The CAP was held for fifty minutes before returning to base. An RAF Fighter Controller was sailing with the Navy during this phase and added a touch of familiar jargon to operations, a previous complaint having centred around the misunderstanding of Fleet Air Arm terminology! During the 'Hill Buzzard' phase the Tigers joined the 'unfriendly' forces and flew twenty-two sorties over two days and nights and were tasked with being both supersonic and subsonic very-high-level targets for RAAF Mirages from Butterworth. During 'Sea Canary 1', 74 provided low-level CAP for the Fleet on a line almost two hundred miles from base. During this phase the Tigers were working in conjunction with Royal Australian Navy Skyhawks from 805 Squadron. Next came 'Bold Robin', which required the Tigers to provide the air defence of Singapore itself against high- and low-level targets. It was split into two parts, the day phase requiring a CAP to be mounted overland for three hours, with four aircraft aloft at any one time. Putting a novel concept into practice, two Phantoms provided airborne early warning of targets penetrating the CAP line at low level. During the ensuing night phase, all targets were above 10,000ft and all fighter sorties were scrambled on telebrief from base for an ADP interception. The Tigers found that the problems here were the supersonic Phantoms, which had now changed sides, and, in their efforts to fly into the best defensive positions, more than one sonic boom was laid across a slumbering Singapore around the midnight hour! Only a few of the attacking force got through 74's defensive screen, however, with the controllers at Bukit Gombak working flat-out to direct the Lightnings on to the waves of incoming aircraft. Those that did succeed in getting through were caught as they tried to escape. The final part of the exercise was 'Sea Canary 2', which followed a very similar format to '1' except that CAP had to be maintained for five and a half hours. 20 Squadron's Single Pioneer Flight assisted in this by taking Russ Peart aloft as controller. He could visually spot incoming low-level raids and radio their height and direction to CAP aircraft to aid their interception of the enemy. The technique worked well, the elderly piston-engined aircraft proving to be an effective asset.

After the completion of 'Bersatu Padu', the Tigers were all set to celebrate their own involvement in the exercise by flying a battle formation around Singapore, but, strangely, the political clearance for this was not forthcoming and the formation contented itself instead with parading around the Tengah zone. Prime Minister Lee Kwang Yew visited the base a few days later to confer his own congratulations for the part the Squadron had played and spent some considerable time with the aircraft. Those who met him found him to be as charming, and indeed inquisitive, as his international image suggested he might be.

After the exercise, Tony Craig and his colleagues were dismayed to find that more serious fuel leaks were appearing on aircraft that were thought to have been cleared. This effectively reduced Squadron strength to four F.6s and the T.5 during the autumn, but to compound the situation still further yet another modification instruction was received which would take six weeks per aircraft to put into effect. This was the Fast Run Fire Integrity system, which was designed finally to eliminate all fire risks. It was pure coincidence that Air Marshal Sir Neil Wheeler should be visiting 74 at this time to present a citation to Dennis Caldwell on behalf of the whole Squadron in recognition of their efforts in extinguishing the fire in Paul Adams' aircraft and pushing the others to safety. By October the situation had improved enough to allow a couple of aircraft to participate in the SEATO Air Display at Bangkok. The Boss and Dave Roome flew to Thailand, the support party travelling by Belfast, and an enjoyable five days were spent at Don Muang International Airport, the Lightnings stimulating a lot of interest. The Thais were excellent hosts and the Tigers' party was pleased to have made the trip.

Meanwhile, at Tengah, a new missile-firing programme was getting under way. Ten Red Tops had been allocated for Exercise 'Redflash', but the initial week's programme produced the customary dismal results. A follow-up programme was spoilt by bad weather and just three sorties were completed, Dave Roome being the only Squadron member to manage a successful launch against a Meteor-towed Rushton target. The year 1970 ended with the Tigers falling 220 hours short of the FEAF's flying task but still having flown a total of 3,229 hours during the year.

TAIL-END TIGERS

As the year turned, everyone was very aware that 74 was now on the run-in to disbandment, for it had been announced that August 1971 would mark the end of the Squadron's stay in the Far East. It was time for the Trappers to visit again to complete check-rides on all Squadron pilots, and Robin Hargreaves was awarded an exceptional rating. He was the only pilot in the whole Lightning force to be so commended. Of the other Tiger pilots, six received an above-average assessment, three a high average and three an average. In addition to this, Robin and Barney Bullock were qualified as Lightning QFIs. All in all, it was a very favourable start to the New Year!

'Tiger Rags', because of other commitments on both sides, had lain dormant for a large part of 1970 but were resurrected for these final few months. On 74's part, the lack of air superiority training became apparent immediately, for in the initial six sorties the Mirages completely outmanoeuvred the Lightnings, literally flying rings round them! This led to some intense discussion and detailed debriefings, which paid dividends because by the end of the detachment the Tigers had clawed their way back to respectability. Immediately the Rag had finished a comprehensive training programme, with the emphasis on fighter leadership in combat, was instituted. Every Squadron pilot flew this programme and on the return visit to Butterworth the following month the balance had been redressed. The Australians had by this time taken delivery of their own Mirage IIID two-seater and they delighted in taking the Tigers aloft and showing off the delta's capabilities. The Tigers could with justification be envious of the Australian serviceability record, particularly when it was learned that those Lightnings that had not been through the Fire Integrity Programme were forbidden to use reheat except in take-off—and that this would be followed by a restriction on the whole fleet to 3g until the No 1 engine mountings had been checked. But there was light at the end of this latest engineering tunnel. On 15 February four Lightnings were airborne at the same time for the first time in 1971; and the following day five Lightnings and the T.5 were up together. All at once, Squadron life took on a new dimension!

Exercise 'Tiger Trek' was to be the last major deployment by 74 in the Far East. It took place during April 1971 and its purpose was to join the Royal Australian Air Force's Golden Jubilee celebrations. Barney Bullocke had already gone ahead to make arrangements, and on Sunday the 11th Dennis Caldwell led the first of two pairs of aircraft to RAAF Darwin and then on to RAAF Edinburgh, where the forty-eight ground crew and reserve pilots were waiting for them. At Edinburgh the Tigers participated in the celebratory air display. All went well except for one mishap when Pete Carter hit a magpie early in the routine. The aircraft was examined in the air by other members of the formation and, apart from a slight dent in one of the leading edges, no damage could be detected. As all engine indications in the cockpit were normal he was authorized to continue. But, after landing, closer examination revealed damage to the intake skin of No 2 engine and the latter was changed, a replacement being sent from Tengah. Work was completed in time to meet the scheduled return to Singapore after a second display had been flown at Melbourne. This visit was the first made by Lightnings to South Australia, and as such it received extensive press and nationwide TV coverage, the two displays being witnessed by a total of 350,000 people. One of the aircraft, XR725/'A', was, as a result of its presence, the most travelled of all Lightnings, having previously visited places as far apart as Toronto (while with 5 Squadron) and Thailand.

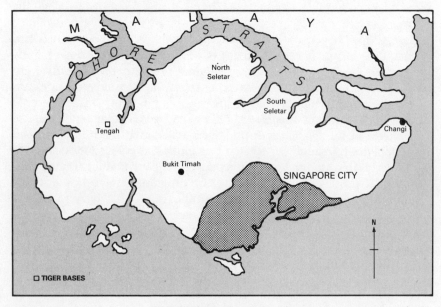

SINGAPORE ISLAND, 1967—1971

During May Kevin Mace organized a Squadron Air Defence Competition which had pilots and controllers working together in small teams, resulting in an exchange of information and ideas between 74 and Bukit Gombak which stood the Singaporean controllers in very good stead. The last 'Tiger Rag' was held during June, four Lightnings deploying to Butterworth and the Australians organizing a seemingly endless stream of parties, functions and beer as their way of saying *au revoir* to the Tigers. July was the last month that 74 enjoyed operational status prior to its disbandment. HMS *Eagle* berthed off Seletar for the first two weeks and Navy aircraft flew from Tengah, combined operations being planned and executed with the Gannets on airborne early warning sorties, with the Buccaneers on air-to-air refuelling and with the Sea Vixens as targets. This was *Eagle*'s farewell visit to Singapore piror to her sailing home for scrapping, and 74's low-flying specialist, Dave Roome, marked the occasion in typically spectacular fashion. He was with Tony Craig in the T.5 when he saw *Eagle*, took over the controls and roared towards the carrier, passing at high speed just a few feet in front of the bridge. It was unfortunate that the Captain was watching at the time! Incensed at what he considered to be a reckless and dangerous stunt, he immediately called Tengah's Station Commander (now Peter Latham) who in turn called Dennis Caldwell. Literally within minutes of the 'flypast' Dave was on the carpet and Tony was reprimanded for not stopping him from doing it!

It was planned that, in the best Tiger tradition, 74 Squadron would come off operational status with a nine-ship flypast over HQ FEAF on its last flying day, 25 August 1971. All engineering support was organized towards this end whilst at the same time achieving the monthly flying task. Unfortunately, as so often in the past, the aircraft upset the schedule when they had to be grounded for a week, each having its No 1 engine removed twice for checks. However, slowly but surely, the aircraft emerged from the hangars, all checks and modifications once again completed. After air-testing they were flown only occasionally and kept fully serviceable, ready for the disbandment parade flypast and the subsequent transit to Cyprus and their new owners, the old adversaries, 56 Squadron.

Any disbandment of a famous squadron is a sad affair. 74 had been in continuous operation since 1935. They had seen other squadrons at Tengah gradually disappear during their four years' tenure and now it was happening to them. On 6 August an Open Day was held to allow the families a last look at the Tigers, and between the 7th and the 9th the final trip to the 'Islands' took place. On the 19th a Tiger ten-ship was led around Singapore by the Boss, the plan to overfly the Air Commander's house at 1200 being executed exactly on time. And so to 25 August and the disbandment parade itself, which was reviewed by the Commander of the Far Eastern Air Force, Air Vice Marshal Nigel Maynard. As a single flypast was made by four Lightnings, a General Salute was given and then, at dusk, with a glorious Singapore sunset adorning the skies and with the band playing 'Auld Lang Syne', a lone Lightning appeared almost silently from behind the saluting dais on reduced power as the

Standard was being marched off in slow time, carried proudly by Flight Sergeant Ron Bradley. At the last moment Barney Bullocke selected 100 per cent power and pulled the Lightning into the vertical, climbing spectacularly skywards with reheat aglow in the gathering darkness. A very poignant moment. At 20,000ft reheat was cancelled—at, coincidentally, exactly the same time as the floodlights on the parade ground were switched off and the band stopped playing. A 75 Squadron Australian pilot had watched the whole episode awestruck, but this final symbolic gesture was too much for him to handle. Turning to Roger Pope, he simply said: 'Strewth blue! Now that *was* bloody clever!'

An RAF press release summed up the epilogue very neatly:

> The final task of the Tiger pilots in the Far East theatre will be to fly their Lightning F. Mk 6s from Tengah to Akrotiri Cyprus, where they are to be taken over by 56 Squadron. The Lightnings will be air-to-air refuelled by Victors of Strike Command during their 6,000-mile flight, on which they will stage through Gan, the RAF's remote island station in the Indian Ocean. Flight Lieutenant Munyard will fly home as a passenger aboard an Air Support Command transport aircraft, entrusted with the task of delivering the Squadron Standard to the RAF College at Cranwell. He will also take the Malan Memorial Sword to Bentley Priory.

The flight to Cyrpus was codenamed 'Panther Trail'. Dennis Caldwell and Paul Adams arrived at Akrotiri on 2 September (followed later that day by Robin Hargreaves and Russ Peart) and were met and escorted in by two 56 Squadron aircraft. The following day saw the arrival of Kevin Mace and Mike Rigg and on the 5th Dave Roome, Roger Pope, Nigel Holder and Nick Buckley arrived, Tony Ellender bringing up the rear on the 6th. Tony Craig was amongst the last of 74's complement to leave Tengah and was therefore able to witness the Lightnings' departure. The briefings were straightforward and, once completed, the observers retired to the balcony of the Control Tower to watch. The pairs take-off of Dave Roome and his No 2, Roger Pope, was routine but, once airborne, Dave led his wingman on to a course which brought the Lightnings round until they could be seen heading back towards Tengah. Accelerating, they lost height as they sped toward the tower. The first murmurings of unease passed between those on the verandah. At barely twenty feet and close to supersonic speed, the pair of silver Lightnings flashed by the tower with everyone looking *down* on to the top surfaces. The pair then went on to pass 74's hangar at less than rooftop height before roaring off towards Gan, a flight which was completed in four hours. The Gan-to-Akrotiri leg was completed the following day. There had been plans to make a further stop at Bahrain but, knowing the Lightning's record for becoming unserviceable on the ground, Dennis Caldwell vetoed that idea and decided to fly direct to Cyprus instead. Sheepskin seat covers were provided to improve comfort and absorb sweat, making the flight a bearable one despite its being 8hr 5min long!

The Lightning T.5 returned to Britain the way it had arrived—by sea. Flown in to RAF Changi, it was again loaded on to a barge which had been driven up to the Changi beach at high tide, watched by bemused sunbathers and swimmers. It then set off at a sedate five knots along the Singapore coast and through the busy harbour where the crews of the many ships at anchor lined the rails to watch its progress. The T.5 was craned aboard a cargo vessel, secured and cocooned on deck, and set sail for Liverpool.

The dispersal of the crews from Akrotiri was an occasion tinged with the inevitable sadness. A proportion of the ground crews had applied for positions within the Singapore Air Force and were accepted, along with a considerable amount of mainly administrative equipment left behind by the RAF, piled in the centre of the now deserted Tigers' hangar. Of the majority staying in the RAF, each went to his new posting proud to have been associated with the Tigers and each wondering what the future held in store for such a famous squadron. Already rumours were circulating that within a few months it would be back, flying the new SEPECAT Jaguar. But by the time the first Squadron reunion had been held (on 13 November 1971 at Bentley Priory), nothing had happened and there were fears that 74 would be out of commission for a long time. Which it was—for more than a decade.

But what of the eleven years with the Lightning? Dennis Caldwell:

> Without doubt it was the finest flying machine in the world. And once the gun was reintroduced and made to work it became one of the best Mach 2 air superiority fighters of any air force. And remember, despite the engineering problems, the Tigers met all of their operational commitments in the Far East and completed 95 per cent of their allotted flying task. That was only possible by dedication and sheer hard work on the part of every member of No 74 Squadron and something of which I will forever be proud to have been associated.

Now the only tiger's roar to be heard in the area comes from the Malayan jungle just across the Straits from Singapore Island.

CHAPTER 11

Phantom Tigers

Down in sunny Suffolk where the grass is green,
There is a fighter squadron that is cool and mean.
We live in a HAS site made of metal and wood,
We've no need to be modest 'cos we're so bloody good!

We're in our F-4Js loaded 4 by 4,
Tornados are lead-nosed, they know the score.
We're rapping all the tankers and flying all day,
Splashing all the bandits in our F-4J.
The missiles are expended and the fuel's run dry—
It's a pretty tough life being Kings of the Sky . . .

AFTER THE DISBANDMENT of 74 Squadron in 1971 there were periodic rumours concerning its re-formation. Old Squadron members remained in touch individually and the occasional reunion, organized by Mike Cooke, would bring all together to voice their collective optimism that it would not be too long before the famous Tigers were back as a front-line unit. It was the Falklands crisis of 1982 that eventually precipitated their return. After the defeat of the Argentinians it became clear that a permanent air defence presence was required in the South Atlantic. Initially 29 Squadron provided this; then Wattisham's 23 Squadron was sent down to patrol the exclusion zone. But, as tensions lessened, the squadron presence was commuted to that of a flight of four aircraft. 23 did not return to Suffolk: instead, its colour was transferred directly from Mount Pleasant to Leeming in preparation for eventual re-equipment with the Tornado F.3, with the overall result that a gap was created in Britain's own air defence capability which 11 Group urgently needed to fill. The F.3 was too far away, the Phantom was out of production and so as a short-term measure it was decided to buy ex-US Navy Phantoms, to serve until the Tornado was available. In storage at MASDC (the Military Aircraft Storage and Disposition Centre) at Davis Monthan AFB in Arizona and at NARF (the Naval Air Rework Facility) at San Diego were a quantity of F-4Js which had been retired after the introduction into service by the Americans of the F-14 Tomcat, and these suited the RAF's requirement very well. A deal was struck to bring them out of the desert, subject them to a complete rebuild at NARF and ferry them back to Britain to replace the missing squadron.

In late 1982 a team of RAF personnel led by the Vice Chief of the Air Staff, Sir Peter Harding, visited the United States to establish the condition of the Phantoms that were on offer and to evaluate their ability to meet requirements. To provide an acceptable life for the aircraft (envisaged at that time as being five years), it was established that the fifteen airframes chosen would have to have a package of fatigue modifications embodied. One aspect of the aircraft which did not come up to expectations was that of its avionics and the AWG-10 radar. The latter problem was overcome when Ferranti (as lead contractor) and Westinghouse undertook to provide, within an acceptable timescale, kits to convert the AWG-10s to 10B standard. Digitally controlled and up-to-date technologically, the 10B was extremely expensive but considerably clearer and rather more reliable than the radar in the RAF's Phantom FGR.2s. It was to be the jewel in the F-4J's crown.

When the RAF team returned home and prepared its report, the recommendation was that a formal request be submitted to the US Navy for the Phantoms together with a logistics support package. Two Letters of Offer were subsequently sent. The first, covering the purchase of the aircraft and their rework, was presented on 3 March 1983; the offer, valued at £45,000,000, was accepted on 15 April. The second, covering the support package and valued at some £40,000,000, was forwarded in September. In addition there was separate funding for Ferranti and Westinghouse as well as for British Aerospace for the part they would each play in the programme and for the purchase of British gunpods. In all, Ministerial approval for the project was for a total of £125,000,000.

The support package was conceived as an eighteen-month 'get you going' programme based on US Navy usage but modified to try to reflect the RAF's proposed method of operation. This in itself was always going to be difficult, given the lack of experience of the Americans in the day-to-day ways of the British. The imbalance of the package, when details became available, was all too apparent. There were plenty of spares relating to the strengthened undercarriage for carrier landings but a drastic shortage of radios and airframe spares in general! In fairness, it did indeed get the Tigers going but after the initial period had expired there were still considerable engineering problems, so much so that for the first two years of operation there was one aircraft permanently LOG to be robbed of components. When the situation did improve enough to rebuild the 'hangar queen', it took nine months to do so. The initial 'suck it and see' concept of the support package, with its wrongly anticipated requirements, exacted a harsh penalty.

At the time the purchase of the Phantoms was authorized there was considerable discussion within RAF circles of the designation that should be applied to the aircraft. It was evident that the FG.1 and FGR.2 designations currently applied to RAF F-4s was inappropriate for the F-4Js as the latter were not going to be employed in the ground attack or reconnaissance roles. So should 74's aircraft be Phantom F.3s? Or should an exception be made and the American F-4J designation be retained? But, if that were adopted, would there be confusion with servicing manuals and subsequent modifications and directives which may relate to the

American version but not the British or *vice versa*? Then again, all US Navy Js were being converted to S standard, leaving only the British aircraft as Js. British Aerospace were at pains to point out the dangers in not allocating a unique designation to the British aircraft, and in particular the need to be able quickly to identify drawings and parts. It was this argument which ultimately won the day and the F-4J(UK) designation was confirmed as the one to be adopted. Even so, this nomenclature proved to be too cumbersome for most and the aircraft was known simply as 'The J'.

The Naval Air Rework Facility at North Island, San Diego, was responsible for the F-4J engineering programme. Basically this consisted of the implementation of the F-4S Service Life Extension Program (SLEP) which the US Navy had adopted (but excluding the introduction of the leading-edge slats), the deletion of unwanted American systems and the incorporation of those required by the RAF (although a look inside the wheel well of an F-4J after delivery still showed evidence of the aircraft's US Navy ancestry!) Not visible, but also a legacy of the aircraft's carrier operations, was the lack of an anti-skid braking system.

The Phantoms were completely stripped, allowing anti-corrosive treatment to be applied and exhaustive tests on the integrity of the airframe to be completed. Fatigue meters were fitted to facilitate the future monitoring of the fleet, and additional wiring was incorporated to allow the carriage of Sky Flash missiles in RAF service. Provision was also made for the SUU-23A gunpod, a different model from that used by the US Navy. And TESS was installed, a Telescopic Sighting System situated in the rear cockpit and used for the visual identification of targets. 74 Squadron crews would point to two major factors contributing to advantages of the J over the British-configured FGR.2. One was the superlative radar; the other was the powerplant. Two General Electric J79-GE-10B engines not only gave the Phantom a different fuselage contour because of their smaller dimensions but also an immediate ($1\frac{1}{2}$sec) response in reheat, giving the J the edge in combat. At high level the J79, being a pure jet as opposed to a turbofan such as the FGR.2's Spey, retained much better thrust. It was also a smokeless engine, a fact which also had considerable benefits in air combat.

One problem requiring urgent consideration was the non-availability in the UK of the high-pressure air starter needed for the engine. The F-4J in US Navy service used a static piped system on base airfields and carriers but this option was far too expensive for installation in the Wattisham HAS area, particularly in view of the expected short life of the aircraft in RAF service. Unfortunately the US Navy also had a shortfall in its own requirement for mobile starters and was hard pressed to find any as part of the support package. For a while it seemed as though the RAF might have bought fifteen aircraft which they were unable to start! So an Engineering Requirement was issued for such a starter, which had to meet transportability requirements by road, rail and air: without that capability there would be no Tiger deployments and recoveries into airfields other than Wattisham.

The ejection seat fitted to the F-4J was the Martin Baker Mk 7A, similar to that in Spey Phantoms although it did not have the 'dial your weight' adjustment. Command Ejection, which enabled either pilot or navigator to initiate the ejection sequence, was retained. The American harness was different too, being attached to a torso garment donned over the flying gear. Much discussion initially centred around the need to replace the American air crew equipment and escape system with the British equivalent, but it was decided that this should not be done immediately, retrofitting taking place once the Phantoms had been delivered. In general, the crews found the American kit to be far more comfortable and practical in the cockpit environment, but that did not ultimately prevent full replacement with British kit in 1989. In particular, the US-style flying helmets were great favourites with those who used them. They were lighter and more comfortable than the British Mk 4B helmet, and it was only with great reluctance that they were eventually surrendered!

TIGER TRAILS

A team from the Central Servicing Development Establishment (CSDE) at RAF Swanton Morley went to North Island to monitor the progress of the re-work. Headed by Squadron Leader Ted Stickley, it was *in situ* at the end of 1983, by which time the first of the Phantoms was undergoing strip-down and corrosion control. All the aircraft involved had been built between 1966 and 1969 and each had a distinguished career in US Navy or Marine Corps service. Some of those Phantoms in storage at Davis Monthan were airlifted to San Diego by helicopter (others were still capable of being flown in). One was lost when, during the course of the transfer, the front canopy detached, flew back and struck the main shackle that was supporting the webbing holding the F-4 and broke it. The Phantom fell away into the sea and was not subsequently salvaged. A replacement airframe was found. The incident was viewed by members of the Royal Family on board the Royal Yacht *Britannia*, in the area at the time during the course of a West Coast tour.

While negotiations for the purchase of the F-4J package had been in progress, Squadron Leader Dick Northcote was working as Staff Officer to the Director General of Organization (DGO), one of whose responsibilities was the allocation of squadron number plates to new units. Knowing that he was in line to command the F-4J-equipped squadron, Dick viewed the proceedings with considerable interest! Decisions on squadron nomenclature are based largely on historical precedent and the length of time a standard has been laid up at Cranwell. Normally those squadrons longest out of commission are the first to be considered. In this instance the Tigers' cause was being helped by the constant lobbying of ex-Lightning crews who, once news of a new air defence squadron had been received, had rallied behind 74. It came as something of a shock, therefore, when DGO recommended to his immediate superior, the Air Member for Supply and Organization, that 39 Squadron (a *bomber* squadron which had previously flown Canberras!) should re-form on the F-4J. Fortunately, the Chief of the Air Staff himself intervened, decided that formal precedents should take a back seat on this occasion and instructed that the new squadron would be No 74. The Tigers were back! Shortly afterwards, Dick Northcote was promoted to Wing Commander and appointed as the unit's Commanding Officer. His background and experience were well suited to the task in hand—over 2,000 hours on F-4s, including two tours on 54(F) Squadron, an exchange tour as an instructor on F-4Es at McDill AFB in Florida and a tour as Flight Commander on 111 Squadron.

The responsibility for the formation of the new squadron was a challenge to which Dick Northcote rose superbly. After a refresher course with the Phantom OCU at Coningsby in May 1984, he went on to Wattisham the following month where SEngO Sqn Ldr Dave Allan and Warrant Officer Geoff Bland were already in residence. Ground crews were in the USA on F-4J courses to learn servicing and maintenance procedures in preparation for the arrival of the air crews who would air-test the aircraft and fly them to Britain. Keith Griffin, Mike Parkin and Clive Bairsto were tasked with the initial preparation for the lead-in training at North Island and Yuma, and Dick Northcote spent a month at Wattisham working with Dave Allan and Dave Hurley, overseeing the arrival and tasking of new squadron personnel and ensuring that the hangar allocated to them would be ready for the Phantoms. Initially the Tigers would operate from the flight line as the Hardened Aircraft Shelter (HAS) site which would ultimately house them was still under construction.

The setting-up of a fighter squadron is no easy task. As well as the normal considerations in terms of equipment, manpower and administration, there are many other aspects to the process. From the Tigers' point of view, the hangar and accommodation had not been used for over a year, personnel were arriving in ones and twos and the aircraft had to be flown in from the United States in batches of three over a six-month period. The Squadron silver had to be collected from store and the Squadron's diaries and memorabilia (held by ex-Tiger Dave Roome) had to be delivered. The Standard had been laid up at Cranwell, and Gordon James and Nigel Marks were nominated as Standard Bearers for the re-formation parade, to be held in October. Gordon went to Cranwell to collect the Standard, an event which itself involved a fair degree of ceremonial, and this was first paraded on 9 September 1984. Everyone at Wattisham pulled out all the stops, and the Station Commander, Group Captain Tony Park, ensured that all possible support was given. And Esso Petroleum, so supportive of the Tigers over the years, stepped in with sponsorship to help fund the acquisition of such diverse items as air crew and ground crew cloth patches, Squadron prints and the preparation and stocking of the coffee bars in both the air- and ground-crew rooms.

Happy that all was well at Wattisham and that an administration divided by the Atlantic and the Continental USA was feasible, Dick then flew to the West Coast to familiarize himself with the new aircraft and to lead the team bringing the first of the aircraft back from San Diego. The plan was to have all fifteen F-4J(UK)s back in England by the end of December 1984, and this goal was to be achieved by mounting a series of 'Tiger Trails', ferrying three aircraft at a time across the Atlantic after their acceptance. No 11 Group had decided that only highly experienced personnel should be posted to the new Tigers over a phased six-month period, not only in terms of air crews (where 750 hours' first-pilot time was a minimum requirement) but of engineering staff and administrators as well. Men were being asked to fly a different mark of Phantom, and their experience in dealing with unforeseen problems and reacting appropriately on the air tests, on the work-up and, probably most importantly, on the long transoceanic ferry flights was vital. Ground crews had been sent to the Westinghouse and General Electric companies and to the US Navy at Oceana for practical training as instructors so that they could, in turn, train engineers in the different trades themselves. Dave Allan spent a lot of time at NARF watching the rebuild in progress. Many lasting friendships were struck up amongst the CSDE team, Tiger personnel and the North Island workforce. All the employees at San Diego were civilians, and they took a fierce pride in the job they did, particularly as they all knew that these were the last F-4s that would pass through their hands.

As the aircraft were released from the workshops, air-testing by Tiger crews began. Many a snag was uncovered on these shake-down flights, although many of the minor problems would not have taken on such dramatic proportions had the prospect of a long Atlantic crossing not faced the crews. Some of the problems were not so minor! The hydraulic system, the piping for which had been changed from alloy to stainless steel, proved troublesome, as did the air bleed system, and one of the most serious incidents involved hot air bleeding directly on to the airframe after a blanking plate failed, burning a hole in the skin and subsequently taking many hours to repair.

Conversion for the crews to the F-4J was reasonably quick and straightforward. New Tiger Gordon James' experience was typical. He flew out to the United States in mid-1984 for an eight-week detachment, commencing with two weeks in San Diego for the issue of F-4J flying kit, and to undergo the stringent US Navy medical tests and lectures necessary to obtain clearance to fly US Navy aircraft. Miramar is the home of the Flight Physiology and Water Survival Training Center, and here the Tigers were lectured further on medical matters before moving on to Marine Corps Fighter Attack Training Squadron VMFAT-101 at Yuma in the Arizona desert, where the British crews spent four weeks converting to the F-4J—although, in the absence of that type in Navy or Marine Corps service, much of the flying was conducted on the sixty F-4S Phantoms with leading-edge slats (something the J lacked). Following a week's ground school, ten sorties per crew were scheduled, and these included two initial flights with an instructor pilot followed by an instrument sortie, pilot interceptions at medium and low level, a low-level NAVEX and air-to-air refuelling.

The official roll-out for the F-4Js took place at North Island on Friday 10 August 1984. Ceremonial over, the job of air-testing the first three aircraft began and, once this had been completed, Tiger Trail 1 got under way. Dick Northcote (with Pete Smith in the back seat) led the three aircraft into Wattisham on 30 August to an official welcoming party. Dick had almost been delayed at Wright Patterson after the high-pressure hose to the air starter became detached during start-up and, flailing madly around under the Phantom, had damaged one of the fuel tanks. Determined not to fall behind schedule, he sought out the CO of the resident USAF F-4 squadron, asked for assistance, was given a spare tank and the men to fit it and, just four hours later, was on his way again. Arriving at Wattisham at dusk after the long flight from Goose Bay, the Tigers were invariably subject to considerable attention off base as well as on. A local observer described their arrival:

> The setting sun is just tipping the distant fields, murky through purple haze from Suffolk stubble burning, when the peace of the early autumn evening is broken as five Phantoms burst across Wattisham in a loose V formation. Three aircraft are in an unusual blue-grey finish whilst the others are wearing the customary dull two-tone grey. These two latter (of 56 Squadron) pull up into an impressive vertical climb, quickly gaining thousands of feet, whilst the other three swing round through north to east to settle down in echelon starboard for the run-in and break on Wattisham's runway. Few among the group of watchers spared a glance across to Wattisham's north side, where XM139 and XM147 stood, two forlorn Lightning F.1 decoys which 24 years previously had been the pride of 74 at Coltishall.

Previously used to wearing striking colours whilst in US Navy or Marine Corps service, the F-4Js now had a unique paint scheme which had been applied to the aircraft in the United States and was immediately noticeable upon their arrival at Wattisham. It had not been possible to read British colour specifications directly across to the American specifications, and it was therefore necessary to send samples and allow the US Navy to mix paints to reach the desired effect. When the Js emerged from NARF, however, it was immediately obvious that the Americans had contrived to use a splendid colour that looked almost light green in certain conditions! The discrepancy was realized and attempts were subsequently made to change the scheme from the sixth aircraft onwards, but even this was not entirely accurate. The Tigers' Js continued to be distinguishable by their paintwork alone.

The pattern for all the Tiger Trails was for the Phantoms to fly from San Diego to Goose Bay, where crews would link up with new VC10 K.2 tankers of 101 Squadron for the 5,500-mile crossing of the Atlantic. Gordon James' experience on Tiger Trail 3 was typical:

> It was really deadly boring across the sea. It was a long sector with diversions planned for Greenland, Iceland and Scotland in case of any problems, the need for always flying within diversion range of these places adding perhaps 20 per cent journey time. Flying five hundred yards from the VC10, the effort of keeping mentally alert was akin to motorway driving, a most dangerous

regime but one in which it is the easiest to fall asleep because there is so little to keep the mind alert. When trimmed out behind the tanker the aircraft simply sits there, with no relative movement at all. It's rather like the VC10 has been painted on to your canopy! In those circumstances time goes very slowly. There is no radio to tune in to listen to and with the autopilot working you don't even have to hold the controls. Just endless clouds, or the sea glinting far below, droning on and on and on . . .

One hundred miles from Britain, and with sufficient fuel on board, the Js said goodbye to their tanker and flew the length of the country down to Wattisham.

The Tiger Trail 1 Phantoms were quickly put to good use. One was grounded to familiarize new engineers on the type under the instruction of the American-trained tradesmen who were now back home. A team from Boscombe Down arrived to work on another, helping the Tigers to bring the F-4J up to operational levels by proving systems, the equipment fit and stores carriage. As the subsequent Tiger Trails arrived, the flying programme steadily increased. One problem quickly highlighted as this got underway was that caused by the lack of an anti-skid system, and cable arrests became a common feature in wet or cross-wind conditions.

All the F-4J(UK)s were at Wattisham by 4 January 1985, the last aircraft being flown in by Mike Parkin and Pete Smith who had been delayed at Goose Bay with a broken flap. Not all Tiger Trails had been flown by 74 Squadron crews. Wattisham's Station Commander, Tony Park, flew as navigator to Dick Northcote on Tiger Trail 5, whilst OC Ops, Bob Paine, had flown across with Merv Paine. Once all the Js had arrived, fin codes were applied in a sequence which left nobody in any doubt as to whom the aircraft belonged: ZE350/'T', ZE351/'I', ZE352/'G', ZE353/'E', ZE354/'R', ZE355/'S', ZE356/'Q', ZE357/'N'. Other letter codes were chosen at random. Three of the aircraft also briefly sported names, applied to the port intake. ZE357/'N' had been christened *Avenida Arrow*, ZE361/'P' *Mulvaney's Missile* and ZE363 *Brigantine Bomber*, these names relating to favourite bars used by Squadron personnel in the States! ZE363 was not initially coded as it had acquired a black fin in the time-honoured Tiger tradition by the time it reached Wattisham when, on Tiger Trail 3, it had had an enforced stop-over at Wright Patterson AFB with hydraulic problems. A good beer call resulted in a plot being hatched by the ground crew allocated to fixing the problem to decorate '363 with aerosol paint. Needless to say, it was not a particularly professional job, and once back at Wattisham the whole fin was repainted in a proper manner. For some time 'Whiskey' was the sole black-finned Phantom.

WORKING UP

During 74 Squadron's re-formation parade on 19 October 1984, Dick Northcote was presented with the Malan Memorial Sword as three F-4Js performed a flypast. It was a memorable occasion which showed all the ex-Tigers present that this new body of men was quite capable of continuing the traditions of the past. Formalities over, the Squadron concentrated on its programme of working up. 74's first *ab initio* crew members were already training with 56 Squadron, ready to join 74 in the New Year, by which time the full complement of fifteen aircraft would be present. An initial problem for those crews who had not been involved in Tiger Trails was the difficulty in getting hold of the necessary American flying clothing: this was overcome by sending four crews to Pensacola to be fitted with suit, harness and helmet which in the American services is custom-made for each individual. Such a popular expedient was only practised once, however, for the supply chain was subsequently sufficiently established to allow future kitting out to take place in the United Kingdom.

The year 1985 was, predictably, particularly busy for the Squadron; it was also to be a very successful one, and by March 11 Group was able to declare six of the Phantoms to NATO, with a further three at the end of June and the remainder by the end of December. Dick Northcote's leadership as he brought his boys up to scratch was inspired: he was a very punchy character who led by instinct and was not afraid to act first and take the consequences later if he felt that he was right. 1985 was also the year of a fuel moratorium, which resulted in a reduction in the number of flying hours for all squadrons. An additional problem for 74 was the fact that it had more crews than were normally allocated to fighter squadrons. This allocation had been made in order to build in a degree of flexibility and to allow for some phasing of air crews so that all the experienced hands would not leave at the end of their tours at the same time, the additional bodies being used to act as a 'buffer' between old and new personnel. It also meant a measure of harder flying for the jets, and more fuel consumed. The day was saved indirectly by the cancellation of the Nimrod AEW programme, which freed a considerable quantity of fuel for other use. 74 was amongst the grateful recipients.

Mike Castle recalls his first twelve months with the Tigers:

> They were exciting days for the Squadron—hard work, lots of fun and we were able to surprise a lot of people with what we achieved and how quickly we achieved it. Remember, our aircraft were all equivalent to being brand spanking new and they performed differently from Phantoms the RAF were used to: they had smokeless engines and they could actually *turn*, which, when one remembers that at the time many of the service's Spey Phantoms were restricted to 3*g* with stores on, was significant. This meant that other types were virtually used to discounting Phantoms as a threat, but suddenly they had a force of F-4s that could turn hard, that they couldn't see because of the blue camouflage and smokeless engines and a radar that worked well. Add to this the fact that Squadron pilots were predominantly second-tourists and therefore very experienced, and you start to get some idea of the threat we were now posing.

The Squadron was welding itself into a first class team. Morale was high and everyone looked forward to the ensuing months with considerable anticipation. The traditions of the Tigers and their own and other squadrons' awareness of them were very much to the fore in the early stages. 'We're the boys who make most noise' was not an unprofessional, 'gung-ho' attitude to the flying they did but rather it represented the Squadron spirit and their outlook on the job they were tasked with. There were shades of things to come towards the end of January, when a small-scale Tiger Meet was held at RAF Gutersloh in Germany and 74 was able to send representatives for the first time to such a function since 1966 (although whilst the Squadron had been abroad during the late 1960s and early 1970s, old Tigers had managed to keep 74's flag flying at such functions by attending in an unofficial capacity!). The first operational milestone was a Missile Practice Camp in March, firing two Sparrow and two Sidewinder AAMs successfully, although no aircraft detached to Valley as was customary for such camps, operating instead directly from Wattisham and the newly opened HAS site. Station Commander Tony Park saw the achievement as being worthy of mention. He wrote to Dick Northcote:

> I could not let this moment in 74's history pass without saying well done for achieving a faultless MPC. I know that it was not easy and I also know how hard your engineers worked and the overtime that was accumulated simply to check the aircraft out in time for the first firing. The difficulties that your chaps encountered and mastered make the successful conclusion all the sweeter. Congratulations 74, you have proved that the present Standard is in the hands of a proud and professional bunch.

Following MPC, the Squadron was able to pit the J against the Coltishall Jaguars during a period of Dissimilar Air Combat Training (DACT). This detachment to their old Lightning base lasted for two weeks and served quickly to reinforce the confidence they felt in their aircraft and its systems. Ever open to the suggestion that success in the air should be matched by celebration on the ground, the Tigers rounded off the fortnight with a huge party, which was concluded with an attempt on the world record for the number of officers able to stay aboard a dumper truck as it was driven across an (inactive) runway—and attempts by one Tiger (with a little help from a 6 Squadron colleague) to tamp out the flames of a blazing wreck of a car with the bucket of a JCB!

During the early spring of 1985 the Tigers became involved in major exercises, such as 'Priory' and 'Central Enterprise'. A pair of Phantoms was detached to RAF Binbrook on gun trials, using the ranges off the Lincolnshire coast, whilst during May much of the effort was directed towards an impending Royal visit. In many ways a rehearsal for this was the much-delayed arrival of the Chief of the Air Staff, Sir Keith Williamson, who on 10 May inspected men and machines in the new HAS complex and pronounced himself well pleased by all that he saw. The visit of Her Majesty the Queen to Wattisham on 7 June marked the first occasion on which the presence of a member of the Royal Family had graced the Squadron since the visit of Princess Margaret in 1965. This visit was the last official function involving Group Captain Park, who the following week moved on to Rheindahlen in West Germany. He had been a great champion of the Tigers' cause and had been instrumental in ensuring that the Squadron's transition back to operational status at Wattisham had been a smooth one.

At the beginning of July the 1985 NATO Tiger Meet (the twenty-fifth in the series) was held at Kleine Brogel. 74 was unable to send any aircraft, its programme of working-up being too involved to allow it to do so, but a couple of crews did hitch a lift to Belgium with their fellow RAF Tigers from 230 Squadron before moving on to Cyprus to join their own colleagues who had flown out there on Exercise 'Flying Bengal' for Armament Practice Camp. It must be said that the main purpose of the APC was not a success. The lack of development of the F-4J gunnery software meant that the crews did not have a reliable aiming pipper, and after a week of missing the banner target the gunnery part of the Camp was cancelled. However, USS *Nimitz* was in the area at the time and the F-4Js spent a lot of time working with the F-14s of VF-41 and VF-84, part of the Air Wing of the supercarrier. The Tigers were pleasantly surprised to find that their capabilities were by no means lacking against the Navy aircraft: in fact, they got the better of the Tomcats on virtually every encounter, partly because of the tactics they employed but mainly because of the faulty and inflexible tactics of the American crews who seriously underestimated the capabilities of their RAF adversaries. On 24 July the Tigers were asked to provide a flypast for the United Services Organization show and they obliged by sending six Phantoms. The Commander of Carrier Air Wing 8 was afterwards disposed to send a telex to the Tigers:

The RAF flyby was, in today's vernacular, 'awesome'. Many thanks for a spectacular display of British airmanship and flair. It was literally a show stopper.

The Tigers were able to visit *Nimitz* and responded by inviting seven officers from the two Navy squadrons to Akrotiri, where they duly arrived by CH-46 Sea Knight helicopter. All US Navy ships are 'dry' ships, and the seven had not been ashore for over a month, so it can be imagined that they were soon making up for lost time! Other than operating with the US Navy whilst in Cyprus, 74 did advanced escort work with Canberras, completed AEW sorties with 8 Squadron Shackletons and intercepted their first 'live' Warsaw Pact 'Mays' and 'Badgers'.

Part of every APC has traditionally involved a two-day maximum flying period where squadrons demonstrate that they can fly at least twenty-four sorties each day. This has predictably led to something of a competition between 11 Group squadrons: for example, 43 Squadron had previously flown forty-three sorties on *each* day and 111 Squadron one hundred and eleven sorties over the *two* days (organized by Dick Northcote when he was Flight Commander). The challenge was there for all the Tigers to see—seventy-four sorties in *one* day! Thanks to some brilliant organization by Keith Griffin, the target was comfortably reached on Tigerthon Day, 24 July. The sorties, all taking place between 0700 and

1400, were flown 'clean-wing' and each lasted twenty minutes or so. Some were taken up with a short session of one v. one combat and in other cases the opportunity was taken to give ground crewmen a ride and a quick aeros session if they could cope with it! Followed in the afternoon by the *Nimitz* flyby, the whole episode proved the serviceability levels achieved by the engineers.

When it returned to Britain, 74 issued a challenge to all Strike Command squadrons. Mike Castle:

> We decided to man a CAP at Blakeney off the North Norfolk coast and Lowestoft off the Suffolk coast and sent out a signal to virtually every unit saying, in essence, 'be there or be square: the threat directions are . . .' It was amazing the trade that we got: lots of Jaguars and Tornado GR.1s coming out of the ranges, Buccaneers from Lossiemouth—in fact virtually everything we could have hoped for. They were keeping a few thousand pounds of fuel spare to come the long way round for us. We also had 360 Squadron Canberras on communications jamming, a couple of tankers available for those aircraft that needed it and even a NATO AWACS aircraft overhead. The Canberras got a little fed up with the whistles, cracks and bangs they were putting out as the day progressed and so asked for requests. The result was Dire Straits over the airwaves at the Blakeney CAP and Pink Floyd at Lowestoft! But the highlight for us was Dick Northcote being shot down by a Spitfire! Paul Day of the Battle of Britain Memorial Flight was flying one in the area on a general handling sortie, became aware of what was going on and decided to join in the fun. Den Bannister was in the back seat of Dick's aircraft and you can imagine the scene when he suddenly announced 'Here Boss! I think we have just been shot by a Spit!' 'Bloody nonsense! What are you on about, Den?' 'Check your 7 o'clock then.' And there was Paul.
>
> As a squadron, we were launching aircraft throughout the day, the next Tiger being scrambled ten minutes before the preceding aircraft was due to return. On the day we had lots of serviceable aeroplanes and very quick turnrounds were achieved. We also had a reputation, born of previous Tiger eras, to live up to and that we most certainly did! Everyone now knew that 74 were back with a vengeance.

The American exchange pilot George Patterson arrived in time to participate, and his first experiences with the Squadron showed him that he was with a unit which meant business in all that it did.

Later in the year the Tigers were back in the Mediterranean on two occasions, firstly for a squadron exchange with Italian Air Force F-104s at Cameri (four Starfighters visiting Wattisham during September) and subsequently at the Air Combat Manoeuvering Instrumentation (ACMI) Range at Decimomannu in Sardinia—as with Cyprus, a regular deployment for all the RAF's air defence squadrons. Here six aircraft and eight crews had the opportunity of working with (or against) aircraft of USAFE and other NATO squadrons. It was during this first period of DACT in Sardinia that Mike Parkin and Den Bannister had to abort a mission when a fire caption registered in the cockpit. The problem was a fault in the boundary layer control system, which began bleeding red-hot air over the wing and flaps to such a degree that if they had not been able to land quickly they would have been in danger of flying an aircraft that was literally melting. Both crew members were later awarded Green Endorsements for their handling of the incident.

Back in Britain in the autumn, four Tigers took part in 'Ocean Safari', the joint Navy, US Marine Corps and Air Force exercise that takes place in the Western Approaches. The F-4Js flew CAP with Royal Navy Sea Harriers as part of the defence of the fleet below. After more dissimilar combat with Coltishall's Jaguars, a Mineval, Taceval and Staneval confirmed that the Squadron was ready to be declared fully operational. Once again, 74 had taken its place in the RAF's front line, responsible for the air defence of the United Kingdom in support of the growing Tornado F.3 force.

CAMBRAI TIGERS

Two crews spent a month at Jever in Germany in January 1986 to participate in the Tactical Leadership Programme which is regularly held there. For the rest of the Squadron, 1986 started with the annual MPC at Valley, during which a pair of Sparrows and a pair of Sidewinders were once again successfully fired. Mike Castle and Tony Fulford went into the history books when they were involved in the Squadron's first QRA live scramble with the Phantom, although they missed the actual interception. Hellenic Aerospace Industries visited the Squadron and, as fourth-line contractors for the American engines, discussed the possibility of modifying the J79s for self-start. Such proposals never progressed beyond the talking stage. Leaving all engineering debate behind them, seven aircraft left a cold Wattisham for a rather warmer Decimomannu on 17 February and entered into another period of Dissimilar Air Combat Training, primarily with F-5s and F-15s. And those who were not able to go to the Sardinian ranges had the opportunity of working with the American Aggressors on their own ground at Alconbury using the training areas over the North Sea.

The Tigers were placed on short-notice QRA on 26 March as a result of 29 Squadron's being alerted for possible duty in Cyprus during a period of heightening tension in the Middle East. Several live scrambles were called, but the only interception was on 7 April when Dougie Hunter, with Tony Evans in the back seat, intercepted a 'Bear-F', the first such interception by 74 from Wattisham. On another occasion a failed interception led to a diversion into Leuchars. Poor weather or fuel state often made such diversions inevitable, and they were always programmed to be into a QRA airfield: so, when operating in the Faeroes gap, Keflavik in Iceland was an option, as was Norway when operating further to the north.

Following the Falklands conflict a large proportion of the RAF's C-130 Hercules fleet had been converted to give them a tanking capability. Techniques with the C-130 differ considerably from those employed with the faster Victors and VC10s, so time was progressively set aside to bring crews up to standard with them. Other commitments at this time included live firing on the Hebridean ranges against high-level, high-speed Stiletto targets launched by 100 Squadron Canberras on Operation 'Granular'. Flying from Leuchars, six aircraft were involved, the aim being to investigate the capabilities of the F-4J against types such as the MiG-25 'Foxbat'. It is worth making the distinction between 'Granular' and the normal regimes of the Missile Practice Camp held at Valley. In the latter, firing was at a heat or radar reflector towed by a Jindivik, the object being to hit the source and not the drone. In 'Granular', usually mounted from Leuchars, the aim was to hit and destroy the high-flying Stiletto target.

The AOC's inspection on 22 May at Wattisham included a nine-ship flypast, with Dick Northcote leading the formation of five Tigers and four Firebirds. Shortly afterwards the Squadron sent an aircraft to the huge Mildenhall Air Show on static display. Other statics during 1986 were mounted at Brawdy, Alconbury and Culdrose. At the end of the month a pair of F-4Js was sent to Keflavik to work with the F-15 Eagles of the 57th FIS. Then, for the first time in 20 years, the Squadron was able to attend a Tiger Meet. Since the mid-1960s the fortunes of the annual convention had fluctuated considerably, the fuel crisis of the mid-1970s, for example, forcing the demise of the flying aspect of the Meets. In 1977 it was organized in conjunction with the Silver Jubilee International Air Tattoo at Greenham Common, during which the Silver Tiger Trophy was donated to the Tiger Association by Mappin and Webb Ltd. This valuable challenge trophy has subsequently been awarded annually to the Tiger squadron,that shows the highest degree of professionalism and in which the spirit of the Tiger is best represented. The first squadron to win this award in 1977 was 439 from Sollingen. 74 Squadron was to be the proud winner in 1988. By the mid-1980s flying was back on the agenda and the Tiger Association was growing bigger and the Meets even better patronized—so much so that, in 1986, 74 were one of fourteen NATO Tiger Squadrons to deploy to Cambrai as guests of Esc 1/12. The four jets selected were painted and polished until they shone and they also all acquired black tails. This was just the occasion the Squadron had been waiting for: ZE363 had continued in solitary possession of a black fin and now five more aircraft were prepared for the Meet (allowing for spares). The remaining aircraft were subsequently painted up, too, purely on the premise that any visiting brass would assume that somebody else had authorized it! The ruse worked and the famous black fins were permanently restored!

Flying at Cambrai constituted a progressive build-up to a final scenario involving a sixteen-v.-sixteen exercise with a package of air defence aircraft defending against a similar number of ground-attack types. An Open Day and a flying display at the end of the Meet attracted a large crowd, and the Phantom held its own against the likes of Falcons and Hornets. Operationally, too, the crews came to realize that an aircraft that can carry eight missiles and possesses a good pulse-Doppler radar keeps it very much in the front line, despite the pretensions of the new-generation types. Socially, the French excelled themselves. A hangar was completely decorated in Tiger fashion in readiness for a splendid all-ranks Tiger Ball. Another feature of the week was the commandeering of the local nightspot, where regular Tiger Discos were held with the waitresses beguilingly dressed in Tiger flying suits!

Whilst this was going on the crews left at Wattisham were holding southern QRA for most of the month. This coincided with the sailing of a Soviet naval task force from the Mediterranean to join the Northern Fleet, with a consequent unprecedented number of Russian aircraft accompanying it. 74 executed sixteen live launches during this period and intercepted no fewer than ten 'Bear-Ds' and two 'Bear-As'. A month later the Colchester Tattoo asked for 74's participation, and the Squadron took considerable delight in making a mock attack on the parade ground with two pairs in full reheat at 10 o'clock at night:

> . . . and speaking about noise, your participation in the 'battle' was nothing short of stupendous. I have never seen such a display.

It was around this time that Sergeant Barney Barnes decided that 74 needed a real tiger as its mascot. In February Knaresborough Zoo had closed and all the animals had had to be rehoused or destroyed. Linton Zoo (near Cambridge) had agreed to take Roma, the Sumatran tigress, and an appeal was launched to raise the £20,000 necessary to build the special enclosures. 74's ground crews (amongst speculation as to whether Roma would eat Warrant Officers) decided to play an active part and, with Dick Northcote's blessing, the tigress was adopted.

The Squadron was holding QRA again during July and continued with more successful interceptions. On the 17th six 'Bear-Fs' were photographed, and a week later Dave Best, on his first QRA sortie and with Bunny Warren in the back seat, intercepted two 'Bear-As', two F-15s and a US Navy Orion in the course of a six-hour sortie! Runway repairs at Wattisham meant that the Squadron was using Coningsby as a bolthole, a move which gave them the chance of working with the ADV Tornados of 229 OCU. A further bout of QRA proved as uneventful and unexciting as the previous two sessions had been rewarding. The sunshine returned for many during October when another visit to Decimomannu brought the crews into more aerial contact with F-15s and F-16s. Yet again the Js acquitted themselves well, having paid heed to the old maxim of 'fight in your arena: if you fight in his, he'll win'. Also during October, the Squadron was delighted to learn that it had won the Aberporth Trophy for efficiency and results at the MPC at Valley, with Treble One being beaten into second place:

> The staff there see the way the squadrons operate, their serviceability, the way they conduct their MPC, the way they prepare their aircraft, the way they conduct their firing—in other words, all aspects of the detachment which in the final analysis lead to the choice of squadron that performs the best.

The Belgians of 350 Squadron brought four of their F-16s to Wattisham on a NATO exchange on 21 October, 74 simultaneously sending four Phantoms to Beauvechain. The Squadron diarist recorded the event:

> These were hectic times. During the course of several very enjoyable evenings the Belgians lived up to their spirited reputation, as indeed they did in the air during the flying phases of the exchange.

Just prior to the Belgians' arrival, the Tigers CO-elect, Wing Commander Cliff Spink, made his first flight in an F-4J. It was 7 November before he formally took over as Boss of 74: this was an airborne take-over, Dick Northcote handing over the Tiger One position in a four-ship formation to Cliff and his navigator Martin Routledge who had taken off as Tiger Two. A nice touch was the changing of all the names on office doors, Squadron signs and parking spaces from 'Dick Northcote' to 'Cliff Spink' between the time the hand-over formation took off and landed; this activity included the updating of the CO's Roll of Honour in the crew room. Dick Northcote moved on to the Falklands and was subsequently awarded the OBE for his and the Squadron's success in bringing the F-4J into service.

Cliff Spink's Tiger links had started with the Lightning OCU at Coltishall, where the T.4 had provided his introduction to the supersonic interceptor at the hands of ex-Tiger Jim Jewell, and was followed by Wattisham and $2\frac{1}{2}$ years on 111 Squadron, where his Flight Commander was ex-Tiger Martin Bee. Shortly afterwards, Ken Goodwin arrived to become the Wattisham Station Commander. In mid-1973 Cliff took the Intercept Weapons Instructor course at Coltishall before a spell back with 111 and then 56 Squadron at Akrotiri, flying the Lightning F.6s which had been handed over by the Tigers on their disbandment. Another link with 74's past was via 56's CO at the time, Martin Bee once again, whilst his Flight Commander was now ex-Tiger Henry Ploszek. Subsequently Cliff's Flight Commanders were ex-Tigers Clive Mitchell and Maurice Williams. A few years on and Cliff made his first acquaintance with the F-4—with 111 Squadron once again and this time as a Flight Commander himself. For much of his stay with Treble One he was at Coningsby, with ex-Tigers Bill Maish and then Jerry Cohu as Station Commanders. In 1982 he was posted to the Staff College prior to a move in January 1983 to Rheindahlen, where he was appointed Wing Commander Air Defence at RAF Germany's HQ. His Boss here was Mike Shaw, an early Lightning Tiger. It was whilst in Germany that he was told that he had been given command of 74. Given the many links with the Tigers' old boys' network throughout his career, it was almost inevitable that he should eventually join the Squadron himself!

Cliff took his first 'passenger' aloft in an F-4J on 21 November—Air Marshal Sir Brendon Jackson, the Deputy Commander in Chief of Strike Command who had been very much involved in the decision to purchase the F-4J. Unfortunately the flight had to be aborted when an engine fire warning light activated. Soon afterwards the Squadron was standing Southern QRA once more, intercepting a pair of 'Bear-As' on 19 November. And WRAF JEngO Julie Gibson arrived during the month. She was part of a significant piece of RAF history a few years later when she became one of the first women to undergo pilot training, successfully passing out from Cranwell on the Jet Provost.

ENGINEERING PERSPECTIVES

Dave Allan was with the Tigers until February 1987. By the time he had departed, the Squadron had come to terms with the engineering problems thrown up by the 'new' Phantom. He reflects:

I thought I knew a lot about aircraft until I became involved in the F-4J programme! But the response of all the engineers to the challenge was superb and we mastered everything that could be thrown at us. We all took a great deal of pride in the fact that we had been involved in a unique project, unique in the sense that the RAF had never bought second-hand aircraft before. The novelty of the project ensured a general high level of morale, and that despite having to work around the clock on more than one occasion. What was very noticeable was that air crew and ground crew enjoyed each other's company and there was considerably more interaction between the two than normal at squadron level.

One of the big problems encountered as we climbed the learning curve was the necessity of having to follow the American system of maintenance from extremely poor photostated copies of the manuals. Not only were there very few of them, but they were incomplete inasmuch as amendments had often been missed out. The manuals were never rewritten (which in itself would have been a mammoth task), a decision taken because of the initial five-year life expectancy of the F-4J and the attendant cost-efficiency of doing it. The F-4J(UK) was not quite like any other Phantom and the US Navy publications did not reflect the standard of aircraft we got. Moreover, from the word go these publications were out of date, even for their own F-4Js and F-4Ss, and there were an additional 1,500 amendments necessary following our purchase of the aircraft and the rework. So from our point of view it was a matter of drawing information from several sources and relying on the experience and ingenuity of our own men. Identifying components was another parallel problem. A lot of the parts for the F-4J were numbered differently within the US Navy system, a legacy of buying the same components from different manufacturers—necessary because of the sheer quantities involved. And commonality between the different marks of Phantom serving with the RAF was the exception rather than the rule. Indeed, a favourite saying of Phantom engineers highlighted this: 'When is a Phantom not a Phantom?' they asked. 'When it is an F-4J!'

It seems almost incredible now to realize that, despite everything, within six months 74 Squadron had the highest serviceability rate of any air defence squadron in the RAF. That made my demands for better back-up and my complaints about chronic lack of spares the harder to accept by my seniors. The Squadron, as such, was a victim of its own success!

It had been assumed from the beginning that the F-4J would serve only as an interim and be retired within five years; but, as other programmes slipped, as defence spending priorities changed and while forward planning remained as flexible and volatile as it often does, the decision had been made in January 1986 to extend the aircraft's life for a further five years.

After 74 had settled into operations, and after the original severe supply and support problems had been largely overcome, the aircraft became a very serviceable and cost-effective machine which would often keep going for weeks at a time: they were, in fact, a far better option than the FGR.2 and FG.1, which were becoming expensive. The choice open to the Air Staff boiled down to retaining the F-4J at the expense of the FG.1, which was already restricted in what it could do because of airframe problems.

January 1987 opened with the worst snow at Wattisham for twenty-five years, rendering the HAS site inaccessible for three days. Snow ploughs and blowers managed to keep the runways open, and 74 maintained Southern QRA using personnel who lived on base. As the station was totally cut off, those living off-base were told to stay at home. However, sunshine beckoned on 23 February when nine aircraft left Wattisham for the normally equable climate of Cyprus and the APC. After the frustrations of the previous year, when firing had suffered because of unserviceable equipment, it was pleasing to report that a new gun tape which had been integrated into the F-4J system in the meantime had had the desired effect and that results were as they should have been. Everyone acquitted himself very well and all qualified to NATO standards. The Tigers were also able successfully to renew their acquaintance with elements of the US Sixth Fleet and particularly enjoyed DACTing again with the Tomcat squadrons. 74 also stood 'Q' in the Mediterranean, intercepting three 'Badgers' in the process. One aspect of the deployment which failed to live up to expectations was the weather, which was uncharacteristically wet and, indeed, was the worst that had ever been recorded on the island during March. Socially the Squadron put on a highly acclaimed Tiger Review along the lines of those performed by the Cambridge Footlights and the brainchild of long-serving Tiger Ned Kelly. Appropriately described as a roaring success, these entertainments are only worth doing when they can be done well. Ned's ability to conceive highly original material and then persuade and cajole his colleagues to perform to similarly high standards was the secret of success. The Squadron has been fortunate in that Ken Moore has been similarly blessed with the gift of putting on very successful reviews, maintaining a tradition which says that Tiger Reviews are the best in the RAF.

Eagles came to Wattisham during April when four F-15s of the 53rd TFS from Bitburg arrived on a squadron exchange; four Phantoms made the reciprocal journey. Although the operational aspect of the Americans' visit was adversely affected by poor weather, demands by the Britons for back-seat rides in the two-seat F-15D were not curtailed and their enthusiastic reaction to the performance of the superlative fighter was predictable. The exchange coincided with Exercise 'Mallet Blow', and on one sortie that did proceed Mark Oliver and Steve Smyth diverted into Newcastle after a nozzle failure led to fuel consumption that went way beyond any acceptable level. It was coincidental that a BBC camera crew were at the airport to record the landing of a 747 which had been diverted from a fogbound Heathrow and which was suffering from an epidemic of hamsters which had chewed their way out of the containers during the flight and were running amok in the cargo hold! Mark and Steve's emergency arrival certainly attracted the interest of the waiting media, so much so that it became national news. Rarely has an emergency diversion attracted so much public attention!

TRAGIC ANNIVERSARY

The year 1987 marked 74's seventieth birthday, and it was fitting that the Squadron should be chosen by the Ministry of Defence to be the season's Phantom display unit. On 7 May Cliff Spink checked out Geoff Telford's programme, which had taken over three months to conceive and work up. Robin Birtwhistle was Geoff's navigator throughout, stoically enduring all the violent manoeuvres that go to make up a visually exciting routine on at least sixteen occasions, which would include appearances at Biggin Hill, at Halton, at Coningsby, at Montijo in Portugal for the Tiger Meet and at Kleine Brogel in Belgium as well as at the 'Farewell to the Lightning' show at Binbrook. The season would end with the RAF Battle of Britain Days at St Athan, Abingdon, Leuchars and Finningley. It was important to keep the same team throughout: Robin's job was primarily to watch all the parameters of speed and direction and advise Geoff of any deviation from the normal (so that instant rectification could be made) by conducting a running commentary throughout the display and taking a considerable workload off the pilot's shoulders as he looked for visual references during a routine in which he would have been unable to keep a constant check on instruments. For a back-seater, the flying of such routines can be very trying. The Phantom has a tradition of making 'passengers' sick; indeed, there are some navigators serving today who are regularly affected in this way.

Geoff had started to practise the planned sequence at 5,000ft during February, and over the ensuing weeks this was gradually brought down to a minimum of 500ft. The rules dictate that approval by the Station Commander should precede permission from 11 Group to fly before the public, and this was granted on 1 June when the AOC came to Wattisham to watch. Three separate displays had to be practised because of the unpredictability of English summers—the Full, the Rolling (no looping manoeuvres) and the Flat. ZE361/'I' became the preferred 'aeros' aeroplane for, like cars, aircraft have subtle differences of performance and handling, even amongst those of the same 'model'.

An examination of the diaries and records of any RAF squadron highlights the wide diversity of tasks it is expected to undertake. So it was, for example, that during May 1987, at one end of the spectrum, 74 provided three aircraft for a flypast of the Winter Gardens at Margate as part of the ceremonies to mark the granting of the Freedom of Thanet to

RAF Manston, and, at the other, the Tigers were once again busily intercepting Russian 'Bears'. On 12 May two of the 'Alpha' variant were photographed. In the late 1980s these 'Bear-As', which are pure bombers and which had not been seen for many years, suddenly started to reappear. Initial concern was tempered by the realization that they were being utilized by the Russian equivalent of the RAF's OCUs and that the flights now being intercepted were probably in fact the final long-range training sorties by crews prior to their joining a squadron.

June opened with Wattisham's Taceval. It lasted three days and nights, and all aspects of the capability to operate and survive under total wartime conditions were tested, including ground injects, air raids and intruder play. 74 and 56 operated from the secure area of their HAS sites, which can withstand nuclear, biological or chemical attack. Everyone was required to wear NBC clothing, and for air crews this included the ARS, which is in simple terms a rubber hood with a clear visor and face mask containing all necessary electrical connections. Cleaned air generated by portable compressors such as those carried on the American space programme and popularly known as 'Whistling Handbags' is blown through the hood.

June was also Tiger Meet month again, and this time the Portuguese Air Force hosted a bevy of aircraft, guests of 301 Squadron with their G.91s. 74 sent an experienced team of six crews with four aircraft in response to the growing number of participants at the Meets and the intense competition that the flying and ground handling produced. New Tigers to Portugal were the Norwegians of 338 Squadron with their F-5s, Spanish Mirage F-1s from Albacete, a trio of FB-111s from the 509th BW, a lone PC-3 from the United States Navy patrol squadron VP-8 and the Royal Navy's 814 Squadron with two Sea Kings. Every squadron felt the need to produce the best results in the best-looking aircraft. Once again it was a quartet of gleaming Js that were conspicuous amongst the HASs at Wattisham in the days prior to departure, in stark contrast to the well-worn machines that were usually seen there! These same aircraft had participated in a flypast of the Squadron's adopted Type 42 destroyer HMS *York* as she lay off the Humber a few days previously. Having landed at Binbrook, Cliff Spink and his men were later escorted on board for a cocktail party in the evening to enjoy the very special brand of hospitality that only the Navy can provide!

An already busy schedule became even busier during July and August as the Squadron's birthday celebrations reached their peak and as operations continued unabated. As part of the celebrations, a successful attempt on the London-to-Edinburgh speed record was made on 1 July. Cliff Spink, flying ZE361/'I' with Steve Smyth in the back seat, and Flight Lieutenant Ian Gale, in ZE360/'O' with Ned Kelly (who was celebrating his own birthday in some style!), were the participants. The idea had been conceived by Ian Gale and he set up the logistics of the attempt, with all the military radar establishments that were to be involved, so that a clear passage could be arranged, and with the FAI, who would monitor the attempt and ratify any claims made. Once airborne from Wattisham, the two Phantoms rendezvoused with a waiting tanker (the F-4s were 'clean' and carried no tanks) and set themselves up abeam London for a M0.6 subsonic passage to the Wash then a sustained-reheat M1.6 (1,150mph) dash at 40,000ft up the East Coast to a predetermined point abeam Edinburgh. The record was theirs at 27min 3sec, with Cliff a few seconds ahead of Ian Gale across the line. A legacy of the attempt was the stripping of the paint off the rear fuselages of the two aircraft by the sustained use of reheat over the North Sea!

The first weekend in August was set aside for the 70th Anniversary celebrations proper, starting with a reunion dinner on the Friday evening. The Saturday was given over to a flying display and mini-Tiger Meet, a list of participating aircraft being brought together by Phil Leadbetter that would rival any full-blown air show. The Squadron had worked up a formation team for the day, too, with Cliff Spink as Tiger 1, Barney Barnard as 2, Mike Castle as 3 and Pete MacNamara as 4 and with Mark Oliver as 5 acting as the singleton to impress the watchers with the noise and power of the F-4J! As a complete contrast, a church service on Sunday, during which the Standard was paraded, formed a fitting climax to a memorable weekend.

It is a sad and tragic irony that, just three weeks later, the Tigers were to lose two men and an aircraft in West Wales. Euan Murdoch and Jerry Ogg took off from Wattisham on 26 August in ZE358/'H' in company with two other aircraft. Shortly afterwards they crashed into a hillside at Pont y Gwiar, ten miles south-east of Aberystwyth, and were killed instantly. The formation of three was undertaking a training sortie to practise low-level interceptions. The general weather in the area, although not good, was considered acceptable for such an exercise. Dave Sullivan, with Robin Birtwhistle navigating, acted as formation leader, and Euan and Jerry, as No 2, set up a patrol to the east of Aberystwyth, aiming to be as high as possible so as to be in clear weather. The third aircraft, flown by Rich Lepman, the current USAF exchange officer, went to an agreed point in the south to act as the target. Prior to commencing the exercise, Dave climbed to check the cloud base and reported small amounts in a thin layer between 1,500 and 2,500ft above ground level. As the intercepting pair approached the target point, he saw Euan flying to his right and below him at a range of about four miles. He initiated a turn to the left and, half-way round, looked for his No 2 again but could not see him. Dave continued the turn and called Euan on the radio. In the absence of any answer, he immediately called the emergency services. Euan and Jerry had crashed. The subsequent investigation concluded that, just before impact, Euan had made a violent attempt to roll the aircraft to the right and pull up, a manoeuvre which failed to achieve any appreciable alteration to the flight path. The high yaw angle at impact indicated a departure from controlled flight brought about by the demand for the abrupt roll. There was no evidence to suggest any pre-impact failure of the aircraft, and neither crew member had attempted to eject. The cause has never been positively determined, but the most probable reason was a misjudgement of ground clearance. The seemingly insignificant layer of cloud would have made Euan's task of maintaining visual contact with Dave Sullivan more difficult, and the absence of visual cues on a feature-less ridge-line could have led to a miscalculation of distance: the slight hump of the impact point, being of the same featureless terrain, could have remained indistinct and have merged with the background until just before the crash.

Low-flying and military jet crashes usually lead to calls for enquiries, demands for the halting of military training and an increase in complaints to the RAF about jet noise and disturbance to wildlife and farm stock. There was the usual element of this in the aftermath of the accident, but the Squadron was also very grateful to receive so many letters of support, not only from ex-Tigers and close friends but also from members of the public, and particularly those in Wales who live with military training from day to day. In particular, the suggestion by the Williams and Wall families, who live near the crash site, that a cairn be erected in memory of Euan and Jerry was warmly welcomed by the Tigers. This memorial was duly established and on 28 April the following year 74 participated in its dedication by attending a short but moving service on the windblown hillside.

The Squadron continued with its busy training schedule. Five aircraft were deployed to Valley for MPC while the remainder of the Squadron flew to a very warm Decimomannu for DACT, taking three Jaguars from 226 OCU with them as their own personal Aggressor Squadron! Deci is always hot, but on this occasion it seemed to be excessively so, with recorded temperatures of 49°C. Engineers encountered considerable problems with the ground conditioning equipment, which proved to be incapable of keeping the radars cool enough. The high-pressure air starters could not cope with the heat either. When the Js went on detach-ment the Squadron took the 'Solar' starter with it, a smaller version of the massive 'Houchin'. The latter were of such a size that they were very difficult to transport and for this reason were left at strategic airfields throughout Britain and Europe for use in case of diversion or at airfields that the Tigers regularly used. Conversely the 'Solar' could be flown by Hercules to deployments abroad or in Great Britain. In an emergency there was a technique that could be used to start the F-4J safely, utilizing the more usual low-pressure starting systems found on some RAF air-fields for other types of aircraft. This method sometimes led to spectacular results, fires developing in the jetpipes, with temperatures approaching 1,000°C, requiring the shutting off of the engines. Ground crews had to be carefully briefed about the real possibility of flaming, for whilst this was a perfectly legitimate way of starting, care and an awareness of the consequences was essential!

After the return from Sardinia, the crews enjoyed a brief respite from travelling until the end of September, when four aircraft flew north to Gardemoen in Norway on Exercise 'Whiskey Troll', involving affiliation work with F-5s and F-16s of the Royal Norwegian Air Force. Phil Leadbetter led the main detachment over some spectacularly beautiful country, whilst Cliff Spink and Tim Wilkinson followed later:

We arrived at Gardemoen after the long transit in very poor weather, low cloud and raining, and we could hear on the frequency that 74's aeroplanes were operating and diverting to Orland. We shot an approach at Gardemoen, which was fairly limited in its approach aids, and Tim did an excellent job of positioning us on the centreline. When we broke cloud we could see a very wet runway in front of us. I used every available bit of it, including quite a bit of the undershoot, to put the aeroplane down on. We rolled down the runway with the 'chute streaming, but conscious of the lack of an anti-skid system and leaving the braking until the very last minute at a relatively slow speed, one of the tyres blew. A civilian aircraft was about to taxi to take off: to the great credit of the Squadron engineers who were operating with the detachment, they were on the runway and had the wheel changed before that aircraft called for take off clearance. Three minutes from start to finish!

The remainder of the Squadron stood QRA during Exercise 'Ocean Safari'. Whenever a big NATO exercise is in progress, the Russians predictably become quite active as they shadow the Western fleet, and the Tigers intercepted six 'Bears' and one 'May', the latter type not having been seen over British waters since the Squadron's re-formation on the F-4J. On a completely different tack, Flight Lieutenants MacNamara, Oliver, Whitmore, Lightbody and Stear went down to Uxbridge for three·days to re-learn how to march in preparation for the Battle of Britain Memorial Service in Westminster Abbey. The duty was an important one as the five officers were bearers and escorts for the Battle of Britain Roll of Honour and Fighter Command Ensign. Further QRA duties during October were a backdrop to the ever-present training programme, which slowed considerably during November as a spell of bad weather grounded the aircraft for prolonged periods. Four F-18s from Sollingen came across to Wattisham to participate in 'Mallet Blow', although this too was affected by the weather and the exercise was eventually cancelled after two Harriers crashed on the Northumberland ranges.

74 Squadron ended a year of heavy commitment to Southern QRA by standing duty over Christmas. Several scrambles were called, but no legitimate interceptions were made although the diaries do record tally-hos on a succession of sleighs and reindeer! Two crews lived in The Shed (as the QRA accommodation for men and machine was known) with another on standby at home. Those on duty were rarely allowed to forget that it was the Christmas season as their colleagues and families visited throughout the day, descending on the Q facility with plates of mince pies and Christmas cake. The small table overflowed with fare and the cramped quarters overflowed with people! Then the alarm was sounded and the aircraft scrambled . . . ! Such a scenario is a thing of the past now. The Phantoms at Wattisham ceased to stand QRA in August 1990 as the Tornado F.3 squadrons at Leeming and Leuchars were declared to NATO, although they did continue to operate from Leuchars with the Js for a while whilst 43 and 111 Squadrons were converting to the Tornado.

SILVER TIGERS

In the New Year, new crews continued to arrive, and much of the Squadron's work involved their conversion. A total of 127 hours of sunshine was recorded at Wattisham during February, more than twice the seasonal average, and the Tigers took full advantage by setting up another period of DACT with Coltishall's Jaguars. March was busy in terms of a succession of exercises at squadron, station and NATO level—'Ricochets', 'Active Edge', 'Flintstone' and a Macex (Maritime Air Control Exercise) in collaboration with the Royal Navy. The Tigers regularly sent crews down to the Falklands too, flying the FGR.2 version of the Phantom which equipped 1435 Flight. Tony Dixon:

> New pilots, those on their first tour, completed a dual check with 56 Squadron in one of their twin-stickers before a Falklands tour to remind them of the British Phantom's characteristics. If the navigator heading south was a new man, he went across to 56 as well. But once a couple of tours were safely under the belt or the crews had been on the FGR.2 elsewhere recently, then it was not a requirement to be checked out. It was simply a matter of taking a little bit more care with the systems of the FGR.2 for the first few trips.

Over the Falklands, height restrictions are the same as in Britain and there are areas which crews try to avoid, such as farms (particularly in December and January, when farmers are in the process of rounding up their sheep) and nature areas. Tony Dixon again:

> Nowadays there are not so many aircraft around so you are not continually trying to avoid them, but, having said that, there is still some civilian activity, mainly in the form of the three FIGAS BN-2As—although if you meet one it is quite a surprise! Obviously, in the early days after the war it was an active place militarily, but numbers were soon reduced. What hasn't diminished is the experience of flying in the Falklands—it can be quite exhilarating and crews quickly adapt to the environment!

In the Northern Hemisphere, the liaison with the Norwegian Air Force continued with a non-simultaneous squadron exchange with the F-16s of 332 Squadron from Rygge, an exchange notable for the multiple bird-strike suffered by the Norwegian CO as he left for Wattisham in marginal weather. Engine performance in the climb-out was drastically affected; but, pulling the aircraft round, he made a safe landing on the *taxiway* in a piece of inspired airmanship. Undaunted by the experience, the Norwegian immediately requisitioned a spare aircraft and set off once again, arriving safely and in time for the welcoming party! Mixed fighter-force work against large formations of Jaguars and Tornados was organized. The F-16's combination of agility and avionics made it something of a formidable adversary and the Tigers certainly found it wise to have these aircraft on their side! Once the Scandinavians had returned home, the Tigers flew out to their favourite playground, Cyprus. This proved to be a highly successful APC, particularly memorable for the occasion when American Rich Lepman lost his canopy as he climbed out of Akrotiri *en route* for the exercise area. A successful emergency landing was made (in the new F-4J Convertible, as Squadron wags quickly christened the aircraft), Rich summing up the situation by letting out a low whistle of relief and the words 'Gee! That was awesome!' The failure was subsequently attributed to problems with the canopy locking system. The deployment out to the Mediterranean immediately after the annual AOC's inspection had been, with one exception, trouble-free, with six Victors, seven Hercules and one VC10 available to shepherd the Js across. The exception was the aircraft that diverted to Decimomannu with a double utilities failure.

As is customary, QRA is held by the squadron on APC, and on this occasion the Tigers intercepted a pair of Russian 'Mays' during live scrambles. And as is also customary for the squadron in residence at the time of Her Majesty the Queen's birthday, a five-ship sunset flypast was made at Episcopi. In gun-firing, some very good scores were registered—the Boss with 58 per cent, John Sims with 65 and Russ Allchorne with 60, which were good for the Phantom with its fast-firing podded gun. The return to Britain on 16 June was accompanied by incident, this time involving Ian Gale and Mike Whitmore. After receiving fuel from a Victor, Ian attempted to break contact from the wing hose but was unable to separate from the basket; instead, the hose broke adjacent to the wing pod but with the strengthening wires intact. As the aircraft was heavy with fuel he was unable to check the rearward movement of the Phantom and the bracing wires continued to unravel from the severed end of the hose until, at twice the normal hose length, they too detached from the pod. The whole 70ft length of hose then passed over the right-hand side of the aircraft and sheared off just in front of the basket, which remained firmly attached to the probe. Providentially, there was no damage to the aircraft. The probe remained intact and a safe landing was made at Palermo.

Meanwhile preparations had been completed at Wattisham for both 74 and 56 to operate from a Honington 'bolthole' whilst runway repair and reconstruction work was carried out at their home base. Honington proved to be an interesting deployment as both squadrons were forced to share the same HAS site, crew room and operations room—not an easy situation to work in by any means and one which was looked forward to with some apprehension. Efforts were made by both squadrons to relieve the inevitable congestion by planning their detachments and deployments so as to alleviate matters. So, for example, as the Tigers returned to Honington from Cyprus, 56 flew out. In retrospect, any apprehension was unjustified and it all worked very well, the only problems occurring because Wattisham, 45 minutes away by road, was still providing engineering and MT support.

As a welcome respite from unseasonable Suffolk rainfall, four aircraft, six air crews and twenty-nine ground crews left for Cameri in Italy on 5 July to participate in the 1988 Tiger Meet. Once again this proved to be a highly successful social and flying week (low-level work through the Alps and mixed fighter force operations predominating), with more newcomers in the form of New Jersey Air National Guard Phantoms and

Mirage 2000s of the French test squadron CEAM. The Italian F-104S Starfighters provided the centrepiece of the final day's air show, with flying the likes of which is rarely seen elsewhere—very extrovert and full of Italian flair! The event had included a fifty-aircraft flyby in not ideal weather. Cliff Spink:

> The Italians have got a fairly *laissez-faire* attitude towards leading formations. I flew with Russ Allchorne. We were the two representatives from 74 and I led a box with my two wingmen, which were F-18s (from Sollingen) and Russ as No 4. To try and get the formation together was hard work, and it actually finished up with the F-18 Boss and my navigator giving information to aircraft which were not radar-equipped on how to join the formation—and we were three or four elements behind the leaders! Young Russ learnt a lot about flying that day!

As far as 74 Squadron was concerned, Cameri could be counted amongst its best Meets, for it came away with the much-prized Silver Tiger Trophy. The award is particularly significant as the judges are the squadrons themselves—a factor which considerably increases the value of the trophy to the winner.

Cameri apart, 74 ventured into Europe during that damp summer to Gutersloh to participate in 230 'Tiger' Squadron's Families' Day and also to provide a static aircraft at the Mont de Marson air display in France. It was while returning from this very pleasant weekend that the baggage pod on Steve Noujaim's aircraft, which had not been properly fastened by ground crew at the French base, flew open. Steve lost half his kit, scattered widely over the French countryside, including his Pentax camera. The camera was subsequently recovered and, despite its free-fall from height, was found still to be working!

QUICK-REACTION TIGERS

Chris Laidlaw Bell is probably best remembered on 74 for the hair-raising experience he and Tim Wilkinson had when a flap jack broke during finals into Wattisham. This initiated a violent rolling of the aircraft which CLB had difficulty holding; nevertheless, he had the presence of mind to get the flap up, engage reheat and climb away. Chris went on to complete a flapless arrested landing which he almost executed first time. The hook slipped the RHAG and Chris engaged full power, having decided to go round again, but the hook dangled and caught the PAAG (Pneumatically assisted Airfield Arresting Gear) further along the runway instead! The F-4J, in full reheat, came to a stop in a very short distance! It says much for the strength of the airframe, undercarriage and arrester hook (designed to cope with the high dump loads of carrier-landing operations) that there was no damage at all to the aircraft, just a very scorched runway!

At the end of August a few tanking sorties were conducted with KC-135s from nearby Mildenhall. Louis McQuade (later posted to United States Marine Corps F-18s in Hawaii on an exchange) managed to emulate the trick first performed by Ian Gale (who also went on to fly F-18s, this time in Australia) of pulling the basket from the hose, although on this occasion the fuel continued to flow briefly before being shut off—not before a considerable quantity was ingested by the Phantom's right-hand engine, producing a spectacular one hundred-foot flame to the rear. The whole aircraft was briefly engulfed as the fuel-saturated air flamed, but it all happened so quickly that Louis was·out of it before the J could catch fire. Fortunately it was a low-pressure fireball as opposed to a high-pressure explosion, the consequences of which would have been disastrous. Incredibly, no damage was done to the aircraft, but for the occupants it was an experience they would rather have avoided.

Ken Moore travelled up to Lossiemouth to share 8 Squadron's celebrations on 8 August—8/8/88. Martin Routledge led five aircraft on the return part of the exchange with Norway's 332 Squadron shortly afterwards, whilst at the month's end a mini-Tiger Meet was held at Kleine Brogel. Still at Honington, the Tigers mounted Southern QRA, and live scrambles uncovered an Il-18 'Coot' in full Aeroflot colours, the interception of which the Russians complained about, maintaining that the aircraft was on a civilian flight. The fact remained that it was not flying along any airway and so was almost certainly an intelligence-gathering aircraft. However, during 1988 there was an overall reduction in the number of infringements by Russian aircraft, although whether this was a result of *glasnost* or simply because of atrocious weather in the north of the USSR was difficult to analyse. Whatever the reasons, the QRA readiness state was increased to fifteen minutes from ten, an extension which allowed the alert to be operated from HAS sites as opposed to QRA barns and sheds where the doors open that much more quickly!

Those standing QRA at Wattisham followed a set routine. Coming on duty, new crews (who operate in pairs) accepted the aircraft from their colleagues standing down. This procedure included checking the loaded missiles, putting the power on and checking instrumentation and, if the ground crew dictated, running the engines for a while. The opportunity was also taken to set the cockpit up for both men's individual comfort. The waiting game then started. When the alert klaxon went, all four men zipped up their immersion suits (which were worn all the time) and ran to the shed with the engineers. The first one in hit the button to open the doors; Mae Wests and helmets were donned while the air starter built up pressure. Pilots and navigators strapped in, ground crew up on the port side helping them. The right-hand engine was spooled up first as the pilot talked to Neatishead, asking for details of the threat. Both Q1 and Q2 taxied out of the shed the short distance to the runway and Q1 launched. The second Phantom returned to the shed only after its companion was airborne with all systems fully serviceable. Meanwhile a tanker had taken off from Marham or Brize Norton, ready for the rendezvous which was necessary at the start of most sorties from Southern QRA.

Russian 'Bears' usually fly in pairs, and intercepting British aircraft are tasked with the job of identifying the model (there are numerous variants) and noting the serial of the aircraft. The interceptors take up a position on the left-hand wing, the Russian is scanned for unusual aerials or modifications and photographs are taken from various angles. The process is repeated for the second aircraft, and once that is over both intruders are left to continue on their way. Provided they stay in international airspace they are bothered no more: the brief is purely to intercept and identify, not to intervene and prevent the 'Bears' from continuing on their flight-path.

The annual migration of half the Squadron's complement to Decimomannu at the end of September 1988 further reduced overcrowding at Honington and, with 56 Squadron on their travels too, the bolthole became pleasantly quiet for a while! The opportunity was taken for those crews who had not done so before to fly on affiliation training with Hercules tankers. As foggy November days took their annual toll on flying hours, a pair of Mirage F1s from Rheims in northern France arrived to fly with the Phantoms, which had by now all regrouped at Wattisham. Both 74 and 56 had combined to make up the largest ever RAF Phantom formation of nineteen aircraft (plus two air spares) to mark the return, a record that still stands even after the 1990 Battle of Britain Flypast (which involved just sixteen aircraft plus two air spares). Cliff Spink took the lead of 74's Black Section and Russ Allchorne the Yellow for the occasion. Station Commander Group Captain Mike Donaldson led. Cliff had only recently returned from the Americans' Icelandic base at Keflavik, where he and Russ had taken an aircraft apiece (with Steve McLoughlin and Martin Routledge as navigators) on Exercise 'Hot Spring' in conjunction with 5 Squadron Tornados and 57 FIS F-15s. Many DACT sorties were flown against the Eagles, and for all that aircraft's phenomenal climb and turn capabilities no successful engagement was made against the Tigers!

There were now just three months to readjust to operations from home base and prepare for Taceval, the successful Battle Phase of which was eventually called in the early hours of 20 March. Exercises apart, a pair of Tigers flew across to Beauvechain in Belgium to work with F-16s but were prevented from doing so by some atrocious weather. Colonel Bartrand, Rich Lepman's USAF Exchange Programme Boss, came to visit 74 at the same time as Rich flew Ken Slattum, himself an American exchange officer who was in command of the ASF at Wattisham, a post traditionally filled by a USAF officer—an all-American crew flying a Royal Air Force aeroplane! Four aircraft (and six crews) were sent to Valley to fire Sky Flash missiles for the first time. The initial launch succeeded in destroying a Jindivik which got in the way of the towed radar target during a head-on attack. The Squadron was a little less destructive and rather more constructive in its participation in the annual 11 Group Recognition Contest! The Boss scored 100 per cent, the Flight Commanders 97, participating Flight Lieutenants 95 and Flying Officers 92. The Tigers were quite confident that similar scores would have been achieved even if the examiner had not been an ex-Tiger! As a result of sweeping the board in such a comprehensive manner, representatives from 74 then went on to represent 11 Group in the RAF Aircrew and Regiment competition at Cranwell. This took on a completely different complexion. There were four papers—one on aircraft, one on shipping, one on armoured fighting vehicles and one with a mixture of all three. The Tigers did not maintain their previous success rate.

FLYING BENGALS

April 1989 marked the beginning of the process of deep-servicing the Js following their service life extension to ten years. This meant that at least two or three aircraft would be out of commission for months at a time whilst they were at St Athan. There were occasions when the Squadron was down to just ten aircraft, and not all these fully serviceable all the time, which resulted in increasing difficulties scheduling crews and aircraft to meet the heavy demands still being placed upon it. The demands transcended the routine day-to-day training and included a requirement for two aircraft to be at Cambrai for mixed fighter-force operations with the French Tiger Squadron's Mirage F1s as part of the annual French air defence exercise, 'Datex'. At the same time crews and aircraft had to be available to work with the Tornado F.3 OEU (Operational Evaluation Unit) which the Tigers hosted at Wattisham for a week in April.

The New Year had certainly proved to be a significant one for Cliff Spink, his promotion to Group Captain being confirmed. For four months the Tigers had a Group Captain as Boss—certainly the first time in their history this had happened, and a rare occurrence indeed for any squadron in the RAF. Cliff was formally dined out on a memorable 7 April and three weeks later he handed over command of the Tigers to Wing Commander Graham Clarke. Cliff went on to command RAF Mount Pleasant in the Falklands, and shortly after he flew south news came through of an OBE. The Dining Out took the form of a 'This is Your Life' presentation, organized and researched by Ken Moore. There is no doubting that Cliff Spink was a very hard act to follow. The genial Graham Clarke took a different approach to the job in many ways, but there is no doubting his popularity too, nor the success with which he pushed the Squadron along on its permanently busy schedule. Graham came to the Tigers after a career on Lightnings and Phantoms with 11, 29, 19 and 92 Squadrons.

In 1989 a Tiger Meet had been planned for Oldenburg. It was bad luck that the planning meeting for this was held on the very day that two Alpha Jets and a Tornado collided over Germany, leading to a renewed outcry from the German populace about military flying over the country. The Tiger Meet, as part of a programme of appeasement, was promptly cancelled. The 79th TFS at Upper Heyford stepped in and suggested that it could hold the Meet in the United Kingdom later in the year, but the Ministry of Defence in turn ruled that as 74 was scheduled to hold the 1990 Meet at Wattisham the Americans could not do it in 1989. A secondary reason quoted was the increasingly-heard one of reluctance to 'import additional jet noise into an already sensitive environment'. The same reason was quoted for the eventual cancellation of the proposed

1990 Wattisham Meet. This left something of a bitter taste in the mouths of the Tiger community, compounded the following year by 74's inability to attend a mini-Meet at Upper Heyford. Reputations were put to rights in 1991, however, when the United Kingdom finally played host to the Tiger community once again, the Meet being organized as part of the International Air Tattoo at Fairford. Indeed, this proved to be a special gathering for several reasons, not least because it included representatives from Czechoslovakia's Tiger Wing (flying MiG-23s and 29s), whom 74 had the honour of meeting and escorting into British airspace, albeit in the face of considerable communications problems!

In May 1989, 74 operated once again with the 527th Aggressor Squadron, which by this time had swapped its ageing F-5s for the modern F-16 and had moved from Alconbury to Bentwaters. However, there was still no electronic debriefing available as at Decimomannu, although in 1990 British Aerospace opened a new electronic Air Combat Instrumentation Range over the North Sea. Ironically, by this time the American Aggressors had disbanded in the wake of *glasnost* and defence spending cuts and in the light of stabilizing relations between East and West.

Four aircraft and eleven air crews spent a week at Sollingen at the end of May 1989 on a one-way exchange with the Canadian Tigers of 439 Squadron. 74 came very close to writing off an aircraft during the course of operations here when Steve Noujaim, with Mike Whitmore in the back seat, lost lateral control immediately after take-off when the cable operating the engine bellmouth broke and inhibited the ailerons. Steve decided to attempt an approach but on short finals the stick seized completely, leaving him with rudder control only. He still felt he had a chance of getting the Phantom down safely—which he did, successfully engaging the approach-end cable. The decision was a marginal one, for if the controls had frozen just a few seconds earlier there would have been no option but to have ejected. Steve Noujaim was subsequently awarded the Queen's Commendation for Valuable Service in the Air.

At the end of June the Staneval team arrived at Wattisham. Staneval is Standards Evaluation, and the team is the equivalent of the old Trappers from Central Flying School, checking out pilots and navigators to ensure that constant standards, in terms of both operations and capability, are maintained. Less stressfully, 74 was able to enjoy Wattisham's Open Day on 24 June, a splendid day, with kind weather and a good variety of participating aircraft. The Tigers provided one of the highlights when they raced a Phantom against a TVR Triumph driven by local garage-owner John Kerridge over a quarter of a mile from a standing start. Graham Clarke and Bill Medland in the F-4J won—just. The race was sponsored and the proceeds went to local charities. Air show over, the next major commitment facing the Squadron was Cyprus once again, and preparations for this went into top gear. Extensive trials were flown with another new gun tape for the computerized aiming and firing system, and preparations for the Mediterranean also included cine sorties over the North Sea for new pilots in an FGR.2 with a QWI (Qualified Weapons

Instructor) in the back seat. The Squadron was participating in a 'Flint-stone' generation exercise, a Navy liaison exercise under the control of HMS *Manchester* and an 'Ample Gain' to Coningsby as well. 'Ample Gain' is another of those NATO-wide exercises, this time to test the cross-servicing capabilities of ground crews. It was essential that other bases could ground-handle adequately the unique F-4J, so 74 regularly flew into Coningsby, Leuchars or Leeming to enable its crews to rearm, refuel and turn round the aircraft as part of routine training. Three days of combat with the 527th Aggressors for the last time and more QRA (with four 'Bear-Ds' intercepted) completed an active July.

On 14 August eight Phantoms took off *en route* for Cyprus on the latest exercise, 'Flying Bengal'. Only six made it at the first attempt. Graham Clarke could not persuade his undercarriage to retract so had to return to Wattisham, and Dai Whittingham had a single reheat failure, resulting in the need for a ground abort. Once fully assembled, the detachment followed a normal course and standard air-to-air gunnery was successfully completed, enabling everyone to qualify for a further year whilst maintaining the customary political presence in the Eastern Mediterranean—a presence which was becoming more significant as tensions in the Middle East continued to fluctuate. The usual opportunities were taken to relax on the beaches when not on duty, to swim and scuba dive, to socialize and to acquire the best tan on the Squadron! The Engineering Warrant Officer, John Kent, was taken aloft to celebrate thirty-five years' service in the Royal Air Force. Squadron Leader John Sims, who had taken the author aloft for an experience flight in ZE363/'W', flew his last sortie in Cyprus before leaving the RAF to fly with Air UK. One problem which strangely manifested itself in Cyprus involved the braking parachute. The aircraft were using a British 'chute which, with a few minor differences, is the same as its American counterpart. Why it should suddenly fail twenty-one times defied explanation. In each case the aircraft had to take the arresting cable; indeed, they used it so often that they contrived to break it! A subsequent return to the American-designed 'chute seemed to solve the problem.

The return to the UK was scheduled for 12 September. Tony Dixon recalls:

> There was no air-to-air refuelling support available to bring us back. It was therefore planned to transit through Sigonella in Sicily, although there were some misgivings amongst Squadron navigators that the Sigonella–Wattisham leg was just a little too far. Nevertheless 11 Group had the final say and we were instructed to go ahead. The problems started when the C-130 taking the ground crew from Akrotiri to Sicily became unserviceable. The Boss decided not to launch until the Hercules had arrived so there was a five-hour delay. Sigonella were not too happy to see us anyway, protesting that they did not have adequate ramp space, so the Phantoms were parked very tightly together with their wings folded.

The wing folding facility was one rarely used by the Squadron. Evidence of this became apparent as the hydraulics operating the system leaked as the Js stood overnight and the folded sections collapsed on to each other! During routine servicing at Wattisham wing-folding was regularly checked but because it was hardly used there were frequent problems getting the tips to lock into the 'down' position again. This was generally cured by requisitioning a couple of ground crewmen to hang on until the locking pins slipped into place! Tony Dixon continues:

It had not been our intention to stay overnight at Sigonella, but a combination of factors, including our late departure from Akrotiri and problems with the Italians as far as refuelling was concerned, meant that it was the morning of the 13th before we were airborne again. We all still felt that we wouldn't make it directly to the UK, given that weather reports were none too promising. We had the Canadian base at Lahr in southern Germany as a diversion, and the first wave of four decided that they would go there anyway; however, after being airborne for a couple of hours, they received reports that Lahr itself was deteriorating with a 200-foot cloudbase and thunderstorms. French Air Traffic directed them into Dijon instead, despite this in itself necessitating flying through a pretty severe storm. The second wave of aircraft left Sigonella happy in the knowledge that the UK was not possible because of their fuel state—the Italians had not fully topped the Js up—and, once airborne, ATC had kept the formation at a fuel-thirsty low level. They too had decided on Lahr until they found that the first wave had been directed into Dijon and so elected to follow them there. No such luck! Almost perversely, the French controllers insisted that they divert to Colmar, by which time they had found that Lahr, only twenty-eight miles away, was, contrary to all reports, in fine weather.

The second wave landed at 1600 after the airfield had just completed a three-day exercise, although there was a reluctance to receive Phantoms requesting fuel. Things looked particularly bleak when the air crews discovered that the airfield was to close within fifteen minutes of their arrival, but here fate stepped in in the shape of a RAF exchange officer who was able to pull a few strings and enable the Js to get off again that evening. The low-pressure start technique worked for all the Phantoms. They elected to route back via German airspace rather than risk more confusion with the French and finally called up Wattisham 150 miles out. Ops were more than surprised to hear them, not having been notified of their return that day; nor had the Squadron, who were expecting the whole deployment the next morning. Everyone had gone home, but someone got hold of Bill Medland, who returned to the site, called back any ground crews he could contact and saw them in. Meanwhile those crews at Dijon had been more than pleased to see the Hercules arrive with the starters on board, and the four aircraft got airborne the next morning on the final leg of their extended journey!

BLUE FORCE AT RED FLAG

The next item on the Tigers' agenda was participation in Red Flag, the realistic American air defence and attack exercise which takes place over the Nevada desert. The Cyprus detachment had been back in Britain for barely a week when the Squadron moved to Leuchars to fly its Phantoms against large packages of aircraft of all types across northern England and southern Scotland as part of the work-up. 74 also practised intensively against Tornado F.3s in preparation for its role as part of the Blue Force in the States, defending airspace against American F-15s. Another week of working up at Wattisham preceded the departure on 17 October of four crews in FGR.2s of 56, 19 and 92 Squadrons to Nellis AFB. Other crews flew out by TriStar. It was a matter of regret that they would not be taking any F-4Js to the USA but, with crews from the other RAF Phantom squadrons who were not F-4J-compatible also participating, this was not possible. The deployment involved a crossing to Goose Bay accompanied by TriStar tankers.

The following morning it was found that two of the eight FGR.2s involved (Graham Clarke/Tony Dixon and Dai Whittingham/Stan Ralph) had become unserviceable, as Graham Clarke recalls:

We were faced with a 3,000-mile flight to Nellis. There was no planned route or any support. So we were forced into stopping another night, planning our own route and making many phone calls to obtain clearances and so forth. We eventually flew via Griffiss AFB, where we lunch-stopped in pouring rain and then went on to Offutt and across to Nellis.

Tony Dixon:

We were airborne for 6½ hours, which was extremely tiring, but I, along with the others, was fascinated by the aerial views of America once we had emerged from the great blankets of cloud covering Canada and the northern States. The Plains are phenomenal in scale. The fields are circular by virtue of the irrigation methods used and we got to the stage where, at 30,000ft-plus, all we could see in unlimited visibility in every direction across Utah, Nevada and Colorado were these fields—thousands of square miles of them! The flatness of the plains stopped abruptly at Denver with the formidable barrier of the Rockies. It was a real treat for us to be able to appreciate the sheer beauty of the country.

Air crews do without doubt have an eye for such things.

Two-thirds of the Squadron were involved in Red Flag. It is an American requirement for participating crews to have attained a specific level of experience, so some of the newer Tigers were not eligible. Eight out of the Tigers' complement of thirteen crews made the journey, and with one crew in the South Atlantic that left just four to fly a restricted programme in the UK, including participation in 'Elder Joust' at the beginning of the month. Two aircraft and two crews then went to Albacete in Spain to visit the Spanish Tigers of 142 Squadron, a boisterous social call that involved no flying. Meanwhile those at Nellis did very well, operating as they did against packages of Italian and German Tornados, Singaporean F-16s and USAF EF-111As and F-111s and lots of F-16s of both the ground-attack and air defence variety. Alaskan F-15s, B-1Bs of Strategic Air Command, Air National Guard Phantoms, Marine Corps AV-8Bs and Navy Prowlers also formed part of a very impressive line-up. Graham Clarke relished the opportunity of putting the Eagles down on the last day of the exercise:

Those F-15s we were up against were the latest version of the type and their pilots had been almost offensively cocky all week, claiming shots against anybody and everybody. On this final day we were escorting Blue Force ground-attack types against eight of these Eagles and a pair of Aggressor F-16s. We had a Navy Prowler ECM aircraft with us, whose primary job was to launch Harm missiles against SAM sites, but he had also indicated before we took off that he could do a pretty good job against Eagles too. And he did. At fifteen miles, when the F-15s were thinking about launching missiles, he turned his jammers on and we, as a force, did a split and then began mixing it. At the end, out of the seven F-4s there were three left whilst out of the eight Eagles there was just one left. Both F-16s had been 'shot down'. What is more, only three of the ground-attack types had been hit. The Eagle guys were very sad about the whole thing!

After three weeks in the intense heat of the desert (and resisting the temptations of nearby Las Vegas), the Red Flag crews returned to the United Kingdom. Once again there was just one week's respite before a large part of the Squadron was off on detachment again, this time to Decimomannu. Five aircraft spent a fortnight in Sardinia with, amongst others, F-16s from the new Dutch Tiger Squadron at Twente and Tiger Mirage F1s from Cambrai.

The second half of 1989 had been an extremely hectic one for the Tigers, the programme comprising four weeks at APC Cyprus, one week at Wattisham, one week at Leuchars, two weeks at Wattisham, three weeks at Nellis, one week at Wattisham again and two weeks at ACMI Deci. Some crews had only just returned from Falkland Islands duties prior to Cyprus. The net result was that many did not see their wives and families for weeks on end, and so it was with considerable relief that they could look forward to less travelling once they had returned from the DACT in the Mediterranean. With the advent of Christmas, the festivities began with a

> . . . very good Ops Wing luncheon. There were some very high spirits, raucous singing and a cracking water pistol fight between two Mark 9 Fire Engines in front of the Mess . . .

With gales sweeping the country in early 1990, an attempt was made to deploy to Valley for MPC. It took two days to do so, and once there a succession of firing slots was lost as bad weather continued. Sidewinders and Sparrows were the missiles to be fired, but such were the problems with the weather that hard-pressed ground crews loaded and unloaded the aircraft no fewer than twenty-eight times as sorties were progressively cancelled prior to the first successful launch. However, by the end of the Camp the Squadron had fired four of the five missiles allocated, the fifth due to be launched later in the year on a no-notice firing. Shortly afterwards, Operation 'Joint Venture' involved practice-refuelling from USAF KC-135s. This was a requirement for 'Elder Forest', during which the RAF's tanking fleet was largely committed to the refuelling of ground-attack aircraft. Four AFRES KC-135s from March AFB in California were detached to Cottesmore for the duration of the exercise and a high proportion of air defence tanking was conducted with them. As the Lightning crews had discovered twenty years earlier, refuelling from an inflexible short hose was no easy matter.

CHAPTER 12

Uncertain World

ON 11 MAY 1990 a new Standard was presented to 74 Squadron. The weather did not play its part, as prolonged heavy rain necessitated the adoption of a wet-weather programme which involved parading in a HAS. The presentation, in front of a small number of guests, was made by ex-Tiger Air Vice Marshal B. L. Robinson, the Standard being received by Will Jonas; the old Standard was marched off by Harry Day. Two Phantoms, led by Gordon James, managed a flypast in spite of the atrocious conditions. The ceremony was followed by informal drinks in an adjoining HAS and a formal dinner in the Officers' Mess.

Graham Clarke's response to Boz Robinson's address to the parade very succinctly sums up the Tiger ethos:

> 74 has a fine tradition dating back to its formation in 1917. Because of the Squadron's aggressive fighting spirit in the First World War, it was awarded the Tiger motif for its crest and honoured with the motto 'I Fear No Man'. In the Second World War No 74 played a major part in the Battle of Britain under the leadership of Sailor Malan, whose Memorial Sword I now carry. The same fighting spirit ensured success in various campaigns during the rest of the war and in the part it played in the eventual downfall of Nazi Germany. Since then, 74 has been part of the NATO deterrent that has now proved to have been so successful. We are seeing our most likely aggressor, the Warsaw Pact, disintegrate and its individual members seek democracy and peace. Just as in both World Wars, our more recent predecessors on the Squadron responded to the challenge of the Warsaw Pact by providing a part of that formidable NATO deterrence. Today, on the presentation of our new Standard, we look to the future and in this uncertain world we in 74 Squadron promise to continue to defend our country to the best of our ability, to maintain that Tiger spirit and to honour our new Standard whenever and wherever it is unfurled.

Uncertain world indeed. Within eight months the RAF would be at war in the Middle East and the Tigers would be flying different aeroplanes—and their own survival in a restructured Air Force would be in doubt.

The Tigers returned to a green and pleasant East Anglia on 20 June after another month in Cyprus, and it would not be many weeks before they were involved in helping to train those crews selected to fly Tornado F.3s in the Gulf in the wake of Saddam Hussein's invasion of Kuwait. Operation 'Granby' placed more demands on 74's expertise as the year progressed; it also saw a subtle change in tactics as the Tigers launched four aircraft to man a CAP and fly against eight or ten Tornados. In the early summer, before Iraq's invasion, such work (against Harriers and Jaguars) had been seen as very good training for Red Flag, which 74 were scheduled to attend once again, but that exercise was promptly cancelled following the Iraqis' Middle East belligerence. At the same time, the improvement in East–West relations reduced generation requirements throughout NATO and eased the pressure on RAF squadrons at an opportune moment. For 74 this meant that almost the entire effort could be devoted to working with the desert-bound squadrons.

A visit by the Chief of the Air Staff, Sir Peter Harding, in mid-July had helped to reassure the Tigers that there would be little likelihood of their being affected by the widely reported defence cuts which were probable in the wake of the thaw in relations with Moscow. Within a fortnight of Sir Peter's visit, the Secretary of State for Defence announced that the Phantom force would be phased out over a two-year period. Suddenly the Tigers' future was in doubt; speculation was rife, but by the year's end the situation was as unclear as it had been after the initial announcement. The prospect of all-out war with Iraq added to the uncertainty. Once Operation 'Granby', the deployment of troops and equipment to Saudi Arabia, had been approved and activated, the Tigers worked with Tornado F.3 crews at Leeming and Leuchars with renewed vigour. 74 also sent crews to Sardinia, although it was a muted detachment in the sense that the USAFE F-16s with which they were scheduled to operate did not arrive, a direct consequence of the American build-up in Saudi Arabia ('Desert Shield'). The Squadron also managed to squeeze in a 'Mallet Blow' commitment, although pre-planned exercises for the rest of the year were cancelled. On 31 August Southern QRA was suspended and a UK QRA set up at Leuchars which would be filled exclusively by Phantoms, thus releasing all Tornado F.3s for 'Granby'. For ease of operation, 'Q' was flown with FGR.2s and crews from both 74 and 56 rotated through the Scottish base to share the duty with the resident OCU.

One thing that the Gulf Crisis did not affect was the flypast commemorating the 50th anniversary of the Battle of Britain. It had been intended that the participants should include representation from all fixed-wing squadrons still serving which had taken part in the Battle, although this was not possible given that some had already deployed to the desert. Practice for the flypast, which had been meticulously planned months previously, had started during August when Wattisham (which was the designated 'home' for all participating Phantoms) put up sixteen aircraft and flew them in a tight diamond with few problems. From 10 to 14 September, 74 and its sister-F-4 units were involved with the full practices which brought together the complete formation of 168 aircraft for the first time. On the day itself the flypast commenced at an initial point over the southern section of the River Blyth at Southwold in Suffolk, maintaining a track whereby the first element (the Battle of Britain Memorial Flight Spitfires and Hurricanes) overflew Buckingham Palace at 1200 precisely. From London the participating aircraft took up different routes to enable the majority of the aircraft to overfly RAF Abingdon as part of that station's Battle of Britain At Home Day. The co-ordination required to carry out such a flypast was considerable, not only from the point of view of getting several aircraft formations with varying speeds in the right place at the right time but also in reserving the large amount of airspace required and in ensuring that diversion airfields were available if required. On the ground in London, Will Jonas paraded 74's Standard outside Buckingham Palace, while Iain Walsh and Clive Stinchcombe represented the Squadron the following day at the Memorial Service in Westminster Abbey.

FGR.2s

Shortly before Christmas 1990, Graham Clarke and SEngO David Smith were called down to Strike Command HQ for a progress meeting and were informed that 74 Squadron was to be a Phantom FGR.2 unit by the year's end. This effectively gave the Tigers four days in which to get aircraft out of Leuchars (where the Phantom OCU had disbanded) and into Wattisham, have them checked over and painted up in squadron colours and have all crews converted! Reason prevailed, however, and a further month was allocated for the changeover, a month during which the Squadron was down-declared. By 31 January 1991 all the F-4Js had been retired and placed in short-term storage at Wattisham prior to their allocation to various airfields in Britain and Germany for battle damage and fire training. The first of the F-4Js to be flown away to such a sudden and ignominious end was ZE354/'R', which Barry Cross took to Coningsby and which by way of farewell he pushed to Mach 2 on a high-speed run and took up to 64,000ft at Mach 1.6. He was still going strong when forced to call a halt to the climb, demonstrating a performance which the Tornado F.3 would find it difficult to match.

The J's place was taken by the Spey-engined Phantom FGR.2. Ground crews had been systematically sent away for quick courses on aspects of the aircraft with which they were not familiar. The aircraft behaved well on acceptance by the Tigers. Given that they were all old airframes, the only major problems encountered related to the radar, which would not have been used to the full by the OCU. Chief Tech 'Dixie' Dean and his men worked wonders, and the difference in the radar between the time the aircraft came on charge to the Squadron and six weeks afterwards was quite remarkable. Back-seaters were quick to notice the change, though, from the AWG-10A equipment they had been used to on the F-4J: in terms of clarity and interference, the AWG-12 was a poor system in comparison.

Pilot and navigator conversion was straightforward and Graham Clarke and his Flight Commanders evolved a programme which was quickly completed. Most pilots started with a general handling sortie to re-familiarize themselves with the different cockpit layout. Less-experienced pilots underwent a dual check with Graham, Dai Whittingham, Barry Cross or Russ Allchorne, each of whom had checked each other first. Each Tiger then flew two weapons sorties. These were not high-demand sorties but comprised straightforward intercepts to check out the weapons system and some work against ECM Canberras to allow the navigators to check the different ECM features of the FGR.2. Most air crews were able to fly the F-4J and the FGR.2 whilst the transition from one type to the other was in progress, but only on separate days. Within the first batch of Phantom FGR.2s that 74 received there were nine twin-stick aircraft which, when it came to full operational flying, were not ideal, for although the rear stick is removable the throttle controls are not and this proved to be restrictive. When 92 and then 19 Squadrons at Wildenrath disbanded, their aircraft were transferred to 74 and the numbers of dual-check examples accordingly fell.

It must be said that there were features of the FGR.2 which crews particularly appreciated in comparison with the F-4J. These included the ability to self-start, doing away with the need for strategically placed 'Houchin' and 'Solar' starters and giving the Squadron rather more flexibility as to where they could go. The presence of a VHF radio was also significant in that it suddenly allowed for more diversion options. Along with the FGR.2 came the requirement to form a Phantom Training Flight. Dai Whittingham was chosen to command it, his place as OC A Flight being taken by ex-Red Arrows Squadron Leader Dominic Riley. Although under the control of OC Operations at Wattisham, the PTF drew its aircraft from 74 Squadron, and when there were no students going through it operated as part of 74. Given that the numbers of students expected were not great, a large proportion of the PTF's time was spent as Tigers.

All on the Squadron were sad to see the F-4Js disappear so quickly. In the final analysis, the reasons for their going were financial, comparisons with statistics for FGR.2 and F-4J operations revealing the high cost of the latter. Arguably the Js could have continued in service for a further six months at least without incurring further major costs other than those of day-to-day maintenance, but, under the 1990 'Options for Change' in the RAF, the run-down of the Phantom force meant that FGR.2s were available to 74 and if only for reasons of commonality it made sense to allocate them to the Tigers.

FINALE?

Since its re-formation in 1984, 74 had been one of the RAF's smallest squadrons in terms of aircraft and personnel but one of the busiest in terms of commitment and achievement. The Tigers' spirit was as potent as it ever was, and the new young crews coming through to join them were keenly aware of the Squadron's heritage and tradition—and all were anxious to maintain 74's élitism. In the face of some apparent opposition from 11 Group, that proved to be difficult: as they flew 'old' aircraft, prestige commitments began to be cancelled during 1991 (for example, participation in the Queen's Birthday Flypast) and there was a growing feeling that the Tigers were being progressively pushed aside by their masters in favour of the emerging F.3 squadrons. With the Squadron's

74th birthday celebrations occurring in mid-1991 and, shortly afterwards, its participation in one of the largest Tiger Meets to date, plans were drawn up to 'tiger-stripe' an entire Phantom, as has become customary for hosting units. Permission was not forthcoming for this, which was a bitter disappointment for all—disappointment heightened by being surrounded at the Fairford Meet by the biggest collection of specially tiger-marked aircraft ever assembled in one place. The Squadron was, however awarded a special commendation in the *concours d'élégance*, which was fitting recognition for the many hours of work which the ground crews had put into preparing the aircraft in the static park. It shone!

The Squadron also put together a four-ship display team for Fairford, the routine they flew drawing on Dom Riley's Red Arrows experience. Tigers' pride was restored somewhat by the many compliments paid them by watching air crews of all nations. This was probably the last occasion on which an RAF Phantom team would display at a public show. Amongst the interested spectators was Prince Michael of Kent, whom 74 had had the honour of flying in the FGR.2 a week previously. An amusing corollary to this was the letter subsequently received by the Squadron from the Prince, thanking them for their hospitality: 'But of course the flight in the Phantom was the obvious *twilight* of the day'—an ironic typist's error given that 1991 was certainly the twilight of the Phantom's career!

Graham Clarke did not see the Tigers through to the end. He was posted out on 7 February 1992 and his place was taken by Wing Commander Nick Spiller, from RAF Germany's recently disbanded 19 Squadron. And as these words are written, Taffy Jones' 'greatest fighter squadron of all time' enters its final months before its own disbandment. The so-called 'peace dividend' has seen the demise of many famous RAF squadrons. The Tigers have the honour of carrying the Phantom flag to the end, being the last to disband with that memorable aircraft. At the 74th Anniversary Guest Night, Graham Clarke addressed assembled Tigers old and new:

> It looks as though the Squadron will just make its 75th Anniversary celebrations before it goes. As for the future, much has been spoken about the European Fighter Aircraft and it is to be hoped that 74 would be one of the forerunners for re-forming on that aircraft towards the end of the century.

If such speculation becomes reality, it means that 74 will continue a proud tradition of introducing new types to squadron usage. Whatever happens, the Tigers' roar will only reluctantly be muted and its memory will be kept alive as old Tigers meet to reminisce about a proud past and consider what the future may bring. May that future be not too far away.

Tiger! Tiger!

APPENDICES

APPENDIX A: TIGER COMMANDERS 1917–1992

Maj. A. J. O'Hara Wood	1 July 1917	Sqn. Ldr. R. T. Llewellyn	1 Sept 1945
Maj. The Hon. L. J. E.	11 Nov 1917	Sqn. Ldr. J. R. Cooksey	27 Jan 1946
Twistelton-Wykeham-		Sqn. Ldr. R. L. W. Baelz	22 Apr 1947
Fiennes		Sqn. Ldr. J. H. Lapsley	22 Feb 1948
Maj. A. S. W. Dore	1 Mar 1918	Sqn. Ldr. R. L. W. Baelz	10 Aug 1948
Maj. K. L. Caldwell	21 Mar 1918	Sqn. Ldr. A. R. de L.	5 Sept 1949
Capt. I. Jones	9 Dec 1918–	Inniss	
	3 July 1919	Maj. G. W. Milholland	13 Sept 1951
Squadron disbands		USAF	
Sqn. Ldr. H. G. Crowe	1 Sept 1935	Sqn. Ldr. W. J. Johnston	30 Nov 1953
Sqn. Ldr. D. S. Brookes	19 July 1936	Sqn. Ldr. K. N. Haselwood	3 Jan 1956
Sqn. Ldr. G. E. Sampson	26 Apr 1938	Sqn. Ldr. C. F. A. Curtis	29 Oct 1957
Sqn. Ldr. F. L. White	1 Mar 1940	Sqn. Ldr. P. W. Carr	20 July 1959
Sqn. Ldr. A. G. Malan	8 Aug 1940	Sqn. Ldr. J. F. G. Howe	22 Feb 1960
Sqn. Ldr. J. N. Mungo	10 Mar 1941	Sqn. Ldr. P. G. Botterill	12 Dec 1961
Park		Sqn. Ldr. W. B. Maish	14 Dec 1964
Sqn. Ldr. S. I. Meares	30 June 1941	Wg. Cdr. K. J. Goodwin	7 Oct 1966
Sqn. Ldr. P. H. M. Richey	23 Aug 1941	Wg Cdr D. E. Caldwell	31 Mar
Sqn. Ldr. P. G. H.	3 Nov 1942		1969–31
Matthews			Aug 1971
Sqn. Ldr. J. Addison	10 July 1942		
Sqn. Ldr. P. F. Illingworth	24 Dec 1942	*Squadron disbands*	
Wg. Cdr. W. Ogden	27 Feb 1943	Wg. Cdr. R. Northcote	1 July 1984
Sqn. Ldr. J. C. F. Hayter	1 Apr 1943	Wg. Cdr. C. Spink	7 Nov 1986
Sqn. Ldr. A. J. Reeves	30 Dec 1944	Wg. Cdr. G. Clarke	28 Apr 1989
Wg. Cdr. H. C. Kennard	31 May 1945	Wg. Cdr. N. Spiller	7 Feb 1992
		Squadron disbands	

APPENDIX B: TIGER LAIRS 1917–1992

Northolt	1 July 1917	Halfar	Sept 1935
London Colney	10 July 1917	Hornchurch	Aug 1936
Goldhanger	Mar 1918	*Frequent detachments to Rochford Oct 1939–*	
St-Omer	Mar 1918	*June 1940*	
Tetenghem	Apr 1918	Leconfield	27 May–5 June
La Lovie	Apr 1918		1940
Clairmarais	Apr 1918	Hornchurch	5 June 1940
La Lovie	Sept 1918	*Detachments to Rochford and Manston 5 June–*	
Clairmarais	Oct 1918	*14 Aug 1940*	
Courtrai	Oct 1918	Wittering	14 Aug 1940
Cuerne	Nov 1918	Kirton-in-Lindsey	21 Aug 1940
Halluin	Nov 1918	Coltishall	9 Sept 1940
Lopcombe Corner	Feb–July 1919	*Occasionally operating from Duxford Sept 1940*	
Squadron disbands; re-forms 3 Sept 1935 on		Biggin Hill	15 Oct 1940
board Neuralia *en route for Malta*		Manston	Feb 1941

Gravesend	1 May 1941	*On board* Devonshire *en route to United King-*	
Acklington	8 July 1941	*dom 1–22 Apr 1944*	
Llanbedr	3 Oct 1941	North Weald	22 Apr 1944
Long Kesh	24 Jan 1942	Lympne	15 May 1944
Atcham	25 Mar 1942	Tangmere	3 July 1944

En route to Middle East on board Rangitata *from 10 Apr 1942. From arrival in Egypt on 4 June 1942 until Dec 1942 the Tigers were a squadron in search of a home—and aircraft to fly.*

		Selsey	17 July 1944
		Southend (APC)	24 July 1944
		Tangmere	6 Aug 1944
		Sommervieux	19 Aug 1944
		Bernay	4 Sept 1944
Geneifa	4 June 1942	Gamaches	11 Sept 1944
Helwan	21 June 1942	Lille (Le Vendeville)	12 Sept 1944

Some pilots flying with 73 Sqn at LG 89, others with Test Unit at Helwan. With ground crews moving on to Ramat David, pilots formed joint 74/145 Sqn operating from Idku until losing 74 Sqn status in Oct 1942.

		Courtrai	17 Sept 1944
		Antwerp-Deurne	25 Nov 1944
		Schijndel	6 Feb 1945
Ramat David	4 July 1942	Drope	14 Apr 1945
Hadera	4 Sept 1942	*En route to United Kingdom via road and sea*	
Doshen Tappeh	3 Oct 1942	*convoy 11–15 May 1945*	
Meherebad	1 Dec 1942	Colerne	16 May 1945

Now operating Hurricanes, detached Flights flew from Abadan and Shaibah between Jan and May 1943

		Horsham St Faith	14 Aug 1946
El Daba	25 May 1943	Coltishall	6 June 1959
Idku	26 Aug 1943	*Operated from Horsham St Faith Mar–July 1960*	

Detachments also operated from El Daba, Nicosia, Kos, Simi and Peristerona 26 Aug–23 Oct

whilst runway repairs and resurfacing undertaken at Coltishall

		Leuchars	26 Jan 1964
Dekheila	1 Nov 1943	Tengah	4 June 1967–
Idku	22 Nov 1943		31 Aug 1971

Detachments also operated from Mariut and El Daba 22 Nov–21 Jan

Squadron disbands; re-forms on F-4J(UK) 1984

Dekheila	21 Jan 1944	Wattisham	May 1984–Oct
			1992

Detachments also operated from Idku and St-Jean 21 Jan–4 Mar

Operated from Honington 16 June–18 Dec 1988

Idku	4 Mar 1944

At the time of writing, it is understood that the Squadron will disband in October 1992. However, the numberplate will be transferred to become a component of 4 FTS at RAF Valley.

APPENDIX C: ROLL OF HONOUR

74 Squadron served with distinction in many theatres throughout the First and Second World Wars, not least in the Battle of Britain in the summer of 1940. Whatever the fate of those who fought as Tigers, there is no doubting their courage and tenacity during those dreadful days when the continuing liberty of the British people was in doubt. 'Never has so much been owed by so many to so few'—including those of 74 Squadron listed below.

P. Off. W. Armstrong	Sgt. I. N. Glendinning	Fg. Off. W. H. Nelson
Sgt. D. H. Ayers	P. Off. H. R. Gunn	Sgt. W. B. Parker
Fg. Off. R. J. E. Boulding	P. Off. D. Hastings	Fg. Off. A. L. Ricalton
Flt. Lt. S. Brzezina	Sgt. C. G. Hilken	Fg. Off. P. C. B. St John
Flt. Sgt. F. P. Burnard	P. Off. J. Howard	Sgt. J. A. Scott
P. Off. P. Chesters	Sub-Lt. D. A. Hutchinson	Sgt. W. M. Skinner
P. Off. E. W. G. Churches	Sqn. Ldr. D. P. D. G. Kelly	P. Off. A. J. Smith
P. Off. D. G. Cobden	Sgt. T. B. Kirk	P. Off. D. N. E. Smith
Fg. Off. D. H. T. Dowding	Flt. Lt. A. G. Malan	Sgt. H. J. Soars
P. Off. B. V. Draper	WO E. Mayne	P. Off. R. L. Spurdle
Sgt. W. Eley	Flt. Lt. W. E. G. Measures	P. Off. H. M. Stephen
Sgt. C. W. Francis	Sgt. N. Morrison	P. Off. P. C. F. Stevenson
Fg. Off. W. D. K. Franklin	Sgt. E. A. Mould	P. Off. H. Szczesny
Fg. Off. J. C. Freeborn	Fg. Off. J. C. Mungo Park	Sqn. Ldr. F. L. White
Sgt. L. E. Freese	Sgt. J. Murray	P. Off. J. H. R. Young

APPENDIX D: TIGER STEEDS

It is no easy matter compiling listings of squadron aircraft especially when looking at an operational period spanning 75 years. Particular problems arise from the First World War, where there are inevitable gaps—as indeed there are for the period the Tigers served in the Middle East during the second conflict. There are several sources which can be used, some of which unfortunately vary in the information they convey. I have also had to contend with anomalies such as aircraft being flown by the Squadron when not officially on charge to it. During the war years there was a very high turnover of aircraft on all Fighter Command squadrons as they moved to and from Maintenance Units, and record cards were not always kept up to date; another problem is that many cards have been lost. In compiling this summary I have taken account of information held at the Air Historical Branch, the Squadron's Operational Record Books, pilots' log books, enthusiasts' loggings and the published listings of organizations such as Air Britain and in books such as the mammoth *Spitfire* by Morgan and Shacklady. I am particularly indebted to Mervyn Hambling for his assistance.

AVRO 504

July 1917–Mar 1918

B3148, B3196, B4434, B9901, C4312, C4374, C4377, C4474, C4734

SOPWITH PUP

Jan 1918–Mar 1918

B5284, B5354

SOPWITH SCOUT

Jan 1918–Mar 1918
B5313, B7432, B7482, B7492

ROYAL AIRCRAFT FACTORY S.E.5a

Mar 1918–Feb 1919

Aircraft finished dark green overall. The Squadron was identified by a white rectangle on the rear fuselage sides, and individual code letters relating to the pilots (e.g. Mannock, 'A'; Taffy Jones, 'T'; Twist Giles, 'L') were shown on the fuselage between the rectangle and the roundels. Codes and roundels were also carried on the upper surface of the top wing. The RAF's red, white and blue flash covered the surface of the rudder.

B173, B574, B670, C1109, C1128, C1139 (coded '2'), C1768, C1791, C1858, C1910, C1932, C5396 (destroyed in mid-air collision between Caldwell and Carlin), C6414, C6468, C6494, C6859, C9616, C9211, C9606, C9618, D263, D271, D276 (coded 'A'), D277, D278, D3438, D6864 (flown by Caldwell; fin of chequered design with white squares), D6880, D6894, D6905, D6908, D6922, D6924, D6958, E1295, E1389, E1400, E4025, E4085, E5552, E5660, E5967, E5976, E7252, F894, F5464, F8990 (coded 'R').

HAWKER DEMON I

Sept 1935–April 1937

Initially in natural metal finish. Camouflage applied from October 1935: no Squadron markings were carried, and toned-down roundels were shown on the fuselage sides and in varying positions on the upper surface of the top wing.

K2846, K2847, K2850, K2853, K2905, K2906, K2907, K3767, K3769, K3770, K3772, K3773, K3777, K3784, K3791, K3792, K3793, K3794, K4539, K4540, K4543

MILES MAGISTER I

1938–1944

L6899 (crashed 18/3/41 on the perimeter at Biggin Hill; Mike Halahan killed and AC Ingham badly injured), L6909, L8270, L8359, N3777, P6344, P6345 (hit high-tension wires 7/11/39 near Rayleigh whilst being flown by P. Off. Browne), R1949 (used by 74 in the Middle East), T9765

GLOSTER GLADIATOR I

1937

On charge briefly in early 1937 before a sudden change in policy directed that the Squadron re-equip with the Gauntlet instead.

K6145, K6146, K6147, K6148, K6150

GLOSTER GAUNTLET II

Mar 1937–Feb 1939

74 was the last squadron to be issued with this aircraft. Silver metal finish with serial on rudder in black and Squadron colours either side of large roundel on rear fuselage sides. This was the first type on which the Tigers showed the newly devised black and yellow asymmetric dicing and the Squadron badge, depicting a tiger's head, on the fin.

K5308, K5332, K5337, K5339, K5350, K5355, K5360, K5363, K7792, K7815, K7816, K7817, K7827, K7834 (crashed 11/12/37 whilst force-landing in Tottenham Grammar School grounds, London), K7836, K7852, K7853, K7855, K7861, K7862, K7863, K7864, K7865, K7874, K7875

SUPERMARINE SPITFIRE Mk I/Ia

Feb 1939–Sept 1940

The Squadron code, 'JH', followed by an individual letter, was carried on each aircraft between April and September 1939; thereafter the code changed to 'ZP'.

A detailed description of the markings recorded as being applied to P9306 (currently preserved in a Chicago museum) during 1940–41 is representative of all Spitfires operating with the Squadron. From July 1940 the fuselage roundels applied were of the Type 'A', 35in type with a 7in diameter red centre. Underwing roundels were of the Type 'A', 50in type; 7in fin flashes were also carried. Squadron codes were painted in light grey, each letter being 24in high and 16in wide. By August 1940 undersurfaces were painted in Sky Blue, the upper surfaces remaining in Dark Green and Dark Earth camouflage. At the same time the fin flashes had been extended to three 8in wide, 27in high stripes. During November 1940 spinners were painted Sky Blue and an 18in fuselage band was added in the same colour. The underside of the port wing was painted black up to the fuselage centre-line and the underwing roundel on that side was encircled with a 2in yellow band. In April 1941 the port underwing reverted to Sky Blue.

K9860	First Spitfire to be delivered to 74, on 13/2/39.
K9861	Written off 30/8/39 at Grays, Essex (Sgt. Gower: killed).
K9862	
K9863	Damaged in landing accident at Hornchurch (Freeborn). Repaired.
K9864	
K9865	Undercarriage collapsed at Hornchurch. Repaired.
K9866	Crashed at Hornchurch shortly after delivery. Eventually repaired.
K9867	
K9868	Written off 21/11/39 whilst landing at Cherbourg. (Don Thom: returned to Squadron).
K9869	Crashed at Rochford (Bill Skinner). Aircraft wrecked.
K9870	
K9871	Coded 'O'.
K9872	Written off 24/3/39 (Johnny Freeborn: neglected to lower undercarriage, having been 'distracted by other aircraft on the ground and in the air').
K9873	
K9874	
K9875	Coded 'N'. Lost 27/5/40 near Lumbres, France (Paddy Treacy: escaped and returned to Eire).
K9876	
K9878	
K9879	
K9927	Coded 'B'. Records show that this aircraft was damaged beyond repair 19/7/40 in a wheels-up landing at Church Fenton whilst on charge to 74.
K9928	Struck by lightning and destroyed 3/7/40 over Margate (Sgt. White: killed).
K9931	
K9932	Destroyed 3/5/40 when force-landed on mudflats off Canvey Island (Peter Stevenson).
K9948	Coded 'H'.
K9951	
K9952	Force-landed 24/5/40 south of Dunkirk (Tony Mould: returned to Squadron by sea).
K9953	
K9957	Force-landed 21/5/40 near Calais (Bertie Aubert: returned to Squadron).
K9992	Air Ministry cards show this aircraft as being shot down 31/5/40 over Dunkirk whilst on charge to 74 but Squadron records do not support this—74 were 'resting' at Leconfield at the time.
K9994	
L1001	
L1084	Missing 27/5/40 (Peter Stevenson: force-landed near Dunkirk and returned to the Squadron later).
L1089	
N3091	Shot down 13/8/40 (Brzezina: baled out following explosion in cockpit but unhurt).
N3243	Shot down 24/5/40 over Dunkirk (Bertie Aubert: killed).
P9306	Preserved in Museum of Science and Industry at Jackson Park, Chicago.
P9321	Force-landed 24/5/40 at Calais

	Marcke (Sammy Hoare: taken prisoner).
P9336	Shot down 28/7/40 (Tony Mould: wounded but baled out successfully).
P9379	Shot down 31/7/40 (P. Off. Gunn: killed).
.P9380	
P9393	Shot down 11/8/40 off Kent coast and written off (Peter Stevenson: rescued by MTB).
P9398	Shot down 31/7/40 over Folkestone (Tim Eley: killed).
P9399	Damaged beyond repair when force-landed at Lympne 26/5/40 (Cobden).
P9427	
P9441	Lost 24/5/40 (Paddy Treacy: baled out and returned to the Squadron).
P9465	Crash-landed 8/7/40 at Manston (Peter Stevenson: uninjured).
P9492	Coded 'S'.
P9547	Shot down 28/7/40 over Goodwin Sands (P. Off. Young: killed).
R6603	
R6606	
R6706	Damaged in combat 28/7/40 with Bf 109 (Freeborn: uninjured).
R6716	
R6757	Shot down 11/8/40 near Harwich (Cobden: killed).
R6759	
R6771	
R6772	
R6773	
R6779	Damaged 28/7/40 in combat (Peter Stevenson: uninjured).
R6780	
R6830	Written off 13/8/40 at Stapleford Abbotts, Essex, on delivery to 74.
R6839	
R6840	
R6917	
R6962	Shot down 11/8/40 (P. Off. D. N. E. Smith: killed).
R6982	
R6983	Damaged 28/7/40 by Bf 109 near Manston (Piers Kelly: safe).
X4022	Collided with X4027 and crashed 30/8/40 whilst operating from Kirton-in-Lindsey. Aircraft burnt out (Bill Skinner: escaped unhurt).
X4024	
X4027	Force-landed after collision with X4022. Aircraft repaired.
X4060	
X4061	
X4068	
X4069	
X4101	
X4167	

SUPERMARINE SPITFIRE Mk IIa/IIb

June 1940–Dec 1941

P7292	
P7306	Shot down 26/11/40 over Chatham by Bf 109s and destroyed.
P7308	
P7310	Damaged 10/4/41 during an offensive sweep over Calais.
P7312	
P7316	Coded 'S'. Damaged 7/5/41 in combat with Bf 109s.
P7328	Missing 27/3/41 (P. Off. A. H. Smith).
P7329	Written off 8/10/40 near Beccles after mid-air collision with P7373 (P. Off. Hastings: killed).
P7352	Damaged 14/9/40 by Bf 110 (Mungo Park: uninjured).
P7353	
P7355	Crash-landed 20/10/40 after oil radiator shot away (Ben Draper).
P7356	
P7360	Shot down 17/10/40 over Maidstone (Alan Ricalton: killed).
P7361	
P7362	Aircraft abandoned 23/9/40 during routine patrol off Southwold, cause of accident unknown (David Ayers: drowned).
P7363	
P7364	Shot down 22/10/40 (Bob Spurdle: baled out unhurt).
P7366	
P7367	
P7368	
P7370	Coded 'A'. Shot down 20/10/40 (Sgt. Kirk: died of injuries). Site near Coxheath excavated in 1976 and Merlin engine, propeller boss and cockpit components recovered.
P7373	Sustained Cat 3 damage 8/10/40 after colliding with P7329 (P. Off. Buckland: killed).

P7376

P7381 Missing 19/4/41 (Wally Churches).

P7385 Force-landed 29/10/40 (Sgt. Soars).

P7386 Shot down 14/11/40 near Sandwich (P. Off. Armstrong: baled out, escaped injury).

P7426 Shot down 20/10/40 over south London (Clive Hilken: recovered from injuries).

P7428

P7431 Shot down 22/10/40 (Peter St John: killed). Complete remains of aircraft have been excavated by Halstead War Museum.

P7494

P7501

P7502

P7504

P7506 Shot down 12/3/41 off Dungeness (Sgt. Glendinning: killed).

P7523 Missing 1/11/40 (Willie Nelson).

P7526 Shot down 27/10/40 over Maidstone (Sgt. Scott: killed).

P7527

P7536 Damaged on patrol 11/11/40.

P7537 Crashed 6/5/41 after a bomber escort mission and written off (Sgt. Wilson: baled out).

P7542

P7551 Missing 26/11/41 (Arthur Williams).

P7553

P7557

P7558

P7559 Crash-landed 24/2/41 near Eastbourne after sustaining combat damage (Jan Rogowski).

P7561 Attempted forced-landing 10/1/41 at Detling (Sgt. Freese: killed).

P7591

P7614

P7618 Missing 24/2/41 (Jock Morrison).

P7623

P7667

P7692

P7740 Hit steel mast of windsock 21/4/41 whilst landing at Manston (Peter May).

P7741 Missing 2/2/41 after fighter sweep (Sqn. Ldr. Michelmore: landed on enemy aerodrome and taken prisoner).

P7744 'Bow Street Home Guard'.

P7751 'City of Bradford VI'. Hit pillbox 9/9/41 on approach to Acklington during night landing practice (Sgt. Coxon: killed).

P7782

P7826 'Sind I'.

P7827 'Sind II'.

P7832 'Enniskillen'.

P7839 'City of Derby'.

P7851

P7854 Aircraft destroyed 10/4/41 when executing a victory roll over Manston (Peter Chesters: killed).

P7883 'Grahams Heath'.

P7895

P7928 Missing 6/5/41 (Sgt. Arnott: taken prisoner).

P7965

P7976

P8016

P8018

P8030

P8033

P8042

P8045 'City of Worcester I'. Crashed 2/8/41 near Ousten, Northumberland on routine training flight, cause CO_2 poisoning or oxygen failure (Douglas Steven: killed).

P8046 'City of Worcester II'.

P8047 'The Malverns'.

P8091 'Miners of Durham 2'.

P8140 'Nuflier'.

P8144

P8146 'Covent Garden'.

P8149 'The Lewis and Harris Fighter'.

P8174 'Baltic Exchange'.

P8183 'Tasmania III'.

P8184 'Transkeian Territories I'.

P8197

P8199

P8200

P8207

P8238 'Borneo'.

P8252

P8257

P8259

P8261 Coded 'N'.

P8274

P8275

P8276

P8294

P8296

P8322

P8363

P8364 Missing 6/5/41 (P. Off. Howard).

P8373

P8377 'Siwabong'.

P8380	'Black Velvet'.
P8388	
P8394	'Gibraltar'.
P8396	'Bermuda II'.
P8421	
P8423	
P8460	Crashed into sea 30/11/41 off Merioneth (John Brown).
P8479	'British Glues and Chemicals'. Coded 'V'.
P8544	
P8601	'Delhi 2'.
P8702	

SUPERMARINE SPITFIRE Mk Vb

May 1941–Mar 1942

P8560	
P8578	
P8585	'Teling Tinggi'.
P8600	'Lady Linlithgow'.
P8604	
P8609	
P8741	'Bhabnagar'.
R7228	
R7278	Missing 17/6/41 (P. Off. Parkes: taken prisoner).
W3120	Shot down 27/6/41 by Bf 109 (Sandeman: taken prisoner).
W3127	
W3168	
W3170	'Henley on Thames'.
W3172	'Huddersfield II'.
W3174	
W3176	Missing 6/7/41 (Bill Skinner: taken prisoner).
W3177	
W3178	
W3186	Crashed into sea 9/6/41 (P. Off. Bergen: killed).
W3208	'Eastbourne'. Missing 6/7/41 (Sgt. Lockhart).
W3210	'Malta'.
W3212	'Ghawdex'.
W3232	Missing from sweep 3/7/41 (Sgt. Cochrane: taken prisoner).
W3250	'Central Provinces and Berar II'.
W3251	
W3252	'Berar III'. Shot down 27/6/41 (Clive Hilken: taken prisoner).
W3258	Missing 4/7/41 (P. Off. Henderson).
W3259	Missing 2/7/41 over St-Omer (P. Off. Krol: taken prisoner).
W3263	Missing 2/7/41 (P. Off. Evans: taken prisoner).
W3305	Coded 'E'.

W3306	
W3317	'Newport Hundreds and Wolverhampton UDC'. Missing 7/7/41.
W3321	'Elcardo the Thistle'.
W3367	
W3380	
W3409	'The Peruvian Oilfields'.
W3411	
W3412	Rhodesian Pioneer'.
W3707	
X4668	'Burbage'. Disappeared 27/6/41 (Mungo Park).
X4670	'The Bright Ventura'. Crashed on landing 7/6/41 (Sgt. Doerr). Aircraft repaired. Shot down 17/6/41 (Roger Boulding: taken prisoner).
AA906	Written off 25/2/42 at Ballyherbert.
AA939	Coded 'Z'.
AA974	Coded 'P'.
AB134	Coded 'M'.
AD327	'Solaire Ross'.
AD473	Coded 'S'.
AD508	
AD535	Coded 'T'.
AD552	AD565
AD568	Crashed into sea 8/2/42 (Sgt. Matthews: drowned).
AD569	
BL243	Coded 'W'.
BL290	
BL325	
BL339	
BL369	Coded 'V'.
BL383	
BL407	Broke up 24/12/41 over Llanbedr (Sgt. Stuart: killed).
BL444	
BL492	Coded 'K'.
BL494	Coded 'R'.
BL499	Damaged beyond repair 18/12/41 (Ian Shand).
BL522	
BL713	

HAWKER HURRICANE Mk I/IIb/IIc

Dec 1942–Sept 1943

No Squadron code was issued in the Middle East, each aircraft carrying only an individual code letter.

Z4144	Coded 'E'.
Z4944	Written off 24/3/43 (Fg. Off. Besley: uninjured).
Z4958	Coded 'Z'.
BA131	Coded 'Y'.
BE226	Coded 'F'.
BE336	Coded 'D'.

BE698	Coded 'C'. Crashed 30/1/43 (Bobby Waugh: killed).	LZ894	
BG904		LZ941	Coded 'X'.
BH283	Coded 'Y'.	MA256	Coded 'K'.
BM624	Coded 'A'.	MA266	'Godiva'.
BM664	Coded 'B'.		
BM968	Coded 'X'.		

The following Spitfire Vcs probably served with the Tigers during the time stated:

BN371			
BP284		EE667	
BP342		EN843	
BP664	Written off 8/6/43 (P. Off. Prendergast: baled out over sea, picked up by Royal Navy cruiser).	JK164	
		JK282	
		JK613	
		JK614	
BP708		JL302	
BW932	Coded 'C'.	JL327	
DG624		JL329	
DW932	Coded 'C' (sic).	JL392	
HL564		LZ985	
HV660		MA287	
HW294			

SUPERMARINE SPITFIRE Mk Vb

Sept 1943–Apr 1944

EP692	Coded 'T'.
EP814	
EP880	
ER128	

The inadequacy of records renders identification of 74 Squadron aircraft serving in the Middle East and North Africa difficult. The following Spitfire Vbs may have served with the Tigers during the time stated:

EP691
EP694
ER482
ER504

SUPERMARINE SPITFIRE Mk Vc

Dec 1942–Sept 1943 (alongside Spitfire Vbs listed above)

EE8801	Coded 'Q'.
EE855	
EP814	Coded 'L'.
EP880	
ER128	
ES200	Coded 'F'.
JG799	Coded 'R'.
JG948	Coded 'R' (sic).
JK111	Coded 'W'.
JK143	Coded 'J'.
JK308	
JK316	Coded 'H'.
JK608	Coded 'E'.
JL308	Coded 'G'.
JL312	Coded 'F'.
JL365	Coded 'P'.

SUPERMARINE SPITFIRE Mk IX

Oct 1943–Apr 1944

The following probably served with the Squadron during the time stated:

BS342	Engine fire and undercarriage collapse 13/11/43 (Titch Harris: slightly burned).
EN201	
EN399	Coded 'Q'.
JL228	Coded 'Y'.
MA403	Coded 'A'.
MA455	Coded 'D'.
MA508	
MA603	
MA732	Coded 'T'.

SUPERMARINE SPITFIRE LF Mk IXE

Apr 1944–Mar 1945

The code '4D', followed by an individual letter, was allocated to aircraft flown on the Squadron's return to Europe.

MK266	Damaged on armed recce 9/2/45.
MK288	
MK363	
MK670	
MK681	
MK682	
MK691	Hit by flak 27/5/44 (Guy de Pass: landed safely).
MK694	
ML154	
ML179	
ML200	Crash-landed 10/6/44 in France (Paddy Dalzell: returned to England by American LST).

ML207
ML212
ML230
ML232
ML233
ML236
ML240
ML241
ML245
ML259
ML261
ML296 Coded 'N'.
ML364
ML380
ML412
NH181 Crashed on take off when tyre burst, aircraft striking air raid shelter (David Maxwell: recovered from injuries and returned to Squadron).
NH261
NH314
NH358
NH367 Force-landed 11/8/44 with engine on fire (2nd Lt. Tooke: unhurt).
NH374
NH454 Damaged by flak 10/2/45 (Nick Carter: landed safely).
NH468
NH469
NH477
NH527
NH531
NH546
NH550 Hit by machine-gun fire 16/8/44 (WO Burman: baled out, captured and shot by Germans).
NH553 Shot down 27/8/44 (Jock Malcolm: badly injured, rescued from wreckage by Canadians).
NH576
NH579 Shot down 26/8/44 (Fg. Off. Jackson: returned to Squadron 3/9/44).
NH584
NH609 Coded 'W'. Hit by flak 2/11/44 over Walcheren Island, returned safely.
PK995 5Coded 'X'.
PL123
PL124
PL138
PL152
PL164
PL185
PL196 Damaged by flak 10/2/45.
PL349
PL454 Coded 'V'.
PL497

PT399 Coded 'Z'.
PT548
PT609
PT727
PT732
PT735
PT752 Hit by flak 14/10/44 south-west of Dunkirk (Johnny Johnston: returned safely to base).
PT770 Engine cut out on take-off 29/9/44 and crashed into the Photographic Section's lorry (Fg. Off. Jackson: killed).
PT775
PT823
PT840
PT858 Coded 'P'.
PT889
PT908
PT912
PT937 Coded 'D'.
PT991
PT993
PT995
PT999 Coded 'T'. Wrecked 9/3/45 when engine caught fire in air (Johnny Bennett: burned, landed safety near Dienst, awarded Green Endorsement).
PV121 Damaged 13/10/44 while landing in strong cross-wind (Shanahan).
PV138
PV144
PV147 Coded 'M'.
PV180 Coded 'K'.
PV187
PV291 Shot down 2/2/45 (Frank Hardman: killed).
PV292
PV293
PV294 Shot down 26/2/45 (Bill Cortis: injured, captured, returned to Squadron 8/4/45 after liberation by Americans).
PV311 Shot down 26/2/45 (Ivan Butler: killed).
RK906
RR187 Coded 'G'.
RR200

SUPERMARINE SPITFIRE LF Mk XVIE

Mar–May 1945

SM292
TB279
TB286
TB348

TB353	Hit by flak 20/3/45, damaged beyond repair (Jock Agnew: injured).		EE307	
			EE308	Hit trees 24/7/45 during low-level flypast at Colerne (Taffy Rees: killed).
TB355	Force-landed with oil problems 20/3/45 (Taffy Rees).		EE309	
TB495			EE310	
TB549			EE312	
TB574			EE318	Coded 'Z'.
TB593	Force-landed in enemy territory 5/4/45 (Flt. Sgt. Racy: reached friendly forces).		EE332	
			EE333	Undercarriage collapsed 8/7/47 during single-engine landing (Fg. Off. Hart: uninjured).
TB598			EE334	Tail of the aircraft sheared off 10/7/46 in collision with another during formation practice (David Davies: killed).
TB622				
TB625				
TB631				
TB639				
TB675			EE335	Low flying accident 2/1/46 at Warmwell (Leonard Miller: killed).
TB709				
TB716				
TB738			EE340	
TB739	Crash-landed in flames 19/4/44 near Oldendorf (Fg. Off. Barnes).		EE341	Coded 'G'.
			EE342	
			EE343	
TB741			EE344	Hit tree, crashed and exploded 8/3/46 during low-level practice attack on train (Dinshaw Sorab Bamjee, Royal Indian Air Force: killed).
TB747				
TB859				
TB865				
TB889	Hit by shrapnel 19/4/45, causing explosions in cockpit (Johnny Bennett: returned safely).			
			EE345	
			EE346	
TB903			EE352	
TD136			EE353	Accident 24/9/47 during simulated single-engine flying exercise (Ernest Dennis: killed).
TD143				
TD150				
TD254				
TD258			EE354	
TD262			EE358	
TD324			EE401	
TE116	Hit by flak 24/4/45, forced to land at Twente (Allan Griffin).		EE428	
			EE459	Coded 'S'.
			EE462	Coded 'L'.
			FE473	
			EE478	

GLOSTER METEOR F Mk 3

May 1945–Mar 1948

Camouflaged Dark Green and Medium Sea Grey above with Light Sea Grey undersurfaces and Sky Blue rear fuselage bands and code letters. The '4D' code (which continued postwar) was forward of the fuselage roundel on the port side and aft on the starboard. Individual code letters were repeated in black on the nosewheel door on some aircraft.

EE270	
EE275	
EE279	
EE305	
EE306	Coded 'N'.

GLOSTER METEOR F Mk 4

Dec 1947–Oct 1950

Overall silver scheme with black codes flanking the fuselage roundels (and repeated on the nosewheel door of some aircraft).

RA427	Coded 'E'.
RA439	Coded 'F'.
RA448	
RA451	Lost power in port engine on take-off 14/12/49, written off (P. Off. Jerka).

RA473   Coded 'C'.
RA485   Coded 'N'.
VT106   Coded 'D'.
VT122
VT130
VT133   Coded 'J'.
VT187
VT192   Coded 'C', 'K' and 'X'.
VT193
VT194
VT197
VT198
VT199
VT282   Coded 'T'.
VT303   Coded 'L'.
VT311
VT322   Coded 'J'.
VT324   Coded 'T'.
VW257   Coded 'I'.
VW284
VW311

GLOSTER METEOR F Mk 8

Oct 1950–March 1957

Some aircraft were finished in an overall silver scheme with black codes flanking the fuselage roundels (and sometimes repeated on the nosewheel door); others carried a tiger's head badge on the outside of the engine nacelles flanked by a miniature form of the black and yellow dicing; still others were silver overall with black and yellow dicing either side of the fuselage roundels and code letters in black on the fin beneath the tailplane. The final F.8 scheme was a camouflaged one of Dark Green and Medium Sea Grey with silver undersurfaces and the code letter in yellow on the fin and in black on the nosewheel door. Again, some aircraft also featured the Squadron crest on the nacelles. The '4D' code was discontinued in 1951, following which a single-letter code system was adopted.

VZ443   Coded 'L'.
VZ446   Coded 'T'. Written off 5/5/53
         when it flew into the ground
         during a practice attack on a
         disused airfield at Horham:
         Sgt. Margetts killed.
VZ449   Crashed into sea 5/1/51 off
         North Norfolk coast whilst on
         navigation exercise (P. Off.
         Corn: killed).
VZ452
VZ509   Crashed 19/6/51 into Barton
         Broad (Fg. Off. Turner:
         killed).
VZ512   Coded 'D'.
VZ515
VZ520   Coded 'A'.
VZ521   Coded 'A'.

VZ524   Coded 'P'.
VZ529   Coded 'W'.
VZ540   Coded 'I'.
VZ544   Coded 'Z'.
VZ546   Coded 'I'.
VZ547   Coded 'B'.
VZ548
VZ549
VZ550
VZ551
VZ552
VZ553
VZ554
VZ555
VZ556
VZ557   Coded 'N'.
VZ558   Crashed 7/12/50 whilst
         practising circuits at night at
         Horsham St Faith (Bill Slater:
         killed).
VZ559
VZ577   Coded 'N'.
VZ644   Coded 'C'.
WA772   Coded 'A' and 'N'.
WA814
WA824   Coded 'Q' and 'S'.
WA835   Coded 'R'.
WA836   Written off 19/9/53 whilst
         displaying at Coningsby (Rus
         Ward: killed).
WA838   Coded 'F'.
WA840
WA873   Coded 'V'.
WA874   Coded 'K'.
WA878   Coded 'E'.
WA879   Coded 'C' and 'G'. Collided
         with WE974 3/1/57 (Jock
         Baillie: killed).
WA885   Coded 'T'.
WA891   Coded 'F'.
WA931
WA960
WA981
WA993   Coded 'O'.
WA997   Coded 'R'.
WE878   Coded 'E'.
WE885   Coded 'T'.
WE923   Coded 'C'.
WE960
WE974   Coded 'S'. Collided with
         WA879 3/1/57 (Wally Taylor:
         killed).
WF646
WF647
WF649
WF651   Coded 'T' and 'E'.
WF652   Coded 'Z'.
WF655   Coded 'L'.
WF656   Coded 'Y'.
WF662
WF708
WF709

WF710	Coded 'J'.
WF712	Coded 'H'.
WH304	
WH305	
WH357	Coded 'V'.
WH463	
WK804	Coded 'B'.
WK816	Coded 'M'.
WK874	
WK888	Coded 'U'.
WK932	
WK936	
WK979	
WL163	Coded 'J'.
WL164	Coded 'X'.
WL173	

GLOSTER METEOR T Mk 7

1950–1957

VW430	Coded 'X'.
WA658	
WA659	
WA671	
WA721	
WA725	Assigned to Horsham Station Flight but used by 74 Squadron.
WF787	
WH127	
WL368	
WL380	

HAWKER HUNTER F Mk 4

Mar 1957–Jan 1958

Camouflaged Dark Green and Medium Sea Grey with silver undersurfaces. Dicing markings on the nose flanked a tiger's head. Codes were in yellow on the fin and in black on the nosewheel door.

WT708	Coded 'P'.
WT720	Coded 'B' and 'F'.
WT764	Coded 'J'.
WV262	Coded 'K'.
WV269	Coded 'H'.
WV272	Coded 'L'.
WV281	Coded 'Q'.
WV314	Coded 'JH'.
WV317	Coded 'D'.
WV324	Coded 'C'.
WV326	Coded 'R'.
WV334	Coded 'E'.
WV370	Coded 'M'.
WV371	Coded 'N'.
XE658	
XE661	Coded 'F'. Abandoned 25/5/57 on take-off after overshooting

runway at St Faith (Tony Davies).

XE662	Coded 'S'. Written off 25/5/57 during heavy cross-runway landing at St Faith (Tony Hilton: ejected 'involuntarily', suffered multiple fractures of the arm).
XE683	Coded 'G'.
XE688	Coded 'A'.
XF940	Coded 'F'.
XF993	

HAWKER HUNTER F Mk 6

Nov 1957–Nov 1960

Camouflaged Dark Green and Medium Sea Grey with silver undersurfaces and white wing tips. Some aircraft carried a facsimile of Sailor Malan's signature in black beside the tiger's head on the nose. The pilot's name was often reproduced in yellow beneath the port cockpit sill.

XE559	Coded 'D'.
XE589	Coded 'R' and 'Q'.
XE591	Coded 'G'.
XE599	
XE606	
XE610	Coded 'J'.
XE612	Coded 'M'. Lost power 17/5/60 on take off at St Faith, overshot, caught fire (Tim Nelson).
XE613	Coded 'C' and 'K'.
XF419	Coded 'C'.
XF425	Coded 'H'. Collided with XF502 25/8/59 at night (Peter Rayner: ejected successfully).
XF448	Coded 'N'. Crashed 21/8/58 into sea off Winterton, Norfolk, during tail chase (Nick Tester: killed).
XF450	
XF502	Coded 'R' and 'K'. Collided with XF425 25/8/59 over Cantley, destroyed (Pete Budd: killed).
XF504	Coded 'B'.
XF511	Coded 'P'.
XG164	Coded 'H'.
XG198	Coded 'Q'.
XK136	Coded 'A'.
XK140	Coded 'E'.
XK141	Coded 'F'. The Hunter 6s had pilots' names painted on the cockpit sills. XK141 was allocated to Ian Cadwallader who was also tasked with designing the stencils for the application of the tiger to each aircraft. The first stencil

consisted of the outline shape of the head. This was sprayed on in yellow. The second stencil incorporated cut-outs to give the black stripes across the forehead and down the cheeks, plus the mouth and nose. When all spraying was complete each application was finished by hand—red tongue, white teeth and white fur down each cheek and black and white whiskers.

XK142   Coded 'L'.

HAWKER HUNTER T Mk 7

1958–1966

Silver with yellow trainer bands and a tiger's head on the nose. The fin flash of XL620 was swept back.

XL568   Converted to Hunter T.7A in 1963, coded 'X' when returned to Tigers.
XL620   Coded 'Z'.

ENGLISH ELECTRIC LIGHTNING F Mk 1

June 1960–Apr 1964

74 was the only squadron to use the F.1 operationally, other recipients including the AFDS and 226 OCU. All aircraft were in natural metal finish with a large tiger's head on a white circle on the tail fin, a black fin code and black and yellow dicing on the nose. Black was added to the fin in July 1962 and the code letters were changed to yellow.

XM134   Coded 'A'.
XM135   Coded 'B'. Preserved at the Imperial War Museum, Duxford, in full 74 Squadron colours.
XM136   Coded 'S'.
XM137   Coded 'D'.
XM138
XM139   Coded 'C' and 'F'.
XM140   Coded 'M'.
XM141   Coded 'D'.
XM142   Coded 'B'. Lost 26/4/63 after control hydraulics failure (Jim Burns: ejected safely).
XM143   Coded 'A'.
XM144   Coded 'J' and 'G'.
XM145   Coded 'Q'.
XM146   Coded 'L'.
XM147   Coded 'P' and 'J'.
XM163   Coded 'Q'.

XM164   Coded 'C' and 'K'.
XM165   Coded 'F'.
XM166   Coded 'G'.
XM167   Coded 'H'.

BAC LIGHTNING T Mk 4

1961–1966

Natural metal finish with a large tiger's head on a white circle on the fin, a black fin code and black/yellow dicing on the nose. Yellow 'T' bands.

XM974   Coded 'T'.

BAC LIGHTNING F Mk 3

April 1964–Sept 1967

The F.3s carried enlarged asymmetric dicing either side of the nose roundel, an enlarged tiger's head on a white disc on the black fin (with yellow coding) and a black spine. The flight refuelling probes were often painted in 74's yellow/black dicing. From January 1966, by order of the Defence Council, the black was removed from the fin and spine, the tiger's head marking was greatly reduced in size and the code letters were changed to black.

XP698   Coded 'F'.
XP700   Coded 'A'.
XP702   Coded 'C'.
XP703   Coded 'G'.
XP704   Coded 'H'. Destroyed 28/8/64 during practice aerobatics at Leuchars (Glyn Owen: killed).
XP705   Coded 'K'.
XP706   Coded 'L'.
XP751   Coded 'B'.
XP752   Coded 'D'.
XP753   Coded 'J'.
XP754   Coded 'M'.
XP755   Coded 'P'.
XP764   Coded 'H'.

BAC LIGHTNING F Mk 6

1966–1971

Originally in an all-silver finish with a tiger's head on a white disc on the fin and black code letters. In mid-1968 the Squadron recovered the black fin and spine (although the spine was subsequently returned to silver) previously carried by the F.3s and the coding was changed to yellow.

XR725   Coded 'A'.
XR758   Coded 'J'.
XR761   Coded 'B'.

XR764   Coded 'E'.
XR767   Coded 'A'. Crashed 26/5/70 in
         Malacca Straits (John
         Webster: killed).
XR768   Coded 'A'.
XR769   Coded 'B'. Later to 11
         Squadron and Binbrook.
         Crashed into North Sea
         11/4/88 after engine fire
         during practice air-to-air
         combat with a 74 Squadron
         Phantom (the F-4J crew
         promptly marking up their
         aircraft with one 'kill'!)
XR770   Coded 'C'.
XR771   Coded 'D'.
XR772   Coded 'E'.
XR773   Coded 'F'.
XS893   Coded 'G'. Crashed into the sea
         12/8/70 off Tengah (Mike
         Rigg: ejected safely).
XS895   Coded 'H'.
XS896   Coded 'J'. Crashed 12/9/68 on
         approach to Tengah (Pete
         Thompson: killed).
XS897   Coded 'K'.
XS920   Coded 'L'.
XS921   Coded 'M'.
XS927   Coded 'N'.
XS928   Coded 'L'.
XS930   Crashed 27/11/70 on take off
         from Tengah (Frank
         Whitehouse: killed).

BAC LIGHTNING T Mk 5

1967–1971

XS416   Coded 'T'.
XV329   Shipped to Singapore 3/3/67.
         Tailplane suffered severe
         corrosion during the voyage
         resulting from the effects of
         salt water and salty
         atmosphere but, after repair,
         aircraft was taken on charge
         by 74 at Tengah and coded
         'T'.

McDONNELL DOUGLAS F-4J(UK) PHANTOM

Aug 1984–Jan 1991

Very distinctive greenish-blue colour scheme applied in error during rework and which was only changed to standard Air Defence Grey when the aircraft passed through deep servicing at St Athan. Not all the Phantoms had been so treated by the time of their sudden withdrawal from service in January 1991. An orange and red (almost stylized) tiger's head with black and yellow dicing was painted on the nose and in a white circle on the fin (which latter was subsequently painted black). Yellow code on rudder and in black on nosewheel door. With the exception of ZE359, the F-4J(UK)s were dispersed around Battle Damage Repair Flights in the UK and Germany on their retirement.

ZE350   Coded 'T'. Ex-BuAer 153768.
ZE351   Coded 'I'. Ex-BuAer 153773.
ZE352   Coded 'G'. Ex-BuAer 153783.
ZE353   Coded 'E'. Ex-BuAer 153785.
ZE354   Coded 'R'. Ex-BuAer 153795.
ZE355   Coded 'S'. Ex-BuAer 153803.
ZE356   Coded 'Q'. Ex-BuAer 153850.
ZE357   Coded 'N'. Ex-BuAer 153892.
ZE358   Coded 'H'. Ex-BuAer 155510.
         Crashed 25/8/87 near
         Aberystwyth (Euan Murdoch
         and Jerry Ogg: killed).
ZE359   Coded 'J'. Ex-BuAer 155529.
         Preserved at Imperial War
         Museum Duxford, returned
         to USMC livery.
ZE360   Coded 'O'. Ex-BuAer 155574.
ZE361   Coded 'P'. Ex-BuAer 155734.
ZE363   Coded 'W'. Ex-BuAer 155868.
ZE364   Coded 'Z'. Ex-BuAer 155894.

McDONNELL DOUGLAS PHANTOM FGR Mk 2

Jan 1991–

Standard Air Defence Grey overall. Markings as for F-4J(UK) except yellow and black dicing on radar warning receiver on top of fin.

XT891   Coded 'S'. Twin-stick aircraft.
XT892   Coded 'J'. Twin-stick aircraft.
XT895   Coded 'Q'. Twin-stick aircraft.
XT896   Coded 'V'. Twin-stick aircraft.
XT897   Coded 'N'. Twin-stick aircraft.
XT900   Coded 'J'. Twin-stick aircraft.
XT901   Coded 'O'. Twin-stick aircraft.
XT905   Coded 'P'. Twin-stick aircraft.
XT907   Coded 'W'. Twin-stick aircraft.
XT914   Coded 'Z'. Twin-stick aircraft.
XV393   Coded 'T'. Twin-stick aircraft.
XV398   Coded 'V'.
XV401   Coded 'I'.
XV409   Coded 'G'.
XV415   Coded 'O'.
XV423   Coded 'Y'.
XV433   Coded 'E'.
XV460   Coded 'I'.
XV465   Coded 'S'.
XV469   Coded 'N'.
XV487   Coded 'G'.
XV490   Coded 'R'.
XV497   Coded 'W'.
XV499

INDEXES

INDEX OF PERSONNEL

Note: In official records, personnel are frequently referred to by surname only, and it is regretted that, in some instances, no further details are known. Generally, ranks have been omitted from this index, since one man may hold many during a career.

INDEX OF PLACENAMES

Hassum, 151
Helwan, 99, 100, 130
Heydakrug, 126
Honiley, 173
Honington, 278, 280
Hornchurch
  Sqn. re-forms at, 47
  description of, 48
  life at, 48–9
  at outbreak of war, 57
  refuelling at, 62
  NAAFI at, 64
  entertainment at, 64
  night flying at, 68
  visit by King George VI to, 68
  visit by Churchill to, 74
Horsham St Faith
  Sqn. moves to, 162
  severe winter at, 162–3
  Open Days at, 164, 176, 178
  Sqn. returns to, 194
Hounslow, 19

Idku (LG 154)
  Sqn. moves to, 115
  split detachments at, 128
  flooding at, 129
Izel-le Hameau, 40

Jever, 266
Juvincourt, 153

Kastrup, 168
Kreevil, 160
Keflavik, 266, 281
Kinloss, 220

La Lovie
  Sqn. moves to, 25
  Sqn. returns to, 38
Lahr, 285
Le Bourget, 56
Le Havre, 24, 142, 143
Le Vendeville (Lille) (ALG
  B51), 144
Leconfield, 178
  rest and training at, 68
Leeming, 276, 284, 290
Leeuwarden, 150
Lens, 139
Leros, 121
Leuchars, 185, 266, 267, 272,
  276, 284, 286, 287, 290, 291
  Sqn. moves to, 204–5
  operations from, 208
  as first Lightning F.3 base,
  210
  'raid' on Wattisham from,
  227
Lille, 132
Linselles, 38
Llanbedr
  Sqn. moves to, 96
  aircraft scrambles at, 96
  drogue towing at, 97
Locking, 160
London Colney
  Sqn. moves to, 19
  Giles crashes at, 20
Long Kesh, 98

Lopcombe Corner, 42
Lumbres, 68
Lympne, 132
Lubeck, 163, 168

Manston
  as forward operating base, 69
  Sqn. detaches to, 87
  bombed by Me 109s, 88
  accommodation at, 89
  refuelling at, 138
March, 287
Margo Scirrocco Bay, 43
Marham, 280
Mariut, 127, 129
Marsa (Malta), 46
Marsa Matruh, 128
McDill, 258
Meherebad
  as a camp, 102–3
  recreation at, 105
  food and diet at, 105
Masirah, 226
Menin, 28, 31
Mers, 37
Merville, 26, 27, 30, 37
Middleton St George, 203
Mildenhall, 267
Miramar, 259
Mont de Marsan, 279
Montijo, 272
Mount Pleasant, 282

Nantes, 134
Neatishead, 166, 167
Nellis, 286, 287
Nicosia, 116
Nieuport, 25
Nijverdal, 151
Nordhoek, 148
Nordholz, 155
Northolt
  Sqn. forms at, 19
  Giles force-lands at, 20
  escort to Churchill at, 137,
  153–4
  escort to Eisenhower at, 138
North Weald, 58
  Sqn. re-forms at, 130
  new establishment at, 132

Odiham, 178, 185
Offutt, 286
Oldenburg, 282
Oldendorf, 155

Paphos, 121
Paris, 141
Pas de Calais, 136
Penshurst, 82
Peristerona, 127
Ploegstreet Wood, 31, 34
Port Said, 130
Port Taufik, 99

Qum, 102, 106

Ramat David
  seconded to USAAC, 100,
  101

ground crews diverted to,
  117
Renesse, 150
Rheindahlen, 264, 269
Rheine, 150
Risselghem, 40
Rochford, 24
  detachment to, 60
  low flying competition at, 61
  refuelling at, 61
Rotenburg, 155
Roubaix, 38
Rouen, 136, 140, 141, 142
Rouex, 139
Roulers, 27, 35

St Athan, 272, 282
St-Jean (Acre), 114–15
St-Omer
  Sqn. flies to, 24
  stores recovered from, 25
St-Trono, 138–9
San Diego (Naval Air Rework
  Facility), 254, 256, 257, 259,
  260
Scampton, 216
Scheldt, River, 38, 39, 144
Schijndel
  food supplies at, 139
  crews and aircraft move to,
  151
Schoondyke, 145–6
Sealand, 43, 47
Seletar, 251
Selsey, 137
Shaibah, 108
'Shit Creek', 51
Simi, 118 et seq
Sollingen, 276, 279, 283
Sommervieux (ALG B8)
  Sqn. moves to, 139
  first sortie from, 140
Southampton, 24
Southend, 137
South Mimms, 19
Stradishall, 182

Ta Kali, 46
Tangmere
  coastal defence exercise at,
  51
  joins 134 Wing, 136
  visit by King George VI to,
  137
  Sqn. returns to, 137
Teheran, 105
Teheran-Meherebad, 212
  see also Meherebad
Tengah
  preparation for move to, 225
  arrival at, 226–7
  life at, 229
  operations from, 231
  weather at, 231, 233
  bar competition at, 240–1
  Australians at, 241
  Sqn. leaves, 252
Tetenghem, 24
Tournai, 39
Twente, 156, 287

INDEX OF AIRCRAFT TYPES

flying in, 51; camouflaging of, 53

Gladiator, 47, 50, 53

Javelin, 182, 198, 211, 230, 244

Meteor, 244, 249
 F.Mk 1, conversion to, 159, 160
 F.Mk 3: speed of, 159; deliveries, 160; night flying in, 164; asymmetric problems with, 164; camouflage and markings of, 169
 F.Mk 4: conversion to, 164; visit to Copenhagen with, 168; camouflage and markings of, 169; as high level bomber, 171
 F.Mk 8: conversion to, 172; hangarage of, 174; description of, 175; camouflaging of, 175, 181; modifications to, 178; bubble canopies on, 181
 T.Mk 7: delivery of, 171; dual sorties on, 175, 185

Gotha, 26, 40

Grumman
 EA-6B Prowler, 286, 287
 F-9F Panther, 179
 F-14 Tomcat, 254, 264, 271
 S-2 Tracker, 247
 TBM Avenger, 182

Handley Page
 Heyford, 51
 Victor, 209, 211, 220, 226, 235, 241, 242, 244, 247, 266, 278

Hannover, 29, 34

Hawker
 Audax, 51
 Demon: Demon flights, 43; in Malta, 43 et seq; condition of, 44; camouflaging of, 44; flotation gear on, 44; war test with, 45; engine inspections on, 46; dismantling of, 46; fitters and riggers for, 49
 Fury, 52
 Hunter, 180, 182, 183, 191, 192, 204, 215, 230
 F.Mk 4: Sqn. re-equips with, 184; first deliveries of, 185; ground crews' assessment of, 185; engine flame-outs in, 185–6; underpowered aircraft, 186; last Mk 4, 188
 F. Mk 6: Sqn. re-equips with, 188
 T. Mk 7: first use of, 191; training on, 201; flypast with, 211; sad farewell to, 213

Hurricane: other Sqn. usage, 53, 57; first examples for 74 Sqn., 102; spares problems with, 105, 106; spares package for, 107; BBMF aircraft, 211, 220, 290

Typhoon, 114, 149, 152

Hawker Siddeley Buccaneer, 265

Heinkel
 He 111, 61, 64, 65, 68, 69, 70, 82, 92, 114
 He 177, 155

Henschel Hs 126, 65, 66, 67

Hunting Jet Provost, 270

Ilyushin
 Il-14, 191
 Il-18 'Coot', 280
 Il-28 'Beagle', 191
 Il-38 'May', 264, 276, 278

Junkers
 Ju 87, 83, 84
 Ju 88, 64, 67, 77, 90, 95, 98, 116, 117, 150, 155

LVG, 28, 34, 35, 36–7

Lockheed
 C-130 Hercules, 212, 241, 244, 247, 266, 278, 281, 284
 F-80, 170
 F-104 Starfighter, 210, 218, 219, 220, 265, 279
 L.1011 TriStar, 286
 P-2 Neptune, 247
 P-3 Orion, 268, 273
 T-33, 218, 219, 220

Martin
 B-26 Marauder, 134, 138
 RB-57 Canberra, 241, 244
 Baltimore, 129

McDonnell Douglas
 AV-8B Harrier, 286
 F-4 Phantom, 218, 219, 220, 247, 248, 255, 258, 259, 270, 271, 279
 FGR. Mk 2: in the Falklands, 277; in Nevada, 286, 290; ground crews' conversion to, 291; radar snags with, 291; pilots' conversion to, 291–2; comparison with F-4J of, 292; display flying by, 292
 F-4J(UK): first two-seater since Demon, 45; at NARF, 254; radar for, 255; purchase of, 255; support package for, 255; designation of, 256; engines for, 256; air starter for, 256, 275; ejection seat in, 257; ground crews' conversion to, 258, 259; roll out of, 260; paint scheme for,

260; coding of, 261; wing folding on, 284–5; retirement of, 291

F-15 Eagle, 266, 267, 268, 271, 281, 286–7

F-18 Hornet, 267, 276, 279

Messerschmitt
 Me 109, 68, 69–70, 71, 74, 75, 80 et seq, 117, 145, 149, 151, 152, 155
 Me 110, 69, 76, 77, 87, 91

Mikoyan
 MiG-23, 283
 MiG-25, 267
 MiG-29, 283

Miles
 Magister, 65, 90, 128
 Martinet, 163

Myasishchev M4 'Bison', 190, 210

North American
 B-25 Mitchell, 133, 148
 B-45 Tornado, 176
 F-86 Sabre, 180, 182, 188, 204, 218
 F-100 Super Sabre, 182, 218, 219, 220
 P-51 Mustang, 160

Northrop F-5, 212, 266, 273, 276, 283

Panavia
 Tornado F.3, 254, 266, 276, 281, 286, 289, 290, 291, 292
 Tornado GR.1, 265, 271

Pfalz, 26, 27, 28, 29, 33

Republic
 F-84 Thunderjet, 178, 182
 P-47 Thunderbolt, 128

Rockwell International B-1B, 286

Royal Aircraft Factory
 R.E.8, 37
 S.E.5a: first deliveries of, 19; Vickers gun fitted to, 19; bomb racks fitted to, 26; markings of, 32; in Wing attacks, 37–8

Rumpler, 34

Scottish Aviation Pioneer, 248

SEPECAT Jaguar, 253, 263, 265, 266, 275, 277, 289

Short
 Belfast, 249
 Stirling, 135

Sikorsky S-61, 247

Sopwith
 Pup, 19
 Scout, 19

Supermarine
 Scapa, 45
 Spitfire, 265
 BBMF aircraft, 192, 211, 220, 290
 Mk I: first delivery of, 54; conversion to, 54;

GENERAL INDEX